# ELSWICK-HOPPER
# OF
# BARTON-ON-HUMBER

## THE STORY OF A GREAT BRITISH BICYCLE MAKER

NIGEL LAND

Published by
Fathom Writers Press, The Ropewalk, Barton-on-Humber

2010

Published by Fathom Writers Press,
The Ropewalk, Barton-on-Humber, DN18 5JT

Printed by G W Belton Ltd, Gainsborough, Lincolnshire.

# ACKNOWLEDGEMENTS

Firstly I must thank my wife for her tolerance of the hours I have spent on research and writing and for doing an initial proof read. My thanks go to everyone who has contributed to this book, for your stories, loans of material, and most of all for your support and encouragement. If I have missed your name from the list I apologise.

So warm thanks to:

Eva Adlard, John Andrew, Rick Appleyard, Bryan Ashton, Doreen Atkin, Stewart Atkinson, Jack Austin, Tony Baines, Dr John Ball, Francis Barratt, Steven Bell, Bob Blackburn, Ruby Bland, Ben Blow, Colin Booth, Phil Bradley, Gordon Brooks, Peter Brotherton, Norman Broughton, Linda Brown, Peter Brown, Geoff Bryant, Roger Bugg, Bill Carter, Andrew and Betty Clark, Keith and Sheila Clark, Sandra Clayton (for meticulous proof reading), Ernest, Rosemary and Edward Clements, Walter Clements, Frank Clements, Jean Clipson, Terry Clipson, Audrey Cole, Roy Cox, Sid and Eileen Credland, Peter and Ruby Credland, Jeremy Crook, Gordon Crow, Mark Daniels, Nick Davenport, Herbert Dent, Jack Dimoline, Queenie Dixon (through a WEA tape made in 1994), Hamish Easdale, Christine Ellis, Emlyn Evans, Mary French, John French, Eddie Gaunt, Bernard Gouldthorpe, Bob Griffiths, Harry Haddock, Nigel Haddock, Stan Havercroft, Herbert and Gladys Hedley, Tim Higgins, Maud Hildred, Richard Holland, Dennis Holtby, Walter and Joan Horne, Dan Kehew, Marjorie Kirkby, Geoff Lago, Alan Laundon, Scotford Lawrence, Jim Leach, Gordon Linley, Noel Loxley, John Malseed, Frank and Janice Martinson, Janet Mathias, Mary Mayo, Ray Miller, Dave Orford, Audrey Peck, Brian and Muriel Peeps, Ray Pettit, Barrie Portas, Alan Potts, Margaret Rodmell, Harry Reynolds, Brian Robinson, Robert Seaman, Leslie Shakesby, Aspoèe Simelli, Colin Slater, Barry Smith, Catherine Smith, Tony Snelling, Dorothy Sobey, Jack Stead, Peter Stow, Tony Speight, Trevor Stow, Arthur Such, Eva and Bertha Such, Peter Sweetman, Janice Taylor, Nora Thompson, Jack Tighe, Nev Tong, Veronica Turnbull, Jim Turner, Sir Reginald Tyrwhitt, Don Tyson, John Waghorn, Tony Wall, Ken Waller, Charles Watkinson, Stan Weatherall, Susan Webster, Brian Wiles, Nigel Wilson, Max Withrington, Barry Wood, Alan Worfolk, Colin Wright and finally, John Wilson and his staff at North East Lincolnshire Archives for their patience in dealing with a novice cycle historian.

I have included photographs from <u>many</u> sources, but special mention must go to Brian Peeps and Dr John Ball for free access to their collections. My thanks to David and Michael Lee, of David Lee Photography Ltd, for permission to use some of their large collection of Elswick-Hopper and Falcon photographs. Their photographs are marked '© David Lee' and copies are available from the company. My thanks also to Taylor and Francis for permission to reprint extracts from 'F Hopper And Co - The Problems of Capital Supply in the Cycle Manufacturing Industry, 1891-1914' by A E Harrison, *Business History*, vol 24 no 1 pp 3-22 (1982). See: http://tandf.co.uk/journals

# CONTENTS

# FOREWORD

Who would have thought that a cycle manufacturer working in a small market town in North Lincolnshire could develop a business with enormous world-wide markets? By the early 20th century Fred Hopper's cycle works in Barton on Humber had achieved this remarkable position. The bicycle, unlike the previously used horse, gave the world a relatively cheap, reliable and adaptable form of personal transport. Hopper's bicycles were well-built and reliable and after leaving Barton went on to be sold in the four corners of the globe.

Cyclists could visit friends, could shop, could go for a healthy 'spin', could race, or, for the more energetic, could load up and go on holiday. Local clubs like the Barton Cycling Club, later the Wheelers, or national bodies like the Cyclists' Touring Club quickly sprang up and provided opportunities for organised cycling – a social as well as healthy activity. At its height the works employed some 800 workers – almost one in eight of the town's total population – and it is hard to imagine that such a large workforce will ever again be assembled at a single Barton business. Fred Hopper's legacy can still be seen in the firm's former office building at the bottom of Brigg Road, in the machine and assembly rooms which remain standing in Marsh Lane and in his workers' housing in Butts Road and Queen's Avenue.

Tragically this book also details the demise of this once mighty concern – a story of bad decisions and under-investment which can be mirrored again and again amongst Britain's manufacturers and which have allowed foreign businesses, perhaps inevitably, to take over many of our markets. The 'might-have-beens' include a possible co-operative working agreement with what became the mighty Honda – now there's a thought to be conjured with!

Nigel Land has left no stone unturned to detail the story of the Barton Cycle Works. Here is a book which will form a long-lasting resource for our town's local historians as well as for cycle historians the world over.

Would that more Bartonians would put pen to paper and similarly record the history of some of our town's other shortly to be forgotten industries.

Well done, Nigel – I offer you the thanks of all Bartonians for your years of hard work in producing this splendid book. Long may we continue to see you pedalling our streets, always it seems on a different, often old, often Hopper, bicycle.

**Geoffrey F. Bryant**

## INTRODUCTION

It was after an evening meeting of the executive committee of Barton Civic Society at the beginning of June 2001 that I agreed to write this book. It was customary to adjourn to the Wheatsheaf (just round the corner from Fred Hopper's first workshop) after such meetings and committee member Ro Bryant's husband Geoff, historian, WEA organiser, and accomplished church bell ringer, was in the habit of joining us after practice. I have always cycled and been interested in bikes and someone mentioned Elswick-Hopper. I asked Geoff if anyone had written a history of the company. His response is engraved on my brain: "No, why don't you write one?" How could I not rise to the challenge, though little did I know it would take the next nine years to complete. He started me off with the name of an ex-employee of Hopper's and Nora Thompson proved an enthusiastic and valuable contact, supplying old catalogues that she had saved from destruction, her memories and the names of several more people to pester.

Neither Geoff nor I are from Barton, but we have both developed a deep interest in this oddly situated market town, with its closer historical links with the north bank than with the hinterland of Lincolnshire. Appropriately Geoff is Yorkshire born and I spent the first 16 years of my life in Boston, just 50 or so miles to the south. There is evidence that the Hopper family moved to Barton via Bridlington and Hull, so all this animosity between the north and south banks of the Humber is, in reality, just nonsense – ferries and market boats provided a ready means of travel across the estuary until the opening of the Humber Bridge in 1982. Now the centre of Hull is just 30 minutes away by bus.

I wish I had started my research a few years earlier when people who had worked for the company since the First World War were still alive. Fred Hopper Junr was still active when I first moved to Barton – as direct a link with the founder as you could wish to find. Another regret is that several of my contributors are no longer with us, a sad consequence of taking nine years to produce it.

This is primarily a history of the Elswick-Hopper company in all its forms. My objective was to compile a comprehensive record of this important company that competed for many years with the likes of Raleigh and Hercules, both nationally and internationally, from its home in Barton on Humber. I have used company records where available, contemporary newspaper and journal reports, and oral accounts. Indeed, one of the most enjoyable tasks was recording the stories of those who worked for the company, and the final chapter includes many of these. I was sustained in my researches by three factors – the academic research done by Dr Tony Harrison in the early 1980s on the early years, the sheer energy that Fred Hopper clearly put into the business, and the enthusiasm and fondness for the firm that is still apparent in local people who worked for Hopper's.

It is likely that I have made mistakes, misinterpreted some facts and missed some things out. For this I take full responsibility and would be delighted to hear from readers with more accurate information. I can be contacted at ndland@btinternet.com.


**Nigel Land**

# CHAPTER 1

## THE EARLY DAYS

This first chapter traces the early years of the business up to 1900, beginning with Fred Hopper's apprenticeship, his initial start as a whitesmith, and his entry into bicycle manufacture. For much of the detail in the first two chapters I am indebted to the late Professor A E Harrison[1] of York University, who spent many hours during 1962 at the Marsh Lane offices studying the company archives. I am also indebted to the late Leslie Green, company secretary, for donating them to the County Archives in Grimsby.

To set the context for the Hopper cycle works we start with a short review of the early development of the bicycle industry in England.

## The Bicycle in the Nineteenth Century

*Fig. 1.1 From The Evolution of the Bicycle 1867-1938, this is probably an English Boneshaker from 1869.*

Machines known as velocipedes were introduced in France in the early 1860s and were a development of the earlier hobbyhorses, which were simply propelled by the feet pushing against the ground. It was not until towards the end of the decade that this new development was seen in Britain. Velocipedes were simple machines propelled by cranks and pedals attached to the front wheel (Fig. 1.1). Once domestic manufacture got underway this novel form of locomotion was enthusiastically taken up by members of the growing middle class. The velocipede soon acquired the sobriquet 'boneshaker', as due to the poorly surfaced roads it did not provide the most comfortable of rides, though the introduction of solid rubber tyres around 1869 brought some improvement. The cushioning effect of larger front wheels was soon discovered, and of course, meant that more ground was covered with every turn of the pedals – a benefit that found favour with the growing number of young male cyclists, especially those involved in the new sport of bicycle racing.[2] Before the end of the 1870s the diameter of the front wheel had grown to the largest size that could be comfortably pedalled, typically to a maximum of 58″, depending on the length

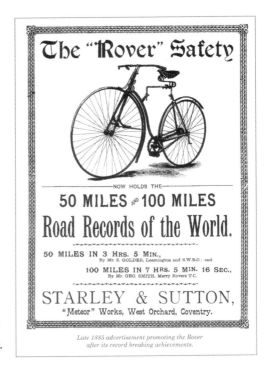

*Fig. 1.2 (left)*
*A Scottish rider of a*
*Rudge ordinary.*

*Fig. 1.3 An 1885*
*Rover advertisement,*
*showing the*
*importance of records.*

The "Rover" Safety

NOW HOLDS THE

## 50 MILES AND 100 MILES
## Road Records of the World.

50 MILES IN 3 HRS. 5 MIN.,
By Mr. S. GOLDER, Leamington and S.W.B.C.: and
100 MILES IN 7 HRS. 5 MIN. 16 SEC.,
By Mr. GEO. SMITH, Merry Rovers T.C.

## STARLEY & SUTTON,
"Meteor" Works, West Orchard, Coventry.

*Late 1885 advertisement promoting the Rover*
*after its record breaking achievements.*

of the rider's leg. The 'high bicycle' (Fig. 1.2), had become the choice of the serious cyclist.[3] Bicycle racing, long distance rides, weekend club runs and just pottering around the lanes, were increasingly popular activities for those with the money to buy what were quite expensive machines. Road surfaces were poor as even the main roads and turnpikes had fallen into disrepair, due to the popularity and reliability of the railways. Roads had become the preserve of local horse and pedestrian traffic, until the growing and influential cycling lobby pressed the local authorities to make much needed improvements. The high bicycle required a certain degree of athleticism and so mainly appealed to young men, who could cope with the occasional 'cropper'. This hazard was the biggest drawback to the machine and was caused by an obstruction in the road, such as a stone, or pothole. The sudden loss of forward motion caused the small back wheel to lift, throwing the unfortunate rider forward, when he would invariably entangle his legs with the handle bars and be deposited unceremoniously head first on the road. Understandably, those men of more mature years, and women of all ages, preferred the tricycle, which had developed alongside the high bicycle, and was widely used until the 1890s.

The big breakthrough came in 1885 when the bicycle as we know it today made its first appearance; this was the Rover, designed by J K Starley of Coventry, a city that had become a major centre of bicycle manufacture.[4] These low-slung machines were called 'safety bicycles' to distinguish them from the high bicycle, which then became known as an 'ordinary,' or by what was initially intended as a derogatory term, a 'penny-farthing'. The Rover was equipped with elegantly curved top and down tubes, but was clearly closely related to the modern bicycle (Fig. 1.3). The development that allowed the two wheels to get back to the more-or-less equal diameters of the velocipede, and yet achieve the speed of an ordinary was, of course, the transfer of pedal power to the rear wheel via chain driven gear wheels, with a larger number of teeth on the chain wheel than on the rear sprocket providing the gearing. The ordinary was still being made at the end of the 1880s, although as early as 1888 there were six times more safeties being made, showing how quickly the new design found favour. In the same year John Boyd Dunlop patented the pneumatic bicycle tyre, which after a few years became sufficiently reliable to supersede the solid rubber tyre.[5] Improved comfort was a clear benefit of the new invention, and by 1890 superior speed capability was also demonstrated in track events. In September of that year C A Smith rode a pneumatic tyred safety from London to Brighton and back in 7 hours 50 minutes, beating by nearly an hour the coach's best time, achieved in 1888 with 16 changes of horses.[6]

By the mid-1890s the popularity of the safety bicycle was firmly established and many new companies were formed to cash in on booming demand. This was due in no small measure to the feeling of security that came with the lower seating position. It has been estimated that in 1895 there were 1,500,000 bicycle riders in the country,[7] at a time when the cost of a machine was still beyond the reach of most people. To quote John Woodforde from his *Story of the Bicycle*:

> The year 1896 was a phenomenal one for the cycle trade: agents hurried from factory to factory, cash in hand, pleased if they secured even a couple of machines out of the dozens on order. Gunsmiths and locksmiths deserted their trades for work in the booming cycle industry, which was backed by the investments of clergymen no less than financial adventurers. Then, the following year, a slump set in; and such was the degree of over investment that the effects on many were disastrous.

One of the factors causing the slump was that the boom had been driven by fashion, with fickle London society in the vanguard. The industry's problems were further exacerbated by a flood of cheap American imports,[8] and it was not until prices fell to a much lower level that a mass market could develop. New production methods were slowly introduced and prices fell steadily up to the First World War.

The boom of 1896 also saw the start of a dramatic demonstration of the ability of the bicycle to circumnavigate the globe. An incredible ride of 19,237 miles was recorded by John Foster Fraser in *Round the World on a Wheel*. This odyssey was made in the company of two friends. Starting in 1896 it lasted for two years and took them through 17 countries, including Romania, Russia, Persia, India, Japan, China and America:

> Our wheels were good sturdy roadsters, painted black. In the diamond frames were leather bags stuffed with repairing materials. Over the rear wheels had been fixed luggage carriers, and to these were strapped bags containing underclothing. We were clad in brown woollen garb, guaranteed by the tailor to wear forever and a fortnight, and we each wore big, bell shaped helmets.

Such trips are still made today and books published about them. However, it is not hard to imagine that the challenge of cycling around the world in 1896 was immensely more difficult than now.

## And so to Barton

The story of Elswick-Hopper Cycles begins in the small town of Barton on Humber, far from the main nineteenth century manufacturing centres of Coventry, Birmingham, Nottingham and London. Bicycle manufacture no longer takes place in the town, although it is home to a very successful wheel building company, Target Wheel Products and on the same industrial estate is the factory of bicycle tool and accessory manufacturer Weldtite. Fred Hopper's enduring legacy is buildings – the housing he built for his employees, the large office building, now converted to apartments and an industrial estate almost in the town centre that will probably become a brown field housing development. In its heyday the bicycle factory employed 800 – in a town with a population of around 6,000. Bicycles were despatched to all parts of the country and to most countries in the world. Fred Hopper was a classic Victorian entrepreneur, starting with little and creating a large business, but also caring for his town and its people.

## Fred Hopper, Apprentice

The only son of Robert and Mary Hopper was christened plain Fred. He was born on 28 September 1859, and had a sister, Annie, three years older. Fred's grandfather, born in Hull in 1804, was also called Robert. Movement of goods and people had always been easy across the Humber, well served as it was by ferries, and Hull was a source of employment and access to markets for the sale and purchase of goods and produce. By the time of Fred's birth a regular ferry service had been established from New Holland to Hull, with New Holland being situated on the MS&LR Company's railway line from Barton to Grimsby.[9] From census records it seems that the family moved to Barton between 1824 and 1827. We know that in 1851 both father and son Robert were living in one of the houses in the Butchery, directly north of Barton Market Place and that they were both employed as tallow chandlers.[10] Fred's father worked 48 years for the local candle factory owned by William Rawson. According to his obituary he was a well-known townsman and had been a very energetic member of St Mary's church choir.[11] His son also took a keen interest in this church and in later years provided the St. Matthew screen, an altar cross that he made with his own hands, altar candlesticks and a large silver chalice and paten.

Young Fred attended the National School in Queen Street (now restored as the Wilderspin National School Museum) and then served an apprenticeship with Henry Neave. After the repeal of the Apprenticeship Laws in 1814 there was no longer a fixed term of seven years to acquire his Master's skills, and there was no fixed school leaving age. It is possible to reconstruct Fred's early years as a craftsman on the following information:

1. Henry Neave is first recorded in Barton as an engineer, millwright and agricultural implement manufacturer in George Street in 1872. From there he moved to Fleetgate, where the business was recorded in the 1881 census, but in White's Directory of 1882 he was an engineer and machinist based in Brigg Road.

2. From various sources it seems that after finishing his apprenticeship Hopper found work as a journeyman with a Hull boilermaker, and also with Marshall's of Gainsborough, a large and successful engineering works founded in 1855 and renowned for its steam traction engines.

3. Fred Hopper was recorded as living at his parent's house on King Street, age 21, in the 1881 census, employed as a blacksmith. Given the long working hours of those times it would seem likely that rather than just visiting his parents on census day he was living and working in Barton in 1881.

4. The foundation of Hopper's bicycle business has been consistently recorded in the company records as 1880. For example, in the 1936 Hopper catalogue: 'It is a little more than 56 years ago since the first Hopper bicycle was manufactured in a small workshop at Barton on Humber.' Given that Hopper only reached the age of 21 in September 1880, and what we know from newspaper reports, it seems that he acquired the habit of many Victorian companies of overstating their seniority.

The probability is that Fred Hopper returned to Neave's business on completion of his two years as a journeyman, which would tally with local oral history, and took over the business at some date after 1882. If he returned in 1880 it could account for the later insistence that this is when his company started.

## Fred Hopper, Whitesmith and Machinist

The first mention of Fred Hopper in his own right is in Kelly's Directory of 1885, where he is listed as a machinist in Brigg Road. The 1796 Enclosure map for Barton shows that the workshop was adjacent to the foundry used by James Harrison, younger brother of longitude clockmaker John, for casting bells. The site of the workshop was, until 2006, occupied by John Keal's decorator's shop and the site of the bell foundry is that of the adjacent town housing. Keal's old building was demolished in 2009 and has been replaced by an apartment building. Lee's almanac of 1908 carried an article on 'A Great Barton Industry' in which it was stated that 'Mr Fred Hopper had his services frequently requisitioned for repairing damages (that occurred on the roads, which at that time were not nearly so well kept as now) to the old high bicycles, and constant contact with different makes and an inborn knowledge of mechanics, induced him to make a speciality of the new means of locomotion, with the result that general bicycle making or repairing soon absorbed the greater part of his time.'

The earliest known photograph of the business (Fig. 1.4) must have been taken in the early 1880s, and shows a proud proprietor with his staff of four outside the workshop. Fred Hopper was keen on recording events through photographs and many have survived to provide evidence of his activities. This photograph was probably intended for advertising purposes as the tools are displayed *outside* the

*Fig. 1.4 Fred Hopper (4th from left) and staff outside the Brigg Road workshop.*

shop and Fred is posed with hammer and tongs. We can recognise in this picture the flywheel of a tile extruding machine (brick and tiles were a major industry at the time) and the forks of a high bicycle. Hopper's business has been described as both blacksmith and whitesmith, the latter being verified by the photograph. Referring to the 1818 edition of *A Book of English Trades* on Smiths: 'some are called black-smiths...others are called white-smiths, or bright smiths; these polish their work to a considerable degree of nicety...' There were undoubtedly overlaps in both trades, but the notion of using tubing and then polishing and plating a finished product is definitely not blacksmith work.

Fred's first wife, Margaret Ann, died on 22 August 1888 at the age of 29, three weeks after the birth of her first child, Fred Forster Hopper. The baby followed his mother to the grave on 2 September. His second marriage was to 19 year old Hannah Elizabeth Jackson, the second of six daughters born to the wife of a hairdresser and toy dealer in George Street, Barton on Humber. They married in 1890, and Hannah gave birth to their only child, Fred, on 7 November 1891. The Hopper's new home was in Brigg Road, conveniently next door to his workshop. The present town house development that replaced the old houses echoes the old home with its modern oriel window.

## Cycling in Barton

Growing up in the 1870s Fred Hopper would have witnessed the development of the 'high bicycle', so it is not surprising that local tales tell us that he covered many miles on one, probably on both sides of the Humber. The Yarborough Bicycle Club was formed in Grimsby in 1878, the same year as Hull Amateur and a year after Hull Bicycle Club, and in his home town the Barton and District Cycling Club was founded in 1880,[12] by, it is reported,[13] Fred Hopper himself, the same year that he claimed as his first year in business. We also know that the Barton Cycle Club[14] was formed on 2 May 1881, so this relatively small town supported two clubs for a time.[15] During his time in Gainsborough Fred Hopper

*Fig. 1.5  A E Barraclough with a cross frame safety – possibly a Hopper prototype as it has no top stay. Arthur was a successful member of Barton & District CC, and died of TB at the young age of 28.*

would have been aware of Baines & Sons, a firm that had been connected with the cycle trade since the days of the velocipede.[16] At some time in the 1880s he became an agent for Humber, Singer and Rudge bicycles and no doubt learned much from the machines that passed through his hands. We know that he repaired ordinaries, and we know that he was involved with the new cycling club(s). An interesting insight into his promotion of cycling as a sport comes from the *Lincoln, Rutland and Stamford Mercury*, 2 January 1888, presumably on behalf of the Barton and District Cycling Club:

> Home Trainer Handicap. Mr F Hopper held his first handicap last week at the Volunteer's Hall, Barton. There were 25 entries, most of which competed. The first prize, a silver medal, was won by A Barraclough (Fig. 1.5). The second prize, a bicycle lamp, was secured by A G Poole. There was a good attendance and interest was shown in the competition.

Significantly Mr Poole of George Street was the local consul for the Eastern Central Division of the Cyclists' Touring Club. In the CTC Gazette for March 1885 the local 'Place for Repairs' is given as 'Engineering Co, Brigg Road', denoting a competent cycle repairer, and surely referring to Fred Hopper's workshop. Towards the end of the year the edition of 26 October reported on the first road handicap of the Barton and District CC, run the previous Saturday, 'when the weather being fine, the members turned out in force, and some good sport ensued'. The course was about 9½ miles and the fastest time was by H Frank in 37¾ minutes. His handicap time gave him third place, first going to G Underwood.

The *North Lindsey Star* of 10 October 1891 reported the annual Lantern Parade of the Barton and District and Barton Wheelers Cycling Clubs on Saturday night, 3 October. A parade of 47 brilliantly illuminated machines met at Brigg Road and made their way through the town. They included a quadri-cycle and several 'good old ordinaries'. It attracted thousands of spectators and raised £3 for the provision of a dinner for the 'men who work on the roads', with any surplus to be given to the Barton Nursing Association. As already recorded the roads were poorly surfaced and Mr Dunlop's new pneumatic tyres were expensive and prone to puncture, so to the rider of a solid rubber tyred bicycle the road mender was an indispensable friend. The dinner took place at the White Swan on 16 October when about 30 sat down to a 'capital spread' provided by host Ross. For the parade itself 'Mr F Hopper, with his usual generosity, gives a valuable prize for the best decorated machine.'[17] Other reports tell of rides to Hull and Beverley (via New Holland ferry) and to Cleethorpes – a return distance of about 30 miles – not an insignificant distance given the road conditions.

A further indication of the growing interest in cycling and other sports is an advert in the same paper, 24 October for the Wheatsheaf Hotel on the corner of Holydyke and Brigg Road:

> Est. 1793, 'The Cyclists' House' F W Hope. Good accommodation for Cyclists, Cricket, Football and Fishing Clubs. Good stabling for horses.

By the time he became a cycle manufacturer Fred had been in business for almost 10 years and was 30 years old. Whatever thought processes convinced him that making bicycles in Barton was a viable proposition, by 1890 he was ready to go.

## Fred Hopper, Bicycle Manufacturer

Barton was still a predominantly rural area in 1890 with the majority of the male workforce engaged in agricultural work. A substantial number of factories had developed in Barton during the nineteenth century, such as brick and tile works, rope making, a large maltings, a cement works, a chalk quarry and a fertiliser manufacturer, mostly based to the north along Waterside, the road connecting the town centre to the Humber estuary. They provided mainly low-skilled jobs that were poorly paid. The *Lincoln, Rutland and Stamford Mercury* reported on 30 December 1888 that unemployment was high,

> 'partly owing to the farmers employing as few hands as possible in these depressed times. The Ropery works have only been working about half-time lately, and there has been no employment at the Barton chalk quarry for the last two or three weeks.'

It is clear that Hopper would need to pay little more than a small premium to attract the best workers to his new business. From solicitors' records we know that Robert Hopper had an interest in the Brigg Road workshop as he took out a mortgage on the whitesmith's shop, which contained two forges, and an adjoining fitting shop – all occupied by 'F. Hopper, machinist'. The document is dated 20 March 1889 and recorded the mortgage value as £100. The money was needed for his son's new venture.

The first evidence of actual bicycle manufacture in Barton is to be found in the *North Lindsey Star* of 1 February 1890. It carries an advertisement for the 'North Lincolnshire Cycle Works, Barton-on-Humber, F Hopper Proprietor. Branch Depots:- Brigg, Scunthorpe and Winterton.' The detail (Fig. 1.6) corroborates local oral history that Hopper's first bicycle was called 'Ajax'. It is reproduced from a microfiche copy and shows a cross frame design that was favoured by many manufacturers of the time, including Singer, over the Rover diamond frame. It also refers to Hopper being sole agent for Singer,

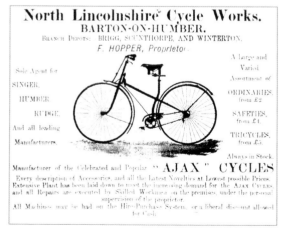
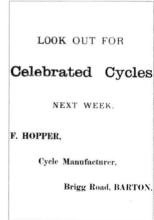

*Fig. 1.6 (far left) Advertisement in the North Lindsey Star of 1 February 1890.*
*Fig. 1.7 (left) A 'taster' advertisement in the North Lindsey Star of 25 January 1890.*

Humber and Rudge, and states that 'extensive plant has been laid down to meet the increasing demand for the Ajax Cycles.' Hire purchase was offered as well as a liberal discount for cash. Interestingly the price of a second-hand ordinary had fallen to half that of a safety. The launch of the Ajax had been preceded for a number of weeks through 'trailer' advertisements in the *Star*, showing that Hopper was well aware of the need to publicise his machines (Fig. 1.7).

A similar advert appeared on 14 March 1891 (Fig. 1.8). It refers to the North Lincolnshire Cycle Depot with branches at Brigg and Winterton, and exhorts readers to "Ride the 'Ajax Safety' Everybody's Favourite Mount." The Ajax had become a more sturdy looking machine with an additional top tube strut and the head tube to bottom bracket strut had almost become a full down tube; however, it was still recognisably a cross frame. The 1891 season got off to a bad start if the advertisement in the *Star* of 10 January is to be believed (Fig. 1.9). Lee's almanac for 1908 also tells the story of the Ajax:

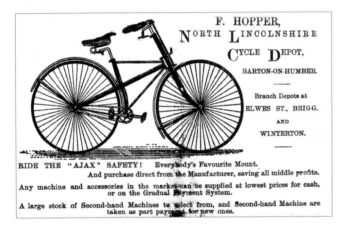

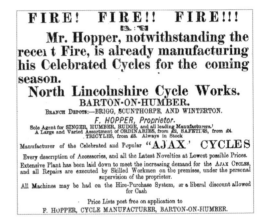

Fig. 1.8   *The second generation Ajax from an advert 14 March 1891.*
Fig. 1.9   *This refers to what may have been the first fire at Hoppers, but it was by no means the last.*

Most people will well remember the early safety cycles which followed in the wake of the high Ordinary, and now after many years, one occasionally comes across a specimen of the first local cross frame safety, the 'Ajax', which was made in Barton, reminding us of the times before pneumatic tyres were introduced. The Ajax safety was one of the machines that helped to build the reputation of the Barton firm, and the success encouraged Mr Hopper to seek business outside the local sphere, with the result that in 1888 he commenced doing a wholesale trade, and two years later the first consignment of Barton-made cycles was shipped abroad.

This was printed just 18 years after the Ajax was launched, and when Hopper was very much in command of the company, but it does beg the question of why he appears to have consistently brought forward some major milestones in the company's history.

Hopper's entry into manufacture was clearly well planned, given the build up in advertising, his promotion of cycling events and the opening of a new showroom reported in the *North Lindsey Star* on 21 February 1891, just a year into manufacture. Headlined 'Mr Hopper's Cycle Works', it continues:

The new showrooms and clubroom have been opened. The rooms are large and handsome and reflect great credit on the ability and taste of the proprietor. Mr Hopper's fame as a maker and inventor of improved Safety Bicycles is by no means confined to Lincolnshire. Mr Hopper has a branch establishment in Elwes St, Brigg, managed by Mr F Walker and also branches at Caistor, Louth and Market Rasen. It would well repay anyone to visit the establishment and be shown round by the courteous proprietor, the stock of cycles is large and of the very best kind in the market.

*Fig. 1.10 Barton & District Cycling Club outside the White Swan, c 1891, © David Lee.*
*Fig. 1.11 William Abey, born in Thornton Curtis in 1867, with what appears to be an 1890 solid tyre Ajax.*

Prior to the provision of a clubroom at Brigg Road, Barton and District CC had met at the White Swan, situated at the junction of Waterside Road, Fleetgate and Butts Road, and a photograph (Fig. 1.10) was taken outside the hotel of what is probably the club at the start of a weekend run. Most of the bicycles are of cross frame design, with just two ordinaries, and Fred Hopper is present, sixth from the right. Close scrutiny reveals both 1890 and 1891 models, assuming that they are indeed Ajax bicycles. All have solid tyres so it is most likely that it was taken in 1891. A year later and pneumatic tyres would have been in use on some of the mounts. As the bicycle in front appears to be an 1891 model perhaps the photograph was also intended to commemorate its appearance.

William Abey was born in the nearby village of Thornton Curtis in 1867. He is undoubtedly pictured in Fig. 1.11 with a Mk 1 Ajax and was probably a member of one of the Barton cycling clubs. An early letter (Fig. 1.12) from Hopper to the Hyde Rubber Co written in 1892 carries a picture of the 1890 Ajax, along with illustrations of Lucas oil lamps, a horn and an adjustable spanner. It would seem from this that he planned to be a factor for all things cycling from the onset, rather than simply a supplier of bicycles.

An idea of the significance of Hopper's promotion of local cycling clubs can be gained from a report in the *North Lindsey Star* of 11 July 1891:

The run last Saturday was to Winterton where the members were met by the Scunthorpe and Ashby clubs. Much interest was taken in the Bicycle Handicap by the Bartonians seeing that all the heats were won by Mr Hopper's celebrated Ajax machines. This speaks very highly of the Ajax and reflects great credit upon the energy, perseverance and inventive genius shown by our respected townsman. Mr Hopper deserves the fame he has achieved in the Cycling world. The return journey was much enjoyed in the cool of the evening.'

In 1892 the Barton and District CC was still headquartered at Hopper's Cycle Works and the Club Captain was local printer T H Ball.[18]

In the 1892 *Kelly's Directory of Lincolnshire* Fred Hopper is listed as a cycle manufacturer, agent and electroplater in Brigg Road. However, an analysis of the 1891 census reveals just six men were employed in the cycle trade in Barton, though there are well over 100 recorded as general labourers. This indicates that the business got off to a slow start. The main employment for Barton men in the

*Fig. 1.12 Hopper letter dated 11 November 1892 advertising the Ajax and accessories.*
*Fig. 1.13 The workshop, house/office and showroom along the west side of Brigg Road,
early 1890s.*

census year was equally split between agriculture and the many brick and tile works. Hall's Ropery took third place. As bicycle sales have always been seasonal, it is likely that Fred initially employed his workers for only part of each year. The Brigg Road premises are shown in Fig. 1.13 at around this time, and the window posters advertise Humber and Singer bicycles. The single storey workshop of 1880 is still the same and the house to the right with the oriel window is where Fred lived with his family until 1898. After that date it became the main office until 1905. The premises to the right of the house were the shop and showroom, opened in 1891.

A E Harrison was most fortunate to find an 1892 catalogue for Hopper cycles, since lost, and noted that:

> Hopper obtained a local reputation for the manufacture of a reliable and cheap machine without frills and accessories. He kept abreast of the main improvements in cycle design of the 1880s and 1890s including the 'safety' bicycle, the diamond frame, (though Hopper thought the cross-frame was technically better) ball bearings and pneumatic tyres. During the early 1890s the retail prices of his bicycles ranged from £21 to £10 and there were five different models. The enamelled cycle frames were made in his Barton workshops, but tyres, saddles and most other components were purchased from the much larger cycle component makers located in the West Midlands.

On 5 April 1893 Robert Hopper[19] took out a further £200 mortgage with the Independent Order of Oddfellows on -

> A Whitesmith's Shop, one forge therein, brick and tiled;
> A Machine Shop, adjoining and communicating, brick, timber and tiled;
> A Fitting Shop adjoining and communicating, timber and galvanised iron roof
> A Plating Shop, adjoining and communicating, timber and galvanised iron roof;
> A Polishing Shop, adjoining and communicating, brick and tiled;
> All occupied by Fred Hopper, Cycle Manufacturer and Whitesmith.

Drawings dated 20 May 1893, and stored at the North East Lincolnshire Archives Office in Grimsby, show plans for new privies to be built at the back of the Brigg Road cottages. Business must have been brisk as it was in June 1893 that Fred Hopper had a brush with the law, being fined 10s and 4s 6d costs for employing a young person after 6pm.[20] Not a good thing for a future JP, especially as the regulation had been in place since 1874, when the Factory Act of that year decreed that children must work no more than 10 hours a day, to be between the hours of 6am and 6pm.

It appears that manufacture of bicycles saw a steady build up from 1890 until it took off in 1895, when Hopper was struggling to cope with demand, just as the national 'boom' commenced. The local situation was described in the record of a visit made to the Brigg Road Cycle Works by a reporter from the *Lindsey and Lincolnshire Star*. This was published 15 June 1895, and is reproduced in full, as it is a unique contemporary record of the business:

## ROUND THE NORTH LINCOLNSHIRE CYCLE MANUFACTORY
## A CHAT WITH MR FRED HOPPER OF BARTON-ON-HUMBER

Amongst the great cycle makers in England Fred Hopper, of Barton-on-Humber, takes a prominent place. Some idea of the extent of the buildings may be derived from the fact that they occupy an area of 600 square yards. Mr Hopper, who has always been an enthusiastic wheelman, is a well-built man, who thoroughly understands the business throughout, and looks after the details of every machine himself so as to be assured of its accurate build. When I called on him a few days ago and asked him, in the interests of the readers of the Lindsey and Lincolnshire Star, to allow me to look over his premises, he said that he had not the time to spare, but kindly placed at my disposal his overseer, who showed me round the premises explaining in a lucid manner the various stages a cycle has to go through before being handed over to the agent. The first place we examined was the Store-room, which had boxes all neatly numbered containing things necessary for the trade. We left there and made our way to the smiths' shop, which is a lofty apartment containing forges in full swing. In close proximity a splendid specimen of one of Crossley's latest 12 horse power gas engines running at a very high speed in order to keep the various machines up to full pitch. The turning shop was next visited. It contains turning, milling and capstan machines for the manufacture of ball bearings, all the cups and cones for the bearings being turned out of solid bar steel. Close at hand another shop is being prepared for the reception of more machinery. The demand for the 'Advance' cycles is so great that the present machinery is totally inadequate. As we went into the brazing shops the forges were working. This department is fitted with the latest and best gas-brazing appliances and Mr Hopper has laid himself out for the manufacture of all kinds of fittings and parts of cycles for outside supply as well as his own use, and consequently is doing a very large business with 'the trade'. The grinding and polishing room is most interesting. My guide kindly showed me a crank in its rough state, then put it successively through the hands of the rough and fine polisher, the effect being marvellous. In going through the plating room I noticed the roof was covered with shafting, which my guide said was made with swivel bearings to run at the required speed. Here the plated goods are put on a wheel running at 200 revolutions per minute in order to complete the burnishing. My informant said that with proper care the nickel plated goods turned out by My Hopper would last half a century. For his plating Mr Hopper has a big reputation, indeed he claims to have one of the best plants in the North of England and he does a lot of work in this department outside the cycle trade. There is also in the plating room a large stove heated with gas, in which wool is pressed for polishing purposes. Going forward into the tube bending room, I found several men at work bending tubes. The next place I visited was the fitting shop, which is recognised as the finest of its kind in Lincolnshire. It is considerably over 100 feet in length, having ample accommodation for forty fitters, each man having a patent stand just behind him. The floor is asphalt covered and kept in clean condition. On the beams running across the top of this shop are quantities of tubing and steel stowed away, the stock being constantly replenished, as the vast number of machines are turned out. The enamelling department contains several vats filled with enamel and one of the most modern enamelling stoves heated with gas by improved Bunsen burners to 450 degrees Fahrenheit. In connection with this branch of the business is a large store-room containing every requisite necessary for the quick manufacture of enamelled goods. We next visited the paint shop, where the men were busy putting the finishing touches to a batch of beautiful juvenile cycles ordered for London that night. The show-room is a most capacious department, capable of showing off to the best advantage 200 machines. In the present rush of business, however, it is worth to note that it only contained two machines, and these were being packed ready to send away by rail that night. One of these was a novelty in the way of ladies' cycles. It had been specially designed by Mr Hopper himself in order to assist ladies mounting: the back wheel and chain were covered with a patent leather case, neatly laced so as to allow of no possibility whatever of a lady's dress catching. The other machine was a 'racer' and had an entirely new design of frame, specially adapted for racing purposes, which, in the opinion of the inventor, will become universally popular with racing men; the weight of the machine is only 26 lbs. The machinery in all the shops was scrupulously clean and everything was in first rate order, whilst a fresh country breeze swept through the capitally-lighted and well-ventilated premises and kept even the polishing department comfortable. There are not less than 100 labour-saving metal working tools run by overhead gearing and lacking nothing but human intelligence. For the best machinery that mechanical genius has devised for the rapid turning, screwing, planing, boring and wheel-making have been pressed into service. These machines are most systematically arranged and are governed by the most skilful mechanics to be found. All along Mr Hopper has been keeping well abreast of this utilitarian and artistic age and the proprietor of the 'Advance' machines has introduced, and is introducing, many novelties, all adding to the beauty, grace and strength of his cycles. The 'Advance' is not only so by name, but is undoubtedly in advance of the times. Hopper's machines are all built with the latest pattern of diamond frames, fine steel tubing and are fitted with all up-to-date improvements. From enquiries, I found that Mr Hopper has agents in all parts of Great Britain and is being besieged with letters day by day by cycle agents wishing to become his representative for their respective districts. His chief agent in the district is Mr George Layne, Elwes St, Brigg, who always has a good show of his latest machines. I then went into the office to have a chat with Mr Hopper. Although the hour was getting late he was still busy and assured me he was up to his eyes in work and scarcely knew which way to turn. With his men working late, he said he had orders that would keep them going for a month ahead and had to absolutely refuse several offers. Mr Hopper said he always made a point of refusing an order if he could not get it done within the time the customer wanted. 'You see,' he smilingly replied, 'I make frames for so many firms, that with my present staff and machinery it is utterly impossible for me to supply all. I hope, however,' he continued, 'to considerably enlarge my plant and increase the staff, then I will be able to put out just double what I do at the present time.' I asked how he could turn out such excellent well-built machines at such a low price and command so large a sale for them in face of the keen competition amongst the high-class makers. 'Well,' said Mr Hopper, without the slightest hesitation, 'I make everything connected with a bicycle on the premises and look after all details myself so that there is a minimum of waste. I have no high salaried managers, nor track riders to pay for booming my machines, but rely entirely on the merits of the machine, and by carefully examining every machine myself before it goes out of the place give universal satisfaction to my customers. Then another thing – and not the least – is that our expenses are so much lighter in Barton and I have not the same heavy rents and rates as some of my competitors have in London, Coventry and other large places.' The conversation then turned upon racing machines and Mr Hopper was very enthusiastic about his new 'racer', which he intends to place in the market at once. On being invited to try the machine, I just had a short spin and I certainly think it will perform all Mr Hopper claims it to do and should have a splendid future before it. As the hour was getting late, I was almost reluctantly compelled to take leave of the genial manufacturer of the 'Advance' cycle and did so wishing him every success in his great undertaking.

**THOMAS McDOUGALL**
**June 12th 1895**

What is interesting from this article is that Hopper had, at this early stage, commenced manufacture of components, rather than buying them from established Midlands manufacturers. This trend was made possible by the labour cost differential, a situation that continued for more than half of the next century. What is also clear is the very hands-on approach taken by Hopper in the early days, and his enthusiasm for new developments. His works were powered by gas engines, which also drove generators for electric lighting – not available in the town until 1913, and then by a company of which Fred Hopper was chairman. Two early photographs have survived of the Brigg Road factory (Fig. 1.14) and are thought to date from the mid-1890s.

*Fig. 1.14 These two photographs of a busy and overcrowded factory both include Fred Hopper (partly obscured behind a ladder in the machine shop, and standing in the centre of the frame shop) and an unknown top hatted visitor. A customer, or a potential investor? It may even be his partner Henry Wilson, © David Lee.*

## Expansion Plans

In pursuit of expansion, plans to extend the Brigg Road workshop by adding a 17ft by 71 ft bay to an existing building were passed in June 1896.

Tony Harrison recorded that Fred Hopper's considerable talents as a manufacturer and salesman were not matched by a corresponding financial acumen, and that his efforts to expand the firm were constantly constrained by difficulties in raising the necessary capital. This shortcoming ultimately proved to be his undoing. His first attempt at expansion, to double the output, resulted in Fred Hopper selling the business to the Cycle Industries Corporation. This was a finance company, registered 12 May 1896, and formed at the height of the bicycle boom for the purpose of carrying on business as manufacturers of cycles, vehicles, carriages and parts. The directors were mainly based in London and comprised two accountants, two engineers, a draughtsman and an agent.[21] The sale was reported in *The Cyclist* on 9 September 1896, which stated that the business of Mr Hopper of Barton had been purchased by a syndicate with the intention of opening a depot in Hull. Hopper was retained as managing director and in November the cycle business was floated as the ABC Cycle Fittings Ltd, with a nominal capital of 50,000 £1 shares and the intention 'to manufacture, sell and deal in pneumatic and other tyres, wheels, accessories, parts, fittings, cycles, perambulators, bath chairs, carriages, motors, motor cars and vehicles'.[22] Plans for a second storey to the old workshop fronting Brigg Road were passed in August 1896, so money <u>was</u> being invested in the business. An illustration of the extension plans, unfortunately from an unrecorded source, shows the Brigg Road frontage very much as an artist's impression (Fig. 1.15), though the old workshop to the left was indeed made into a two storey building. It appears that things did not go well between Hopper and the new owners and within a very few months he quit, to start afresh as the MS&L Cycle Manufacturing Company. The name was an abbreviation of Manchester, Sheffield and Lincolnshire, taken from the railway company situated next to the new works on Butts Road, just to the east of the Barton railway station buildings (Fig. 1.16). The site for the new factory had been part of Briggs' brick and tile works and Fred Hopper purchased a two acre plot on 5 February 1897 for £150. From the deeds it appears that construction of the new works was already underway – the plans had only been reviewed by the local authority in January. He needed financial backing and was successful in finding four investors. The key person was Henry Wilson, who first appeared in the town in the 1881 census as a guest of solicitor and local historian, Robert Brown

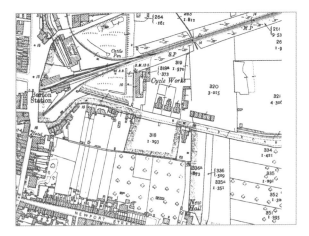

*Fig. 1.15 Artist's impression of the 1896 Brigg Road expansion plans.*
*Fig. 1.16 From a 1908 map showing the site of the Butts Road factory on Butts Road. The houses to the east were also built by Hopper for senior staff, and the hotel near the railway station is the White Swan.*

Junr of Priestgate House. Wilson was born in Armitage, Staffordshire, the son of the local vicar and third of five children. By the time of his birth Armitage had a thriving clay based industry and 1851 saw the start of the sanitary ware business that is still known as Armitage Shanks. He had found employment with Frankish and Kingdon, in Hull, becoming a junior partner in that company. He was also married the same year to Blanche Annie Standfield, an artist, and daughter of a successful saddle and harness maker from Exeter. Working in Hull simply involved a short train ride to New Holland, followed by a relaxing ferry trip on the licensed Hull paddle steamer. Wilson was initiated into the St Matthew Masonic Lodge in 1888, and the proximity of the Lodge to Hopper's Brigg Road house and workshop is probably how the two became acquainted. Just seven years older than Fred Hopper, he seems to have taken the younger man under his wing. In January 1897 Hopper was also initiated into the Masonic Lodge, having been proposed by Henry Wilson.[23] Further evidence of his influence on Hopper's business is that two of the other investors were prominent Hull businessmen. The fourth was a civil engineer from London, George Hughes. Fred Hopper sold the two acre site, complete with 'Workshops Offices Storerooms and premises erected upon the said plot or parcel of land' to Hughes on 17 March 1897 for £3,000. Just one month later Hughes sold it to the MS&L Cycle Manufacturing Company for £5,000, payable by £2,000 cash and the balance by the allotment of 3,000 fully paid up shares in the Hull and Barton Cycle Manufacturing Company Ltd. This new company was in the process of being floated to acquire the assets of MS&L, and to provide Hopper with capital for yet further expansion. The prospectus appeared in *The Cyclist* of 28 April 1897. The objective was to issue 10,000 shares to a capital value of £10,000, and the public offering was for 7,000 £1 7% preference shares, with the ordinary shares reserved for the vendor (Fred Hopper), as fully paid. The four investors were appointed directors of the new company alongside Fred Hopper:

Walter Owbridge,[24] of Hull and Cottingham, Manufacturing Chemist and Sheriff of Hull.
William Wellsted CE, JP, of Hull, Chairman of the Kingston Steam Trawling Co Ltd.
Henry Wilson, of Barton on Humber, Solicitor, Frankish, Kingdon and Wilson.
George Hughes, of the Park, Kimpton, Herts, Civil Engineer, Hughes & Young, London.

The Solicitors for the new Company were, of course, Frankish, Kingdon and Wilson, 12, Bowlalley Lane, Hull, and the prospectus provided the following information on the business :

> To acquire, as a going concern, the business and assets of The MS&L Cycle Manufacturing Company,
> consisting of freehold premises in Barton-on-Humber, Lincolnshire, Plant, Machinery, Stock-in-Trade,

orders for machines, trade connections, and the goodwill generally.

The Company will commence business with orders for the supply of their cycles, the profits from which alone, the Directors are advised, will be sufficient to pay a dividend on its capital.

The works are situated at Barton on Humber and adjoining the MS&L Railway Station, and have just recently been specially built for the manufacture of Cycles, Motor Cars, etc and with facilities for the output of between 200 and 250 Machines per week. The prosperity and development of the business has been such that it is now found impossible to execute the orders from customers with the dispatch that is necessary for the conduct of such a business. It has therefore become necessary to convert the business into a Joint Stock Company, for the purpose of providing the additional Working Capital which is required in order to keep pace with the increasing demand.

The Cycles manufactured by this Company are well known to the trade and public, and their 'ADVANCE CYCLE' has the reputation of being one of the best on the market, and is in high favour with many of the leading riders, numerous wins and records having been made upon it.

The Company will take over an agreement made between the Vendor and the ABC Cycle Fittings Co Ltd, whereby the latter have agreed to transfer all orders they have or may receive for complete machines to this Company.

*The Cyclist* commented that: 'No figures whatever are given as to the profits made by the business, which is being acquired and this, we think, should have been done in order to give confidence to those intending to invest.' While it is difficult to see how a profit record could have been built up for such a new company at that stage of the boom, it is clear that anything to do with cycle manufacture attracted investment. The observation was, however, prescient, and, if acted upon may have convinced Hopper of the need to actively promote investment in his business by being more open with his financial figures. As noted in the prospectus, Fred had already negotiated an agreement with the ABC Cycle Fittings Co that existing orders would be transferred to the new company. The prospectus also reveals that his ambitions were already turning to motor transport. It had been quite a year for Fred Hopper, but by the end of 1897 he was once again running his own cycle factory. Perhaps the most startling part of the move from Brigg Road is the speed with which the new factory was erected and commissioned.

## Consolidation

The end of the first of many boom and bust cycles in the industry, in mid-1897, saw ABC Cycle Fittings struggling to survive and, along with many of the new companies formed to cash in on the new craze, it went into liquidation. *The Cyclist* of 16 March 1898 announced that:

The ABC Cycle Fittings Co. Ltd. was ordered to be compulsorily wound up subject to the production of further affidavit of service. The petitioner, H W Crane, is a holder of dishonoured acceptances of £120 and £128.

The Hull and Barton Cycle Manufacturing Co of Barton-on-Humber announce that they are not in any way connected with any cycle firms or companies in any shape or form either in Barton-on-Humber or elsewhere.

The situation in the industry at that time was summed up in the following week's edition:

Not a ray of sunshine brightens the deadly dull conditions of the share markets.

Despite attempts at reconstruction the ABC Company went into liquidation in May 1898 and the Cycle Industries Corporation followed the same month. When the Brigg Road premises were subsequently put up for auction Fred seized the opportunity to reclaim the business he had built up over 16 long years. The auction was conducted by the Hull firm of solicitors, Frankish, Kingdon and Wilson and the successful bidders were Fred Hopper and Henry Wilson. Quite how this squared ethically with Henry Wilson's business involvement with the Hull and Barton Cycle Manufacturing Company is open to conjecture, but it did set the seal on the business partnership between a local bicycle manufacturer and a Cambridge educated lawyer from Staffordshire; a partnership that was to last until Fred's death in 1925. Hopper and Wilson operated as a private partnership under the name of F Hopper & Co and appear to have restarted production at Brigg Road in December of 1898, concurrent with the operation of the Hull and Barton Company. The Butts Road operation continued until the end of 1900, when at an extraordinary general meeting on 9 November at the offices of WR Locking and Scott in Bowlalley Lane, Hull, it was agreed that the company be wound up voluntarily, with the task assigned to WR Locking and Scott as liquidators. On 19 February 1901 a final EGM was held to confirm the sale of the property and effects of the Hull and Barton Co were to be sold to F Hopper & Co for £1,500. The new buildings were surplus to requirements with Brigg Road again under Hopper management. For a few years they were used for storage and offices and on Monday 23 December 1907 a major fire broke out, one of many fires at Hopper's over the years but the first to be found recorded in detail (Fig. 1.17). From *The Star* 28 December 1907:

> On Monday morning a fire broke out at the Butts Road premises of Messrs Hopper and Co, cycle manufacturers, Barton. The fire seemed to have got a good hold at the station end of the building, which is a two-storeyed one and contains a large value in bicycle frames stored in the top room. Gradually the flames spread and smoke was seen issuing from all parts of the building. The outbreak was first discovered by Foreman Porter West at the station, who immediately warned the owners. A clerk was dispatched to the captain of the fire brigade and West proceeded to the cycle works office. By this time, however, the fire had got a very firm hold of the building at the station end. Assistance soon arrived and Mr Hopper, the head of the firm, with Mr Powell, solicitor, rendered considerable help.
>
> The building seems to be an ill-fated one, for in the process of construction some ten years ago it was, during a very severe gale, largely demolished. Since the expansion of the St Mary's Works, however, the Butts Road building has been employed as a stores department and here, at the time of the fire, were in keeping no less than 3000 pairs of rubber tyres and a similar number of machines and frames. The latter were principally stored in the portion most damaged and it is estimated that the damage will not be less than £1000. Half of the building itself has been razed to the ground, and unquestionably the whole would

Fig. 1.17 Fire damage to the Butts Road factory.

have been destroyed had it not been for a brick partition wall, which did much to check the progress of the flames.

The damage was repaired and in December 1908 the building was leased to the Lincolnshire Territorial Force Association for use as a Drill Hall by 'E' Company of the 5th Lincolnshire Regiment. The Territorials used the Drill Hall for many years, and it also doubled as a popular venue for dances. It was eventually sold off in the 1970s to a chemical cleaning company, Atlas Chemicals, and was later demolished.

Hopper announced his return to Brigg Road with a notice in the 1899 edition of Lee's Barton Almanac:

. . F. HOPPER & Co., . .

Beg to announce that they have purchased the Cycle Factory on BRIGG ROAD which was formerly carried on for many years by them.

They intend placing on the market Cycles of the very Highest Degree of Perfection, and intending Purchasers will find it to their advantage to deal direct with the Manufacturers, and save the many intermediate profits which they have to pay indirectly when they buy from anyone but bona fide Manufacturers. They also intend putting on the market a Machine which will

Revolutionize the Cycle Trade.

We cannot give full particulars here, but we can say that it will be a Machine suitable for lord or labourer. It will be fitted with Pneumatic Tyres of the Highest Grade, materials throughout the best that money can buy. It will be Fully Guaranteed, and the price will be

£6 : 6s.

We can do, and intend doing, what no other firm has hitherto done, and that is to put a Sound, Reliable, and Up-to-Date Machine within the reach of everybody. We shall study no agents in this matter, but shall go bang for the Public, who will save at the least £4 on every machine by purchasing direct.

Arrangements have also been made for a very large output of Machines built with BSA Fittings, and these will also be sold at a price that will be an eye-opener to the public. Further notice will be given in due course.

F. HOPPER & Co.,
Cycle Manufacturers,
Barton-on-Humber

So, a strongly worded statement that Hopper saw the need to go for the mass market, now that the bicycle was no longer 'fashionable'. The comment about bona fide manufacturers may have been aimed at another local company advertising in the same almanac – 'W Shaw builds his machines from the best materials at a reasonable price.' 'Shaw' Cycles were based in Chapel Lane in Barton, though they do not appear to have been in business long.

## Henry Wilson

Once established as a practising solicitor Henry Wilson moved to Elm Tree House situated on the corner of High Street and Marsh Lane, and built in 1844 by George Ingram, a brick and tile manufacturer from the north bank of the Humber.

Henry Wilson was a Liberal and a strong supporter of the working class. A letter written by him has survived and is in the possession of Mr G Crow of Barton:

Dear Sir,

I'm sorry to be unable to attend the meeting of the Liberal Association tonight. Had I been able to be present I should have strongly supported the proposal for the amalgamation of the Barton Working Men's Club with the Barton Liberal Association. I think myself that the good cause will be better served, and that there will be a greater probability of strong united action being taken, by an undivided Association, than would be the case were the two bodies to remain as at present constituted. It will not do to find us unprepared for battle; the Tories will endeavour to make capital out of poor General Gordon's death,

*Fig. 1.18 The Hopper family in the garden of Elm Tree House, on Barton's High Street c 1898.*
*Fig. 1.19 Fred Hopper Junr aboard one of his father's creations, c 1898.*

and there is no knowing how many weak kneed Liberals may be talked over into supporting a vote of censure on the Government. I may mention that I have seen Mr Brown, and he is also strongly in favour of amalgamation.

This letter is dated 16 February 1885 and was addressed to Mr Joseph Flower, Honorary Secretary of the Barton Liberal Association, and perhaps explains the care that was taken to provide the best possible conditions for the work force at the new St. Mary's Works, when it was built in the early years of the next century. At the time the Liberal Party was in power, only to lose to Lord Salisbury's Tories in 1886. Upward mobility was common in late Victorian England, given the opportunities that abounded for setting up new ventures.

December 1898 must have been something of a watershed for Fred Hopper: Henry Wilson moved to The Hall, built by the Hall family, owners of Hall's Barton Ropery, and Elm Tree House was sold to Hannah Elizabeth Hopper. Fred Hopper had truly joined Barton 'society'. The photograph shown in Fig. 1.18, was taken in the garden of Elm Tree House, probably during 1898, and is of Hannah and Fred Hopper, with Fred Junr, who would have been seven. The ladies sitting on the bench are most probably sisters of Hannah Hopper.

Wilson's liberal attitudes clearly had a major impact on Hopper's treatment of the cycle works employees, as evidenced by the setting up of the recreation club and other such 'improvement' opportunities for his employees, once they were outside the factory.

## The Shows

What little we know of the early Hopper bicycles comes from the national show reports that appeared in the cycling magazines. It is unlikely that many of his workers could afford to buy the fruits of their labour, because until competition and more efficient production methods started to take effect, the bicycle was something of a luxury item.

The first national show attended by Fred Hopper seems to have been the Stanley Show at the Royal Agricultural Hall, Islington, in November 1897. This was an important showcase for the industry, and stand 12 was occupied by the Hull and Barton Manufacturing Co Ltd.

> The 14 machines staged are under the trade name of 'Manchester' cycles. The '98 curved frame is used on the ladies' mounts and the gentlemen's machines are built with forward handlebars on the racers and flat bars on the roadsters. They are solidly constructed mounts upon ordinary lines, possessing no very special construction features.[25]

The report was more positive for the 1899 Stanley Show, where Fred was again attending under the Hull and Barton Cycle Manufacturing banner.

> A good display of finished machines and parts is found on this stand, and a leading line is made of the supply of made-up frames to the trade, with BSA or the firm's own fittings. They have a new box crown of their own design, which has extended sides, and they also push BSA or Harrison's free-wheels and brakes. The whole of the machines show very good finish. Small tools for the trade are also dealt in largely. Those concerned in the making of cycles will find this exhibit interesting.[26]

It was not until the 1901 Stanley Show that a stand was hired under the name of F Hopper and Co.

## Endnotes

1   *F Hopper & Co. – The Problems of Capital Supply in the Cycle Manufacturing Industry, 1891 – 1914.* A E Harrison 1982 Business History Vol 24, No 1 pp 3 – 23.

2   *The Origins of Bicycle racing in England: Technology, Entertainment, Sponsorship and Publicity.* Andrew Ritchie JPMPF 2007 for more information.

3   *On Your Bicycle* McGurn 1987 Chapter 3.

4   *On your Bicycle* McGurn 1987 p 86.

5   Ibid p 89.

6   *The Story of the Bicycle* Woodforde 1970 p 90.

7   Ibid p 92.

8   *On Your Bicycle* McGurn 1987 p 130.

9   The Manchester, Sheffield and Lincolnshire Railway Company was formed in 1847 becoming the Great Central Railway in 1897.

10  A tallow chandler is a maker of animal fat candles, though it can also mean a seller of such candles. As Rawson's was quite a large concern it can be concluded that the Hoppers were employed at the time as candle makers.

11  *Lincolnshire Star* 25 November 1893.

12  *Lynepropp's Luck, Cyclist Annual & Year Book for 1892.*

13  *Bicycling News and Motor Review* 16 July 1902.

14  It is presumed that this club changed its name to the Barton Wheelers Cycling Club as both this club and Barton and District co-existed for several years.

15  *Cyclist and Wheelworld Annual* 1882.

16  *The Cyclist* 10 February 1897.

17  *North Lindsey Star* 3 October 1891.

18  *Lynepropp's Luck, Cyclist Annual & Year Book for 1892.*

19  *The Star* 25 November 1893 reported the death of Fred Hopper's father on 19 November at the age of 66. It states that he had been manager of Rawson's candle factory for 48 years. (This is unlikely, though he must have reached a management position at some stage, which would explain his ability to help his son financially in the early years of his business.)

20  *Lincoln, Rutland & Stamford Mercury* 23 June 1893.

21  *The Cyclist* 27 May 1896.

22  *The Cyclist* 9 December 1896.

23  Information provided by Mr Holtby from the St Matthew Lodge records.

24  Walter Owbridge was born in Haxey, Lincs and devised the popular Owbridge's Lung Tonic.

25  *The Cyclist*, 24 November 1897.

26  *The Cyclist* 22 November 1899.

# CHAPTER 2

## THE YEARS OF GROWTH

The Edwardian years saw rapid growth of the bicycle industry as improved manufacturing techniques and increased competition resulted in more affordable products, thereby creating a much larger market. Under the direction of Frank Bowden, Raleigh increased output through a factory modernisation programme, and in 1901 was employing between 550 and 850, depending on the season. Raleigh's export markets had been developed by the mid-1890s and product quality and innovations like the three-speed hub gear were linked to a marketing strategy that emphasised best value for money, rather than lowest price.[1]

Given the time lost in establishing a new factory in Butts Road and the work involved in returning to Brigg Road, not to mention the need to supply existing customers, it is doubtful whether Hopper gave much thought to export trade before the turn of the century. However, the trade was well served by journals and magazines and he would be well aware of the progress made by Raleigh in Nottingham and by his many competitors in the west Midlands. He had built a sizeable wholesale trade domestically and this continued to grow throughout the pre-war years. With easy access to the large port of Hull by boat, to Liverpool by rail, and to Immingham by local rail, after that port opened in 1912, Hopper was in an excellent location to trade with overseas agents and could compete with the larger established companies.

During the Edwardian years Hopper undertook a construction programme that was unprecedented in Barton. A new factory, new head offices and domestic housing for the growing work force (Fig. 2.1) were just some of the projects that placed a considerable strain on the financial resources of the business. Like many cycle makers of the time, such as Singer, Austin and Humber, Hopper was convinced that motorised transport was the way forward (Fig. 2.2). However, these ventures required more investment than he was able to attract, and this chapter ends with his company in receivership, on the eve of a world war.

Fred Hopper retained an interest in the mechanical development of the bicycle well into this period, when he should perhaps have been more concerned with the financial management of the business. He developed a design for a folding bicycle for which Patent No 20,926 was approved in September 1909, though folding bicycles never appeared in the catalogues during his lifetime (Fig. 2.3).

Much of the material for this chapter is drawn from Dr A E Harrison's 1982 paper on F

*Fig. 2.1  'Park View', Barrow Road, also referred to in early postcards as Hopper's Row, built by Hopper in 1907, © David Lee.*

*Fig. 2.2   Taken around 1902 this photograph encapsulates Hopper's ambitions. The car could be a Delahaye and the motorised bicycle may have a Minerva engine. Fred Hopper is to the extreme right. Note the second storey on the workshop, later improved with facing bricks, © David Lee.*

Hopper and Co and I am grateful to Taylor and Francis (www.tandf.co.uk/journals), the publishers of *Business History* for permission to quote extensively from his work.

## July 1902

The situation in 1902 was described in a report on 'A Group of Lincolnshire Traders' in *Bicycling News and Motor Review* of 16 July.

> Very well known factors are F Hopper & Co of Barton. Mr Hopper has been in the trade since 1880, and his business has grown to such an extent that we are informed that the output now reaches 12,000 annually. Two years ago the business and premises of the Hull & Barton Cycle Manufacturing Co Ltd of Barton on Humber were absorbed, so that the factories and stores now cover several acres of ground. The machines manufactured are known as the Advance and Torpedo, but being principally manufacturers to the trade a large business in frames and machine built from Eadie and BSA fittings is done; the wholesale agencies for these, as well as the agency for the principal proprietary articles, being held. Two years ago they commenced stocking side lines. Mr Hopper issued to the whole of the trade of the United Kingdom a letter on this subject, pointing out that during the winter months anyone connected with the cycle trade can purchase suitable side lines for selling in cycle shops during the off season. The list of these articles includes everything from sewing machines to pianos and organs. The movement has met with great success, and there are many cycle dealers up and down the country who, last winter, were working a successful side line business; whereas, on the other hand, their shops would probably have been comparatively idle. Mr Hopper was the founder of the Barton & District Cycling Club, which, at one time was a very important club in the district. He promoted road racing and took great interest in the sport, but like many other cycle clubs this has had to give way to the times, and is now defunct. Mr Hopper is still an ardent supporter of the sport and his name generally appears in any subscription list. He has taken great interest in his workmen, and two years ago built them a news room, adjoining the works, which is supplied with daily papers and weekly pictorials. He bought a full set of brass instruments, engaged a practical teacher and commenced what is known as the Barton Cycle Works Brass band. This he has pushed with energy, and the band has already appeared in many contests with success. They have won many prizes and are accepted to

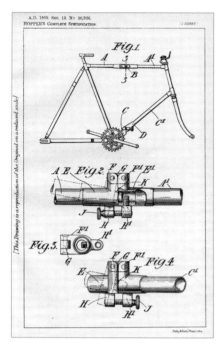

Fig. 2.3   Fred Hopper's patent application for an improved folding mechanism.

compete at the Belle Vue contest at Manchester in July. Mr Hopper is well known at the Stanley Show, always having a stand there. Motor cycles are being made, and although not having commenced the manufacture of motor cars some trade is being done, and Hopper's are making arrangements next year to be able to put on the market a first class car of their own manufacture.

Smith's 1902 *Barton Family Almanac* carried an interesting advertisement for F Hopper – proclaiming it to have 'The Largest Cycle Manufactory in the North of England.' One suspects that Elswick of Newcastle may also have made the same claim.

## Growth

F Hopper & Co grew significantly in terms of sales and profits in the first seven years of the new century:[2]

| Trading Year | Trading Profits £ | Sales less Returns £ |
|---|---|---|
| 1900/1 | 2,228 | 34,804 |
| 1903/4 | 5,939 | 45,353 |
| 1904/5 | 6,779 | 71,141 |
| 1905/6 | 8,340 | 101,741 |
| 1906/7 | 10,475 | 124,458 |
| 1907/8 | 8,843 | 117,996 |
| 1908/9 | 9,852 | 123,848 |
| 1909/10 | 8,823 | 112,919 |
| 1910/11 | 11,237 | 148,863 |
| 1911/12 | 11,614 | 158,209 |
| 1912/13★ | 4,354 | 160,152 |

★ 5 August 1912 to 7 October 1913

While trade sales had grown in the domestic market Hopper could see from the lead set by Raleigh that to become a serious player in the industry he must start exporting. H W Allkin was hired early in the decade to develop the growing overseas markets in the Far East and Australasia. Naturally, such trips were expensive and time consuming due to the slow pace of sea travel and the huge distances involved. An undated itinerary of what may have been Allkin's first trip is stored in Lincoln Archives and is reproduced here. It shows that Hopper was serious about establishing new markets and was prepared to invest the necessary resources, including the manufacture and transport of 4,200 bicycles. Mr Allkin's background is not known but it seems likely that he was already in business in Cape Town. I have found no record of him visiting the UK, but, the firm, H W Allkin of Cape Town, is listed as an Elswick-Hopper customer in files dating from 1914 to 1932, with purchases that included both Torpedo and Elswick motorcycles. The spelling of the original has been retained:

Proposed tour of H W Allkin commencing and concluding at Cape Town.

| New Zealand | Dutch East Indies | Cochin China |
|---|---|---|
| * Invercargill | *Batavia | Saigon |
| *Port Chalmers | *Soerabaya | |
| Dunedin | Samarang | Siam |
| *Christchurch | Padang | *Bangkok |
| *Wellington | *Medan | |
| Palmerston North | Balawan | Straits Settlements |
| *Auckland | *Palembang | *Singapore |
| Fielding | | Kuala Lumpur |
| | Japan | *Port Swettenham |
| Australia | *Yokohama | Selangor |
| *Perth | Tokio | Klang |
| *Adelaide | *Kobe | Taiping |
| Ballarat | Kioto | *Penang |
| *Melbourne | Osaka | |
| *Sydney | Kiogo | India |
| *Brisbane | | *Colombo |
| Maryboro | China | Tuticorin |
| Rockhampton | *Shanghai | *Trinchinopoly |
| Townsville | *Tientsin | *Madras |
| Charters Towers | Peking | *Bangalore |
| | *Hong Kong | *Bombay |
| | Canton | |

Sample cases to be sent to all places marked * = 28 cases, say 150 machines.

| | £ |
|---|---|
| Estimated cost of ocean travel | 180 |
| Estimated cost of expenses 150 days at £2 | 300 |

Fig. 2.4   *A consignment of 130 packing cases en route to Shanghai 1907.*

Fig. 2.5   *Wrapping at Brigg Road c 1907.*

The investment paid off and from a negligible level of exports in 1900, overseas sales reached £78,000 in 1911/12, close to 50%. As with home sales the strategy pursued was to deal with intermediaries and within a few years Hopper had a network of overseas trading houses as customers. One of the largest was the Atherton Group, with offices in Liverpool and bases in Burma and India. In August 1908 George W Brockhurst was authorised to act on the firm's behalf in Japan. This was followed two years later by an application for registration of trademarks in Japan. The first catalogue issued purely for the export market is dated February 1907 and during that year Hopper won a large export order for Shanghai (Fig. 2.4), which would have been transported along Waterside Road to Barton Haven, and transferred from there by boat to Hull Docks. According to the photograph it comprised 130 cases, containing 600 bicycles and one Torpedo motor car. The packing shop photograph (Fig. 2.5) shows similar lettering on the cases and may have been taken during the process of packing what was clearly a significant order.

Two Hull men with business credentials were hired to develop the UK and European markets: Charles Herbert Atkinson and Charles William Shakesby. C W Shakesby was involved with the East Riding Cycle Depot on Holderness Road, Hull[3] in 1892 and was later noted as manager of the Butts Road factory. He is pictured in a prominent position in an early photograph with Fred Hopper and the workforce (Fig. 2.6). It would seem from this evidence that he was one of the first 'white collar' employees. He remained a traveller for many years, still residing in Hull and was followed into the business by his son Clarence V Shakesby. C H Atkinson made the move to Barton in 1898 and eventually became foreign sales manager. He bought White Cross House on Barrow Road in 1910 and stayed with the company until after the First World War, when he left to start his own bicycle and garage business at his home, trading initially as White Cross Cycles. The family recalls tales of his trips to Holland, occasionally accompanied by his wife, so we can assume that sales to European agents were given his personal touch.

The most significant effects of growth on the town of Barton were in rising employment and the need for new factory buildings and housing. The 1891 census shows a mere half dozen declaring employment in the nascent Hopper cycle manufactory. According to the 1901 census the population stood at 5,700 and by 1905, Hopper employed 400; by 1912, 800. Skilled men were brought in from Yorkshire and from the Midlands, probably attracted by the fresher air of rural Lincolnshire, and

*Fig. 2.6  Fred Hopper (right) and Charles W Shakesby with the workforce c 1902. It was taken against the south wall of Keal's building, facing the entrance to Beretun Green. It was demolished in 2009.*

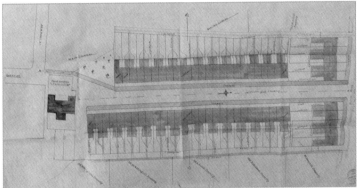

*Fig. 2.7  'Block plan showing development on New Hall Estate for Messrs. F Hopper.' Initially called New Street it was later called Queens Avenue, an extension of Queen Street.*

cheaper housing, especially as the company embarked on a series of house building projects. The best example is the development of Queen's Avenue as a northwards extension of Queen Street. It was built for Hopper employees in what had been the grounds of the magnificent Georgian house known as New Hall, one of Barton's earliest large brick dwellings. The property came on the market in 1903, was bought by Fred Hopper and occupied by one of his foremen, Albert Wall, for a few years. The large orchard situated to the east of the house was split off for housing and the residual property eventually resold. Plans were submitted to the Urban District Council in 1906 for the construction of houses in 'New Street' for rental to cycle workers, with simpler, cheaper houses on the west side and more elaborate ones on the east for the better paid (Fig. 2.7 & 2.8). Management houses were also built just to the east of the Butts Road factory – a row of eight semi-detached properties – for, amongst others, the company secretary (Fig. 2.9). Other houses were constructed from 1903 onwards on Soutergate, Barrow Road, and Catherine Street. The provision of modern dwellings would have provided a strong incentive to work for Hopper, especially for skilled workers from outside the area. The ownership of the Hopper houses has not been investigated in any depth as it is outside the scope of this book. However, they were undoubtedly built as rental properties, as before 1914 less than 10% of housing was owner occupied.[4] It is known that some were owned by the company for many years and it is probable that the rest were either sold on as sources of investment income, developed by local builders in the knowledge that Hopper's workers would fill them, or bought by prudent employees.

*Fig. 2.8 'New Street' has been driven through the New Hall grounds as the first step in the creation of Queens Avenue. Houses on Butts Road are seen at the end.*

*Fig. 2.9 Management houses built by Hopper c 1905 at the west end of Butts Road, adjacent to the Hull and Barton Manufacturing Co Ltd factory.*

An idea of the growth in sales, and the advantage of a factory sited on an estuary, was reported in *The Cyclist Trade Review* of 23 March 1905. With the title 'Cheap Rates' the article continued:

> Owing to the increase of their trade in London Messrs Hopper & Co of Barton on Humber inform us that they have had to extend their premises in St John St, Clerkenwell. In addition to keeping a varied stock of machines and accessories there, novelties as they come out are immediately sent out to Mr England, their London depot manager. For the convenience of London traders and with an idea to overcome the difficulty of carriage, consignments of cycles are sent regularly twice a week from Barton to London by boat and London agents are not slow to take advantage of the benefits of the cheap carriage. Incidentally, Messrs Hopper and Co inform us that they have a means of getting machines from Barton to London at sixpence each.

So it is clear that based close to a busy estuary, with excellent marine links to London, Hopper was able to use his location to advantage.

## Public Life

As well as developing his business Fred Hopper found the time and energy to become deeply involved in Barton's public life, possibly with the encouragement of Henry Wilson. He was elected to Barton Urban District Council in 1902 shortly before a visit to the factory reported in the *Lincolnshire and Lindsey Star* of 5 April 1902. The report recorded the regret of the Fire and Lighting Committee of the UDC "as to the 'hostile manner' in which the Committee had been met by Councillor Hopper when they made an official visit to his works for the purpose of inspection as to the means of escape etc., in the event of an outbreak of fire. A rather lively discussion took place on this point, Mr Hopper's contention being that the committee visited his works at an inconvenient time. Mr Hopper's explanation was accepted." He could clearly be a prickly character.

In 1904 Hopper purchased the Lordship of the Manor of Barton on Humber, succeeding George Martinson. The title had been held by the crown until 1859 when it was sold to Adam Jessop and George Bradley; Fred Hopper was the seventh holder of the Lordship. While something of an honorary title by this time, as the UDC, established in 1894, was the governing body, it would have endowed the holder with a significant position in local society. The title passed to Fred Hopper Junr on his father's death and he eventually sold it to Barton UDC in 1936 for £100.

Fig 2.10 *Fred Hopper, every inch the Edwardian patrician – JP and Lord of the Manor.*

Finally, he was made a Justice of the Peace, qualifying at the Lincoln Quarter Sessions on 20 June 1907. The studio photograph, Fig. 2.10, was most likely taken at this time as it shows him every inch the Edwardian gentleman with his waxed moustache, morning coat and gold Albert. It was an expensive day for the new JP, as a £2 fee was payable to the Commission of the Peace of the Parts of Lindsey as part of the qualification process, and he also paid a two guinea subscription to the Lindsey Wine Fund. Whereas the role of magistrates had once been the preserve of the landed gentry and the clergy, by 1900 it was possible for merchants, industrialists and retired professionals to be appointed, signifying a shift in power from a rural ruling class to a partly urban elite.[5] Hopper qualified extraordinarily well as a local industrialist and at the age of 47 seemed to have the world at his 'wheels', having set up a grassroots business in rural Lincolnshire to compete with the best of the Midlands manufacturers. Public service was, of course, very much in the Victorian tradition of philanthropy and Fred Hopper did give much to Barton in the provision and maintenance of facilities in the town,

Fig. 2.11 *A fanciful view of the Brigg Road establishment as it appeared on the back of the 1903 catalogue, clearly to impress customers who were unlikely to visit Barton.*

Fig. 2.12 *Letter heading from 1905. Note the absence of the Brigg Road offices, which were constructed later that year.*

especially where his workers' welfare was concerned. His partner, Henry Wilson, joined the bench as a JP a few years later in January 1911, the same year that Rev W E Varah, (father of Chad Varah, who founded the Samaritans in 1953), accepted the vicariate of Barton. Fred Hopper also took education very seriously and for many years was a manager of the National School on Queen Street.

## A New Factory – St Mary's Works

Development at Brigg Road was limited by lack of space on the west side and in 1900 a new building was erected on the east side at the junction with Castledyke South. The land was leased to Hopper and Wilson by Robert Brown Junr, the local solicitor and historian, with whom Henry Wilson had first stayed when he arrived in Barton. According to the records the building was rented from Henry Woodcock, a local farmer and also a Councillor, so it is likely that he agreed to pay for the building in return for a regular rental income. The terms were agreed on 12 May 1900, according to a letter in the Lincolnshire Archives from Henry Wilson to 'Dear Hopper', for a term of 21 years. From a highly inaccurate artist's impression of 1903 (Fig. 2.11) it accommodated a new frame building shop and a store for accessories. In later years it was used as a packing shop and store for the domestic market, known as 'the English' to distinguish it from 'the Foreign' packing shop, built in 1907 further up Castledyke South and on the south side (Fig. 2.13).

This development was not sufficient to keep pace with demand and a major step was taken to move production to a new site to the north of Soutergate, bounded to the east by housing and the Anchor Brewery buildings on Pasture Road, and to the west by Manby House and its land towards Marsh Lane. Houses on Soutergate, giving access to the old tan yard site, had been acquired by the partners some time before, indicating that they had done some serious long-term planning. This relatively narrow site (east to west) was named the St Mary's Works after the Parish Church on the south side of Soutergate and the original main entrance was off that street (Fig. 2.14). From archive material we know that construction started in 1903, with the erection of water closets, and continued

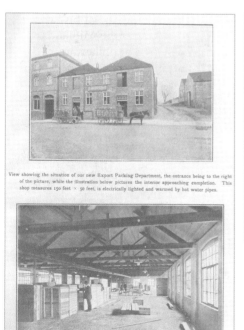

View showing the situation of our new Export Packing Department, the entrance being to the right of the picture, while the illustration below pictures the interior approaching completion. This shop measures 150 feet × 50 feet, is electrically lighted and warmed by hot water pipes.

*Fig. 2.13 From the 1908 catalogue this shows the building leased from Henry Woodcock, with motor dray and horse drawn rully outside. The office was built adjacent to it to the left, and the export packing shop is visible on the south side of Castledyke South.*

*Fig. 2.14 The entrance to the new works was originally on Soutergate. Note the proximity to St Mary's church.*

The Recent Extension at our St. Mary's Works, from an actual photograph.

*Fig. 2.15 A photograph of St Mary's Works taken from St Mary's church tower in 1906. The new machine shop is seen under construction to the left of the photograph.*

*Fig. 2.16 The same view taken in 1907.*

in stages until 1908, when a new machine shop was constructed. A 'K type' Crossley gas engine was ordered in December 1902 and a letter from Barton Gas Co, dated 27 January confirmed that a new gas main was to be laid to the tan yard premises and that the charge would be 2s 8½d per 1,000 cu ft. Correspondence also took place with the Varnish and Colour Works of Wolverhampton in December 1902 concerning the best way to achieve a stoving temperature of 200°F using steam or gas at the new factory. Waste water disposal was also considered and William Harrison of Harrison and Robb, consulting engineers of 21 Scale Lane, Hull, was hired to establish the best way to carry waste water from the Works into the Humber. Whatever scheme he came up with it is clear that waste water was piped into the Butts Road drain and thence to the Haven and Humber.[6]

Some buildings had two storeys, with workshops on both floors, and some were single storey. Some were of substantial brick construction with tie rods and ornate cast iron plates denoting the year of construction; others were steel clad. An article in *The Cyclist* of 17 November 1904 recorded that Hopper had:

> been noted for many years for the production of low priced machines, and whose annual production exceeds 18,000 machines and frames. Mr Hopper has made a special study of the requirements of this class of trade, and is perhaps the largest specialiser in frames in this country. His system throughout is based on specialising methods and he is fortunate in having perfected a means of liquid brazing which enables him to reduce cost and give the exceptional value he offers. His factories at Barton on Humber are organised on up-to-date lines, one of the latest being a plant for enamelling by superheated steam. Recently Mr Hopper became lord of the manor of Barton by purchasing the manorial rights to the township – a barony which dates back to the days of William the Conqueror. The manorial rights include market tolls, quit rents, etc, on copyhold, land minerals, fishing and shooting rights, and proprietorship of the haven of Barton on Humber, where thousands of tons are annually landed. Less than half a century ago the manorial rights of Barton were sold for £5,050. The purchase by Mr Hopper has given great satisfaction to the townspeople of Barton, where he takes great interest in municipal affairs, and is the largest employer of labour. Mr Hopper is a keen business man, of indomitable energy, and his unfailing courtesy has earned for him the highest respect of all those cycle agents with whom he has had business dealings.

The factory was photographed from the tower of St Mary's church for the January 1907 and 1908 catalogues and a comparison clearly shows the rapid pace of building (Fig. 2.15 and 2.16). Crossley Otto gas engines powered electrical generators as they had for the Brigg Road workshops, and this power was supplied to dc motors, used to drive the many lay shafts around the works, to the plating shop, stove enamelling ovens and to the lighting circuits. It was not until 1913 that the Barton on Humber Electric Supply Co Ltd began to supply the town with electric street lighting, with, almost inevitably, Fred Hopper as chairman, following an agreement between Hopper and the UDC signed on 5 September 1912. Clearly not concerned with upsetting a major customer the gas company had objected to the parliamentary bill to authorise electric lighting on the grounds that such schemes were not economic in towns with populations below 12,000, and that if the new cables were laid in close proximity to the gas mains it could prove highly dangerous in the event of 'electric wires fusing.' The gas company may, of course, have been just a little worried at the prospect of competition, having enjoyed a monopoly since 1846.

The speed of development at St Mary's is best described by quoting from *The Cycle and Motor Trade Review*, of 12 September 1907, entitled 'The Growth of Hopper's Works':

The last time we went to Barton on Humber to see the factory of F Hopper and Co was in July 1906, and we were very much impressed by the size of the works and the arrangements generally. We then noted that there was still available land for further extensions of the works, and that certain enlargements were contemplated, but we were in no way prepared for the huge extensions which we inspected a week or so ago. Mr Hopper himself was good enough to devote the morning showing us round, and, in spite of our making the tour of the works as quickly as possible, it took several hours to do so.

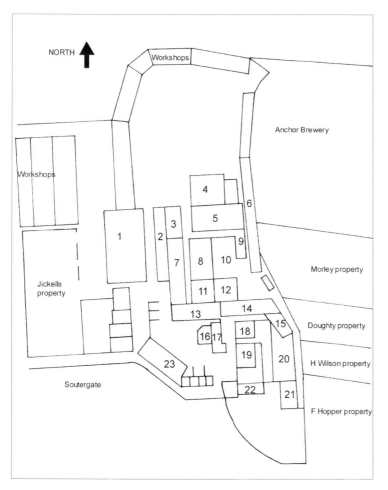

*Fig. 2.17 Plan of St Mary's Works c 1907 before the extension west through to Marsh Lane.*

*Key:*
1.  New machine shop
2.  Stores
3.  Lining
4.  Foreign enamelling room
5.  Enamelling and lining
6.  Frame making and filing
7.  Machine room
8.  Polishing
9.  Gas producing
10.  Polishing
11.  Plating shop
12.  Engine room
13.  Stores
14.  Frame building
15.  Blacksmith shop
16.  Office
17.  Tube store
18.  Enamelling
19.  Enamelling
20.  Liquid brazing and black leading
21.  Bricklayer store and joiners' shop
22.  Handlebar shop
23.  Machine shop

The first extension we came across was a new store for complete machines which had just been started on, and will be completed in about three and a half months – in good time to receive a stock of 1908 models. This storehouse is 150ft long by 50ft broad, and will be arranged so that machines can be stacked in several tiers. It is situated alongside the chief offices and stock rooms, whence all the despatching is done. [This would have been an extension to the Woodcock building on Brigg Road.]

From here Mr Hopper took us down to St Mary's Works, of which we gave a bird's-eye view last year. The big machine shop, which we then showed in a half-finished condition, has now been running for nearly a season, and, big as it is, a still larger shop has had to be built to relieve the pressure upon it. This new shop is 125ft by 55ft, and is arranged with a wide gallery all round and a glass roof, quite in the style of the most modern factory practice, thus ensuring that the work shall be done under the best possible conditions. This shop and all the other main shops are fitted with an installation of big arc lamps, so that when working overtime, as is the general rule here for most months of the year, the men can see their work almost as well as by day. The contrast between this and the old-fashioned 'one man one gas jet' method is, of course, very great, and seems more remarkable in such an old-world place as Barton, which is, in outward appearance, the same old-fashioned market town it has been for hundreds of years, for Hopper and Co's works do not disfigure the landscape with reeking chimneys.

All the power is obtained from dynamos driven by gas engines, which are supplied from suction plants on the premises. For the main power plant a new 100hp gas engine has been put in since our last visit, in addition to the engines in the power station, which we then illustrated. This new engine is now driving a 65kw Siemens dynamo, which has just been installed to replace another of smaller power. One of the engines then in the central power station is also being replaced by a much larger engine of 70hp, which will be used exclusively for the electric lighting plant.

A new and much larger air compressor for the sand-blast and brazing plants is being put in, and a 60hp engine is being located outside the works altogether, simply to drive a suction arrangement to extract the dust from the polishing shops.

During the first week in August, while the works were shut down for stocktaking, the old polishing lathes were taken out of one of the several polishing shops, fourteen new double-spindle lathes were put in, and a complete system of brick-lined trenches was laid through all the polishing shops, on which the suction-cowls for the dust-extractors will be fitted as soon as the rest of the plant is ready.

Mr Hopper's watchword is 'Efficiency' and he is convinced that he gets a better and larger output when the work is done under the best conditions; hence the excellent lighting arrangements

*Fig. 2.18 Fork brazing at St Mary's Works.*

*Fig. 2.19 The lining shop. Note the ample window light and numerous electric lamps.*

and the new dust-suction plant. For the same reason he arranges all his shops so that each workman has plenty of room in which to move, and to us, accustomed to the economy of room necessary in the Midland factories owing to cost of land, the arrangements for the men at Barton seem quite generous in their spaciousness. Still, there can be no doubt that better results are obtained thereby.

Further extensions have been made in the plating shops. Several new vats have been put in during the last twelve months, among them a new vat for plating rims, in which the rims roll round and round slowly in the vat, and do not stir up the sediment, which is the objection to those vats with revolving anodes. The enamelling plant can now only be described as 'vast'. In several weeks during the past season over 1,400 frames and forks were actually enamelled in these shops each week. A new shop has just been erected specially for lining frames, forks, and guards. This shop has glass sides like a conservatory, so that the liners have regular unshadowed light by which to work (Fig. 2.19). The floor is kept tarred to prevent dust from rising. Another new shop has been added specially for the liquid brazing process in which the frames are dipped in a bath of molten brass.

As an example of the thorough system in the works Mr Hopper showed us that, in the event of a complaint from a customer (which rarely occurs), a frame can be traced to the actual builder, filer, finisher, enameller, etc, who is responsible for its turn-out. As Mr Hopper pointed out, this involves a lot of clerical work, but the end justifies the means, for men will not scamp work when they know that the actual piece of work can be traced to them, even if many months have passed since the work was done.

The men seem to appreciate Mr Hopper's labours for their betterment, as they stay with the firm for long periods. Several of the machine-shop men are working alongside their own sons, who were apprenticed to the business years ago, and one man, from whom Mr Hopper enquired how long he had been with the firm, told us he had been there for twenty five years.

A healthy sign of the past season's trade is the fact that, in spite of the big weekly output, there are scarcely any finished machines in stock, and very few finished frames, thus showing that sales have been well up to the output. At present the works are running with the full complement of hands, and parts are coming through in quantities which will mean a fine stock of frames and machines ready for the 1908 season, so that buyers need have no fear of slow deliveries next year. It is estimated that when the few extensions that still remain to be completed are in full running order, the output will be up to 2,000 frames per week.

The foreign trade is growing steadily and rapidly, and while we were there quite a number of big cases were sent off to Barton Haven for transport across the Humber to Hull, whence they would be shipped direct to their destinations abroad. This method of shipment is a gain to the overseas buyer, for it minimises the carriage from the place of production to the port of shipment, on which cost the foreign buyer has, in many cases, to pay duty, as it is added to the invoice price on which duty is paid.

Since last year this business has been transformed into a public company under the title of F Hopper and Co Ltd. The additional capital thus acquired enables the scope of the business to be further extended, so that altogether, with the increased power and space, and improved methods of production, the prospects of the firm seem very bright indeed.

Mr Hopper deserves the greatest credit for the way in which he has built up in a small country town from very small beginnings a business which will bear comparison with the biggest businesses in the recognised centres of manufacture, and from the firm's customers we learn that the goods turned out compare very favourably in value for money with anything produced elsewhere.

Given that this article appeared in a trade journal, supported by advertisements from firms like F Hopper and Co Ltd, it was not likely to be critical. However, it does provide a first hand picture of the factory after just four years. The provision of dust extraction and good lighting and the statement concerning 'Efficiency' show that Hopper understood well the link between good working conditions and high rates of production. The system of traceability shows that Hopper took quality seriously, and with reliance on piece work there would indeed have been a temptation to 'scamp work. Tracing a frame back to its makers relied on each one being stamped with a letter and serial number, typically at the

*Fig. 2.20 Henry and Blanche Wilson's Silver Wedding celebration in the newly erected machine shop at St Mary's Works.*

top of the seat tube (see Appendix 1). The 1906 photograph must have been taken much earlier than July as the machine shop was used for Henry Wilson's silver wedding party (Fig. 2.20). The photograph taken from the balcony shows the band at the far end behind the top table. Henry is directly in front of the conductor and Fred to the left. The completion of the building must have coincided with the event, which took place in June. It was rapidly filled with machine tools and put to work (Fig. 2.21).

The Hopper and Wilson partnership, joined in 1907 by local solicitor Gilbert Nowell, had negotiated the purchase of Manby House and its land during 1908 and in February 1909 leased it to the new limited company, F Hopper & Co Ltd, registered in 1907, for seven years, with an option to buy. The option was exercised in October 1909, by which time new polishing shops had already been erected on this new area of the St Mary's site, which now extended through to Marsh Lane.

Increased production required additional equipment and Hopper bought the best machine tools available, such as those supplied by Charles Churchill & Co and Alfred Herbert, both of Coventry. What equipment he could devise and make himself he did. He had an operational liquid brazing plant set up in 1904,[7] though this was not new technology, as Raleigh had perfected the technique as early as January 1900.[8] He built his own enamelling stove heated by superheated steam and by 1908 had

*Fig. 2.21 The St Mary's machine shop in full swing c 1914. Note the exposed belt drives, but also the excellent lighting.*

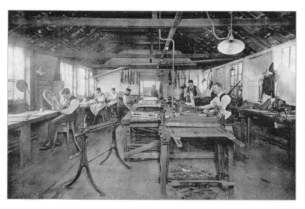

*Fig. 2.22    Gearcase making 1912.*

*Fig. 2.23    Hopper wheelbuilders. Note the predominance of men – during the war many were replaced by women, and the practice continued after 1918.*

devised an electrically heated stove and built and installed two of them. Six more were added in 1909, three in 1910 and two in 1911, giving an idea of the growth in production capacity over these years. As an example of his entrepreneurial approach to business Hopper added the stoves to the list of products advertised in the thick trade catalogues of the period; in 1908 there were four different sizes available. Above all Hopper was a practical and experienced mechanic who knew his product from personal use and so had no need for expensive back room designers and draftsmen. What he did need was hands-on labourers and craftsmen, especially as he knew that the lower wages paid in Lincolnshire could give him a competitive edge if he made more of the components previously bought from Midland suppliers such as BSA, Bown, and Eadie. This strategy, which we have seen was implemented as early as 1895, allowed him to lower prices even further and so remain competitive. As a percentage of the value of total output, component purchases fell from 58.6% to 44.9% between 1900 and 1913, while the wage bill rose from 13.5% to 18.2%. By 1913, only special gears, saddles, chains and pneumatic tyres were purchased fully manufactured from specialist producers.

*Fig. 2.24 Soutergate, west of the entrance, at home time.*

*Fig. 2.25 The new office under construction in 1905. Note the shipment to India loaded on to rullies. The George Hotel can be seen across the road.*

## A New Office

Burgeoning production required additional administration to handle the mass of purchase orders, sales invoices and other such paperwork and Hopper set the mould for the next 60 years by building a new and prestigious office block on the corner of Holydyke and Brigg Road, directly opposite the George Hotel, and following northwards the building line of the Woodcock building. Why did Fred choose to separate the offices from the main production centre? Perhaps because he was so well established on Brigg Road, had created a showroom there and already had plans to further develop the Castledyke South land. Given his stated ambitions to take the company into motorised transport it is most likely that Hopper was carefully assessing the potential of all available land in the town, and decided that there was insufficient space on a single site for his ultimate vision. Whatever the rationale, his home at Elm Tree House on High Street was ideally situated, lying roughly midway between the two centres of operation. Plans for the offices were drawn up by local architect Arthur Stamp in May 1905 and passed by the UDC on 1 June 1905. The completed building was occupied later that year, surely a fast track project that would be impossible to accomplish in the 21st century. The office construction is captured in Fig. 2.25, which shows continued use of the adjacent Woodcock building during construction, and the completed building is shown in Fig. 2.26. The builders clearly did a good job as it was deemed

*Fig. 2.26 The completed office building on the corner of Brigg Road.*

suitable for redevelopment by Barry Smith of Copperfield Developments as apartments in 2006, a task which took more than twice as long as the original construction. The Woodcock building had been stripped of its tiles a few years before and was deemed beyond repair. It was rebuilt using old bricks and incorporated into the apartment scheme. Barry sadly died, age 62, on 3 December 2009, while in the midst of a similar project at the old Anchor Brewery site. The Hopper offices are now known as Copperfield House and are a tribute to Barry Smith's expertise.

Fred Hopper once told Canon W E Varah that when excavating for foundations the builders dug out a considerable collection of chips of bell metal.[9] The conclusion drawn by the Vicar was that this must have been the site of the James Harrison bell foundry, which, as stated in Chapter 1, was actually on the opposite side of Brigg Road. It is probable that the vacant site had been used for the disposal of waste material. The office building was reported in the *Hull Times* of 16 December 1905, and despite some repetition of facts already covered it is given in full to capture the Edwardian flavour:

> You mount an Enchanter or a Torpedo 'bike' and you free-wheel to your heart's content. Take a gear of about 75, and all ordinary hill-climbing is accomplished with ease and grace; it really is surprising the manner in which the Torpedo responds to one's feelings, but the secret is all in the making. You buy a Torpedo or an Enchanter and immediately you fill the saddle you feel wedded to that machine for life.
>
> At the birthplace of the Enchanter and Torpedo very extensive additions have just been made, and in alluding to these improvements it may be opportune to trace the building of these machines from their early history to their final stages. The historic town of Barton on Humber was never in so flourishing a condition as it is today. It may have been an important agricultural centre, say, 50 years ago, but now the old order has changed, and given place to the new, with a result that the metropolis of North Lincolnshire, as it is designated, is decidedly a commercial place, with little or no corn market. The manufacture of bikes has given it a world-wide reputation, and in some parts of Japan, South Africa, Russia, New Zealand, India, Australia, and many other climes the name of Messrs F Hopper and Co is more familiar than it is even some 15 to 20 miles away from the scene of the firm's huge premises. The reason for this is chiefly due to the enormous foreign trade the firm has merited, and only those who watch the daily packages away from Barton to abroad can have any idea of the business carried out by Messrs Hopper.
>
> The head of the firm, Mr F Hopper, a personage who has accomplished much for the advancement of his native place, is the son of the late Mr Robert Hopper, who was a tallow chandler for Mr William Rawson in the building now occupied by the Humber Candle Company. Serving his apprenticeship with Mr Neave, whitesmith, Mr Hopper afterwards worked for a time at one of the large boiler-making shops in Hull, also at Marshall's, Gainsborough, and ultimately settled in Barton again. Possessing great tenacity of purpose, and one who understood not the meaning of the word 'failure' he commenced a little forge of his own on the very site where the Brigg Road works now stand. He had as an apprentice a young fellow named Wilson, who is not only with the firm today, but has a son also as apprentice. In his modest beginning Mr Hopper took to repairing bicycles, and, being convinced that there was a great future for the 'wheel' resolved upon the manufacture of bikes as his chief pursuit. Soon Mr Hopper's fame found extensive circulation, and it was necessary to enlarge his then small workshop, and from that time to the present has the story been a continuous one of extensions and improvements, until now the firm – including that valued member Mr Henry Wilson – are the proud owners of one of the most complete and up-to-date outfits for cycle building in the country.
>
> The value of their plant is little dreamed of at Barton, and only those in the inner workings of the trade can form anything like a correct idea of the money invested. The whole of Mr Hopper's business abilities have been directed towards the production of a really sound, recommendable machine at the lowest possible price and that his labours have been crowned with success is proof abundant in a Torpedo. In spite of all enlargements and additions to the Brigg Road premises, including the erection of a large warehouse and offices, it was found absolutely necessary some time ago to purchase and construct other works. The St Mary's Works then came into existence on the

site of the old tan yard, which had been closed for some years. The pits were filled in, and much expense entered into before the present splendid array of some twenty-five odd departments was completed ready for use. The St Mary's venue is a 'colony' in itself, and the outsider would marvel if he saw therein. Practically speaking all the frames are built here, and, although it would no doubt be interesting, the various processes through which a frame has to go before being sent to Brigg Road for completion as a machine are too numerous by far to allow of special description. Suffice it to say that there are many parts in a frame and each particular part is attended to by men skilled at their work. System governs everything, and here is presented a fine example of what proper order can accomplish. Some 200 men are at work, and the buzz of machinery as one passes along reminds one more of the interior of the 'Black Country' rather than rural Lincolnshire. It is a veritable beehive, where the sting of 'vim' is manifest in every inhabitant. Some idea of the magnitude of the frame department may be gathered from the fact that the weekly average turn-out is some 900 machines and frames, and at times even more than 1,000 are completed in a week. Here are some of the sections of the department: the receiving of the material in its rough form, the knocking together of the frame, brazing (much of this is done by hand), shot blasting, filing, edging, polishing, and latterly enamelling, lining and plating (wheels and handlebars &c.). The processes are exceedingly interesting, but they would take too much space for description.

In another part of town the firm have stored something like £9,000 worth of rubber, whilst it is not an uncommon occurrence to give orders after the style of 20,000 crank wheels at a time, and when one considers that between 340 and 400 hands are regularly employed full time, one need hardly be surprised at such colossal orders. The clerical staff numbers some 20 persons, including eight lady typists, and shorthand writers, and it is to extend the accommodation for these pen-workers that the new handsome and commodious offices have been erected at the corner of Brigg Road and Bank Street.[10] Without any unnecessary ceremony one may designate this building as the finest set of offices in North Lincolnshire, and that to Barton they add importance and dignity to the town. Of a commanding appearance they stand out as the hall-mark of progress, and anyone entering the town cannot help being deeply impressed.

Insignificant though Barton may still be to some of the people across the Humber, it can, at any rate, teach them much in the matter of the cycle industry. Barton residents have a right to honour the head of the firm, for in divers ways has he placed what was surely in some ways a retrograde place on an entirely advanced footing. He has built in many quarters, and his enthusiasm in this respect is still going ahead. As a member of the Urban Council he has a strong and earnest desire for a better state of sanitation, and the scheme suggested by him should ere long find favour, as it certainly deserves. In its present antiquated method of sanitation Barton would in the event of an epidemic arising cut a very sorry figure. An ardent Churchman Mr Hopper has held various religious offices. In this, as in his business matters, he is all for progress, and what is a particularly happy feature is that he demonstrates an earnest endeavour at comradeship for his employees after working hours. In his brass band – which has gained prizes without number (including a third at Crystal Palace this year) – he offers every inducement to the individual to succeed – inducements which are recognised in appreciable manner.

It was the original intention to mark the opening of the new offices by a convivial evening, but the pressure of business just at the present hardly allows of such an occasion, though at the first opportunity there will be a loyal celebration.

The new erection is a three-storeyed one, the ground floor being entirely reserved for the clerical staff, and the second storey as a general stores, and the third as an erecting room. The total length of the front of the building is 105ft, and the height from the footpath to the eaves is about 40ft, the span being 50ft. The building is of brick, with Howley Park stone dressings, all the facing bricks being selected stock from the yard of Mr J B Tombleson JP. All the girders are of steel, supported by cast iron columns in the centre. The office fittings throughout are of pitch pine, and the two principal entrances contain some fine ornamental work. The heating of the building is accomplished by the hot water low pressure system, and the rooms are lighted by electricity. A modern system of ventilation has been employed, and the whole building carried out on a scale to ensure comfort to those working therein, and for a speedier transmission of the piles of correspondence to be got through day by day. To Mr John Stamp, the sole contractor, the building is a great credit, and to Mr Arthur Stamp, the architect and director of the work, high praise is also due. They have had under them the following local tradesmen and sub-contractors: Messrs H Pickard and Sons, W King and Son, H Flower, and D K Austin. By the opening of these offices Barton has, at any rate, finished the year 1905 in a style which augurs well for the future. Messrs Hopper assure one that there are already orders booked to provide work for all until well into the New Year. At the recent Stanley Show in London many large and valuable orders were taken.

W. A. T.

Hopper also believed that it was the right time to create a presence in the London market by establishing an office and showroom. This was achieved with the signing of a five-year lease to run from Christmas Day 1905 on a shop and offices at 88 and 90 Tabernacle Street, London. The annual rent was set at £135.

## Capital for Expansion – F Hopper & Co Ltd.

A lack of understanding of the financial markets, and consequent difficulties in raising capital for expansion, was the Achilles' heel of the early Hopper enterprise and though Henry Wilson undoubtedly brought a different perspective to the business he was versed in law, not finance, and seems to have been swept along by Fred Hopper's enthusiasm for growth. According to A E Harrison, Henry Wilson had the greater personal income and from the records he made the bigger financial contribution to the business. At the start of the 1900/01 financial year the balance on his capital account stood at £5,247, increasing to £8,664 at the start of 1903/4 and £9,996 a year later. Fred Hopper's account stood at £3,265, £3,464 and £4,255 on the corresponding dates. From Harrison's paper:

> Wilson was also ploughing back more of the interest and profits accruing to the partners and also paying in some further sums of capital. In addition to his personal stake Wilson also secured small sums from his wife and sister and from his firm of solicitors.
>
> Apart from the capital accounts of Fred Hopper and Henry Wilson and family, there was by July 1900 a mortgage on certain of the firm's buildings of £2,000 but this was paid off a couple of years later. There were also overdrafts from the Stamford, Spalding and Boston Bank and from the National Provincial. The partnership never managed to eliminate these overdrafts and during 1902 the banks demanded security. The National Provincial got a mortgage on the Butts Road property (the ex Hull and Barton Cycle Works), while the Stamford Bank obtained a mortgage on certain of the Brigg Road premises and the deposit of the deeds relating to the firm's Soutergate property. On the balance sheets of 1901, 1904 and 1905 bank overdrafts stood as follows:

|  | 1901 | 1904 | 1905 |
| --- | --- | --- | --- |
| The Stamford, Spalding & Boston Bank | £1,289 | £4,734 | £5,562 |
| The National Provincial Bank of England | £1,608 | £1,574 | £2,432 |

The burst of fixed capital expenditure by F Hopper and Co during 1905/7 was prompted by the general prosperity of the cycle trade and of the firm in those years. In order to accommodate their investment programme, the partners looked initially to the mortgage market. In May 1905 £450 was obtained from a local spinster, Sabina Westoby, by way of a mortgage (interest at 4% per annum) on five cottages owned by the partnership. In 1906 Wilson's professional connections brought in two relatively large mortgages. The first came in July from Thomas S Whitaker at Everthorpe Hall, near Brough, Yorkshire, who loaned £1,200 (at 4½% per annum). The second was provided in September jointly by John C Anderson, a woollen manufacturer in Huddersfield and Auley Macauley, a solicitor of Heckmondwike and was for £5,500 at 5% per annum. Both loans were made on the security of property owned by the firm.

This was still insufficient capital for Fred Hopper's St Mary's Works projects, but most of the property was already mortgaged and the personal liabilities of the two partners were becoming too much of a burden. They decided to create a joint-stock limited liability company and the papers were signed on 20 February 1907. The agreement simply transferred the assets, contracts and liabilities of the Hopper and Wilson partnership to the new company. The partners' consideration was to be:[11]

> the sum of £43,539 (of which the sum of £11,535 shall be the amount payable for the goodwill of the said business) which shall be paid and satisfied in manner following that is to say:- The sum of £5,500 shall be paid in cash within 30 days after the allotment of Debenture Stock to be issued by the said Company to the amount of £25,000 as hereinafter mentioned but in the event of the full amount of such £25,000 Debenture Stock not being subscribed within 30 days from the last day limited for subscriptions on such issue being made the Company will pay to the Vendors such sum in cash as will represent one-third of the amount subscribed in respect of such issue and the balance of such sum of £5,500 shall be satisfied by the issue to the Vendors or their nominees of Debenture Stock to that amount and the sum of £38,035 the residue of such purchase money shall be satisfied by the issue to the Vendors of fully paid shares in the said Company to that amount in the proportions following namely to the said Fred Hopper 16,878 of such fully paid shares and to the said Henry Wilson 21,157 of like fully paid shares.'

The vendors also entered into a covenant that they would not engage in the manufacture of cycles for a period of five years if they ceased to be Directors of the company.

A E Harrison again:

> Upon incorporation the Company had a nominal capital of £22,000 First Mortgage Debentures, £25,000 Second Debenture Stock and 50,000 Ordinary shares of £1 each. The First Debentures were intended to pay off the property mortgages and the bank overdraft. The Second Debenture Stock was to provide new fixed and working capital, plus £5,500 payable to Hopper and Wilson as part-payment for the business. The Ordinary shares were mostly allocated to the partners as further payments for their business and as only these shares carried voting rights, the control of the company was firmly in the hands of Hopper and Wilson, who became Chairman (plus managing director) and Vice-Chairman respectively.

Two other directors were appointed: William Tomlinson, manager of the St Mary's works and Gilbert Nowell, the Barton solicitor, but relative to Hopper and Wilson they had little financial stake in the new company.

> The arrangements made with respect to the Ordinary shares were the only ones that went according to plan. Part of the subsequent financial history of the firm concerned the problems created by the difficulty experienced in getting the First and Second Debentures issued.
>
> During the week ending 2 March 1907, the company made a public issue of its Second Debenture Stock on the London Capital market. In the opinion of *The Economist*: 'The stock will not, we imagine, prove tempting to the majority of investors at a distance, as it is not a first-class security and will be of quite unmarketable character.'[12] This was a fairly accurate forecast, as out of the £25,000 nominal worth of stock issued, only £5,100 was subscribed by the beginning of August and Hopper and Wilson regarded the issue as a failure. They took the £5,500 owing to them as part of the purchase consideration in the form of Second Debenture Stock and, via Richard Barnes and Edward Preston – solicitors of London and the nominees of the Finance and Construction Company Ltd of London – had the stock distributed among various people during the course of the next three years.
>
> There were, however, subsequent allotments of the Second Debenture Stock, which had raised £6,490 new capital for the business by October 1913. These were not the result of public issues, as the firm had chosen in 1908 to be a 'private' limited liability company under the terms of the 1907 Companies Act, and so public issues were forbidden to it. This had the more-or-less inevitable effect of restricting further increments of capital to local sources.
>
> Out of the £5,100 raised by the public issues, £1,780 came from people either living in Hull or North Lincolnshire, or having identifiable personal or business connections with the Company. The £6,490 of new capital subsequently raised by issues of Second Debentures, and the £3,341 by issues of

Ordinary shares came, by and large, from the same sources, with only £1,040 coming from people with no identifiable geographical, personal or business connection with the company. Fred Hopper and Henry Wilson were the most significant contributors of capital during this period, taking out their Ordinary share dividends in 1907 in the form of Ordinary shares (£1,771), and in 1909 in the form of Second Debenture Stock (£2,430).

By the time of the first Annual General Meeting, held on 21 December 1907 it must have been clear that the objective of becoming a limited company had not been achieved as the two original partners were still too heavily invested in the business. They did succeed in getting Gilbert Nowell on board and he became, in effect, the third member of the private partnership that continued to drive the business forward. The tone of the minutes of the first AGM reflected an optimistic meeting. It was attended by the five directors, the company secretary, and two shareholders – Hopper's sister-in-law, Edith Ann Jackson, and the Barton surgeon, W G Loveridge. A dividend of 10% was declared on the share capital, free of income tax, with a bonus of £1 per share. A sum of 50 guineas was set aside for Directors fees leaving a balance of £1306 4s 5d carried forward. The auditors' report showed that the vendors (Hopper and Wilson) had been overpaid by £3,938 and this amount was to be deducted from the bonus payable to each of them. Whether due to misplaced trust or naivety the new company relied on Barnes and Preston to sort out the problems of Debenture issue, a mistake that was to be repeated with a similar company a few years later. More from Harrison:

> During 1907/08 a finance company, the Motor Investments Exchange Limited (with which R Barnes and E O Preston were involved) took £500 of Second Debenture Stock at par with an option on a further £15,000 worth at 90. Via its advertising and its business connections, the Exchange Company planned to distribute the stock to investors at par.
>
> Unfortunately, its plans went awry, and F Hopper and Co. got no more stock issued by this method after the original £500.

From the minutes of a board meeting on 25 January 1908 Barnes had written to the company contending that the original application by the MIE for £500 might be satisfied by the allotment of £90 per £100. As they had already received £440 from investors they suggested that an additional payment of £10 would square the accounts. The proposal was rejected and MIE called on to pay the £60 balance. The situation as of January 1908 was that the company had just seven shareholders, all local. These were Hopper with 14,499, Henry Wilson 18,776, Tomlinson 402, Nowell 202, Harold Wilson (Henry's son) 202, Edith Jackon 2 and William Loveridge 2. The first company secretary was Herbert Bell, who stayed with the business until appointed accountant to the Cleveland Bridge and Engineering Co, Darlington in 1913.[13] By the end of 1908 there were 18 shareholders, though the new ones held small amounts. By the end of 1912 this had grown to 27, with the same directors and secretary. What is surprising is that the growth that took place in the intervening years was possible with so little external investment – a tribute to the cash generating capabilities of the business and to the management for reinvesting profits.

By 1907 the company was already of a substantial size. There were 58 staff employed, of whom 11 were foremen and eight typists; the number of hands-on employees was probably around 400, though it was not recorded as many were employed on piecework, effectively paid by their foreman. Hopper's weekly pay was £16, with Charles Atkinson the next highest at £4. Junior typists made just 6s per week.

An insight into company discipline comes from the minutes of a directors meeting on 5 December 1908 attended by Hopper, Wilson, Tomlinson, Nowell and Bell:

> The suspension by the MD of Potts and Marshall, the works joiners, was then discussed. Mr Hopper explained to the meeting that on the evening of 19 November he discovered these men leaving the works at 8.40pm and booking full time on their work sheets to 9pm, Potts, the foreman, having signed the sheets. In addition to this both were taking away quantities of wood, which was against the strict instructions to the contrary. Mr Wilson proposed, seconded by Mr Nowell, 'That both of these men be instantly dismissed and the Secretary was thereupon instructed to acquaint them of the decision

of the Directors.'

Mr Wilson was most emphatic on this point and of the upholding of the action the Managing Director had taken in the matter in suspending the men until this meeting had had the facts placed before it.

Hopper was well placed, living at Elm Tree House, to keep an eye on what was going on at the factory just down the lane. What is surprising is that the men were not summarily dismissed by him, rather than by the company secretary more than two weeks later. Fred Hopper certainly cared for his employees, as proven by the provision of a social club, but was he also worried that the factory might become unionised and thereby drive up pay rates? Given that the Amalgamated Society of Engineers was becoming stronger by the year and that agricultural labourers formed a new union in 1906,[14] this is a strong possibility. Employment continued to grow and staff numbers were up to 77 by 1913, including 12 typists and a draughtsman.

Back to Professor Harrison we learn that :

Despite the amount of capital that was raised from local and business sources, there is no doubt that for the firm it was a difficult process and that it was not sufficient:

> . . . the difficulty is, there seems to be absolutely no money about, nobody seems to have any. I know plenty of personal friends who know the business, and who would be very glad to get hold of the Second Debenture Stocks at a few pounds under par but they have money locked up in property, they cannot sell any, and, as I above mentioned, there seems to be absolutely no money to be got hold of at all."[15]

The Second Debenture Stock bore an annual interest rate of 6%, and was redeemable after 15 years at a premium of 7½%; while the Ordinary shares bore an annual dividend of 10% in 1907, and of 7½% during 1908/1912 – a stability almost unique in the cycle trade. These terms were quite favourable to investors when compared, say, with the paper issues of other cycle companies. On this criterion, the firms' stocks and shares should have sold well with people not closely connected with the business, but, on the other hand, the rather secretive attitude of the firm to the publication of its affairs militated against successful issues. In the 1907 prospectus, potential investors were told that the total assets of the Company were valued at £67,045 and that there were prior charges amounting to £22,000. In a private circular issued in October 1912, they were given a valuation of the business (£122,619 7s 11d), and some idea of the firm's weekly physical output, and of the extensions to fixed capital assets made during the previous five years. In neither document were potential investors informed of the profits and sales history of the firm, nor were they given a detailed breakdown of the firm's liabilities and assets. Indeed, upon enquiring about balance-sheets and other information, prospective stockholders were told, as on one occasion in 1910:

> I may state that as this is a private company the stockholders are not entitled to a balance sheet, and further seeing that there are only about ten holders of Ordinary Shares, no balance sheet has been printed ... You will probably be aware that at the time this Debenture Stock was offered to the public, it was on the occasion of the business being converted into a private company, and it was not the intention of the founders and owners of the business that it should ever be any other than a private one.[16]

They had to be content with affirmations that the stock was 'a valuable investment and readily saleable', or 'as safe as the Bank of England', and 'a first-class security'.[17]

Hopper did not feel obliged to cut back on his expansionary plans because the Debenture Stock issue of 1907 was a failure, nor when he experienced two years (1907/08 and 1909/10) of falling sales. But with additions to fixed capital assets sometimes exceeding the amount of finance from retained profits and stock and share subscriptions, he had to look to the commercial banks a great deal for increments in working capital.

The partnership's bank overdraft stood at £7,993 at the end of July 1905, and this increased to approximately £15,000 by August 1907. All of this extra overdraft was obtained from the Stamford, Spalding and Boston Bank (in return for which the firm directed most of its turnover in cheques and acceptances through the Bank), and the account at the National Provincial stagnated.[18] Finally, however, the Stamford Bank decided that £15,000 was enough and fixed this sum as, in general, the firm's overdraft limit. During the next three years, Hopper applied each autumn – when stocks began to accumulate – for more credit, but the Bank conceded very grudgingly, if at all, and only on the basis that overdrafts above the £15,000 were to be 'temporary' and/or that the directors of the cycle company would give personal guarantees as to their repayment backed by their own securities.

From Harrison's work we can see how Hopper was financing his fixed capital assets between 1907 and 1913:

| | Additions to Fixed Capital Assets at Cost | First Debentures | Second Debenture Stock | Ordinary Shares | Other Loans | Retained Profits | Excess of Capital Raised over Capital Expended[1] |
|---|---|---|---|---|---|---|---|
| 1 March 1907 – 3 Aug. 1907 | 5,476 | | 5,100 | 200 | | | -176 |
| 5 Aug. 1907 – 1 Aug. 1908 | 2,863 | | 1,350 | 1,771 | 500[2] | 1,306 | +2,064 |
| 3 Aug. 1908 – 31 July 1909 | 2,736 | | | | 600[3] | 527 | -1,609 |
| 2 Aug. 1909 – 30 July 1910 | 5,154 | 500 | 2,430 | 1,050 | | 834 | -340 |
| 1 Aug. 1910 – 5 Aug. 1911 | 2,827 | | 600 | | | -523 | -2,750 |
| 7 Aug. 1911 – 3 Aug. 1912 | 2,086 | | | | | 267 | -1,819 |
| 5 Aug. 1912 – 7 Oct. 1913 | 1,851 | | 2,110 | 320 | | 2,354 | +2,933 |

Note:
1. Sum of columns 2 – 6 minus column 1
2. A loan from H S Vernon later taken in the form of First Debentures.
3. A mortgage from T T Gray, a client of Nowell's on some buildings and land on Marsh Lane. (Letter of 2 February 1912 company secretary to M Bilton of Hull.)

It does appear that Hopper's disdain for the financial markets bordered on arrogance or was it just overconfidence? At the board meeting on 13 February 1909 the situation on overdrafts was discussed by the directors present, Hopper, Wilson and Tomlinson. Due to the heavy stock of finished goods, and the large amount of goods forward dated, the bank overdraft was over the limit. As a temporary solution it was resolved that Hopper, Wilson and Nowell would place £500 each into a private account to be called the 'Hopper, Wilson and Nowell Account'. This account was to be used to keep the company within the agreed overdraft limits, though the amount was nowhere near enough. All through this period the two, and then three partners, operated at two levels: as a private business partnership, and as directors of a company. More from Harrison:

> In December of 1909/10 – the last of these three trading years – the Stamford Bank granted a temporary extra overdraft of £4,000,[19] but by the following month it was demanding that the Company's total overdraft be reduced to £17,000 at the rate of £50 per week.[20] The firm did not comply with the Bank's demand, as the relatively heavy fixed investment expenditures at that time, combined with the stockpiling of goods, had rendered it acutely short of liquid capital. The ensuing summer turned out to be poor and the company's home sales suffered correspondingly. Its trading profits were cut, and, in order to maintain its ordinary dividend at 7½% no allowance was made for depreciation when the firm's accounts appeared in October 1910. Immediately, the Stamford Bank demanded a reduction of the firm's overdraft by at least £500, and registered its disappointment at the balance sheet.

Hopper replied by requesting, in view of the seasonal pressures on finance, an extra overdraft of £5,000, which the Bank declined to give, with the additional demand that the total overdraft be reduced to £15,000 in two weeks. Two weeks later, the total overdraft stood at £17,075, and soon afterwards the Bank raised consternation in the company by demanding the closure of its whole account by 1 December:[21]

> What they, Hopper and Wilson, choose to describe as our 'unreasonable' attitude has been forced upon us by their conduct of the Company's account, the persistent non-fulfilment of their promises made to us, and their utter disregard for any fixed schemes for the reduction of the Company's indebtedness. They seem to look upon us not as Bankers, but as financiers, whose bounden duty it is to furnish them with such extra capital they require ... Week after week, in spite of warnings and threats, we are 'rushed' with cheques and acceptances in excess of their limit. Our cautions seem to be treated with something very near contempt. We now refuse to keep the account under these conditions.[22]

Hopper and his colleagues refused to close their account at such short notice as it was financially impossible for them to do so, and threatened to defend their action in court.[23] With considerable lack of grace, and on the grounds that 'we do not wish to embarrass the Company by closing it on December 1st, if this course can be possibly avoided', the Bank gave way, and consented to an overdraft limit of £17,000, but with the promise that 'at the end of six months the advance will only be continued if reduced to £15,000. .. It must, moreover, be understood that the Company shall not purchase any new properties ... without first obtaining the consent, in writing, of the Bank.[24]

In view of these restrictions imposed by the Stamford Bank, and of the tension of a crisis which made Hopper ill,[25] the Company decided it was high time to reduce their overdraft by an issue of the First Debentures, and thereby get on more favourable terms with the Bank. Apart from two allotments of £500 each to H S Vernon, and their use as security for bank overdrafts, the First Debentures had not been 'placed' – an attempt with the Law Guarantee and Trust Society in December 1907 having failed.[26] At first, Henry Wilson, in whose hands the matter initially rested, again tried the insurance companies. He applied to the Norwich Union Life Assurance Company, the Royal Insurance Company, and the Scottish Law Life Assurance Association. The Norwich Union seemed interested, but wanted personal guarantees from the Principal shareholders for the £22,000, and a life policy for £22,000 on Fred Hopper. As to the former, Wilson wrote, ... 'you and I could not take that awful load. . .', and the latter, '. . . is I think out of the question.'.[27] The Royal declined to consider the firm's offer as '...they won't invest in manufacturing concerns'[28] and the Scottish, though interested to the extent of asking for balance sheets and property valuations, again desired personal guarantees for the £22,000.[29] No further contact with the insurance companies was made.

In 1911 the expenditure that followed the purchase of the bankrupt Elswick Cycle Co. created further need for capital. Shops and offices for the manufacture and assembly of cycles and motor-cycles were constructed on the St Mary's site in Marsh Lane. The partners applied to the Halifax Permanent Building Society for a loan but were told:

> They (the directors of the Society) do not grant advances upon works properties except under very special circumstances where there is a large margin of security, and only when they are short of securities. I might say that at the present time the applications for loans upon good house properties are in excess of the number which the Society requires,[30]

and, ultimately, Hopper and Wilson had to persuade Nowell to provide the requisite £2,500 by way of a private mortgage.

At the turn of 1911/12, Hopper and Wilson were put into contact with a London firm of solicitors, Warwick Webb, Son and Company[31] through the good offices of George H Hiles, a small-time company promoter of Hull. They undertook the commission of 'placing' the First Debentures. Warwick Webb could not '... help feeling that there is little chance of dealing with an issue of this sort except among people directly interested in this class of business',[32] and accordingly interested a director of Messrs Singer Limited. Singer was a relatively large cycle and motor-car manufacturing concern, but, as Warwick Webb explained:

> It is not, however, to be supposed that he will personally put up the money, but there is no doubt

that he can influence the investment of the amount required in the present issue if satisfied with the proposal. Accordingly, his association with Messrs Singer Limited is in our opinion distinctly an advantage rather than the reverse, as he is thereby qualified to appreciate the points of a business of a kind with which he is already intimately acquainted, while at the same time he is in a position to influence the money required.[33]

The alternative, as Warwick Webb saw it, was '. . . to try a public issue well backed by advertisement ... though we should regret the loss of the previous opening'.[34] The Singer connection proved unfruitful:

...the question of this issue was mentioned in the quarter indicated but only in the most general details in view of the extraordinary depression of business in London at the present time, and as the general reception was not favourable no details were given as it was eminently undesirable to hawk your business without any prospect of success.

You will of course realise that the sum asked for is too small for a public issue, but is a considerable sum for a private individual to look up in these uncertain times. Nevertheless we feel that the matter might very well be re-opened in the same quarter with a very fair chance of success sometime after Easter, assuming that the present unrest and lack of confidence in the business world has passed off, if you have done nothing in the meantime.[35] [The 'depression of business' was due to the national coal strike.]

By June 1912, however, it was clear that the Singer director was no longer interested, and Warwick Webb had achieved another opening in the form of a manager of a London Company (who remained nameless). Negotiations with this institutional investor went so far as a detailed inspection of the firm's accounts, and Warwick Webb finally announced in the November: 'He gave us distinctly to understand that ... the proposed lenders will complete the matter as they are evidently keen upon it.[36] At this juncture, however, the Company broke off the negotiations as the National Provincial Bank had accepted their First Debentures as security for a much larger overdraft.

During the time in which attempts to place the First Debentures were going on, the firm never did fulfil the Stamford Bank's condition that its overdraft should eventually be reduced to £15,000. But the £17,000 limit still operated, and the firm got no further accommodation except for a temporary loan of £3,000 granted in March 1912 and guaranteed by Hopper, Wilson and Nowell jointly.[37] The inflexible attitude of the Bank was decidedly irritating to Hopper and his colleagues, especially in view of the fact that they needed more working capital to finance the record orders for cycles, cycle frames and motor cycles that were received during 1910/11 and 1911/12. Without adequate working capital, the firm relied more heavily on the trade credit of its suppliers, but by the spring of 1912 this source was being pushed to its limit, and forthright letters began to arrive on Hopper's desk demanding a settlement of accounts.[38] These demands became even more pressing when the coal strike of that year closed Hopper's works for a fortnight, and when rumours began to circulate in the cycle trade that the firm had to send to the USA for its components.[39] [American cycles had a poor reputation in the UK at that time].

To add to its problems, there was the fact that the firm '... this year had to date many more thousands of pounds worth of goods forward than we have done in previous years, and consequently this had its effect on the cash receipts',[40] and the continuing process of fixed capital investment:

You are quite right, our enormous outlays these last few years in capital expenditure to meet the increased business, has made it very difficult for us. We have been putting more money in buildings and machinery, which is a proper thing to do, but of course there comes a time, however well you may be doing, and however sound you may be financially, when your liquid cash is not sufficient to enable one to handle a business with that degree of comfort, which is necessary with a concern of this kind, and I am anxious therefore to get this additional Capital to enable us to work in a more easy manner.[41]

In November 1912, the National Provincial offered to take over completely the firm's bank accounts, and extend its overdraft to £25,000, with all the First Debentures, £5,000 of Second Debentures, and the insurance policies on the life of Fred Hopper as security.[42] The Bank was planning to open a branch in Barton and hoped to make it commercially viable by handling the town's largest account. Given their problems the directors accepted this proposition with alacrity.

In terms of overdraft the National Provincial proved more generous than the Stamford Bank - it awarded the firm a three-month extra overdraft of £10,000 in February 1913, for instance[43] - but it also exacted stiff conditions. The most irksome of these to Hopper, with his cycle-car ambitions, was '. . . that our capital expenditure shall not in any one year exceed £500, and no capital expenditure over these figures shall be entertained before first consulting with you on the matter.'[44] [Hopper planned to spend some £5,000 on fixed investment during 1912/13.] Furthermore, Hopper felt that:

> ... this £25,000 is entirely inadequate for the needs of this business – growing as it is – and we shall have to provide more capital. When you take into consideration that our total overdraft of £25,000 is very little more than about six or seven weeks' sales, and that we have to give a reasonable credit, you will quite see the difficulties we have to contend with.[45]

He was, therefore, decidedly interested when Warwick Webb and Son announced that a Mr. Cowperthwaite of London was in a position to formulate a scheme in order to raise extra capital for the company.[46]

The partners' lack of financial acumen, an adverse money market and an impatience to expand had led to a situation where a clash with the banks and suppliers was inevitable. But far from reining back on expansion Hopper carried on regardless. An earlier investment by the partners in land on Castledyke South was developed as a sawmill, joiners shop, stables and foreign packing shop, all leased to F Hopper & Co Ltd for 10 years from 16 July 1910 for £120 quarterly. The buildings were of brick, wood and corrugated iron. The stables were for the horse and rulley[47] teams which moved finished goods from St Mary's Works to the packing shops on Brigg Road and packaged machines from Brigg Road to the railway station. Further expenditure was incurred when the lease on Tabernacle Street expired. Alternative premises were leased from Charles Richard John, the Duke of Marlborough, at 8 Great Eastern Street for an annual rent of £140 in September 1910. This was close to the Tabernacle Street property and the terms of the lease were quite specific and rigorous, demanding that at the end of the lease the lessor would:

> 'paint the outside wood and iron work of the said demised premises and all additions thereto with two coats of good oil and white lead paint in a proper and workmanlike manner and also at the expiration of the said term paint all the inside wood and ironwork..'

The Duke also insisted that no part of the building would be used as a beershop or public house or, indeed for any 'dangerous noxious noisome hazardous or offensive trade business.'

At the end of 1912, based on research by local historian Dr John Ball, industrial employment in Barton was as follows:

Hopper's 800+

Shelsey's Adamant cement works 100-150

Farmers' Company (fertilisers) 100

Clapson's shipyard 50

Hall's Ropery 100

brick and tile works 12 (a low number due to the time of year).

It can be seen that the Cycle Works was by far the dominant industrial business, providing more than twice the number of jobs.

## Purchase of Elswick Cycles

The acquisition of Elswick Cycles Co Ltd brought into the company a range of bicycles that had achieved a reputation for excellent quality and novel designs that could command a premium price. Despite chronic financial problems Hopper, Wilson and Nowell formed a new venture in 1910, quite separate from F Hopper and Co Ltd, called the Elswick Cycles and Manufacturing Co to acquire the patents, trademarks and goodwill of the bankrupt company. Elswick Cycles started life as William Newton & Co in premises at Elswick Court,[48] behind what later became Fenwick's Department Store

*Fig. 2.27 & 2.28    Two views of the Elswick building under construction during 1911.*

on Northumberland Street, Newcastle on Tyne, with the Elswick brand name first applied to ordinaries. Elswick safety bicycles were highly regarded for their fine workmanship and finish and particularly for the special shade of paint known as Elswick Green. The firm was innovative in the use of forged lugs and in building frames from duplex tubes, some of which crossed over and were known as truss frames. This gave stiffness with lightness and during the 1890s boom the Elswick became very popular with the upper classes. To cope with home and export demand a separate company was set up and floated on the Stock Market in 1896 – Elswick Cycles Co Ltd, with Mr F Buckingham as manager. The capital raised was used to build new offices and workshops but the available space was soon filled. In 1900 the company moved to new premises in Shields Road. This was just at the time when prices were falling and mass markets opening up. Unfortunately Elswick's wealthy patrons were no longer interested in pedal power and the demand for the expensive machines plummeted. Liquidation followed. Just why Elswick could not adapt to new market conditions is not clear. The company had diversified into motorcycles and small cars, so was not averse to change; it is likely that they just ran into insurmountable liquidity problems, similar to those about to stop Hopper in his tracks.

The purchase of Elswick does not seem to have been made public until late in 1911. *Bicycling News and Motor Review* carried an article on 11 October under the heading 'Elswick Evolution', noting that 'a syndicate has acquired everything and a large factory is in course of erection'. The issue of 8 November carried the full story:

> It is a pleasure to know that the famous Elswick bicycles will not be a lost design, for the old business, with all patents, goodwill, etc, has been lately purchased by a Northern Syndicate, an up-to-date factory secured at Barton-on-Humber, and progress established so far that the new firm with the old name is actually showing at Olympia, where its reappearance will be welcomed by many agents. Under the new management Elswicks should quickly re-establish themselves with all traders, for their reputation was ever of the soundest, and the lapse has not been long enough for that fact to be forgotten....The selling policy of the firm is to be on the sole agency plan, and several contracts have already been booked, while, of course, the firm anticipate a busy time at the Show. Deliveries will be made at the end of the year in ample time for an agent's earliest requirements of new models. We may mention that the late works manager of the old firm has taken up his quarters at Barton.

So in the midst of an ambitious expansion programme Hopper and partners now needed to build a separate range of machines – bicycles and motorcycles – and the Elswick factory was rapidly constructed in 1911 in a prominent position on Marsh Lane, at the western end of the enlarged factory development (Fig. 2.27, 2.28 & 2.29). This building has survived, though the majestic external wall extension, half way along the building, was dismantled many years ago. The building was initially used

*Fig. 2.29 The Elswick building being used for motorcycle assembly in 1915, © David Lee.*

for motorcycle erection, bicycle erection and also to assemble the cycle car. Later it became the main erection shop producing both lines. Whether the original intention had been to maintain the illusion of a separate company, with completely separate manufacturing facilities, is not clear, though highly unlikely, as it would have placed a huge burden on the already shaky capital position. However, the acquisition of the Elswick marque did allow Hopper access to a different market that would warrant higher selling prices than the Hopper marque, which was still being marketed on the basis of price. An advert in *Bicycling News and Motor Review* on 8 February 1911 stated that 'You want PROFIT and the best way to get it – and to get a lot of it – is to sell Hopper's Cycles and Motor Cycles.' It goes on to state that 100,000 complete machines and frames had been made in 1910, and that Hopper's cycles 'can be bought at prices as low as most of the un-named and unreliable machines now being offered, and they can be sold at the same prices as machines that cost twice the money.' With his usual efficiency Hopper did indeed get things moving quickly enough to equip stand 102 at the Olympia Show in November 1911 with a full range of 'The Famous Elswick Cycles', including the special truss frame, and also two models of Elswick motor cycles.[49] The latter were, of course, identical to the Torpedo models, but in different livery. The stand was described thus by *Bicycling News and Motor Review* on 22 November, the show running from 20 to 25 November:

> It is a pleasure to see the Elswick models once more decorating a stand, though in a hasty review one could only observe that little difference has been made in the models we have seen of late years bearing the Elswick transfer. Many little improvements have been incorporated in the designs of the types now shown, but for the main part they retain the symmetrical form and delightful finish which gained for them an enviable reputation. A dozen models grace the stand, ranging from the fully equipped roadster, replete with every modern necessity, to the juvenile type warranted to withstand the antics of the average youth. The cross and truss frame has been retained, not only for its value as a strengthening agent, but on account of its neatness and exclusive appearance. Agents would do well to carefully study the lines of the Elswick before fixing up their arrangements for the coming season. The firm are also showing a couple of models in petrol bicycles.

Some employees relocated from the North-East, including J W Thompson of Byker, Newcastle on Tyne who had worked for the firm in Walker Gate for four years as an assistant in the brake and finishing department. His Newcastle reference letter is dated 27 September 1910 and his Barton offer 9

December 1911. The new company was looking for 'two or three good men as finishers at slightly better prices than formerly paid by the old Company.' This letter was typed on a Saturday and the follow up letter on Tuesday, 12 December, asking him to 'come at once, ready to start work on Thursday morning, which is the beginning of our working week.' He was also asked to 'look up H Scott of 16, Clifton Street, Byker, and bring him along with you if possible'. The company had written to him but had not yet received a reply. It is a measure of the efficiency of the postal service that Thompson received the offer in time to get a reply back to Barton on the Tuesday morning, and that his new employers could be confident of him receiving the instruction to be in Barton on the Thursday morning, bright and early to start work. Thompson later served with the Royal Field Artillery with the British Expeditionary Force and a file letter records that he would be taken back 'as a Cycle Erector immediately on his return to civil life.'

A nice story appeared in the *Lincolnshire and Lindsey Star* of 3 May 1913: 'For the second year in succession a blackbird has built its nest, laid its eggs and reared its young in the Elswick Cycle Shop. Amid the whirr of machinery and the melody of the workmen it is quite at home. It has lined its nest with the cords of which ladies' dress guards are made and one or two of the men who take breakfast in the shop supply its material wants.'

## The Formation of the Elswick-Hopper Cycle and Motor Company Ltd

The search for capital had brought the partners into contact with many London 'money men' involved in the promotion and flotation of companies. The involvement of Mr Cowperthwaite, suggested by Warwick Webb, led to the creation of a new company, intended to take over the assets of both F Hopper & Co Ltd and Elswick Cycles Co Ltd. A E Harrison's paper again takes up the story of the final dramatic stages in the search for financial stability:

> In the event, Cowperthwaite put the firm into contact with a professional company promoter, Sydney Hereford Lavey of Bush Lane, London, and in February 1913 it was agreed that Lavey should form a syndicate to float the company and the Elswick partnership combined upon the London capital market. The syndicate was to get £6,000 for supervising and arranging the flotation, and Lavey £250 in cash and £250 in shares. The Elswick Syndicate Ltd was duly formed, and a prospectus for the new public company drawn up. It was agreed that the company – the 'Elswick-Hopper Cycle and Motor Company' – should have a nominal ordinary share capital of £150,000, of which £130,000 should be issued; and that £98,748 should be paid for the old company and the partnership, as to £55,415 in cash and £43,333 in ordinary shares, plus interest payable on the purchase price from the date of 3 August 1912 at the rate of 5½% per annum. This, it was calculated, would leave approximately £24,000 to be used as extra capital for the cycle business. The directors of the new company were to be Edmund Shaver of Scotstown, Glasgow, late general manager of the shipbuilding firm of William Beardmore and Company, Col. Wellsted of Hessle, Fred Hopper, Henry Wilson and Gilbert Nowell.[50] [Edmund Shaver had no previous connection with the firm.]

The details of the prospectus were reported in the *Cycle Trader* of 27 June 1913 and are reproduced in full as they give a snap shot of the business and present the vendors' view of the company at the time:

> This company has been formed to acquire the business of F Hopper & Co Ltd, of Barton on Humber and the Elswick Cycles & Manufacturing Co, of Barton on Humber and to raise additional capital for extensions and development. The St Mary's Cycle and Motor Works of F Hopper & Company are of considerable extent, covering about 7½ acres of land (six acres freehold) and consisting of a number of buildings mostly one storey. The works of the Elswick Cycles and Manufacturing Company adjoin the St Mary's Works and have only quite recently been erected owing to the expansion of the motorcycles and cycle-car business.
>
> The contiguity of the works to the ports of Hull, Grimsby and Immingham is an advantage over competitors for business with foreign countries, which cannot be overestimated in value. The success of F Hopper & Company, represented by the present-day volume of their output indicates the locale

of the works as eminently suitable and conducive to development. Not only has cheap land allowed of the erection of the most healthy works in the English cycle trade and provided those conditions which are necessary to obtaining the best workmanship, but a body of skilled workers has been trained under the company's supervision. The latest mechanical appliances and equipment and the best materials are other factors in the success of the house. The supply of frames and parts to other manufacturers is an important feature of the business.

F Hopper & Company has for many years specialised in the production of bicycles, tricycles, frames and accessories on a very large scale and has built up a world-wide connection, resulting in a great demand for its products. This is evident from the fact that the financial year ending August 3, 1912, the number of cycles, tricycles, frames, etc., manufactured numbered 64,872, of which no less than 31,555 were exported to 46 countries of the world, including Japan, South Africa, Dutch East Indies, Canada, Holland, Federated Malay States, Siam, New Zealand, Australia, etc.

The development of the business of the company and the organisation for producing on an average 300 cycles, tricycles, frames per day has been gradual over the past 30 years.

The demand for motor cycles and frames from the customers of the company has necessitated the development of this branch of the trade and for the past year there were produced and sold 718 motor cycles and judging from the orders now in hand there appears to be every probability of the sales of motor cycles, as well as of tri-cars, side-cars, rickshaws and frames, being largely increased during the current year.

Coincident with the progress of the motor industry there has been a remarkable demand for the cycle-car. With a view to meeting this demand the company has produced a car with a water-cooled engine and a system of friction drive (dispensing with the expensive gear box and differential axle), which can be sold at a price little in excess of that asked for a motor cycle and side-car and yet leave a handsome margin of profit. The demand for this car will be beyond the present capacity of the works and will necessitate considerable extensions and the provision of additional working capital. Owing to the great demand for this car, the company have to refuse to book further orders for the present.

The company at present employs close on 800 hands. The workshops have been planned to secure production at a minimum of cost.

The books of the vendors have been examined by Messrs. Gourner, Bullock, Andrew and Co. of London and Messrs. Fawley, Judge and Easton, of Hull, chartered accountants and they report as follows:

June 20 1913

We report that we have examined the books and accounts of F Hopper & Co Ltd for the three financial years ending August 3, 1912 and of the Elswick Cycles & Manufacturing Company for the first year's trading ending August 3, 1912 and certify that, after making allowance for depreciation of plant and machinery, but before charging interest, income tax and remuneration of managing and other directors, the net profits were as follows:-

|  | £ | s | d |
|---|---|---|---|
| For the financial year ended July 30, 1910 | 7,403 | 19 | 7 |
| For the financial year ended July 30, 1910 | 8,407 | 5 | 11 |
| For the financial year ended July 30, 1910 | 12,292 | 10 | 3 |

The growth of the business has been considerable during recent years, as is indicated by the annual sales for the past three years having been £112,918, £148,863, and £169,975 respectively and the profits are of an increasing character. In view of the rapid development of the motor cycle and cycle-car sections of the business, Mr F Hopper, the present managing director of F Hopper & Co Ltd, has considered the advantages to be derived from the use of the additional capital provided by this issue and he reports as follows:-

'I beg to report to you that the business of the company continues to increase and that the expansion of the home and foreign trade in cycles, cars and motor cycles, provides exceptional opportunity for the beneficial use of the £24,000 which you are providing for extensions and as additional working capital. Having regard to the percentage of profit obtained on the amount of business done in past years and the demand for the motor cycles and cycle-cars which the company are producing, I estimate that the profit for the year 1913-14 will not be less than £20,000.'

The directors anticipate that a large additional profit will accrue as a result of the execution of the orders in hand for the motor cycle and cycle-car and after making provision for all outgoings and ample reserves for contingencies, it is calculated that the company will be able to pay 10% per annum on the £130,000 shares now offered for subscription.

The assets and undertaking to be taken over as a going concern as on August 3 1912, the date of the last annual stock-taking, subject to this company discharging the current trade liabilities amounting to £37,207 mentioned below, are as follows:-

|  | £ |
|---|---|
| Land, buildings, workmen's houses, machinery and plant. | 68,223 |
| Stocks, work in progress, loose tools, trade utensils and fittings | 45,967 |
| Sundry debtors | 17,035 |
| Cash at bank and in hand | 2,570 |
| Premiums paid on policies for £15,000 on the life of F Hopper | 1,613 |
| Patents, trade marks and registered designs | 547 |
|  | £135,955 |
| Deduct current trade liabilities (including provision for dividend of 7½% declared for the year ended August 3 1912. | 37,207 |
|  | £98,748 |

The purchase price has been fixed at £98,748. The vendors agree to take £43,333 (the maximum proportion allowed to comply with the requirements of the London Stock Exchange rules) in fully-paid shares and the balance of £55,415 in cash. Interest is also payable on the purchase price from August 3, 1912, to completion of the purchase at the rate of 5½% per annum.

As will be seen from the above statement the assets of a floating character exceed £65,000. The additional working capital upon all the shares now offered being subscribed would amount to £24,000, which is considered to be ample for all immediate expansion and development purposes, leaving the remaining unissued capital of £20,000 to be issued as required.

Mr F Hopper has agreed to act as managing director for a period of seven years and thenceforward until determined by either party at the same remuneration as he has received in a similar capacity from F Hopper & Co Ltd (namely, the sum of £1,250 per annum), with a commission of 5% on the profits in excess of 10% per annum on the issued share capital. Continuity is, therefore, assured.

It is a pity that company houses are listed with land, buildings, machinery and plant, but their inclusion does prove that some houses were still owned at this time. It is also interesting that half the value of the company was held in capital assets. For all the optimism of the prospectus the flotation failed dismally, as described by A E Harrison:

Some delay was incurred in making the issue, for developments in the London capital market were not deemed favourable, and Lavey could not get the issue underwritten.[51] He finally abandoned the underwriters and appealed to the market on 23 June, but this was not a wise decision. During the very same week in which the prospectus appeared before the public, The Economist reported that:

... the capital market for the time being has run dry. In spite of the very tempting rates of interest ... many really first-class securities have been left on the underwriters' hands to the extent of 80 or 90 per cent ... There is no obvious source from which the supply of capital may be replenished.[52]

Only the previous week this same journal had observed that the market for industrials had suddenly slumped due to a general panic selling.[53] In retrospect, it was noted that:

> Mr Hopper was entirely ignorant of the condition of the money market here as regards flotations, and having an absolute faith in the business itself needed little persuasion as to the furious demand there would be on the part of the public to take shares in such a company, and Mr Wilson and Mr Nowell were almost equally simple-minded.[54]

In the event only 4,735 of the 130,000 shares issued were subscribed for. Upon the very obvious failure of the flotation, Lavey offered to raise £20,000 by 'making a market' in the new company's shares on the London Stock Exchange, and in view of the £6,000 fee already paid and of the registration expenses, Hopper and his friends assented. On this basis they proceeded to an allotment: 4,735 shares to the public subscribers, 1,000 to the directors in respect of their qualifying shares, 34,592 to F. Hopper and Co. Ltd., 8,741 to the Elswick partnership, and 7 to the signatories to the Memorandum of Association. The Elswick-Hopper Company took over the liabilities and assets of its predecessors. Technically this was quite illegitimate for, prior to the attempted flotation, it was agreed that the new company should pay off the mortgage and Debenture liabilities of the old, which it was manifestly unable to do.[55] Nothing came of Lavey's proposal to raise £20,000, and the National Provincial, as holders of the old company's First Debentures, eventually became uneasy about the legal status of its holding, entered a debenture holders' action, and obtained the appointment of Sir William Peat as Interim Receiver and Manager of the business.[56]

Sir William Barclay Peat, a chartered accountant, was appointed in the High Court of Justice, Chancery Division, on 17 October 1913. The news had been broken by *Bicycling News and Motor Review* on 15 October as 'the sensation of the week'. It goes on to remark that 'the firm has thriven markedly of late years – the principal having always been a firm believer in shows and their value from an advertising point of view; and it is a matter of regret that difficulties should have arisen when their prospects were so bright. However, the statement that the company would attend Olympia the following month as usual, proved incorrect.

As for the National Provincial Bank their plans for an impressive new branch in Barton, on the corner of the Market Place and George Street, were passed by the UDC on 1 May 1913 (Fig. 2.30). The bank merged with the Westminster in 1968 and the Barton branch celebrates its centenary in 2013.

*Fig. 2.30 Barton Market Place c 1920 and the National Provincial Bank built in 1913.*

# Receivership and Reconstruction

It had taken one crisis to finally sort out the liquidity problem that had built up over the years of expansion and yet another world crisis to set the new company securely back on its feet. A E Harrison explains what happened next:

> Hopper was immediately pressed by his trade creditors [of which there were 302], and, in response, drew up a detailed set of accounts relating to the financial position of the firm, and called a meeting of the 18 largest unsecured creditors at Birmingham on 19 November 1913. With the support of T R Canning of Canning and Company, and of W A Davies of the Palmer Tyre Company – the latter was one of the three largest creditors – Hopper obtained the agreement of the creditors that they should carry through a scheme of rearrangement of the Elswick-Hopper Company's affairs. The creditors were empowered to elect the company's board of directors until their accounts were settled, a scheme of rearrangement was devised, and, after some initial opposition from the Bosch Magneto and Dunlop Tyre companies and after a legal process of some nine months duration, a reconstructed Elswick-Hopper Company appeared.
>
> The main aspects of the reconstruction were the creation of £50,000 of 5% 1st Debenture Stock by the new company and the agreement of the National Provincial to subscribe for £45,000 of these in order to discharge the firm's bank overdrafts and its outstanding private mortgages, leaving £15,000 as extra working capital. The Second Debenture Stock holders of the old company took an equivalent asset in the new, and the unsecured creditors, who had promoted the reconstruction, received 5% Third Debenture Stock in satisfaction of their claims. The ordinary shareholders of F Hopper and Co took the ordinary shares of the Elswick-Hopper Company.
>
> In effect, the reconstruction at last provided the cycle firm with the liquid capital it needed, and converted its short-term liabilities into more convenient long-term liabilities. Under the directorate appointed by the creditors – Fred Hopper, Fred Warwick of the Cycle Components Company, and George Poppleton, a chartered accountant of Birmingham, with A H Davies, a man still in his twenties, as company secretary – the Barton cycle works passed into a prosperous period of wartime inflation and munitions contracts and, with a less ambitious rate of fixed capital formation, achieved a financial stability which continued into the inter-war period.
>
> It was thus the National Provincial Bank that finally rescued the company from its financial difficulties and made available the capital which previous resort to banks, building societies, insurance companies, local connections and the London capital market had failed to provide. If Fred Hopper had shown the same flair for finance as he demonstrated in the direction of the technical, manufacturing and sales aspects of the business, many of his problems might never have arisen. As it was his entrepreneurial talents were unable to achieve the degree of success which easier access to capital might have permitted.
>
> The amended scheme of arrangement was dated 4 April 1914 and the receiver was finally discharged on 10 July 1914, but there were many meetings held during the preceding months and many trips to Hull and London for the partners before all the issues were resolved. Several affidavits were filed by the parties involved and Hereford Lavey, the man who set the flotation going, did his best to extract as much as he could in settlement of money owed for his failed efforts.
>
> An archive summary of Counsel's opinion of the preliminary options for reconstruction is worthy of note:
>
> Mr Hopper has two great assets:
> 1. Absolute integrity and complete confidence on the part of his creditors and
> 2. Optimism, but the latter, when highly developed is liable to prove dangerous. It is clear for some time the business has been carried on with a very inadequate working capital and this has only been possible owing to the complete faith in its financial stability, which all the creditors hold and the ease with which they could probably discount its paper.

Fred Hopper had invested 34 years of his life building up a large manufacturing business and the financial crisis must have been a serious blow to his self esteem. However, this practical man, at the

*Fig. 2.31 A tricycle rickshaw being tested by one of the chauffeurs, with perhaps, one of the office staff in the chair.*

peak of his endeavours, had never got to grips with the money markets, and his unwillingness to share information with would-be investors had cost him control of his company, though having Warwick and Poppleton on the board of directors did at least bring experienced outside counsel to the company.

## 1914 Stock Taking

Probably taken on the first anniversary of the new company, and to ensure that the assets of the old company and the partners were fully accounted for, the 1914 stock take reveals some interesting data. There were eight salesmen in the UK at the time and they are listed together with the motorcycles, which they presumably used for business and as samples of the company's products:

A J Kessler, Brighton, 2½hp Torpedo and 4hp twin Torpedo.

H S Knowles, two lightweight Torpedoes.

W J Spurgeon, 3½hp Torpedo, 2½hp Torpedo, 2hp Torpedo. Torpedo Model B sidecar.

L J Turner, Ipswich, 2¾hp Torpedo.

C W Shakesby, Hull.

J H Welsh, Barton, 2½hp Torpedo.

R W Gregg, Greenock.

F C Ransley, Southport.

T Foster, Selby.

In the motorcycle building shop there were 49 motorcycle frames listed, and 42 in the motorcycle stores. This included 'one Elswick Special TT twin frame, fork, guards, back wheel, stand, carrier, tank, handlebars, front brakes and exhaust lifter (requires tank for oil and front wheel.' It is almost certain that this is the machine ridden by T T Laker (see Appendix 2).

Every single transfer was listed and counted, covering 12 pages, and approximately 380 different styles. The total number of transfers came to 66,217 multi-coloured and 56,254 plain gold, with titles reflecting the many countries that were customers of the Barton company.

Rickshaw templates were listed as part of the sidecar building shop inventory, though just when these were supplied is not yet known. Fig. 2.31 is undated, but probably late Edwardian. Between 1914 and 1916 orders were placed with J J Plater & Sons, 262-264 Bradford Street, Birmingham, for baskets and rickshaw bodies.

## War

The Great War brought prosperity to Elswick-Hopper through government contracts and a steady demand for bicycles. It called more than 700 Barton men to arms, and 167 did not return. Many of them had been employed by Fred Hopper. The business continued to prosper due to the willingness of women to take the jobs left vacant by the men.

### Endnotes

1    *Raleigh and the British Bicycle Industry* 2000 R Lloyd-Jones and M J Lewis Ashgate p 84-85.
2    F Hopper & Co. – The Problems of Capital Supply in the Cycle Manufacturing Industry, 1891 – 1914. A E Harrison 1982 *Business History* Vol 24, No 1 p 4.
3    Internet 1892 Hull Trade Directory.
4    *We Danced all Night* Martin Pugh Vintage Books 2009 p 63.
5    *Rural Society and County Government in Nineteenth Century Lincolnshire* R J Olney 1979 The History of Lincolnshire Committee p103.
6    The new drain ran through the site and also carried water from the Beck. This spring fed pond was situated between the two churches and was a very attractive feature. Unfortunately the drain under the works eventually suffered partial collapse, causing flooding of the Beck Hill area due to the Beck overflowing. In 1984 a new drain was installed, bypassing the Hopper system and flooding is now rare.
7    *The Cyclists' Trade Review*, 17 November 1904.
8    *The Story of the Raleigh Cycle* G H Bowden p 23.
9    *The Barton on Humber Magazine* October 1944.
10    Now known as Holydyke.
11    Agreement F Hopper and H Wilson with F Hopper & Co Ltd.
12    *The Economist* 2 March 1907, p 376.
13    *The Star* 15 February 1913.
14    *A Social and Economic History of Britain* 1965 P Gregg p 408.
15    Letter, 10 November 1910. H A Bell, company secretary to Cooke, Enerver and Tulk of London.
16    Letter of 22 February 1910 company secretary to J W Tofts of Paddington, London.
17    Letter of 29 November 1910 company secretary to W Reeves of Sparkbrook, Birmingham and letter of 4 November 1911 company secretary to Miss S M Menneer of Cornwall.
18    Minute Book 13 July 1907.
19    Minute Book 15 December 1909.
20    Letter of 5 January 1910 Stamford Bank to F Hopper and Co.
21    Letters 8 October and 5 October 1910 S S & B Bank to F Hopper & Co.
22    Letter 26 November 1910 B C Praed, general manager S S & B Bank to Grimsby branch manager.
23    Minute Book 18 November 1910.

| | |
|---|---|
| 24 | Letter 28 November 1910 S S & B Bank to F Hopper & Co. |
| 25 | Letter 7 December 1910 F Hopper & Co to S S & B Bank. |
| 26 | Minute Book 14 December 1907. |
| 27 | Letter 1 June 1911 H Wilson to F Hopper. |
| 28 | Ibid. |
| 29 | Letter 27 June H Wilson to F Hopper. |
| 30 | Letter 5 October 1911 Manager, Halifax Permanent Building Society, Hull to Frankish, Kingdon and Wilson, Hull. |
| 31 | Letters of 26 January 1912, 7 February 1912 and 8 February 1912 G H Hiles to F Hopper & Co. |
| 32 | Letter 11 March 1912 Warwick Webb to F Hopper & Co. |
| 32 | Letter 13 March 1912 Warwick Webb to F Hopper & Co. |
| 34 | Letter 11 March 1912 Warwick Webb to F Hopper & Co. |
| 35 | Letters of 23 March 1912 Warwick Webb to F Hopper & Co. |
| 36 | Letters of 4 June, 6 June, 23 October, 24 October, 5 November, 7 November, 9 November, 15 November, 1912. Warwick Webb to F Hopper & Co. |
| 37 | Letter 27 March 1912 Barclays Bank to F Hopper & Co. (Barclays took over the Stamford bank during the winter of 1911/12.) |
| 38 | Letters 20 April, 20 June, 20 June, 20 June, and 4 July 1912. F Hopper to Sturmey Archer Gears Ltd of Lenton, Nottingham; to Wholesale Traders' Association Ltd of Birmingham; to C Barlow of Accles and Pollock of Oldbury, Birmingham; to A E Gelder of the North British Rubber Co Ltd.; to Barton Gas Co of Barton on Humber, respectively. |
| 39 | Letter 29 March 1912 F Hopper to Seabrook Bros of London EC and letter of 31 October 1912 F Hopper to the National Provincial Bank. |
| 40 | Letter 19 March 1912 company secretary to Palmer Tyre Ltd of London WC. |
| 41 | Letter 21 October 1912 F Hopper to A J Kessler of Brighton. |
| 42 | Letter 29 March 1912 company secretary to the National Provincial Bank of Hull; letter of 9 January 1913 F Hopper to Warwick Webb. |
| 43 | Letter 14 February 1913 company secretary to the National Provincial Bank. |
| 44 | Letter 15 November 1912 F Hopper to the National Provincial. |
| 45 | Letter 9 January 1913 F Hopper to Warwick Webb. |
| 46 | Letter 9 January 1913 Warwick Webb to F Hopper & Co. |
| 47 | Rulley was the term applied to a flat bed four wheel wagon pulled by a single horse. |
| 48 | *Cycle Clips – a history of cycling in the north east* Tyne & Wear County Council Museums 1985 p11 and 12. |
| 49 | *Bicycling News and Motor Review* 8 November 1911 supplement. |
| 50 | Prospectus Elswick-Hopper Cycle and Motor Co Ltd May 1913. |
| 51 | Letter 13 June 1913 S H Lavey to G H Nowell. |
| 52 | *The Economist* 28 June 1913. |
| 53 | *The Economist* 21 June 1913. |
| 54 | Bosch Magneto Ltd. Brief to Counsel in opposition to petition to sanction scheme of arrangement in the matter of the Elswick-Hopper Cycle and Motor Company Limited, as presented by the Palmer Tyre Co Ltd before Mr Justice Astbury in the Chancery Division of the High Court of Justice 17 March 1914. |
| 55 | Agreement of 19 June 1913 between the Elswick Syndicate Limited and F Hopper and Co. |
| 56 | In re F Hopper and Co Ltd. Between the National Provincial Bank of England Limited and others, and F Hopper and Co Ltd and others. 7 October 1913. |

# CHAPTER 3

## THE GREAT WAR

The High Court discharged Sir William Barclay Peat as Official Receiver on 10 July 1914, but Fred Hopper had little time to ponder the future of his company as war was declared with Germany less than a month later, on 4 August 1914. Parliament passed the Defence of the Realm Act in the same month and this gave the government ever increasing powers over industry and transport as the war progressed. Initial British strategy was based on a short war with limited involvement of British troops. Lord Kitchener did not agree and, as the new Secretary of War, persuaded parliament to raise a large army of volunteers. By April 1915 Hopper's had lost 103 skilled employees to Kitchener's Army. The company archives contain many government forms and company documents that illustrate just how much control the government took of manufacturing companies during the conflict. Not only were there forms to fill in and submit, but also tribunals to attend, both in Barton and Grimsby. Raw materials were government controlled and shortages a constant anxiety for manufacturers. However, thanks to the survival of two letters (one partial) from Fred Hopper to his son, we can see that money was still to be made and that extricating those close to him from the demands of the war was uppermost in Hopper's mind.

### Company Structure in 1914

The next table illustrates clearly the Hopper manufacturing philosophy of specialisation, with many departments, each performing specific functions. Manufacture was divided into 28 departments, though not all were individually foreman managed. This functional division of labour was reflected in the myriad of small buildings, with some even having one department upstairs and one downstairs. The movement of materials was clearly a chore, and one that was given to school leavers using specially made wooden barrows. These were boys of 13 who were lucky enough to have a relative already working for Hopper's – like other businesses in the town it was very much family oriented.

The practice had been one of specialisation from the early days of the company, so that a handlebar fitter remained a handlebar fitter and became very expert in this narrow field as a result. The key workers were the toolmakers who served an exacting apprenticeship, and were responsible for keeping all manufacturing machinery working properly. They made all the special tools and assembly jigs, set up and repaired machine tools and generally kept the factory wheels turning. This specialisation and the relatively narrow skills of the majority of the men led to problems with government representatives, who often misinterpreted the role of individuals. It also meant that it was not easy to move employees between departments to smooth workflow. It was the very opposite of today's multi-skilled worker philosophy.

Female factory employment was not a major part of Edwardian life, and even within the Brigg Road office only 30% of the staff was female. The figures also show that 61% of the factory staff was of military age and a further 20% underage, but available in due course, though the war <u>was</u> supposed to be over by Christmas. The few men too old to be called to fight – just 14%, is an indication that this was still a young company and many of these older men had worked for Hopper since the early days, before the move to St Mary's Works, and were now employed as foremen and leading hands.

The table is based on a composite of archive data and describes the structure at the start of the war in August 1914.

| Department | Male | | | | Female | Total |
|---|---|---|---|---|---|---|
| | military age | over military age | under military age | total male | | |
| Fork Blade | 4 | 1 | 2 | 7 | 3 | 10 |
| Frame Building | 25 | 15 | 9 | 49 | | 49 |
| Press | 5 | 2 | 5 | 12 | | 12 |
| Back Stay | 4 | 2 | | 6 | | 6 |
| Welding | 1 | 1 | | 2 | | 2 |
| Front Fork | 3 | 4 | 1 | 8 | | 8 |
| Filing | 33 | 3 | 1 | 37 | | 37 |
| Rough Polishing | 13 | 3 | | 16 | | 16 |
| Frame Cleaning | 2 | 4 | | 6 | | 6 |
| Enamelling | 9 | 2 | | 11 | 3 | 14 |
| Lining | 16 | | 8 | 24 | | 24 |
| Crank | 8 | 2 | 8 | 18 | | 18 |
| Handlebar Making | 5 | 3 | 1 | 9 | | 9 |
| Polishing | 37 | 3 | 6 | 46 | | 46 |
| Plating | 4 | 1 | 8 | 13 | | 13 |
| Buffing | 7 | | 4 | 11 | | 11 |
| Frame Erecting | 14 | 1 | 2 | 17 | | 17 |
| Mudguard | 2 | | | 2 | 3 | 5 |
| Brake | 1 | 1 | 2 | 4 | 5 | 9 |
| Handlebar Fitting | 5 | | 1 | 6 | | 6 |
| Wheel Building | 9 | | 3 | 12 | 6 | 18 |
| Machine Erecting | 18 | 2 | 2 | 22 | | 22 |
| Gearcases | 8 | 1 | 1 | 10 | | 10 |
| Motor Cycle Frame | 6 | 1 | 1 | 8 | | 8 |
| Motor Cycle Erecting | 8 | | 6 | 14 | | 14 |
| Repair | 2 | | | 2 | | 2 |
| Machining | 15 | 5 | 16 | 36 | | 36 |
| Turners | 7 | 2 | | 9 | | 9 |
| Toolmakers | 3 | 2 | | 5 | | 5 |
| Electrical | 2 | | 1 | 3 | | 3 |
| Engine Room | 2 | | 1 | 3 | | 3 |
| Blacksmiths | 2 | 2 | 1 | 5 | | 5 |
| General Yard | | 1 | | 1 | | 1 |
| Millwright | | 1 | | 1 | | 1 |
| Stores | 2 | | 1 | 3 | | 3 |
| **Total** | **282** | **65** | **91** | **438** | **20** | **458** |
| Packing & Draying | 9 | 7 | 2 | 18 | 16 | 34 |
| St Mary's Staff | 9 | 10 | 3 | 22 | | 22 |
| Brigg Road Staff | 12 | 5 | 4 | 21 | 9 | 30 |
| **Total** | **30** | **22** | **9** | **61** | **25** | **86** |
| **Overall Total** | **312** | **87** | **100** | **499** | **45** | **544** |

## For King and Country

Hopper's first casualty was Thomas Henry Bate, ex-Royal Navy, retired coastguard and employed as a company chauffeur. He joined the Royal Fleet Reserve and was called up at the start of the war. On 22 November 1914 he was serving as Petty Officer First Class aboard armoured cruiser HMS Hogue on patrol off the coast of Holland, in the company of sister ships HMS Cressy and HMS Aboukir. Early that morning the ships were spotted by German submarine U-9, which fired two torpedoes at Aboukir, immediately disabling her. Hogue stopped to pick up the crew and was also hit by two torpedoes, sinking within 10 minutes. U-9's remaining two torpedoes were fired at Cressy with one hit and she was also sunk, with the loss of a second Barton man, Frederick Speary. From the three ships 837 men were rescued and 1459 lost, among them many cadets and reservists. It appears that the convoy was not following orders to zig-zag and was unable to maintain recommended speed due to the age of the vessels.[1]

In 1914 there were 47 Hopper employees listed as Territorials or reservists. They were under the direction of Lt Harold Wilson, son of Henry Wilson, and a solicitor with the same practice in Hull. With headquarters provided by Hopper in the old Butts Road factory the Territorials were the first to leave the works, though initially, just for annual training at Bridlington (Fig. 3.1). According to Capt Robert Fieldsend's diary[2] the 5th Lincolnshire Territorial Regiment was at camp at Bridlington from 26 June 1914, 'little thinking that its fortnight's training would extend to six months and then be followed by service in the field against the most highly trained military nation in Europe.' From there, after a brief visit to Barton, they headed south, continually moving and taking part in exercises before finally arriving at Le Havre on 4 March 1915.

*Fig. 3.1 Elswick-Hopper & Co men 5th Lincs Regiment. Harold Wilson is sitting directly behind the drum. From the facial expressions this photograph was taken before they saw hostilities.*

Such was the enthusiasm of young British men for giving the Germans a 'bashing', that it was not until January 1916 that conscription was introduced for unmarried men aged 18-41, and extended to married men in May of that year. This change was made essential by the huge losses sustained on the Western Front, the horror of which has been fully documented elsewhere. Conscription led to a doubling of the number of Hopper's men serving in uniform and to a major rearguard action by the company through the tribunal system, in an effort to retain essential skills to operate the business. The attitude of the government was that the loss of skilled men could be made up by what they called 'dilution'. This meant hiring unskilled workers, especially women, girls and boys, and providing whatever training they needed to become effective workers. The volume of paperwork that has survived bears witness to the efforts that were made by the government to conscript, and by the company to retain key employees.

The following table shows the inexorable loss of Hopper's men to the war and the heavy impact of the initial draft of volunteers and reservists with 229 joining HM Forces and 82 (as of November 1917) leaving to work in munitions factories. This represents 61% of the 1914 male workforce and an astonishing 75% of those under the age of 41. While 108 additional women had been employed the total workforce at the end of the war was just 70% of the pre-war level.

| Date | Male Employees | Female Employees | Total Employees | HM Forces | Munitions Factories |
|---|---|---|---|---|---|
| July 1914 | 505 | 58 | 563 | | |
| 16 April 1915 | 351 | 44 | 395 | 103 | |
| 16 July 1915 | 337 | 59 | 396 | | |
| 15 October 1915 | 310 | 45 | 355 | | |
| 10 December 1915 | 301 | 95 | 396 | 117 | |
| 18 February 1916 | 308 | 129 | 437 | 121 | |
| 14 April 1916 | 307 | 144 | 451 | 126 | |
| 14 July 1916 | 304 | 171 | 475 | 139 | |
| 13 October 1916 | 303 | 135 | 438 | 149 | |
| 12 January 1917 | 296 | 142 | 438 | 169 | |
| 13 April 1917 | 279 | 163 | 442 | 186 | |
| 13 July 1917 | 279 | 175 | 454 | 212 | |
| 12 October 1917 | 275 | 168 | 443 | 215 | 82* |
| 25 January 1918 | 264 | 169 | 433 | 220 | |
| 26 April 1918 | 248 | 170 | 418 | 226 | Returning |
| 26 July 1918 | 233 | 171 | 404 | 228 | Men |
| 25 October 1918 | 227 | 166 | 393 | 229 | 0 |
| 3 May 1919 | 281 | 156 | 437 | | 72 |
| 30 August 1919 | 312 | 198 | 510 | | 91 |
| 24 April 1920 | 412 | 215 | 627 | | 150 |

* Quarterly figures are not available for employees leaving as Munitions Volunteers, apart from a letter dated November 1917, giving a total of 82 up to that date. Factories to which volunteers were sent include Bowden Brake Co, Birmingham; Ruston and Proctor, Lincoln; Clayton and Shuttleworth, Lincoln; Richard Sizer, Hull and Sanderson Tractor Company, Bedford.

## Conscription Tribunals

Much management time appears to have been taken in keeping, or trying to keep, key workers from being conscripted, or transferred to other factories engaged in full time war work. There was a procedure in place to decide individual cases of conscription, with an initial local review and then a follow-up, held in Grimsby, or London, if the first one failed, and if leave was given to appeal. Local reviews were handled by Barton solicitor G H Nowell, and as a long time friend and business partner of Fred Hopper it must have been a difficult task for him.

Transfer of employees to munitions factories was handled by the Ministry of Munitions via the Grimsby Employment Exchange. In June 1915 the company wrote to the tribunal in an attempt to retain John Osbourne,

> ...engaged for some time in producing the necessary tools for munitions work. He will in the course of 2 or 3 days be starting work on further tools for the sub-contract for munitions we are taking which will necessitate him working long hours and if this man is taken away we cannot undertake the munitions contract we have arranged for. We have only two tool makers left, the others have gone to different centres. We object to the transfer of this man.

This plea was successful and the response was received on 27 August 1915 on form WMV11:

Sir,

I am directed by the Minister of Munitions to inform you that, after careful consideration of the objection made by you to the transfer of the workman named above in accordance with the conditions of his enrolment as a war munitions volunteer, he has decided that it will not be necessary at present to transfer the workman from your works. The Minister of Munitions will be glad, however, if you will be so good to advise him of any alteration in the circumstances in the man's employment.

Absolute exemptions from military service were applied for on form R-53 and notified on form R-10, while exemptions required form R-27. Arthur Stow was 24 when an R-53 was submitted to keep him out of the clutches of the war machine. He was a protégé of Fred Hopper and something of a favoured 'son' of the company, having joined as an office boy at the age of 13. Hopper gave him a gold watch for his 21st birthday and by 24 he was running the Export Department. Having invested so much time and effort in building a large and profitable export business Hopper was loathe to let him go. On 6 March 1916 a Notice of Decision, form R-29 was received from G H Nowell, who was clearly not unduly affected by a conflict of interest, as he stated that there were not sufficient grounds for allowing the claim. An appeal was lodged and was heard at the County Police Court in Grimsby on 1 May, at which the appeal was dismissed. Not content with this decision Hopper wrote to J Barker, Clerk of the Appeal Tribunal, on 5 May asking for leave to make a further appeal. The two page letter pulled no punches and gives a clear picture of the company's situation nearly two years into the war:

We do not think the position was made quite clear by our Managing Director that should this man be taken from us we have no one who can conduct this foreign business, and it is impossible to get anyone with the necessary knowledge and experience in our industry as well as a knowledge of shipping. For your information, this Department had been staffed with four men, two of them are on Active Service, and a third is called up and goes immediately, which, as above mentioned will leave us with only the head of the Department. The export trade to secure, has cost many thousands of pounds in foreign travel, and it is only this last year that we have begun to see the results of our enterprise and expenditure to secure this class of business, and to have to close down this trade would be a loss which we do not think is fair, nor do we think it is in the best interests of the country that a trade like this should be lost. The Board of Trade repeatedly advise the pushing of this export business so as to equalise foreign credits and keep the exchange normal. We are manufacturing at the present time on an average 600 cycles per week, of which 500 are for export. The whole of the details, foreign correspondence, shipping, checking and arranging has to be done, and we have only this one man to do it.

We have sent from these works 250 units into the Army, we have engaged and are working 150 women, a portion of whom are engaged on the manufacture of 3" shells, and the balance assisting in the export trade. If we close down it will mean the discharge of at least 70 of these women, the discharge of all the packers, the case makers, and many of the other workers, and further it will be a deplorable blow to the town which, in a very great measure, depends on this business, it being the town's principal industry.

We would ask your kind perusal of a speech made by Mr McKenna, the Chancellor of the Exchequer, who says,

'For this country trade and victory are not in opposition but are inter-dependent. Destroy our trade and you will shatter the very foundation of our power to make great advances to our Allies and Dominions. The huge balance can only be met by the maintenance of our trade.'

Also the circular letter of Mr Walter Long, President of the Board of Trade, of 23 March, 1916,

'In deciding cases which come before them Tribunals should recognise the injury that may be done to the industries and commerce of this country, if managers directing important business, and clerks possessing technical knowledge, or otherwise occupying positions of special responsibilities, are removed from their present employment and cannot be replaced.'

We have no doubt, after perusing these facts you may grant our appeal. This person would only make a single unit in the Army whereas in our industry his importance is not to be measured by numbers. We have endeavoured to carry out in fact as well as spirit, the recommendation of the Ministers in respect to dilution of labour, and we were complimented by the Board of Trade representative no less than three weeks ago, on the very effective way in which we had carried through this recommendation of the Government.

Our policy has been to keep simply the heads of the Departments, and we are working the balance of the business by semi or unskilled labour of either under or over military age, but should the policy of taking the principals be adopted, all the efforts we have made would be rendered useless, and it is for this reason we ask you to grant us the appeal we are making.

Signed Managing Director (Fred Hopper JP)

This impassioned plea was successful in gaining leave to appeal to the Central Tribunal. Company secretary A H Davies received a letter after the hearing from J W Reading of the Central Tribunal, based at Queen Anne's Chambers, Tothill Street, Westminster, with the following statement:

In this case Mr Hopper the Managing Director of the Elswick Hopper Cycle & Motor Co Ltd appeared in support of the appeal. The original application, the notice of appeal, and the grounds for the decision of the Local Tribunal were read. Mr Hopper then stated his case to the Tribunal, his statement being substantially that contained in his 'grounds of appeal'.

The only question at issue was as to whether it was expedient in the national interests that the attested man should be retained in his present employment. Mr Hopper's contention was shortly, that the man's services in the export trade were too valuable for him to be taken for the Army. But it appeared that Mr Hopper had been informed that all his output would shortly be required for H M Government in which case the export trade would cease and the attested man's work would also cease. In these circumstances the Appeal Tribunal supported the Local Tribunal's decision that the man be not exempted from service.

At the same time the Central Appeal Tribunal felt that this was an important case and gave the employers leave to appeal, a course they have 'not previously taken although they have dealt with over 250 cases.' There followed a questionnaire that comprised six paragraphs and 14 detailed questions, aimed at probing the efforts made by the company to release men and, in particular, what grounds there were for the exemption from service applying to the individual. The final question was not exactly subtle: 'What would be done by the firm if, for instance, he were to die suddenly.' The response was unequivocal: 'If this eventuality occurred we should immediately apply to the War Office for the release of one of the men who joined His Majesty's Forces in 1914, to enable us to carry on the work of this Department, for which this man has had special training.'

On 1 June 1916 Stow was granted exemption conditional on remaining in his present occupation.

'The face of the war at the beginning of 1917 was little altered from that it had shown the world at the beginning of 1915'...,[3] and fresh troops were desperately needed on all fronts. Arthur Stow was 25 when the company received form R-44 on 23 January 1917, which recorded his occupation as *Clerk* to Foreign Dept. This stated that 'In accordance with R114(C) he is not engaged in work of high National importance and is not irreplaceable.' There was a final hearing at Grimsby on 14 February 1917 where the latest appeal was dismissed, though the job description was corrected to *Manager,* and Stow left shortly after the appeal for Mesopotamia. He survived the war, became a director in 1931, and was appointed managing director in 1936.

The statement by the Central Tribunal referring to H M Government taking the total factory output was never fulfilled, and Hopper's insistence on the importance of exports to his business was validated by events, as will be shown in the next section. His statement concerning success at exporting 'only this last year' was rather short of the truth, however, and an indication of how much Stow meant to him.

The works manager, William Tomlinson, was exempted on the basis that he would be impossible to replace. The appeal on behalf of company secretary and commercial manager, Albert Henry Davies was also successful, on the grounds that he was also in charge of the munitions workshop.

A brief look at two identical tribunal submissions shows the attitude of companies to female employees in 1915. Wheel building employed six women and 12 men in 1914, a higher proportion of women than any other department. Given the small diameter of spokes and the tiny size of spoke nipples there is a big advantage in having small hands when assembling wheels. However, women were apparently not suited to the final job of truing. Frank Sanderson and Harold Lawtey were both employed as wheel truers and the tribunal submission dated 30 December 1915 stated:

> This man is required to complete one of a cycle of operations which is mainly exported, and it has been our experience that the work cannot be learned under 9 to 12 months. Women labour has been experimented with by the foreman in the past and has had to be discarded as practically hopeless. Women take the wheel building up to the finishing process performed by this man and six of the staff of nine engaged on this work have enlisted. We have now reached the absolute minimum and if this man is taken it will disturb the cycle of operations and throw out of work a number of other employees in the factory.

Both men subsequently saw service with the armed forces and wheels continued to be built, presumably without too many problems with wobbly rims.

By February 1917 there were 101 men of military age still employed, of whom 48 had been successful at tribunals, 33 had failed medicals and 20 had not yet been called to arms.

## Personal Letters

Two letters from Fred Senior to Junior reveal the stark contrast between life in the trenches for Hopper's infantry soldiers and life back home for their old boss and his son. I am indebted to Dr John Ball for these, the only personal letters that appear to have survived. It would seem that although Hopper fought hard to retain his export manager, Arthur Stow, through representations to the local tribunal, he adopted a more cautious strategy for his son and heir. It appears that Fred Junr had been sent to work for F E Baker Ltd of Birmingham, maker of the Precision engines that powered Torpedo and Elswick motorcycles. Given that he was just 25 years old when the first letter was written on 30 March 1916, it is likely that a position in a manufacturing company in the industrial centre of the country was considered by his father to be a safer bet than remaining in Barton. The homely content of the letters was in sharp contrast to the slaughter going on in Europe, and it is clear that he would have loved to have his son follow in his footsteps and become better acquainted with the business.

> My dear Fred,
>
> I received your letter and ordered the little trike for you. To-day I went into the packing shop to see it, and got a shock. By some means Slack – who has the drilling of the rims in his hands – had allowed the girls to run riot and the holes were drilled to take a hub about 2ft wide between the flanges. You can imagine the state of the wheels. He had also left the handlebar dropping down at an angle of about 90 degrees instead of about 25. The brake lever was set so that I could just comfortably reach it. I immediately sent it back again, following it, and went for Slack. I found there were 4 or 5 more machines built in a similar way, and I ordered them to be taken down and new wheels fitted. They are putting another through and it will be sent off to-morrow (Friday) the last day of March so it should be at destination to the time required.
>
> I was going to B'ham this week to a Board Meeting, and should have dropped upon you just for a few minutes. Mr Warwick is not well and he wrote to see if we would have the Board Meeting at B'ham instead of Barton. At the last moment I decided I would not go; I did not like to leave the place, and very fortunate it was for me, because Davies got in the blizzard, and instead of getting home on Tuesday night, he did very well to land home on Wednesday at dinner time, and he had had a very rocky time. He had to stay in Sheffield on Tuesday night could not get any further and landed

in Sheffield somewhere about between 12 and 1 in the morning. We did not catch much snow here, but we got a terrible wind and sleet. The wind was so bad that it began to lift the North-East corner of the Elswick shop roof, that we had to get stays and bolt it down to the floor.

We have had a great misfortune this week in being stopped for castings. The blizzard was the cause, there have been no goods in from B'ham to-day or yesterday, the result is we lost a shift on Thursday, and Thursday night, and it looks like losing the Friday shift which is very unfortunate, considering that we are pledged for so many of these shell ends per week.

The cycle part of the business is going very nicely, we are gradually putting in more women workers and the men are gradually disappearing. I suppose you will know that young Parkinson in getting married, and unfortunately for him I am afraid, I am told he is taking a sweet shop in Hull. He has got a pension of 17/6 per week from the Government. I am afraid he is looking for trouble, as sweet shops are not always a profitable investment. It would have been much better for him if he had learned wheel building, where he could have worked a few hours per day, and earned a decent sum every week.

I have just got a new thing going in the works. You will remember that we commenced to make our chain wheels and cranks the same pattern as Williams. The crank had to be turned on a pin and then milled to take the chain wheel. Up to now, we have had a man turning the cranks down in the ordinary method, and we were paying the sum of 5d per dozen for turning these; we have now a fixture on the same principle as a shanking cutter which turns the crank down, we have a cross slide, one set holds the lathe tool and turns the crank down to its proper size before the shanking cutter comes on, then the back slide brings up the knurling wheel, and they are not going to cost much more than a quarter of what we were paying the men, and is a more accurate job.

I am working on a scheme now for turning axles with a drilling machine and a circular mill combined. We have got to turn our machines out with women labour and I think we shall achieve each job. I do not know whether I told you we had got four women filers, but we have had four at work some time, and we are going to put another batch on. The first four are doing 'top notch'.

There is a great field for young men who have got faculties for engineering devices, at this present day, and I have come to the conclusion that the old order is absolutely to be changed, in the times which are looming ahead it will be particular tools which will be made to suit the particular work, and cheap operators with a few skilled operators to look after them. I can see it coming more and more every day but I must confess that the women who are being put on the various jobs are most adaptable, and are doing their work well.

Tombleson's brickyard deal is turning out very well. If you remember I gave £1000 for the lot. I have sold the roofs for £230, we have already got 60 standards of timber loaded up to our timber sheds, and I have refused an offer of £15 per standard, so that you will see the saving works out into hundreds.

The Grassby deal keeps progressing slowly every week, and will come out all right in the end.

Toney the polisher has a boy in the polishing shop. He made an attack on a boy from the frame shop the other day and it so happened that the attacker received two black eyes and a 'bluggy' nose. In the early part of the fight Toney Senr was backing Toney Junr to great slaughter, but when he found Toney Junr was getting the worst of it he made an attack on the frame shop boy, and because Tomlinson would not discharge the frame shop boy, Toney Senr sent in a week's notice, which I have acknowledged to-day by accepting it, so good-bye to Toney, and good riddance.

I was going to Thorne on Wednesday, which – as you know – is over the Trent and near Doncaster. I was going to look at a stock for sale there. I went by car anticipating I could get over the new bridge at Keadby. When I got there I found the Board of Trade officials and the Gt Central directors were all there testing the bridge, with four locomotives coupled together and two traction engines. There was the County Surveyor, Mr Thropp – but although he very kindly went to see if they would give me permission to pass with my car, I drew a blank, and we had to return, so I called at Sir Berkeley's sale which happened to be the same day, and then went round to Brigg, had a little lunch at the 'Angel', and home. Mr Haslam was with me, and I have no doubt you will wish you had been there, and I am sure I wish you had been. I arrived home about 2.30, and had certainly enjoyed the outing very much indeed.

Believe me to be,

Your Loving Father

By this date the company had lost over 120 men to the armed forces plus some to munitions, but it would seem that Hopper was happy with the performance of the female replacements. It is also interesting to note his hands-on involvement with production, at the age of 56, and his vision of a future dominated by automatic machines manned by semi-skilled operators. His purchase of Tombleson's brickyard, known also as West Field Brick Works,[4] appears to be a strange business for a cycle maker. The second letter explains it as part of a strategy to build a substantial holding of land, by reclaiming worked out brick and tile works situated in the low lying area along the Humber Bank, which had originally provided rich grazing under the old three field system until enclosure at the end of the eighteenth century allowed them to be exploited for clay. Clearly the trauma of receivership had not dampened his enthusiasm for new projects, nor his energy to carry them forward, though it is as well that he did not pursue his goal of filling the pits with Humber mud, as the area is now one of the top nature reserves in Europe.

Sunday night. 24/6/17

My dear Fred,

Your letter of this morning was gladly received. First I think that the motor cycle you have is well worth £30, it ought to realise that amount; on the other hand, I was wondering whether, if a sidecar was fitted to it, it would be any use to me running down to my various jobs. I rather think it would, and as you are not using it, I should be rather pleased if you would send it down for me to experiment with and we will arrange about a price later on.

Secondly, the red card which you anticipate getting I don't think you will have any difficulty in getting, the more I see of the position of the country, the more I see that men who are skilled in engineering are not required for the Ranks. This means naturally, that the man who makes himself efficient is the man who will not have to go into the Army; on the other hand, I enclose you a cutting which I have taken from the Sunday Chronicle to-day, from which you will see that the Government are wanting skilled men, so that if you do not get your card the policy would be to volunteer in this line, and I do not think you would have any difficulty in passing the test which they give to these men; then again, I would much prefer you to stay where you are, and speaking to Mr Sangster last week, he could not understand how Mr Baker had got into such a blue funk about the Government fetching the men from him, as they are not experiencing the difficulties there, and when you come to think that I have got some men in my place who are not artizans (sic) and no older than you, I really think you ought to be able to manipulate matters as to keep clear of it; this you want to keep in your mind. I am not unpatriotic by any means, but in my position, you are the only son, and naturally I wanted you to follow me here, and the more you know of the business generally, and the more experienced you become, the more likely you are to fill my position, although the practical commercial experience can only come from years of hard work, but your portion that you are doing now ought to fit you in a very great measure for the future. I shall be glad to hear when you have got your Red Certificate, and when you do get it, hang on to it.

I am sorry to note Mr Baker is so worried, give him my kind regards, every man who is running a business in these times has worries innumerable, and deserves what assistance and help that can be given to them, therefore leave nothing undone that you can do to help him. He is a good little man whom I have a very keen affection for.

You will know of course, that I had Mr Sangster over, and he enlightened me pretty considerably as to the exact state of affairs in Birmingham, but it is very marvellous, but nevertheless true, that

B'ham does not know everything that goes on in the United Kingdom, and there is at present a slight stir on foot with the Assoc. Of Cycle Manufacturers complaining that certain people are turning out a good number of cycles and they wish to curtail it; you can draw your own conclusions from this.

Home affairs are very much as usual. The good ship 'Hamilton' (to be shortly named the 'Saucy Arethusa', or the 'Saucy Sarah') (and numerous other Saucies, EAJ) whichever it is at the moment, left Goxhill on Saturday with her first cargo of timber, bound for New Holland, and I am very pleased that I bought her. She is a clouting good ship, and much more will become of her if the war were to cease within a reasonable period.

Not having much to do in my business (?) I have embarked upon a few speculations to fill up my dead time (??), and the latest is Cade's or otherwise Morris's brickyard. The timber from it will go to B'ham to be made into cases and crates for Birmingham products. I am out on some very good speculations, and my only worry is that you are not here to assist me and get that tuition which only experience can give. Dealing in timber, iron, brass, lead, zinc, and various other details requires a little time to understand, and it would have been of extreme value if you could have been with me, and unfortunately I have lost Arthur Stow. I have installed young French, but although he does his best, he is just about as lively as a funeral. I have only had him a fortnight, and I have had a month too long.

I have at the back of my mind a scheme when I get the whole of the brickyards purchased for fitting the 'Saucy Arethusa' with pumps and engines to pump up the mud out of the Humber and fill up the pits where the clay has been dug out, in a similar way to which they did at Immingham. There is no reason why it could not be done, and I have got my eye on another brickyard, which, if it would be purchased, would make a very nice estate of about 70/80 acres.

In the meantime, I have letters coming addressed to me as 'Brick & Tile Manufacturer', 'Tile Merchant' and so on, and this week I have been forwarding tiles to Scotland; next week I shall be sending them to London and other parts, so by this you will see that I have a little of something to occupy my mind. The great difficulty that I feel, and my greatest trouble is that I have got to have a car with a driver to take me out to the various jobs. A landaulette car is too big in these niggardly times. I have thought of buying a little runabout, but I do not know even then whether my nerves would be just good enough, but with the shortage of petrol, and the state of people's minds, I have the feeling that running a big landaulette car is not 'just it'. I can see quite well that there is money to be made out of breaking these yards up, and as I am the 'Only Richmond in the field' at present, I want to take advantage of it, but, oh, if I only had some help. You can scarcely realise the position, I have men at three different yards at work to be looked after, and the detail attached to it, and of course, the realising of the estates, just gives me a little of something to do.

With reference to the cycle business, we are doing well, in fact we are making a lot of money, how we shall deal with it we shall see later. We are supplying all the Rudge Depots with Elswicks, and we have an open order to supply as many as we can. The shipping trade is.....

It is a great pity the third page did not survive, but Hopper's claim to be making a lot of money is born out by the next section. His determination to keep his son out of the armed services comes over loud and strong, and Fred did avoid call-up. Charles Sangster was managing director and one of the founders of Birmingham based Components Ltd, a major supplier of parts to the cycle industry. The bracketed comment 'EAJ' is by Edith Anne Jackson, Fred's sister-in-law, who typed the letter.

## Trading Conditions

The initial impact of declaration of war is illustrated by an extract from a letter to W H Weight of the Board of Trade, dated 6 February 1917. This records turnover as:

| Year ending 31 July | Turnover £ |
|---|---|
| 1914 | 113,698 |
| 1915 | 73,394 |
| 1916 | 103,273 |

These figures corroborate the statement that exports were badly hit during the first year of the war and then started to pick up. It is clear that the company would have struggled to survive if Hopper had not persevered with his exports. For the last three months of 1916 he records output as:

| Month | Home £ | Export £ | Munitions £ |
|---|---|---|---|
| October | 3,924 | 3,367 | 260 |
| November | 6,575 | 4,865 | 787 |
| December | 5,218 | 4,310 | 0 |

The Chairman's address to the AGM on 12 December 1916 complained of shortage of material and labour, and reduced shipping for overseas trade. By a little creative accounting he claimed that 75% of male employees had joined the colours, but claimed that with the employment of women workers they had been able to maintain an output and execute a portion of the orders on hand. Trading profit for the year before tax was £7,236.

The government had designated certain companies as 'controlled establishments' from early 1915 and essentially took control of their output, in order to turn them over completely to munitions production. This was specialised work that required large machine shop capacity, as most components were produced by machine tools. Bicycles require a much greater variety of equipment in their manufacture and so most companies in the industry were not well suited for total conversion to munitions manufacture.

Government form Z8 reveals something of the frustrations of Fred Hopper in April 1915. The form asked for data on the present state of employment and for comments on the 'prospective state' of the company. Hopper's response to the probable extent of change during the next two months was no change to the home market and a decrease in the foreign and colonial markets. The significant information follows in a page of general remarks to the effect that:

1. We are Manufacturers of Cycles and Motor Cycles and have been established since 1880.
2. Ours is the staple industry in the town, inhabitants 7,000.
3. Our trade is divided as follows: 50% Home, and balance Export.
4. Prior to the outbreak of war the business prospects were very good and factory was employed full time with good forward Contracts. Within one week of outbreak of War all our orders were either cancelled or suspended. During the months of August, September, October, November and December we ran our works and put goods into stock to enable us to keep our workpeople going.
5. During this period we continually endeavoured to obtain an order from the War Office by sending representatives and writing them. We failed to secure an order of any description.
6. In January the trade for both Home and Export began to open out.
7. In February we took a sub-contract for cavalry saddle fittings; quoted for steel presswork for ammunition trays and undertook to make 1,000 (One thousand) sets per week, made all the tools and plant necessary and are now expecting instructions to proceed with the work.
8. Have taken order for presswork for aeroplanes.
9. March. Trade, both Home and Export improving rapidly. Shortage of men felt very severely.
10. April. Trade both Home and Export very good. Difficulties now arise in securing raw materials, and by working long hours with our limited staff we estimate that by the end of our Financial Year that our turnover will be about 50% of a normal year.

Normal hours of work were recorded as 55½ for both males and females, with males working a typical 68½ hour week.

By July 1915 103 men had left for HM Forces with between 50 and 70 of the remaining workforce engaged on government contracts. These included saddle arches for field guns, military cart hubs and spoke sockets, parts for field kitchens and electric stoves for the Royal Flying Corps. The latter were quite elaborate affairs (Fig. 3.2 & 3.3). By October the list of products had grown to include staves and bushes for cart wheels, rifle clips, staple plates, hinges, hasps, machine gun band clips and 50,000, 3 inch Stokes trench shells. The Stokes trench mortar was a widely used weapon on the Western Front, and had been developed by Sir Wilfred Scott-Stokes of Ransome and Rapier, Ipswich. Although a prototype was available by the end of 1914 it was not adopted by the army until the spring of 1915 and lack of munitions manufacturing capacity meant that it was not fully deployed until 1916. The shell weighed 11lb and had a range of 800 yards. However, there were periods when no munitions work was in hand, for example, between October 1916 and June 1917.

*Fig. 3.2 Field stove as supplied to the armed forces – doors closed.*

*Fig. 3.3 Field stove – doors open.*

At this stage Hopper's problems were clearly skills related and partly due to his policy of specialisation. The reliance placed on toolmakers meant that the loss of just one of them was a serious blow. A company letter from the end of 1915 emphasised this problem – 'We are short of toolmakers, if this was not so we could utilise more youth and girl labour and accept more government orders which are continually being offered to us.' The possibility of extending night work was also mentioned as a way of increasing capacity. So the lack of toolmakers, itself an indication of the small number employed at the start of the war, proved a serious barrier to accepting lucrative government contracts, but did not stop the company continuing production of large quantities of bicycles for home and export.

To draw a comparison with another large-scale bicycle producer, Raleigh produced over 60,000 machines in 1914 and in October 1914 250 men had volunteered for active service.[5] However, by the end of 1915 total employees had risen to over 2,000. Most of the new workers were women employed in munitions manufacture at the associated Sturmey-Archer factory. The machine tools for mass production of hubs were well suited for producing munitions.[6] Cecil Twist of Coventry Premier described the problems at his company as follows:[7] 'By reason of the small proportion of machinery to the total plant of a factory equipped for the manufacture of cycles, it is impossible to occupy fully such a factory on the production of munitions.' This was the same problem faced by the Barton factory. It was eminently well suited for the production of bicycles; it was not a general machining factory that could be retooled for munitions production. However, some machine tools were suited for sub-contract work, for example:

3" Stokes trench shells for Rennie Forrestt Shipbuilding and Dry Dock Co Ltd, Wivenhoe, Essex and H W Porter of Newbury, Berks.

Sockets for strut ends for Grahame White Aviation Co Ltd of Hendon.

Various parts for Ruston & Proctor Ltd and Clayton & Shuttleworth Ltd, both of Lincoln.

In 1915 making presswork parts for Grahame-White Aviation Co.

Machining saddle arches for Haynes & Son Ltd of London. Fuse caps for National Radiator Co, Hull.

Women were working on a variety of tasks by early of 1916 and the jobs of 127 female employees were described as:

| drilling | 14 |
| axle turning | 2 |
| polishing | 5 |
| frame filing | 8 |
| frame cleaning | 8 |
| frame erecting | 3 |
| machine erecting | 17 |
| handlebar fitting | 2 |
| shell turning | 68 |

By January 1917 the government wanted to know how many female employees were replacing men (84) and how many employees were engaged in export work (148 men and 71 women). Although German submarines had posed a serious threat early in the war it was not on the scale of the next conflict with Germany and it would appear that the world's appetite for British made bicycles was as healthy as ever. In April the company was complaining that there was no finished stock available, compared to a typical level of £25,000 in 1914. This was an attempt to improve the allocation of raw materials as the company claimed that 'we are restricted owing to shortage of goods manufactured from steel and malleable iron, which at present can only be procured under a Class A certificate.' Given that the war was still finely balanced, it is not surprising that raw materials for the Barton plant were tightly rationed, unless intended for war production. The company was still actively pursuing government contracts and it is a little surprising that so few were forthcoming. Hopper's was probably dismissed by the London based planners as a remote small-town manufacturer, and this is perhaps understandable, as most of the bicycles before 1914 were sold to the trade and the name of Hopper would not have been well known outside the trade. The country was still a major manufacturing centre and well endowed with large factories in the Midlands, the North-East and North-West. The Barton factory was simply allowed to get on with making bicycles as best it could with material shortages, so long as men capable of fighting were released. Comparatively few sub-contract munitions jobs were awarded and none directly.

A few details of the export business are known from Arthur Stow's tribunal evidence. For example, the status of orders on hand in January and February of 1917 were enumerated in a final attempt to produce convincing evidence of the importance to the company of the export department and are shown in the following table. They illustrate just how large an export business Hopper had built up.

| Country | January 1917 | | February 1917 | |
| --- | --- | --- | --- | --- |
| | Cycles | Cycle Frames | Cycles | Cycle Frames |
| Belgian Congo | 26 | | 18 | |
| British West Indies | | | 12 | |
| Canada | 14 | | 14 | |
| Canary Islands | 3 | | 3 | |
| Ceylon | 28 | 2 | 16 | 2 |
| China | 6 | | 42 | |
| Cyprus | 8 | | 8 | |
| Denmark | 56 | 5,962 | 56 | 4162 |
| Dutch East Indies | | | 38 | |
| Egypt | | 58 | | 59 |
| Finland | | 200 | | 200 |
| France | 6 | 235 | 6 | 235 |
| Greece | 6 | | 9 | |
| India | 695 | 50 | 781 | 200 |
| Morocco | 4 | | | |
| Norway | 100 | | 100 | |
| Phillipines | 30 | | 30 | |
| Portuguese East Africa | | 4 | 3 | |
| Portuguese West Africa | | | 8 | |
| Russia | 150 | | 150 | |
| South Africa | 54 | 760 | 54 | 1076 |
| South America | 14 | | 32 | |
| Straits Settlements | 54 | | 179 | |
| Trindad | 12 | | | |
| West Africa | 19 | | 21 | |
| TOTAL | 1,285 | 7,271 | 1,580 | 5,934 |

Denmark was a good customer for many years and these figures show just how important that country was during the war. Monetary value of exports for January 1917 was estimated at £20,000 of which £5,500 represented the wages bill. These orders were simply work in hand but give a picture of the healthy nature of international trade at a time when the war was by no means nearing a conclusion. Reference to a pre-1918 atlas is recommended for readers who wish to know which modern countries comprised 'Portuguese West Africa'. It can be assumed that generalisations, such as 'West Africa' refer to British colonial territories, such as Nigeria and Sierra Leone. It is not known whether the Russian order was ever dispatched as that country was on the point of collapse by that time, even though outright revolution was still a few months away.

Trade with Atherton for India and Burma continued to prosper during the war years, with sales of £4,320 in 1916, £8,251 in 1917 and £11,000 in 1918. This was surpassed in the first year of peace with £14,366.

Marine insurance was important for exports during wartime and some of the policies drawn up in 1916 were for:

| Ship | Voyage |
| --- | --- |
| SS Atsuta Maru | London to Bangkok |
| SS City of Chester | London to Capetown |
| SS Dunvegan Castle | London to Capetown |
| SS Weimar | London to Geneva (part rail) |
| SS Elizabethville | Hull to Kinshasa |
| SS Rinaldo | Hull to Bombay |
| SS Egwanga | Liverpool to Somanyah via Accra |
| SS Manistee | Liverpool to Las Palmas |
| SS Worsley Hall | Liverpool to Khartoum |

Export volumes are further corroborated from the few surviving insurance lists, with 11 ships carrying exports in May 1916. These included bicycles for Accra, Penang, Colombo and Hawkes Bay (New Zealand) and motorcycles to the value of £198 to Colombo aboard 'Clan Farqhuar'. This would equate to approximately seven machines. A similar number was exported the following month.

The healthy state of export orders did not mean that they could be fulfilled with any speed, given the shortage of materials and that is perhaps why Hopper continued to pursue government contracts; he had, after all, been told that his works were to be shortly filled with these. The letter to W H Weight, previously quoted, gives a good picture of the situation as of 6 February 1917 and also shows that Hopper was still coming up with new ideas:

> As explained to you, at the present moment our orders for Munition work, although they appear to be large quantities, do not amount to great cash value, but we manufacture these goods for Messrs Ruston & Proctor Ltd, also Messrs Clayton & Shuttleworth Ltd, both of Lincoln and we are receiving orders from them regularly.
>
> The list of export orders now on our books is about the average amount of standing orders held by us, as repeat orders are regularly received in sufficient quantities to maintain the average shown on the list attached. We have a very good export trade also for a small 2½hp 2-stroke motor cycle which we manufacture: the engine itself is not made in our works, this we purchase, and at the present time are awaiting deliveries.
>
> We enclose an illustration of a machine we had intended showing you, which we have introduced for the use of wounded soldiers. It is a hand-propelled tricycle with either right or left hand control, is capable of being driven at a speed upwards of 6/7 miles an hour with the greatest ease; it is really a very good thing, coming out at a reasonable price. In getting this machine out we have been considerably handicapped owing to the lack of just two or three skilled men for the most important work, but we have almost overcome the difficulty and hope soon to have them going through in quantities.
>
> We omitted also to show you a cycle which is quite a new departure in the cycle industry; this is a lady's carrier machine, for the purpose of carrying out goods from various trades people, work which has hitherto been done by young men. An illustration of this is also enclosed and may be of interest to you. It is quite a new thing and has met with a very good reception, and there is a good demand for the machine.

The lady's carrier is an intriguing idea, and presumably a response to the lack of young men for the delivery of goods. However, there were many boys below conscription age to fill the role and no details have been found of this machine. There followed current data on production and orders at the end of 1916:

WORK PROCEEDING £

| | |
|---|---:|
| For Export Trade | 18,000 |
| For Home Trade | 30,000 |
| For Munitions sub contracts | 162 |
| Total | 48,162 |

OUTPUT 1916 £

| Month | Home | Export | Munitions |
|---|---:|---:|---:|
| October | 3,924 | 3,367 | 260 |
| November | 6,575 | 4,865 | 787 |
| December | 5,218 | 4,310 | 0 |

In August 1917 the company secretary, A H Davies was canvassing for government work, this time through the director of Aeronautical Supplies based in the Air Board, Strand, London. Davies had visited the offices and was following up with a formal request to tender for tube and metal parts for fins, rudders etc. It seems he was not successful as he stated in a letter to the Ministry of Munitions, 14 November, enclosing yet more employee lists that 'we are still negotiating for Aeroplane parts for the Air Board....' However, by 1917 companies such as Raleigh and BSA were under pressure to rebuild their non-munitions work due to falling prices, a difficult task, given government restrictions on supplies.[8] So Elswick-Hopper's lack of machine tools, machinists and toolmakers proved ultimately a commercial advantage as the company continued to produce bicycles and motorcycles for both the home and export market and was thus in a good position for the return to normal business at the end of 1918.

## Armistice

Financially the company did well from this terrible war, despite a poor start, as profit figures show, though 1918 was certainly the icing on the cake:

| Year | Profit £ |
|------|---------|
| 1915 | 144 |
| 1916 | 481 |
| 1917 | 1,277 |
| 1918 | 12,468 |

Although this chapter has concentrated on exports, based on the contents of the archives, it is clear that the home market also remained healthy, as orders placed by Brown Brothers demonstrate. This major factoring company had been a customer of Hopper since 1913 and sales for March 1917, as an example, were worth £2,096. Hopper himself did well from the war. In 1917 he had sufficient funds to buy Park Farm, a large working farm of around 190 acres on the southern edge of Barton, and to move from Elm Tree House in Barton's High Street to a more prestigious dwelling, Cliff House, at the western entrance to the town situated near the top of Ferriby Hill (latterly known as the Humber Bridge Hotel but now sadly demolished to make way for a modern housing estate). Elm Tree House was bought by the company, on a mortgage from Hopper, and until it was sold in the 1960s was the designated home for senior managers. As already noted, his son Fred Hopper Junr was not called to serve the country and his most favoured employee, Arthur Stow, came home from the war to help the company face its post-war challenges.

What is clear from the employment data for the war and post war years is that Hopper realised that future profitability depended on labour costs and that women would work for less money than men – still an issue today. By 1920 Elswick-Hopper was employing more women than during the war and more employees, but fewer men. This was despite hiring back men who had served the country and wished to return. The war had changed the social order forever – women were no longer content to take work as servants, and they were recognised by enlightened employees as valuable assets. It is a pity that it took so much slaughter to prove the point. Although women with property, or married to property owners, and over the age of 30 were given the vote in 1918, they did not achieve universal suffrage until 1928, a breakthrough that Fred Hopper did not live to see.

## Endnotes

1       www.worldwar1.co.uk.

2       *Gunfire* No 17 p 1 to 48.

3       *The First World War* John Keegan p335.

4       *Bricks, Tiles and Bicycles in Barton before 1900*, Geoffrey Bryant and Nigel Land, p31.

5       *The Story of the Raleigh Cycle*, Gregory Bowden p40.

6       Ibid.

7       Ibid p 106.

8       *Raleigh and the British Bicycle Industry* p106.

# CHAPTER 4

## THE INTER-WAR YEARS

The world market for bicycles was strong following the Armistice and company sales for 1919 were 55% up on the previous year. Ironically, munitions demand for the first three months of that year was also higher than for the whole of 1918. This chapter shows the company surviving the industrial turmoil and depression of the inter-war years with remarkable ease – due to the utilitarian nature of its products, its position as the major industrial employer in a still largely agricultural area, and in no small measure to the strength of its export market. It also records the death of Fred Hopper in 1925, weakened, some said, by years of exertion, finally succumbing to a severe cold at the age of 66.

Employment at Hopper's increased rapidly during peacetime, from 393 in October 1918 to 510 in August 1919 and 627 in April 1920, a figure exceeding that of 1914. Returning servicemen comprised the major increase, with male employment up 81% in 1920, but interestingly, female employment also rose during the same period by just under 30%. Little wonder that Chad Varah's parents at Barton's Vicarage found it difficult to hire domestic staff. As he notes in his autobiography, *Before I Die Again*, his father, Canon W E Varah, employed six servants before the war and also a nanny and other casual help, whereas post-war the household was reduced to just a single 'daily' with a woman to help with the washing and ironing two days a week. A combination of better pay and shorter hours for factory work and falling income from church farm land meant a much harder life for the Vicar's wife. It seems that Canon Varah was often seen cycling through the town on his parish visits, presumably on a Hopper machine.

There were slack periods at the cycle works during the depression as related by Francis Barratt, a third generation Hopper employee. A time served Hopper tool maker he records that his father, Francis (Stan) had been a Hopper apprentice in the early 1920s and had been laid off during the early 1930s, finding work in Grimsby building the new dry dock. He returned to Hopper's but left for good in 1938, when 'short time' was imposed, to work for Armstrong Patents in Beverley, makers of shock absorbers.

### Business Environment

To understand how Elswick-Hopper survived the difficult inter-war years it is useful to look at the world economic environment. Falling industrial profits from 1909 to 1914 had resulted in downward pressure on wages and increasing industrial strife, especially in the mines. This had been masked by the war, but the incipient pre-war slump 'returned on a punishing scale'.[1] Overseas demand was shrinking and textile exports by the late 1920s were at half their pre-war level, due to the raw material producing countries starting up their own mills. In 1918 British shipyards had the capability of supplying the ship building needs of the whole world, and yet in 1921 they were working at just 20% capacity.[2] A return to the Gold Standard in 1925 and massive overvaluation of sterling at $4.86 (the five bob dollar) did nothing to help labour intensive export industries, and inevitably jobs were lost and wages cut. Unemployment in shipbuilding approached 30% nationally and in Barrow-in-Furness reached 49%.[3] Falling profits in the coal fields and mine-owners' demands for wage cuts and extended working hours eventually precipitated the nine day National Strike of 1926, with 1.5 million workers called out by the TUC, of whom 90% were miners.[4] Response was most solid in London, the coalfield towns and large cities, including Birmingham, Liverpool and Hull. Barton on Humber, just a ferry ride across the Humber from Hull, was insulated from this unrest.

Though the Gold Standard was dropped in 1932, and duties were imposed on imports, such measures did not stave off the depression that followed the financial crash of 1929, itself caused by lack of regulation of the money markets and stock market over-exuberance, a sequence to be repeated more than once since, and most recently in 2008. While the mighty Tyneside shipyards had produced 238,000 tons of ships in 1913, in 1933 the tonnage was just 7,000, a situation that led to mass unemployment. National unemployment rose from 1.6 million in 1929 to 3.4 million in 1932.[5] However, outside the heavy industrial and mining areas there was also much prosperity, with wages rising and prices falling. Electrical goods were being developed to make use of an expanding National Grid and car ownership grew from 78,000 in 1918[6] to 1,000,000 in 1930[7] and nearly 2,000,000 by 1938, (mainly due to the availability of smaller and cheaper cars within the reach of middle class families, and much expenditure on road building.[8]) This growth in car ownership would undoubtedly have been much greater had the depression not so drastically increased unemployment, and it was not until the late 1950s that ordinary working families could afford a car – resulting, as we shall see in Chapter 6, in declining demand for bicycles.

One impact of the great depression was significant fluctuation in bank rate, used then, as now, to either stimulate or depress demand. The rate in 1919 stood at 6% and between 1920 and 1930 swung between 3% and 7%. 1931 saw four changes within a four month period, from 3% down to 2½% before rising to 6%. The following year there were six changes, with the rate falling in the first six months from 6% down to 2%, where it stayed until 1951, apart from two minor blips in August and September 1939, presumably a reaction to the imminence of another war. It is also useful to look at the Retail Price Index, which is based on a 1974 number of 100. At the start of this period the RPI was 19.9, rising to 25.3 in 1920, falling during the rest of the decade to 17.3 in 1930 and to a low of 15.8 in 1934, before rising to 17.3 in 1939. So by 1934 prices had fallen by a signifcant 20%.

As explained in William Oakley's history of the CTC, *Winged Wheel*, the immediate post-war period saw a boom in bicycle sales spurred by the return of young men unwilling to settle back into the humdrum of urban life. 'A bicycle offered a simple answer to restlessness, a cycling club the means of enjoying that comradeship they had experienced together away from home.' However, before long the CTC feared a decline in membership due to rising unemployment and also to a powerful and antagonistic motor lobby constantly trying to push anti-bicycle legislation. In reality the CTC enjoyed rising membership throughout the period – bicycles were seen as the only affordable way to travel further in search of work; they provided the opportunity to participate in track racing and time trials, and were the means for vast numbers of lower paid people to enjoy weekend breaks and touring holidays across the whole of the British Isles. Distance was no object and local Barton cyclists pedalled off for a tour of a few hundred miles with not a second thought.

For the industry the best summary is provided by Lloyd-Jones and Lewis in their account of Raleigh and the bicycle industry. They explain that cycle exports recovered rapidly after 1918 and increased eightfold between 1918 and 1920, despite the constraints of shortages of raw materials, power and labour – all the consequence of a debilitating war. These factors pushed up prices, accounting for some of the increase in export value, but also allowed foreign manufacturers to compete more effectively. During this inflationary boom the average price for a British export machine rose from £7.25 in 1918 to £9.75 in 1921, an increase of 34.5%. Lloyd-Jones and Lewis observe that the worst period for British cycle manufacturers was between 1921 and 1924 and this is born out by the experience of Elswick-Hopper.

## Peacetime Boom, Bust and Recovery

The Barton factory (Fig. 4.1) did not match an eightfold increase but export sales did increase from £41,183 in 1918 to £171,622 in 1920, a healthy 416% improvement. This immediate post-war boom was short-lived, and the subsequent fall was not helped by the refusal of the government to apply import tariffs, though such measures were applied at 33.3% to imported cars.[9] Elswick-Hopper exports

*Fig. 4.1   An aerial view of Barton showing the large area occupied by St Mary's Works. Note the large Elswick and 'aerodrome' buildings at the lower right hand side and the office near the top, just left of centre. © Aerofilms Ltd.*

followed the industry by falling to £38,104 in 1921, though recovering to £79,270 the following year and to £129,308 in 1925. The 1921 dip meant some short time working at Marsh Lane, though on 25 November 1922 the *Hull Times* was pleased to report that 'ordinary time' had been resumed that week.

Import tariffs certainly helped the growing car manufacturing industry, which had been badly affected by the post-war slump – when both Morris and Austin came close to bankruptcy. However, between 1924 and 1939 80 car manufacturers went out of business and prices fell by an average of 25%.[10] This was in some ways a replay of the bicycle industry following the end of the 1890s bicycle boom, when only those firms capable of cutting costs could survive. Hopper's early misadventure into motorised transport did at least force the company to refocus on its core business. Local conditions enabled the company to avoid some of the strife hitting the Midlands, where BSA's Redditch factory was hit in 1920 by an assemblers' strike for higher piece rates. This was followed by a one month strike in April 1921 of cycle and motor cycle workers in Coventry that caused widespread disruption.[11] The Barton firm's rural location again proved the viability of Hopper's original decision to build bicycles away from the principal areas of industry, and increases in imported power costs were avoided by having his own generating plant. So far as jobs were concerned Hopper's factory was still the best payer, with little local competition. It is likely, however, that material shortages had an unavoidable impact on production costs.

The 1923 AGM was held at the George Hotel in Barton on 20 December with George Poppleton, Fred Warwick and Fred Hopper listed as Directors. The year had not lived up to expectations 'due to various influences that curtailed the Export Trade which are now gradually disappearing – some avoidable, others have been remedied'. Foreign trade for 1924 was showing 'a steady improvement' but taxation and fuel costs had been expensive. However, a trading profit was reported of £6,191.

The 15th AGM was again held at the George Hotel on 21 November 1928, where a trading profit of £12,910 was reported. The chairman was Fred Warwick and the death was reported of the previous incumbent, George Poppleton, on 14 December 1927, shortly after the 1927 AGM. Following his father's death Fred Hopper Junr had been elected to the board on 27 January 1926 – he was already works manager – and Poppleton's place was filled by the company secretary Albert H Davies.

The 1934 AGM was held at the Brigg Road office – perhaps as an economy measure – on 15 November. Fred Warwick was chairman and Fred Hopper Junr managing director, with Arthur Stow replacing A H Davies, who died in 1930. A measure of profitably during the depression is that in six years trading profit had grown to £33,309. J E Gilbert took over the job of company secretary, and was elected to the board in 1931, along with Arthur Stow.

The 23rd AGM was again held at Brigg Road on 30 November 1936 and the composition of the board had changed significantly. Fred Hopper Junr had taken over as chairman and Arthur Stow as managing director. Three new directors had appeared: Ernest Bramwell Ridsdel, Charles Cecil Rawlinson and Walter Marsden Heald. These gentlemen all appear to have been members of the legal profession, and Ridsdel's London based firm of solicitors acted as the company's registrar. J E Gilbert, though still company secretary, was no longer a director. During the year the unissued ordinary share capital of the company, 65,932 shares of £1 each, was offered by way of rights to the shareholders with 100% take up. The issued share capital was then £139,819, of which £33,560 was in the form of 8% cumulative preference shares. The long standing National Provincial loan was finally paid off and the year's trading profit was £29,262.

The 1937 AGM was held on 22 November and was again fairly upbeat, despite a rise in the price of raw materials, which incurred an increase in stock value from £41,631 to £57,521. Profit for the year was £23,534, and a healthy dividend of 15% (less tax) was paid on ordinary shares.

J E Gilbert died suddenly around this time and was replaced by George Clarke, an accountant by training. Born in 1905 Clarke had run a trading company in the Belgian Congo at the age of 19. He then ran a gold mine in Rhodesia and another in Sudan, a tin mine in Burma and worked also for a time in Brussels for Lever Brothers. The way he explained his move to Barton was that the Lever Brothers director he worked with knew someone with an involvement in Elswick-Hopper. They needed someone to replace Gilbert and offered him the job. At the time Clarke wasn't keen on going back to Burma because he was home on leave and could see the storm clouds of war on the horizon.

The 25th AGM was held on 8 December 1938 and no dividend was paid due to 'the present position of the industry', though a small trading profit was made of £5,063 – substantially down on the previous year. The directors thought the year exceptionally disappointing especially as the first three months had shown an advance of 37.5% on the previous year

The final report available is for the 30 December 1940 AGM, which stated that 'trading during the year, although beset with many difficulties, has produced a satisfactory result'. The trading profit was £14,735 compared with £1,485 for 1939.

Although the company was holding its head above water it was facing serious competition from the two largest manufacturers, Raleigh and Hercules. The latter had invested heavily in mass production techniques during the 1920s and by 1935 was a serious rival to Raleigh with an annual capacity of 600,000 bicycles.[12] For their part Raleigh broke with tradition in 1936 by forging agreements with large retailers like Halfords and Currys, to whom Elswick-Hopper had been long term suppliers, and opened a 1,000 machines per week assembly plant in the Republic of Ireland the following year. This was in collaboration with W H Cooper, the Dublin merchants who had distributed Hopper cycles in that country for many years.[13]

Sales figures have survived for the whole of the period, though the Hopper/Elswick split is not available for 1938 onwards.

| Year | Domestic Sales £ | | Total £ | Export | Total Sales | % Export |
| | Hopper | Elswick | Domestic | Sales £ | £ | |
|------|---------|---------|----------|---------|-------------|----------|
| 1918 | 79,500 | 12,511 | 92,011 | 41,183 | 133,194 | 30.9 |
| 1919 | 120,319 | 9,183 | 129,502 | 55,153 | 184,655 | 29.9 |
| 1920 | 89,975 | 11,378 | 101,353 | 171,662 | 273,015 | 62.9 |
| 1921 | 85,643 | 6,018 | 91,661 | 38,104 | 129,765 | 29.4 |
| 1922 | 115,306 | 4,972 | 120,278 | 79,270 | 199,548 | 39.7 |
| 1923 | 84,901 | 7,322 | 92,223 | 77,400 | 169,623 | 45.6 |
| 1924 | 114,526 | 4,797 | 119,323 | 96,804 | 216,127 | 44.8 |

| 1925 | 100,842 | 3,612 | 104,454 | 129,308 | 233,762 | 55.3 |
|---|---|---|---|---|---|---|
| 1926 | 74,983 | 9,276 | 84,259 | 127,308 | 211,567 | 60.2 |
| 1927 | 85,046 | 19,238 | 104,284 | 138,134 | 242,418 | 57.0 |
| 1928 | 93,003 | 20,482 | 113,485 | 168,047 | 281,532 | 59.7 |
| 1929 | 90,050 | 32,193 | 122,243 | 163,868 | 286,111 | 57.3 |
| 1930 | 94,072 | 55,302 | 149,374 | 73,527 | 222,901 | 33.0 |
| 1931 | 81,294 | 56,908 | 138,202 | 58,039 | 196,241 | 29.6 |
| 1932 | 81,007 | 64,716 | 145,723 | 51,786 | 197,509 | 26.2 |
| 1933 | 106,560 | 91,097 | 197,657 | 58,302 | 255,959 | 22.8 |
| 1934 | 123,077 | 100,412 | 223,489 | 72,232 | 295,721 | 24.4 |
| 1935 | 123,440 | 101,839 | 225,279 | 69,776 | 295,055 | 23.6 |
| 1936 | 123,441 | 109,142 | 232,583 | 71,724 | 304,307 | 23.6 |
| 1937 | 100,109 | 85,139 | 185,248 | 77,165 | 262,413 | 29.4 |
| 1938 | | | 157,207 | 45,758 | 202,965 | 22.5 |
| 1939 | | | 162,408 | 56,617 | 219,025 | 25.8 |
| 1941 | | | 222,280 | 58,517 | 280,797 | 20.8 |
| 1942 | | | 146,095 | 85,124 | 231,219 | 36.8 |

These figures show the variable nature of the export market, between 20.8% and 62.9%. Using table C.1 from *Raleigh and the British Bicycle Industry* by Lloyd-Jones and Lewis, it can be calculated that Elswick-Hopper were supplying an average of 10% of British bicycle exports over this period. Given the size of the main competitors, such as Raleigh, Hercules, Phillips and BSA this is probably an accurate representation of their relative size within the industry. The source of this data is *Bicycling News*, 1 July 1937. The marked slump in sales in 1938 was a result of a short domestic and international recession that year, and exports would not have been helped by Hercules and Phillips cutting prices at the end of 1937 for the important Indian market.[14] Two surviving letters show that the company was doing its best to push exports. In one, dated February 1939, the offer of a 17s 11d frame sent to 'The Majestic Bicycle & Supply Company' of Montreal had been declined. Though unable to lower this price an offer was made to supply the gent's 'Canadian Frame Set' with bright parts chromium plated and the usual enamelled parts finished in rust-proofing only, packed in minimum lots of 25 frames to a case for £1 1s. The letter concluded that 'we are sure that you will not find it possible to obtain an English frame set built of British materials at anywhere near this very low price'. The second, also dated February 1939, was to Andre Dewald & Son of Zurich, acknowledging receipt of an order for 10 bicycles and offering special prices on Elswick Model 24 roadsters and the Phoenix roadster. This was in response to Dewald's remark that pricing was the main reason for not placing more orders.

Despite competition from the likes of Hercules, Elswick-Hopper Cycle and Motor Company Ltd entered the Second World War in much better shape than the First and traded profitably during the conflict as we shall see in the next chapter.

## Export Agencies and Trade Mark Protection

To briefly explain the history of trade marks a visit to the Intellectual Property Office website states: 'The marking of goods for various purposes, including identifying them from those of other traders, dates back to ancient times. In the same way, the existence of rules governing the use of such marks goes back to the medieval craft guilds. It was only in the nineteenth century that people began to think of marks, which had become distinctive of a trader's goods, and so attracted valuable goodwill, as a type of property. In the middle of that century, the right to take action in the courts against infringement of a trade mark came about, even when there was no intention to deceive on the part of the infringer.

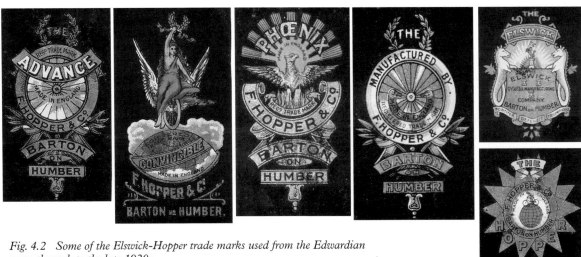

*Fig. 4.2   Some of the Elswick-Hopper trade marks used from the Edwardian years through to the late 1930s.*

The usefulness of such an action was, however, limited by the need for a trader to prove that the mark concerned was in fact capable of distinguishing his goods, and that it belonged to him. The first trade mark registry was established in 1875. Trade mark law was consolidated in 1883, and the Trade Marks Act of 1905 gave the first statutory definition of a 'trade mark'.'

At a time of increasing foreign competition and when the label 'Made in England' still bestowed a stamp of quality it was essential for British manufacturers to protect their patents and trade marks. The registration and ongoing protection of trade marks was also seen as an essential component in building brand loyalty both at home and abroad. If your first bicycle was a 'Famous for Finish' Elswick, with its distinctive Newcastle-on-Tyne coat of arms, and you liked it then perhaps your second one would be from the same company. Given that to most people one bicycle looks very much like another (especially true for export roadsters), the model names, transfers and company trade marks were unique identifiers and their protection vital to prevent locally produced counterfeits – a situation that is as relevant today as it was throughout the last century. Elswick-Hopper employed the London based legal firm of Boult, Wade and Tennant to do this work, and now named Boult Wade Tennant, it is still practising. A selection of trade mark transfers as applied to the head tubes of bicycle frames is shown in Fig. 4.2. Typical work included investigating an infringement of the Phoenix trade mark in 1928 and searches in 1929 relating to trademarks for the China trade. There were no objections to the 'Standard' and 'Winged Wheel' marks, but consent had to be sought from Guy Motors for the 'Invincible' mark.

It was equally important for the growth of exports to work through agencies with local knowledge, and given the relatively slender resources of the company and large export market, the use of agents clearly worked well. On 14 July 1926 an Elswick-Hopper agency was assigned to The China Investment Trust Ltd, a company registered in Shanghai under the Hong Kong ordinances. It seems that the China Investment Trust had a connection with the Dunlop Rubber Co (Far East) Ltd as the agency was 'for the supply of cycles and motor cycles in the whole of the territory covered by the Dunlop Rubber Co (Far East) Ltd'. This comprised the whole of Asia east of Burma, including the Chinese Republic, Hong Kong, Manchuria, Straits Settlements, Federated Malay States, Dutch East Indies and the Philippines. This link with Dunlop is backed up by the Elswick-Hopper archives, which mention the grant of Power of Attorney to Dunlop Rubber Co (Far East) Ltd of Weltevreden, Batavia, Java, Dutch East Indies (DEI), incorporated in Japan and agents for Elswick-Hopper in the DEI for continued protection of trade marks. Trade marks included the Elswick sea horses device and 'Advance'

(1920 with renewal 1940). The China Investment Trust agreement covered the trade marks for 'Convincible', 'Barton-on-Humber' and 'Advance', granted April 1925 and due for renewal 1939. For Burma power of attorney was granted to Isaac Meyer of Rangoon on 30 August 1927 for the Elswick sea horses, 'Advance Wheel', the 'Hopper Star' badge, 'Phoenix', 'Convincible Lady' and 'Barton-on-Humber' device.

The agency for India was awarded to G Atherton & Co (Eastern) Ltd, based at 516 Tower Buildings, Water Street, Liverpool, from as early as 1913, and the archive records show that the company was a major customer through to 1949. Elswick-Hopper instigated a check on Atherton in 1934 following its conversion to a registered company. The response indicated that further research was required into what appears to have been a large trading house:

> Many years ago Mr Murcott of the firm A Murcott & Co Ltd, whilst travelling in India, met George Atherton and some arrangements were entered into between the two concerns. Expenses of an office in Calcutta were shared and Atherton appears to have dealt in certain lines and A Murcott & Co Ltd in others. We believe that when the late George Atherton died, Mr Murcott was Trustee under the will.

G Atherton & Co was awarded power of attorney to protect trademarks within their sphere of influence, which included their agent Isaac Meyer in Rangoon. The remit was to protect the following marks:
21810 'Vivo' (word), 1726 'Advance' (word), 53120 'Barton-on-Humber' (word), 185 Sea Horse (device), 338 'Hopper' (word), and 59/27 'Phoenix' trade mark.

## Land and Buildings
In August 1924 a comprehensive valuation of all Elswick-Hopper property was made. It shows that most of the Edwardian houses built for employees had been sold, though holdings were still extensive.

| Land & Buildings | | £ | s | d |
|---|---|---|---|---|
| | St Mary's | 21695 | 17 | 2 |
| | Brigg Road | 4075 | 10 | 0 |
| | Castledyke South | 1950 | 0 | 0 |
| Sub Total | | 27721 | 7 | 2 |
| | | | | |
| Houses | Elm Tree House | 2500 | 0 | 0 |
| | 12 on Beck Hill | 1337 | 15 | 6 |
| | 6 on Soutergate | 500 | 0 | 0 |
| | Pinfold House (Brigg Road) | 310 | 0 | 0 |
| | 10 on Marsh Lane | 800 | 0 | 0 |
| | Manby House (Marsh Lane) | 900 | 0 | 0 |
| Sub Total | | 6347 | 15 | 6 |
| | | | | |
| Land | St Mary's, Beck Hill & Soutergate | 9310 | 16 | 0 |
| | Brigg Road Offices, Warehouses & Showrooms | 1733 | 2 | 6 |
| | Castledyke Packing Shops | 300 | 0 | 0 |
| Sub Total | | 11443 | 18 | 6 |
| | | | | |
| Grand Total | | 45513 | 1 | 2 |

Pinfold House and the associated Manor Pound were purchased 31 May 1920 for unknown purposes for £310. It was situated on the east side of Brigg Road between 'Southfield' and what is now a funeral parlour (former smithy). Bought from John Andrew it had been leased since 26 August 1902.

Company board meeting minutes record that an agreement was reached in September 1919 to purchase Elm Tree House. It was sold to the company by Fred Hopper in March 1920 for £2,500, of which £2,000 was in the form of a 5% mortgage held by Hopper. It was the home of company secretary A H Davies until his death in 1930 and then of a series of managers, the last being R A McKenna. Upon his death the house was sold in 1967 and was listed Grade II in September 1976.

In November 1928 the 'Back Lane' (Castledyke South) Home Packing Shops, adjoining the offices were finally purchased from Herbert Woodcock for £300. Another self-made Victorian, Woodcock was listed as a plumber and painter in the 1885 Kelly's Directory. He was chairman of the UDC in 1909 and Kelly's 1922 has him living at Hill Farm, Brigg Road, as a JP and farmer. In a rare sale of assets a portion of land at the rear of Elm Tree House, facing on to Catherine Street, was sold to Canon W E Varah in 1931 for £28.

In 1934 four old almshouses and the associated land were bought from the Thomas Holland Charity in exchange for £200 nominal value Consols (Government Bonds). These were situated on Paradise Close, which adjoined the original St Mary's tan yard site to the north. Most of Paradise Close had already been incorporated into St Mary's and these cottages allowed further extension to the north.

The lease on the London showroom at 8 Great Eastern Street continued until 1938, when an application was made to the Metropolitan Borough of Stepney for supply of electricity to 13 Norton Folgate, and 1/3 White Lion Street (later renamed Folgate Street). These properties were quite close to the old showroom, just a stone's throw from Liverpool Street station and are listed as the sole London showrooms in the 1939 catalogue. The move appears to have been short lived as post-war catalogues make no mention of a London showroom.

## Death of the Founder

Fred Hopper died unexpectedly on Sunday 20 December 1925, at 66 years of age, reportedly of a chill and a time when he should have been able to take life a bit easier and enjoy the fruits of his life's work.

A tribute to Fred Hopper exists in the form of a scrap book of his obituaries. It was found by Sir Reginald Tyrwhitt in 2002 in a solicitor's office that had been locked up and left around 1964. He had bought the building, situated next to his own on Whitecross Street, and it proved to be a time capsule, full of valuable records, including the scrapbook – part of Edith Anne Jackson's papers. Fred Hopper's sister-in-law had worked at the Brigg Road office for most of her life. Head of the typing pool she had a reputation as a disciplinarian, but also as a good teacher to the many girls who passed through her hands. Her personal files were also found in the offices. Edith Anne's sister Hannah Elizabeth's obituary is also in the book, and also a funeral pamphlet dated 12 July 1930 relating to the death of Ernest Brown, one of the founders of Brown Brothers. Clipped to the pamphlet is a visiting card from Ernest Brown, with the following hand-written note: '*Xmas 1926 With Best Wishes & happy memories from* Mr. Ernest Brown, *To Mrs Hopper & Miss Jackson.*' Edith Anne had lived with her sister and brother-in law for many years, first at Elm Tree House and then at Cliff House, and continued there until her own death on 22 October 1949, age 73 years. Hannah Elizabeth died on 26 November 1941 age 70. The scrapbook bears the inscription:

**In sweet & loving memory of
a heart of gold.**

----------------------

**Sacred**

**to the Memory of**

**Fred Hopper,**

**Born 28th September 1859**
**Died 20th December 1925.**
**Aged 66 years.**

---------------------

**Interred at the Barton Cemetery on**
**Thursday 24th December 1925.**

---------------------

**R.I.P.**

-----------

The book contains 14 reports from both local and national newspapers and from cycling trade magazines. Even the *News of the World* of 27 December carried a small and inaccurate headline: 'ROMANCE OF TRADE. From Blacksmith to Lord of Manor.' *Bicycling News*, in January 1926, noted that:

> The late Mr Hopper may justly be regarded as one of the pioneers of the cycle trade. He opened his original workshop in Brigg Road, Barton, as long ago as 1880, producing machines with the trade names of 'Miranda', 'Ajax', and later, the 'Advance', the last-named model, incidentally, being still a prominent feature of the firm's programme. Mr Hopper at various times occupied many public offices, notably as Lord of the Manor, chairman of the bench of magistrates, and as a prominent member of the local Urban District Council.
>
> It is not too much to say that the prosperity of the town of Barton has for a considerable time been dependent upon his energy and enterprise.
>
> The late Mr Hopper is survived by his widow and son, Mr F Hopper, jun., to whom we tender our sincere sympathy.'

The geographically inaccurate *Bicycling News and Motor Review* of 20 January 1926, referred to the deceased as the well-known cycle and motor-cycle manufacturer of Hull, who, in the early years of the century made quite a 'splash' in the wheel world by producing bicycles at a figure which seemed impossible for the production of real machines:

> He made his people comfortable, organising all sorts of social functions for them; took a keen delight in public work, having held at various times most of the principal offices in connection with the administration of the affairs of the town. Mr Hopper was a thorough man, and a genuine one, and was among the enterprising ones who made it possible for millions to own machines. He was very popular with his work people and made it part of the business of his life to see to their comfort and happiness.

> This book was intended to be a tribute to Fred Hopper, as much as a record of the company that he founded, so I make no apologies for including the complete report of the funeral, which took place on 24 December, from the *Hull and Lincolnshire Times* of 2 January 1926.

> LATE MR FRED HOPPER
> UNIVERSAL TRIBUTES TO CYCLE PIONEER
> WORKPEOPLE MOURN DEEPLY
> Barton was in mourning on Thursday week when the late Mr Fred Hopper, J.P. was laid to rest in the cemetery.
> The coffin was of solid oak, with brass furniture, and bore the inscription,

'Fred Hopper, died December 20 1925.'

It was carried by Messrs Frank Robinson, John Curtis, Charles Altoft, Johnson, H Pond, J W Booth, J Small and Frank Barratt, all foremen in the cycle works of which the deceased had been the managing director and founder. The grave, which had been bricked, was lined with laurel and chrysanthemums.

Police Superintendent Frank Gostick, with Sgt. Markham, P.C.'s Barsley, Cook, Stubbs, Clark, Falgate and Cox, acted as a body guard, and the magistrates present were Mr Henry Wilson, (chairman of the Bench), Mr O Wass, Mr T Raby, Mrs Grace Schofield, Mr J Dawson, Mr James Barraclough, Mr J C Lee, and Mr W Harvey. Mr Arthur Hudson represented Mr Richard Hudson (the magistrates' clerk).

As the cortege drew up to St Mary's church, the work people from the cycle works lined up in twos, and followed the mourners into the church – the one in which the deceased had taken a particular interest, and after which he had named the works. A full choir met the procession at the door. The Rev. W E Varah (vicar) and the Rev. G H Legge B.A. (curate) conducted the service. To the mournful strains of the Dead March in 'Saul', played by the octogenarian organist (Mr G R Welsh, an old friend of the deceased), the coffin was borne out of the church. Meanwhile, the bells of St Mary's sent forth a muffled peal. It was a beautiful service, and the great church was completely filled with friends and workpeople.

## TEARS OF REGRET

There were many tear-stained faces, and it was pathetic to see strong men so deeply moved. Although there was a covering of snow on the ground, the day was fine, and the sun shone in the chancel where the coffin rested during the service.

The chief mourners were the widow, Mr Fred Hopper (son), Miss E A Jackson (sister-in-law), Miss M Hare and Mrs J Oldridge, (nieces), Mrs Fred Hopper (daughter-in-law), Mrs G W Robinson, Miss B Jackson, Mrs A Bramley, Mr Allbones and Mr E Allbones, (Washingborough), Mr J Oldridge, Mr Arthur Bramley, Nurse Deveraux, Nurse Harrison, Messrs. S Dixon, G Bristow and Mr G Hansley (gardeners) and Mr H Stephenson (chauffeur).

The Elswick-Hopper Cycle and Motor Co. Ltd. was represented by Mr A H Davies (secretary), who also represented Mr G G Poppleton, of Birmingham (chairman of the directors, who was unable to attend due to the inclement weather, and Mr F Warwick of Shirley, who is indisposed. Mr F C Turner (assistant secretary), Mr J A Hammond (cashier), Mr Arthur Stow (sales manager), Mr R W Gregg (Scottish representative), Mr F T Armstrong (London manager), Mr G E Peake (Yorkshire representative), Mr C W Shakesby (senior traveller), Mr G F Franklin (Assistant Works Manager), Mr C V Shakesby (traveller), and Mrs Williams (Lady supervisor at the Works). The St Matthew's Lodge of Freemasons was represented by Messrs. F Hare, Geo. Canty, A H Davies, J W Whitehead, G A A Bradnack, John Haslam, F P H Birtwhistle, G R Usher, E J French, W Stamp, A R McDougall, Hugh C Calthrop, G H Nowell, W H Welsh, J C Stevenson, T H Ball, A Morris and T A Beck (St Lawrence and Industry, Scunthorpe).

## SAD LAST GLANCE

Amongst the large congregation were Mrs A H Davies, Mrs D S Burkitt, Miss Eva Burkitt, Mrs C H Atkinson, Miss C Atkinson, Mrs G H Nowell, Mrs Varah, Mr Joseph Hudson, Mr E Clapson, Mr R H Franklin, Mr G H King, Mr E Rickwood, Mr Harry Flower, Mr T H Grassby, Mr D Jackson, Mr C Collingwood, Mr W D Toogood, Mr R King, Mr L Wood, Mr and Mrs W G Bell, Mr E Foster, Mr John Hogg, Mr D K Austin, Mr E Hurd, Mr Arthur Stamp, Mrs J C Stevenson, Mr W A Witty, Mr T Fawley Judge (Hull), Miss Brown, Mr L Ellis, Mr John Franklin, Mr J W Briggs, Mr A G Poole, Mr Fred Canty, Mr John Lyon, Rev A W Bradnack, Mr Todd (Marsh Lane), Miss Burley, Mr Frank Broadbent (representing the North East Lincolnshire Water Company), and Mr F Peasegood (stationmaster).

The Rev G H Legge preceded the long cortege to the cemetery, where the committal service was read by the Rev W E Varah. The Freemasonry ritual was afterwards recited by Bro. George Canty.

It was indeed sad to witness the last glance in the grave by the hundreds of work people – men, youths, women and girls – and it was more than evident that all realised the loss of a friend.

So numerous were the floral tributes that two of the firm's rullies were used to convey them to the cemetery. These included tributes from: 'The staff, and workpeople at Brigg Road.' 'The works staff, firm and employees.' 'The works club.' 'The sports club.' Mr and Mrs Panton and Miss S Panton (Bridlington), Mr G Canty, 'The directors of the Endless Rim Co. Ltd., Birmingham.' co-directors (Messrs Poppleton and Warwick), Mr S W Farr (representing the Pilot Cycle Co. Maidenhead), Mr and Mrs E J French, Mr F Armstrong and staff (London office), 'Directors of the Components, Ltd.,' W. M. and Brethren, 4622, Scunthorpe, Mr Charles Sangster (Birmingham), Mr and Mrs A H Davies, Mr and Mrs J C Stevenson, Mr and Mrs L J Turner (Ipswich), 'Directors of Midland Tube Forging Co. Ltd., Birmingham,' John Frank and Sons, 'St Matthew's Lodge of Freemasons, 1447, 'Co-directors and secretary of North East Lincolnshire Water Co.,' Miss S J Hopkins, Mr and Mrs Bernard Marsden (Bridlington), Mr Ernest Brown (London), Mr Henry Wilson, Mr and Mrs Hewitt, Mr J Haslam, Mr G H Nowell, Mrs Burkitt and family, Mr F C Pardoe (Hull), Mr G Hopper and sons, Nurse Deveraux and Nurse Harrison, Mr and Mrs Allbones and family, Mr and Mrs A Bramley, Mr Robinson and Miss B Jackson, Mrs J Stow, Mr and Mrs A Stow, 'The gardeners and chauffeur,' Mr C W Shakesby. A beautiful cross from Mrs Hopper and family was lowered with the coffin.

Messrs Ted Dent and Sons were the undertakers.

Barton's *Parish Magazine* for January 1926 recorded the services provided to the two Anglican churches by Fred Hopper. At various times he served as churchwarden, member of the choir (he had a fine baritone voice), and school manager of the local St Peter's church school (built as a National School). He gave substantial help in the restoration of St James's Chapel at St Mary's, St Mary's tower and St Peter's church. The remarkably fine cross on St James's altar, designed by Rev H F Napier, he made with his own hands. He also gave new altar vessels for St Mary's at Advent 1925. These were designed by the Vicar, W E Varah. Fred's grave was marked with an interestingly shaped cross, though whether of his own design is not known. A photograph of the grave, situated in the Barrow Road Cemetery (Fig. 4.3), was found in the scrap book. It has survived well, though has developed a slight lean. The mitred cross must have been a tribute to his skills in metal working, and recognises the thousands of tonnes of steel plate and tube that his company processed into bicycles.

*Fig. 4.3  Fred Hopper's grave, as pictured in Edith Anne Jackson's scrapbook.*

Although Fred Hopper had ultimately built a substantial and successful business it is probable that the severe financial problems before the Great War had been a strain on his health. However, given his constant search for new opportunities, the scale of the business that he built up, and the social ladders he had climbed, it is more likely that he had just burned himself out. It is surprising that it took the death of his father for Fred Junr to be elected a director, but perhaps he knew that his son's heart was not in the business.

The death resulted in the payout of the life insurance policies that had been started in the early years of Fred Hopper & Co Ltd. The total payout from three policies was £27,592 7s 3d. A H Davies, his company secretary since 1913, did not survive him long, dying 17 December 1930 at his home at Elm Tree House. He was buried in a plot very close to Fred Hopper. Earlier that year he had been appointed joint managing director.

## Protecting the Finished Product

A high quality finish was always an important claim for Elswick-Hopper bicycles and had been a proud boast of the original Newcastle Elswick company. For many years the Elswick slogan was 'Famous for Finish', while Hopper machines claimed to be 'The Reliability Cycle', though both lines were produced in the same works and underwent the same processes.

The opportunity to use a chemical system for protecting the bare steel components after sand blasting and polishing, but prior to painting, came in July 1925, when an agreement was signed with the Coslett Anti-Rust Syndicate Ltd of Birmingham for the use of equipment and chemicals to prevent oxidation and rusting. The system used dilute phosphoric acid and iron filings to produce a protective phosphate coating and had been patented by Thomas Watt Coslett in 1906. It was eventually superseded by the bonderising process, first developed in 1929. A new enamelling plant was installed in a custom-built building in 1935 at a total cost of £2,138, along with a new generator. Two years later investments were made in a further new stove, a debrassing plant and a new engine.

Nickel plating had been in use since the company started business and gave a dull sheen, which was durable and improved with age, developing an attractive patina. In line with the rest of the industry chrome was introduced at the end of the 1920s with the start-up of the chrome plating department on 10 August 1929. All bicycles listed for the 1930 model year were chrome plated. Local builders J Stamp were contracted to build the new plating shop at a cost of £603 17s 1d. Total capital cost for the chrome plant was £1,868 and for ancillary rim plating equipment £380, supplied by Canning. Other costs included a new 400hp Ruston & Hornsby vertical oil engine driven generator and transformers to meet the increased power requirements. Overall the move to chrome plating incurred a capital investment of £6,282, a significant sum, equivalent to around £290,000 in 2010 values.

## Selling Bicycles

In 1923 the company employed just five salesmen, F T Armstrong, H W Langfield, F C Ramsley, C V Shakesby and L J Turner, though by 1928 a further six had been taken on. Each salesman was responsible for an area of the country and was paid an annual salary with a sales related bonus.

The foreign market was well served by agents such as Atherton's, but some countries required the efforts of company employees, known as export travellers. One such was F J Dwyer, based in Sutton Coldfield, and just one trip early in 1929 seems to have taken several months to complete. His summary of costs explains the route taken. At the time the trade price of a Hopper Popular Roadster was £3 6s 0d, so this was not a cheap trip.

| Item | £ | s | d |
|---|---|---|---|
| Railway to Marseilles. | 8 | 11 | 0 |
| Boat to Mombasa including tips, subs, bar. | 93 | 0 | 0 |
| Railway in Kenya and Uganda. | 33 | 0 | 0 |
| Railway and steamboat fares. | 65 | 0 | 0 |
| Mombasa to Port Said. | 46 | 0 | 0 |
| Rail and boat from Port Said through Egypt, Syria, Turkey, Cyprus and home. | 60 | 8 | 4 |
| Hotels: | | | |
| Kenya and Uganda. | 66 | 0 | 0 |
| Tanganyika, Zanzibar and Nyasaland. | 55 | 16 | 0 |
| Egypt, Syria, Turkey and Cyprus. | 31 | 8 | 6 |
| Sundry cables, car hire etc. | 125 | 0 | 0 |
| | 122 | 0 | 0 |
| | 102 | 15 | 11 |
| Kit stolen – replacements. | 15 | 0 | 0 |
| Import duties and rail costs of goods. | 218 | 2 | 0 |
| | 78 | 18 | 6 |
| Total costs | 1121 | 0 | 3 |
| | | | |
| Value of goods dispatched on consignment | 1734 | 9 | 9 |

A large quantity of samples, 420 machines, was sent out ahead of Mr Dwyer:

| Country | Elswick Models | Hopper Models |
|---|---|---|
| Nyasaland | 12 | 36 |
| Zanzibar | 6 | 12 |
| Kenya | 24 | 78 |
| Uganda | 24 | 78 |
| Tanganyika (3 lots) | 6 | 18 |
| | 6 | 12 |
| | 12 | 36 |
| Portuguese East Africa | 6 | 18 |
| (3 lots) | 3 | 9 |
| | 6 | 18 |
| | | |
| Invoice value | | £1434 8s 8d |

FJ Dwyer left Elswick-Hopper on 6 March 1939 with a cheque for £250, salary up to 31 March and three months salary in lieu of notice. This was accepted and agreed in final settlement of all monies. His place was taken by F J Armstrong who made a sales visit to Malaya in 1935. He had previously travelled in Europe for the company making one trip in 1928 to the north, first to Helsinki, then on to Warsaw, Riva and Reval, at a total cost of £18 1s 0d.

Many shipping companies carried Elswick-Hopper bicycles to overseas destinations during this period, most now sadly defunct, though at the time prominent lines:
Bibby Bros; City Line, Liverpool; Ellerman's Wilson Line, Hull; Hall Line, Liverpool; Houlder Bros, Hull; Hull and Netherlands Steamship Co; Liverpool Brazil and River Plate Steam Navigation Co; Nederland Steamship Co, Amsterdam; Pacific Steam and Navigation Co, Liverpool; and Union Castle Mail Steamship Co are just a few.

## Barton Cycles Ltd

In September 1928 the company set up Barton Cycles Ltd as an 'Easy Payment Finance Company for Elswick & Hopper Cycles'. Directors were F Hopper and A H Davies and the purpose was to assist dealers 'who for several reasons do not wish to finance their own Easy Payment transactions or yet to utilise the services of one of the Finance Corporations'. It was, of course, a way for the company to boost sales and make a decent margin on the loan. The 1932 catalogue, for example, lists the Hopper Hawk at £8 8s cash, or 12 monthly payments of 16s 9d, no deposit being required, other than the first monthly payment. A payment card (Fig. 4.4) from 1935 records that a Hopper Tall-Boy carrier tricycle, bought through Barton Cycles, cost £25 2s. Business must have been brisk as the transaction was closed in just four months, earning a discount of £1 9s 3d.

## Carrier Tricycles

Tricycles for the carriage of goods were developed during the 1880s with an early user being the Post Office. The first ones were available with the paired wheels either fore or aft, though the former proved to be the most popular configuration. Hopper first listed a carrier tricycle in 1907 (Fig. 4.5) which, given its German inscription, may have been a potential import or simply a check on demand. The

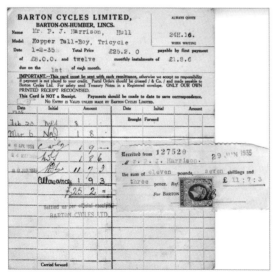

*Fig. 4.4 P J Harrison's payment card from Barton Cycles Ltd for a Tall-Boy Tricycle. This carrier tricycle clearly made him money as the 12 month contract was paid off in six. Thanks to Colin Wright for finding this card in a Hull shop.*

*Fig. 4.5 This box tricycle featured in the 1907 Hopper catalogue.*

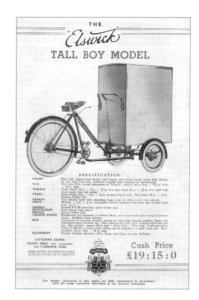

*Fig. 4.6 Definitely Barton made, the description would indicate that it was a new line in 1910.*
*Fig. 4.7 Hopper ice cream tricycle from the 1933 catalogue.*
*Fig. 4.8 1933 Tall-Boy delivery tricycle.*

first 'proper' Hopper machine was listed in the 1910 catalogue (Fig. 4.6). By this time their use was widespread in towns and cities for home deliveries – the equivalent of today's white van. For Elswick-Hopper the boom years for carriers were the 1920s and 1930s; this was also when the ice cream tricycle trade took off after a successful trial by Walls in around 1922 with their slogan 'Stop me and buy one'. Invoices from W Thompson of Finkle Lane, Barton, between 1914 and 1920 indicate that initially the variously shaped wooden boxes were bought in. However, as demand grew manufacture was brought in-house. There were six variations designed to fit the basic chassis, including one specifically for ice cream that included two insulated containers (Fig. 4.7). The dairy model had no need for a box as it was designed to carry a single milk churn within a sturdy frame – these were the days when milk was sold in the street from a churn via a ladle into the householder's jug. One large customer for tricycles was Anglo-Scottish Creameries of Mark Lane London EC3. They were mentioned in a letter to Barton from the London showroom, dated 10 June 1938, as going into liquidation, and that the carriers and tricycles supplied over a long period by Elswick-Hopper would be coming back on the market as second hand sales.

The basic models were supplied with either top opening, or front opening boxes, with the latter fitted with a handy top rack. A tall-boy model (Fig. 4.8) was supplied with a wardrobe rail and was described as 'particularly suitable for valet service', while the produce box was designed with a large capacity for the carriage of groceries. The utility model featured a series of ventilated shelves with louvered doors, designed for the carriage of bread and pastries and also wet and dry fish. These tricycles would have required a good level of fitness to propel, especially in hilly towns – no problem for delivery boys who would use a bicycle for their everyday transport, or else walk, as they would most definitely not have access to a car. Carrier tricycles declined in popularity after the war and few were to be seen once small delivery vans became more affordable. These low impact machines are still produced around the world, even for the sale of ice cream, and with concerns about global warming, and especially the loss of oil as a long term propellant, the carrier tricycle may eventually make a comeback. One local dairyman was using a pre-1914 Hopper box tricycle until 1970. As reported in the *Scunthorpe Evening Telegraph* of 28 May 1970 Harry Leighton used to deliver milk from his father's cows to Habrough homes by bicycle.

> In those days milk was sold from pails hanging from the handlebars of his father's bicycle and it was not until 1950 that he decided to modernise with a second-hand Hopper trike. It had been first used to deliver bread until bought by an Immingham man to carry wireless accumulators to his customers homes. Harry paid £12 for it, rode it back to Habrough and used it for his milk deliveries until he retired in 1970. Initially milk was carried in churns and when bottles were introduced he discovered he could carry about five crates – about half the round.

## London Show Costs

Attendance at the annual Earls Court Cycle Show was mandatory for any serious manufacturer of bicycles and for Elswick-Hopper this involved the construction of a display stand on the top floor of the Brigg Road offices which was then dismantled and transported to London. Typical expenses were £501 for the 1931 Show, including £219 for the hire of the pitch. By 1937 cost had risen to £856 including £377 for the pitch and offices. The increase in cost would indicate a larger space.

## Barton Wheelers

The long absence of a local cycling club did not mean there was no interest in cycling as a sport or recreation in the town and in 1933 a group of riders headed for a weekend rally at Torksey, near Lincoln. They discovered that to take part in racing events club membership was required and so Barton Wheelers was reformed on the spot. At a subsequent meeting at Hopper's Club Dave Farmer was elected club captain, Herbert Dent vice-captain, Harry Houghton chairman, Stan Coulam treasurer and Ben Baldwin secretary. Freddie Hopper agreed to become president, thus reinstating the company to its nineteenth century position of local cycling club patron.

*Fig. 4.9   Henry Wilson and Fred Hopper on holiday in the Isle of Man, probably early 1920s.*

## Henry Wilson

Henry Wilson (Fig. 4.9), who had played such a vital part in the early days of the Hopper enterprise, outlived his partner by seven years, dying 23 November 1932. His estate was valued at £17,966 10s 4d. His best-known offspring was Lieutenant Colonel Harold Graham Wilson, DSO, TD, a veteran of the First World War, resident of Caistor Road and, like his father, a solicitor with Frankish, Kingdon and Wilson.

There is a plaque in the choir of St Mary's Church that states:
'The Rood is placed in this church to the memory of Henry, Blanche and Paley Wilson, March 1937. RIP'

## Barton on Humber Keeps Some Wagon Wheels Moving

W E Newton wrote this article for the *London & North Eastern Railway Magazine*, March 1938 edition.

At this pleasantly situated small township in North Lincolnshire, the terminus of the Immingham Dock-Barton on Humber single line branch railway, within a short distance of New Holland and the Humber ferry service, flourishes one of the largest cycle factories in the country, that of the Elswick-Hopper Cycle & Motor Co. The concern originated in 1880, at a little whitesmith's shop, when the graceful 'Big Wheel' was fashionable, but many wheels have revolved since that time and the present output is about 200,000 cycles per annum. About half this number is sent abroad, consignments being shipped through Grimsby, Immingham, Hull, Goole, London, Liverpool, Birkenhead, and Southampton, to Europe, Ireland, South Africa, Egypt, India, New Zealand, South America, Canada, Japan, China, the Malay States and the Fiji Islands, so that it can be truly stated that Barton on Humber keeps the world's wheels moving.

It is said at Barton that when the founder of the firm, the late Mr Fred Hopper, was busy in his little workshop, he was often visited by seafaring men from ships in the Humber, who would afterwards make known the enterprise of this cycle-maker to traders at their ports of call, and so enquiries would be made, orders given, and wheels set in motion.

Each finished bicycle that leaves Barton on Humber is a real built article; the machines are not just put together, but assembled by skilled mechanics; one machine – one man, is the rule from start to finish of the complete bicycle.

The packing case and crate departments are very important, necessitating huge supplies of timber, which are available at the nearby timber yards at Grimsby, and transported by rail through our New Holland station, at which point all the traffic from and to the Barton cycle works has to be marshalled, either prior to crossing the Humber ferry, for transhipment, or despatch through wagons or containers to all parts of the country. A walk round the despatch shed is very interesting. Nearly whole machines, with only the bars and pedals packed separately in open crates, are for Switzerland; shorter cases, containing complete frames, with one wheel in the fork ends and the other tied to the centre of the frame, were for another market. For the Far East may be seen small boxes, measuring 3ft 6 in by 2ft 9in by 3ft, in which there are 25 complete cycle sets, less wheels. These cases have to be constructed as the packing proceeds, the frames and fitments positioned, packing being added and boards nailed around it, in order to properly fix the contents. The process continues until 25 sets of bicycle parts (less wheels, which are separately encased) have been secured within each box. Other cases are of smaller dimensions and specially shaped, each containing the parts of three machines. These will most likely be intended for shipment to the Middle East, and the last 500 or 600 miles of their journey will be by canal. Large numbers of the cycles are sent away in our specially fitted bicycle containers, which in recent months have been loaded at the firm's works, but formerly all the cycles were conveyed by lorries to Barton on Humber station for loading (Fig. 4.10), either into containers or covered vans. During 1936 there were 84 bicycle containers loaded at Barton station, and up to the end of May 1937 54 containers were utilised. A considerable number of the cycles are forwarded singly, or in small consignments, by passenger train services, and nearly every train leaving Barton for New Holland conveys some of the cycles to the latter station, where they are sorted according to their different destinations.

Special arrangements are carried out prior to Easter, Whitsuntide and Christmas, when it is necessary to utilise the passenger service to a large extent. On these occasions additional brake-vans and pipe-fitted wagons are attached to the principal passenger trains of the day, and large numbers of cycles are loaded through to places such as Banbury, Bristol, Manchester and Sheffield.

At the beginning of January each year the firm despatch more than 14,000 parcels of catalogues by passenger trains. At the time of writing this article the actual number sent in January 1938 is not available, but that for January 1937 was 14,175.

The Elswick-Hopper cycle is 'famous for its fine finish'; even the parts sent abroad are assembled, adjusted for smooth running, and examined before being dismantled for packing. In a gallery round the main assembling floor of the fitting shops, handle-bars are equipped with brake work, and these parts are then sent down by lift to form sets with the frames from the enamelling plant and other parts. The builders, all men of long years of experience and 'wise in their time', are supplied with these complete sets, and from a bin of parts an assembler builds a bicycle, fitting here – if necessary, adjusting there, until the finished article is passed by the inspection department, ready for the Iron Road – and many other roads.

Carrier cycles are a special feature of the Elswick-Hopper Company's manufacture, and this class of cycle is in high demand by the most important multiple shop and public concerns in the British Isles, large numbers also being exported. Another special product of the firm is the Elswick or Hopper toy cycle, and thousands of children are made happy at Christmas-time, both in this country and abroad, when Father Christmas, helped by the LNER, or the Associated Humber Lines brings them a bicycle 'all the way from Barton on Humber'.

Yes, it is true, there are wheels within wheels from Barton on Humber, via the LNER to the utmost parts of the world.

This article shows a little of the complex logistics involved in getting the finished bicycles into the main distribution channels, with just the single line railway connecting the town to New Holland. It describes well some of the procedures involved, and they had changed little since the Edwardian years.

*Fig. 4.10 Bicycles at Barton station ready for dispatch.*

## Factory Employment on 23 November 1939

From a list of wages paid to the factory workers, dated 23 November 1939, it is possible to compare the departmental structure with that at the start of the earlier war.

| Department | Male workers | | Female workers | | Total | |
|---|---|---|---|---|---|---|
| | 1939 | 1914 | 1939 | 1914 | 1939 | 1914 |
| Fork Blade | 13 | 7 | | 3 | 13 | 10 |
| Frame Building | 18 | 49 | | | 18 | 49 |
| Press | 11 | 12 | 4 | | 15 | 12 |
| Back Stay | | 6 | | | | 6 |
| Welding | 6 | 2 | 9 | | 15 | 2 |
| Front Fork | 13 | 8 | | | 13 | 8 |
| Filing | | | | | | 37 |
| Frame Cleaning | | 6 | | | | 6 |
| Enamelling | 9 | 11 | 16 | 3 | 25 | 14 |
| Lining | 17 | 24 | 2 | | 19 | 24 |
| Crank | 10 | 18 | 9 | | 19 | 18 |
| Handlebar Making | 11 | 9 | | | 11 | 9 |
| Polishing | 32 | 46 | 1 | | 33 | 46 |
| Plating | 11 | 13 | 30 | | 41 | 13 |
| Buffing | | 7 | | 4 | | 11 |
| Frame Erecting | 17 | 17 | 3 | | 20 | 17 |
| Mudguard | 1 | 2 | 3 | 3 | 4 | 5 |
| Brake and Hub Fitting | 2 | 4 | 6 | 5 | 8 | 9 |
| Handlebar Fitting | 3 | 6 | 4 | | 7 | 6 |
| Wheel Building | 9 | 12 | 10 | 6 | 19 | 18 |
| Machine Erecting | 31 | 22 | 7 | | 38 | 22 |
| Gearcase | 1 | 10 | 7 | | 8 | 10 |
| Repair | 3 | 2 | | | 3 | 2 |
| Machining | 14 | 36 | 25 | | 39 | 36 |
| Turners | 2 | 9 | 9 | | 11 | 9 |
| Toolmakers | 18 | 5 | | | 18 | 5 |
| Electrical | 2 | 3 | | | 2 | 3 |
| Engine Room | 4 | 3 | | | 4 | 3 |
| Blacksmiths | | 5 | | | | 5 |
| General Yard | 4 | 1 | | | 4 | 1 |
| Millwright | | 1 | | | | 1 |
| Joiners | 2 | | | | 2 | |
| Bricklaying | 10 | | | | 10 | |
| Stores | 2 | 3 | 1 | | 3 | 3 |
| **Overall Total** | **276** | **396** | **146** | **24** | **422** | **420** |

Gone is the back stay department, replaced by the welding department, and the filers and frame cleaners too, due to improved methods of frame production. The machine shop would still be producing many of the components that had given the company its keen competitive edge, though the women now outnumbered the men – as already noted, a legacy of the war, and changing social conditions. The

*Fig. 4.11 Ron Bland's tool room bench in the mid 1930s. Ron was another tool maker who left before the war to join Armstrong Patents in Beverley.*
*Fig. 4.12 Marsh Lane polishing shop c 1938. It includes three of Raymond Eayres' family – his great grandfather, grandfather and a great uncle.*

tool room (Fig. 4.11) saw the largest growth, a reflection of a continued growth in the production of components during the inter-war years. Investment in tools and equipment continued throughout the period, for example, in 1928 £1604 was spent on new equipment, including a press, a hardness tester, lathes and dust extraction equipment (Fig. 4.12).

In common with many large factories Marsh Lane shut down for the first two weeks of August most years, though no break was taken in 1921, presumably due to demand. The opportunity was taken during the breaks to carry out essential maintenance of machinery, including overhaul of all the electrical generators.

## UK Customers & Suppliers

Customer records read like a directory of defunct British companies, though one or two have survived, such as W H Smith, a former purchaser of carrier bicycles. These machines enjoyed good sales throughout the period to the likes of grocers Lipton, Home and Colonial, International, Pearks, and Maypole Dairy Co. From 1932 Freeman, Hardy and Willis, the footwear chain was listed, and Boots of Nottingham from 1931. Large stores included Harrods (from 1913) Army & Navy Stores, John Lewis, and Selfridges & Co, and at least two Selfridges badged Elswick-Hopper made cycles are known to have survived. Jackson's Stores of Leeds was a big Hopper customer during the 1930s with the Light Roadster, Popular and Hawk Racers and the National Roadster purchased in large numbers. Halfords, not surprisingly, had a long relationship with the Barton manufacturer from as early as 1913. Between 1934 and 1936 over 70 machines were supplied to Anglo-Persian Oil Co Ltd, Britannic House, Finsbury Circus. This company is now known as BP and why was it buying a selection of Elswick machines that included a gent's model 17 and 19, model 12, 15, 16, 24, 31, and even a tandem? The mix included racers, light roadsters and full chain case models, so perhaps the company was using its purchasing muscle on behalf of its cycling employees.

At the cycle dealer level the sales ledgers for this period reveal the incredible number of cycle dealers in small towns – 13 customers in Boston, Lincs, for example.

During the first half of the 20th century Brown Brothers grew into the largest wholesale distributor of bicycle and car related goods in the country. The company was founded in 1889, just a year before the appearance of the Hopper Ajax. In 1913 its business with Elswick-Hopper averaged £1,000 per month and continued to grow throughout the war, reaching £2,642 in February 1918. Although sales to Browns fell during the 1920s it started to climb after 1934 and continued through the Second World War.

UK dealer sales were handled by a team of 11 salesmen, including C W Shakesby and his son C V Shakesby, both originally from Hull. Suppliers were many and varied and the sheer number meant that supply logistics were an important part of the business, even though so many parts were manufactured in-house. Mander Brothers of Wolverhampton supplied enamel from 1914, and it is interesting to note the changes in company names; for example, chains were bought from Hans Renold Ltd, Burnage Works, Didsbury, Manchester, until 1932 and after that date from the Renold and Coventry Chain Co Ltd, Spon End Works, Coventry. Similarly, tubes were supplied by the Patent Butted Tube Co Ltd, Tysley until 29 July 1923, when it became Reynolds Tube Co Ltd.

## Another War

The 21 years of peace in Europe covered in this chapter came to an end with a resumption of war with Germany, due in no small measure to the punitive peace treaty signed at Versailles on 28 June 1919. For Elswick-Hopper it had been a case of steady as she goes, with little growth and not much investment. However, the company had survived some difficult trading conditions and was in better shape than it had been at the beginning of the last war.

## Endnotes

1   *A History of Britain* Simon Schama 2002 p 463.
2   *Borrowed Time* Roy Hattersley 2007 p 176.
3   *A History of Britain* Simon Schama 2002 p 465.
4   Ibid. p 466.
5   Ibid. p 466.
6   *Drive On!* L J K Setright 2002 p 48.
7   Ibid. p 66.
8   *The Making of Modern Britain* Jeremy Black p 145.
9   *Raleigh & the British Bicycle Industry an Economic and Business History 1870-1960* Lloyd-Jones and Lewis 2000 p 109.
10  *Borrowed Time* Roy Hattersley 2007 207.
11  *Raleigh & the British Bicycle Industry an Economic and Business History 1870-1960* Lloyd-Jones and Lewis 2000 p 108.
12  Ibid. p 120.
13  Ibid. p 179.
14  Ibid. p 179.

# CHAPTER 5

# SECOND WORLD WAR

The first Hopper casualty of the war was the welfare supervisor, Miss Emily King. A note discovered in old legal documents recorded that 'owing to the blackout of the landing window the stairs were in darkness and she fell down the stairs severing the external cartilage of her right knee.' This occurred at the Cycle Works Club's Laurel House on 2 October 1939 and following two operations at Hull Royal Infirmary she was off work until 7 March 1940. She was duly awarded 12 guineas from the club in compensation.

In the first weeks of the war letters went out to dealers and agents in African countries, Canada, Cyprus and the West Indies advising a 20% increase on all existing quotations, with the proviso that prices ruling at the time of shipment would include any additional transit costs. Danish customers were charged just 15% more, with delivery dependent on supplies of raw material. This letter is dated 3 October 1939:

> All shipments to be insured against Marine and War Risks by us and debited to the customer at cost. We cannot agree to our customers covering on your side under present conditions. Furthermore we could not at any time cable or transmit to you by letter or any other means, the name of steamer and the date of its sailing from any port in this country, for reasons that will be obvious to you. We are informed that the rates of freight to Denmark have gone up 100%...

It was sent to Gode & Co, Rasmussen & Co, Welling & Sondergaard and Stevns & Co. These moves were triggered by the sinking of SS Athenia by U-30 on 3 September, the day that war was declared by Britain. This sinking of a passenger ship off the north-west coast of Ireland, the first of the war, was against the conventions of the time, and resulted in the immediate use of convoys for merchant shipping.

On 19 March 1941 a letter was sent to customers by sales manager Bert Crofts to the effect that: 'It has been found necessary under prevailing conditions to reduce the number of models we were manufacturing, but we are confident that those we are now producing will meet the needs of the public, and that our taking this wartime measure will in no way affect your sales.' He added that prices were to be increased from 21 March and concluded that: 'It is unnecessary for us to enlarge upon the many difficulties we are encountering in regard to production, but we do assure you that everything is being done to give you best possible service, compatible with the raw materials at our command and the labour available for production.'

Concern over war risks prompted George Clarke to write to customers in June 1941 to spell out the liabilities for war damage of goods in transit. He spelled out that 'irrespective of whether goods are sent carriage forward or carriage paid, and loss or damage occurs due to enemy action during the period from handing over to the common carrier until point of delivery according to your instructions, then any such loss would be for your account, and the company would be obliged to recover the invoice value from you as at the time of loss you would be the legal owner'. This must have made a few customers think before placing orders, especially in areas prone to attack by the Luftwaffe.

Although nearby Hull was massively bombed, Barton escaped with just a couple of incidents involving stray hits. One, in February 1940, caused damage to six houses, and on 13 October 1941 a stick of four high explosive bombs created a crater on Ferriby Road. There was a definite advantage in being a bit of a 'back water'.

Not surprisingly, and for obvious reasons, it appears that catalogue production was suspended for the duration. The only ones found are all for 1940 and would have been produced in the first few weeks of the war. They are much smaller than those of the 1930s due to paper rationing and the Elswick cover struck a warlike note (Fig. 5.1), with the introduction stating that: 'Owing to War conditions

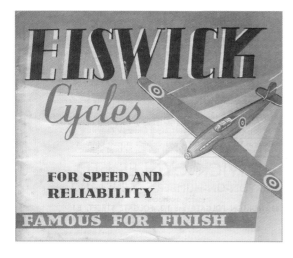

*Fig. 5.1   Cover of a 1940 Elswick catalogue.*
*Fig. 5.2   Marsh Lane staff photograph at the end of the midday break, 1940.*

we reserve the right to make deviations from our catalogue specification where this may be found necessary.' However, the war did not stop the taking of publicity photographs and Fig. 5.2 is believed to date from 1940, taken of the Marsh Lane work force returning from their midday dinner break. The bicycle on the right is thought to be a Brighton Road racing model.

## The Impact of the War on Dealers

Trade fell dramatically during the war, due to material shortages, evacuations and lack of money, exacerbated by hire purchase restrictions, with the Barton Cycles finance subsidiary shut down for the duration. A typical case is shown by a letter to Head Office from Mr Pye, one of the representatives, following a visit to Allen's of Seaford, Sussex. Allen's cycle shop was a sole agent for the company:

> Will you please let Accounts have this sheet? He has paid one cheque and will pay another as soon as he takes a bit. We shall have to carry this account for another month – he is as I have told you before, a good scout – owns his own shop and house – the cash is OK and his stock is OK.

The *Motor Cycle & Cycle Trader* of 19 July 1940 reported under the headline 'Another War Victim':

> Another trader compelled by war conditions to close his business is L J Bayne of 3 Central Buildings, Holland on Sea. Owing to the migration of the greater part of the population Mr Bayne says there is no business left and in consequence he is closing down on July 31. Since the premises will be empty lists etc should not be sent.
>
> Mr Bayne says he has made many good friends in the cycle trade, which he is sorry to leave, but hopes to renew many pleasant associations in happier days.

Holland on Sea is situated between Clacton and Frinton. Most of the population left during the summer of 1940, due to worries that the east coast could be invaded by the Germans, and travel restrictions were in force along both the east and south coasts of England. The Dunkirk evacuation had only just happened, Clacton was designated a restricted military base, road signs were removed, and private car use was severely restricted by petrol rationing. It was not until 1942 that people started returning to their homes.

> The representative for Lincolnshire filed this sad letter:
>
> C F Thornton, New Road, Sutton Bridge
>
> A very big surprise here. The business is closed and locked up. A notice displayed 'Business Closed.' I made enquiries and the cold facts are he was found shot through the face, dead. An inquest was held

and an open verdict returned. He was an LDV [Local Defence Volunteer] and the gentlemen to whom I spoke said in every respect except the verdict it was pure suicide. I can say that Thornton has been a real 'Jitter Bug' for some months. Please delete from Mailing List. No other business here except Fells and all business is transacted at Wisbech.

The sales representative for the southwest and Channel Islands during the war was E Deverell and he wrote several letters that graphically describe the situation in Plymouth in the early years, when Plymouth was heavily targeted by the Luftwaffe. On 8 November 1940 he visited J H Pearce & Co of Pennycomequick, Plymouth:

> I saw Mr Pearce junior, who informed me he was now called for the Air Force and as there was no one else to carry on the business they were gradually clearing the stocks and the business would be closed down at the end of the year for the duration of hostilities. Please note and advise all departments concerned.

On 8 April 1941 he visited Alf Mason's shop at 63 King Street, Plymouth as a follow up to order E16341 for six bicycles:

> I called here chiefly regarding delay in settlement of account, and on seeing Mason he informed me he had already sent on a cheque in clearance. His shop windows have been blown out and a garage and loft which he used as stores has had a direct hit and he has lost a lot of cycle stock, but the tricycles were fortunately in his shop and are undamaged. He gave the order stated to help him carry on for the time being and he will send on a further order later, but hopes you will endeavour to get these through quickly, as he has been left very short of cycle stock.

Deverell was asked by the accounts department to visit S G Shepherd & Co Ltd at 26 Courteney Street, Plymouth, as they had received a postcard informing them that owing to enemy action their depots had been destroyed. As a result they were ceasing to trade. His report is dated 8 April 1941:

> I saw Mr Shepherd at their Union St shop (formerly Raleigh Showroom). Their Courteney St premises are completely destroyed, together with approx. £1200 stock. The Union St premises are also damaged but can carry on under the difficult conditions, but under the terms of the lease they can only sell Raleigh productions and this company will not allow them, even under the present circumstances, to stock any other firms' machines, so that until they can secure fresh premises they would like you to hold their order pending their further instructions.

It seems that Raleigh were not about to let Hitler interfere with a sole agency. But just five weeks later the Luftwaffe put the Raleigh shop out of business too. Deverell sent a letter to the accounts department with an extract from a postcard he had received: 'Owing to Enemy Action our Depots have been destroyed. We are therefore ceasing to trade.'

The final letter from the files referred to a visit to Snell's Motor House at 95/97 Old Town Street, with premises also at Frankfort Street.

> I saw Mrs Snell who is in a very poor state of health for both her Frankfort St and Old Town St premises are completely wiped out.
>
> She and her sister and two grandchildren were in the basement of the Frankfort St shop and were rescued from the debris after several hours and unfortunately her son (Sonnie Snell) has lost his life in the Old Town St premises where he was fire-watching and his remains have not yet been recovered.
>
> They have lost their entire stocks at both places, but for a woman of her age (77) she has wonderful spirits. She has some other premises in St Andrews St, which though damaged are repairable. As soon as these are ready she will open up again and will require a stock of bicycles, which she hopes we will deliver as quickly as possible, and as soon as her premises are ready she will either send on her order or advise you so that I can go down and see her and advise her as to stock, and no doubt you will write her suitably following my call.

In accordance with the Defence Regulations of 1939 the basements of the London premises at 13 Norton Folgate and 1/3 Folgate Street were subject to a possession order on 7 May 1940 by the Metropolitan Borough of Stepney. They were presumably requisitioned for use as air raid shelters.

## War Work

The Marsh Lane factory was treated much as it was during the 1914-18 conflict: as a sub-contractor for other companies. Bicycle production continued, though mainly for forces use, and thousands of Hopper roadsters were painted in military colours for use on the many RAF airfields around the country, especially in Lincolnshire and Norfolk. The US air force was a good customer with 300 cycles sent to Shipdham, near East Dereham, Norfolk in January 1943, followed by 100 to the nearby Wendling base. The scale of such business is demonstrated by a single invoice for £17,174 dated 9 June 1944 for the American base at Fulbeck, Lincolnshire. *Cycling* magazine of 3 March 1943 recorded that American Army Air Services had been supplied with 13,000 bicycles from British factories for the use of their personnel. The 31 March issue noted that the target for 1943 had been set at 800,000 bicycles, about the same level as 1942, with 250,000 destined for the Services. This was similar to the previous year when women employed as munitions workers had been provided with 300,000 machines. A feature of production during the war was the total absence of chromium plating for the normal bright parts, so that rims, hubs, pedals, seat posts, stems and bars were all painted.

*Fig. 5.3 The main machine shop 1942.*

With all these problems it was indeed more difficult for civilians to buy new machines, though Elswick-Hopper did provide several Phoenix export roadsters to local customers. With most of the large export customers out of bounds to shipping it is probable that the company found itself with some surplus export stock to supply local people. To a large extent domestic supply was governed by the availability of frame tubing and components, and based on war-time adverts from small frame builders, their stocks survived well. Cyclists were exhorted in the weekly *Cycling* magazine to take great care of their tyres due to a growing shortage of rubber. By the end of 1942 90% of the world's annual production of 1.39 million tons was in Axis controlled countries, such as the top producer, Malaya, which had produced 540,000 tons in 1940.[1] By 1943 lamp batteries were also in short supply, due to the demand for twin-cell radio batteries by the North African campaign.

Much of the sub-contract work was carried out in the machine shops (Fig. 5.3) and many local women recall making 'bullets' at Hopper's, and indeed the Royal Ordnance Factory at Radway Green, Cheshire ordered 'steel sleeves and brass base plugs' in lots of 1000, for which they paid £10 8s 4d.

Motorcycle forks were produced in large numbers for Ariel Motors Ltd of Selly Oak,

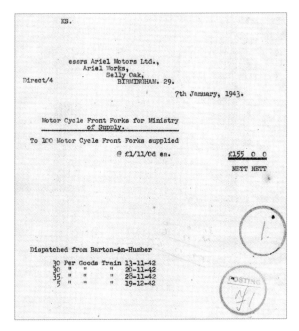

Fig. 5.4   *Ariel invoice for 100 front forks.*

Fig. 5.5   *Credit note issued to BSA dated 26 October 1942 for rejected bracket mountings.*

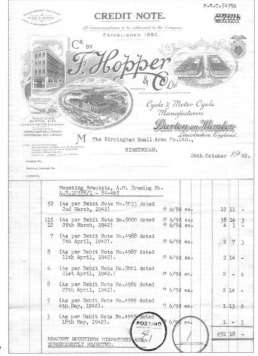

Birmingham (Fig. 5.4). Mounting brackets were manufactured for the Browning gun section of BSA at Redditch (Fig. 5.5) and gate mountings were made for the RASC at Feltham. These were designated in military style: 'Mountings, Gate, AA, LMG, Mk 1'.

Eccentric axles were cadmium plated on sub-contract from Ruston-Bucyrus of Lincoln, destined for use on Crusader II tanks. Toggle arms for filters were brazed and sandblasted for Blackstone & Co Ltd of Stamford, an old-established maker of diesel engines. A steady order was received from Rose Brothers of Gainsborough, for sand blasting, degreasing, bonderising and high temperature stove enamelling (two coats) of 'casing tubes and top covers', apparently an Air Ministry contract.

The most intriguing order was from Messrs A Green of 20 Henry Street, Scunthorpe, dated March 1941. An invoice was raised for £27 17s 0d for 14 experimental 'Bomb Gobblers' hand-produced by the tool room. Nottinghamshire County Council internet site includes an advert for the 'Cotto' Incendiary Bomb Gobbler, a patented device that allowed an individual to scoop up the bomb and deposit it safely in sand, whilst being protected against heat and glare by the Gobbler's asbestos-lined jaws.

The largest customer for war work was Blackburn Aircraft Ltd, of Brough, and many parts were supplied from June 1940 onwards, including control column pivot bracket housings, plungers, links, collars, stabilising plates, pressings for struts, attitude cables, fairlead rollers and various shear bolts, washers and nuts.

Business in the Indian sub-continent through G Atherton continued until January 1941 and had reached a record level during 1940, with a sales value of £23,400. There is also a record of a shipment to East Africa on 27 April 1943 when nine cases of bicycles for Salisbury via Beira were loaded onboard SS 'Clan Macarthur' managed by Cayzer, Irvine & Co Ltd.

## Civil Defence

Elswick-Hopper employees were employed as firewatchers and also formed a team to tackle fires. I am indebted to Charles Watkinson for a copy of the poem compiled by Barbara Towle, one of the team. The other participants are Beaty Chapman, Vera Ashton and Walt Jennings, a veteran of the earlier war.

> We had to do it. It was our duty.
> It ruined our health and spoilt our beauty.
> Fleas came and bit our thighs and our knees,
> but we were amply repaid by Walt's 'Goodnight' squeeze.
> We had some fun, we all agree,
> we really enjoyed Walt's cup of tea.
> For doing our duty we got three times a shilling,
> if they'd given us more t'would have been more filling.
> On the engine we had quite a lark,
> Vera couldn't get the damn thing to spark.
> If we'd had more practice we'd have been experts.
> Walt, not knowing this, made us look twerps.
> 'Now you girls who've been out with the Yanks
> – instead of fire-watching, you've been up to your pranks!'
> We go to bed – it's past midnight,
> the nervous ones need a light.
> Beaty knocks at half past five,
> it's enough to bring the dead alive.
> We open our eyes and crawl out of bed,
> feeling like something three parts dead.
> Going home is just like heaven,
> but we've got to be back by half past seven.
> Thank you, Walt, for a good job over,
> soon there'll be blue birds on the White Cliffs of Dover.
> No more fleas, no more cold.
> Next time we come we'll be getting old.
> Men may come, men may go,
> But Walt will live for ever!

The firewatching teams numbered six and took the duty in turns. Depending on the situation they would be stationed at either the Brigg Road offices, or at Marsh Lane. The girls preferred being on duty at the offices as they could see across the Humber from the top floor. At Marsh Lane, the old 'Aerodrome', so called because it looked like an aircraft hangar, had a scaling ladder on the curved roof. The girls had to climb to the ridge, which made a good vantage point. The problem was there was little to hold on to and Barbara Towle, for one, did not like this duty one bit.

## Management

The firm's final wartime AGM was the 31st held at Brigg Road 28 December 1944. Newly appointed board chairman Arthur Stow reported that in presenting the fifth wartime report the shareholders would 'note with satisfaction that the excellent results of last year have been maintained'. A dividend of 12.5% was paid on ordinary shares and 8% on preference shares. The general reserve was increased to £52,500 by transferring £7,400 from the profit and loss account. Net profit for the year was £41,148, so once again war had significantly improved the profitability of the business. Stow continued:

During the past year the Company's plant has been working to full capacity, and there is every reason to believe that this state of affairs will continue throughout the current year. We have for the time being fulfilled the demands that were made on us by Government Departments for the Services, which now affords us the opportunity of sending our trade friends in the Home Market more frequent deliveries. Furthermore, we are looking forward to the resuscitation and expansion of the export side of our business as the progress of the war permits this to take place.

In my last address I indicated that the question of planning for the future was receiving special attention. In the interim our Tool Room has been re-organised and re-equipped with new Plant. This is the first section of the factory to be re-organised, other departments will be dealt with, and by this time next year I hope to be in a position to advise you that more sections of the Works have been re-planned and re-equipped, in so far as plant may be available, for higher productive capacity.

Finally, I know the Shareholders will be unanimous in extending their good wishes to our Employees who are serving in His Majesty's Forces, and in expressing the hope that in the not too distant future they will be safely home again and we shall be working together once more. Our thanks are also due to our Staff and Employees, many of whom have helped considerably in our Civil Defence Services, for their loyal co-operation during the past year.

Though still a shareholder Fred Hopper Junr relinquished his position as chairman to Arthur Stow in 1943 and had no further direct involvement with the company. Indeed, he had for some time been far more concerned with building a farming empire. His father had kindled this interest with the purchase of Park Farm in 1917, and his son had built up a large holding using his father's estate, which had been held in a trust. A report dated September 1940 listed several agricultural holdings. North Wold farm was situated near Market Rasen and comprised 201 acres, being purchased in 1940. For £1030 some 37 acres on Wold Road, Barrow on Humber had also been bought in 1940. Greenfield Farm, Hibaldstow, had been purchased in August 1940 for £9,000, comprising 363 acres, and, finally Barton Hill Farm was added to the portfolio in April 1941 at a cost of £7,750. Arthur Stow clearly had the good of the company at heart and had learned from his mentor, the first Fred Hopper, that to remain competitive you had to invest in plant and equipment.

Of the three directors appointed in 1936 Charles Rawlinson was the only one left by 1944. In addition to his Elswick-Hopper post he was a director of six other companies. Henry Ernest Spry, a chartered accountant, had joined the board in 1942 and held eight other directorships. The company board thus comprised just three members. With Arthur Stow acting as both chairman and managing director, and with just two fellow directors with no knowledge of the company and not based locally, he was very much in control of the company's future.

**Endnote**

1      *Cycling* 25 November 1942.

# CHAPTER 6

## The World Order Changes, 1945-1958

When the war ended in Europe the country was in poor shape economically. Foreign exchange reserves had been depleted and the war effort had incurred huge debts to the USA and the Commonwealth. It was clear that exports had to take priority over domestic supply and war-time central control continued for some years to ensure that this happened. Raw material allocation and rationing of food and consumer goods were some of the measures that remained in place. The push to manufacture goods for export gave Elswick-Hopper the opportunity to return to its traditional export markets and to make the most of the strong demand for British bicycles.

Further management changes had occurred since the end of hostilities and the directors listed in the 1947 Stock Exchange Year Book were Arthur Stow – chairman and managing director, C C Rawlinson, H E Spry FCA, and J H Bruce. Solicitors were Rawlinson & Son.

*Fig. 6.1   Model W Tradesman's Bicycle from the Hopper catalogue for 1939.*

## A Return to Normality

The Elswick-Hopper archives show that domestic sales picked up quite quickly, despite steel shortages. Elswick Model W carrier bicycles (Fig. 6.1) were sold to Allied Suppliers Ltd, owners of the three chains of grocery stores: Maypole Dairy Co, Liptons, and Home and Colonial Stores; these subsidiaries had branches in most towns in the country. The International Stores chain appears to have favoured Hopper carriers. The Army and Navy Stores in Westminster was an agent for Elswick, as was John Lewis and Co in Oxford St. In the same street Selfridges stocked Hopper cycles, and also had own label models made for them by the company. Boots Pure Drug Co was another customer for Elswick carriers, and Currys

bought Hopper cycles with their own name transfers, in much the same way that Brown Brothers had done for so many years. Looking at dealer lists it is hard to imagine just how big the market was to support the number of bike shops still to be found in most towns, but then bicycles were still the only form of personal transport available to most people.

In 1948 the traditional Earls Court Show returned after a 10-year absence, opened by Viscount Montgomery of Alamein. Elswick-Hopper was situated on stand 20, which featured the top of the range Hopper Vampire and Elswick Rapier racing cycles, as well as traditional roadsters equipped with chain wheels cut out to show either the Hopper or Elswick name.[1] It was a good year that saw national exports of 2 million bicycles. By the following year the industry had turned its back on the traditional blacks and greens – the 1949 Show featured 2,000 models and 'colour was everywhere.'[2] The 1949 Elswick stand can be seen in Fig. 6.2.

Aluminium alloy became very popular after the war for levers, brakes, handlebars, stems and wheel hubs and rims. It was readily available and much lighter than steel. The pursuit of lightness was nothing new, of course, and aluminium frames were first produced in the late nineteenth century. However, Elswick-Hopper's practice of making components in house did not extend to alloy materials and so such parts were bought in – a trend that was to grow significantly over the next decade.

India had gained its independence on 14 August 1947 and a letter to Arthur Stow on 18 September from George Atherton tells a little of the turmoil that followed the resulting partition, as well as confirming the continued shortage of raw materials.

> Dear Arthur,
>
> ...I hardly expected that you would be able to complete the whole lot by the end of December, but as I explained when I sent you the batch covering 1000 for Bombay and 150 for Madras, this would enable you to be making a start. There is such a mix up in the Punjab and around the Delhi area that without further definite instructions from our people there we are not working on old orders lying in our books for so many dealers have left for the purpose of establishing their business in new places.....
> I would suggest Madras be executed in full as that quarter has not had many lately and we have a

number of dealers clamouring for supplies. The result will be that Bombay have out of your present anticipations to the end of December 600 cycles, Madras 250, and this leaves 650 for Calcutta and Karachi, and I really do not expect the latter will have cleared up the mess made by the riots and looting for some time to come......I shall be interested to know if Barton is sharing in the increased steel allocation promised by Stafford Cripps when he was recently in Birmingham, or perhaps he thinks that city makes all the cycles in England.

Good publicity was gained through an article in *British Cycles and Motor Cycles Overseas* in April 1949. Material availability was still an issue and it is no coincidence that Elswick-Hopper stressed the scope of their export market. It is reproduced in full, as it gives an excellent snapshot of the capabilities of the company just a few years after the war.

## SPECIALISTS IN EXPORT
### By L A AYTON

Established nearly 70 years ago, Elswick-Hopper have had long experience in building cycles for markets overseas.

Not many names have been associated with the cycle industry as long and as closely as that of Hopper, for it was as far back as 1880 that Frederick (sic) Hopper started to make bicycles in his small engineering and whitesmith's workshop in Barton-on-Humber, Lincolnshire. The site, now derelict, is opposite the present company's main offices and export department in Brigg Road, which were built shortly before the first world war, well within the memory of the present chairman, Arthur Stow, who completes 46 years' service in May of this year.

The founder himself died in 1926 (sic), and the present parent company, The Elswick-Hopper Cycle & Motor Co Ltd, combines his own F Hopper & Co Ltd, and Elswick Cycles Ltd, the latter being originally the Elswick Cycle Company of Newcastle-on-Tyne, which was acquired in 1910. Manufacture of the two makes continues in the one factory, with corresponding models in each range, but each is marketed by the individual selling organizations and through separate agencies, to retain the brand names which have been established throughout the world.

Through long experience and careful study of market requirements, Elswick-Hopper have always done a large amount of overseas business, and the present export target of 75 per cent of output has been achieved without undue strain on the organization. Both Brazil and India are particularly good customers at present, I was told by H Crook, the export manager, but the stencilling on the cases passing through the export packing department showed that many other markets were also active buyers.

Although it is the final stage in the production at Barton, the export packing department happened to be the first I visited, as it adjoins the head offices which are some hundreds of yards from the works. Normal shipments are made in four types of export packing. The first is of complete

*Fig. 6.3 Harry Plaskitt with one of the rullies outside the Castledyke export packing shop.*

machines with only the front wheel out, the second is similar with both wheels out, the third is of completely unassembled machines with unbuilt wheels, and the fourth of unassembled machines with built wheels.

These latter two classes go to countries where, due to tariff obligations or legislation, a certain amount of local labour is necessarily employed to complete the machines. They are normally packed in cases of 25 sets or in multiples of 25, while the first two types of packing are used for six machines or multiples of six. Many complete machines are delivered to Continental markets in road and rail containers, enabling them to arrive in safe condition with a minimum of packing. All export shipments go by road to ports, mainly to London and Liverpool, while rail delivery is used for the home market.

Complete sets of parts as required for each export order are brought from the main Marsh Lane works on horse-drawn floats (Fig. 6.3). These sets go to the wrapping section of the export packing department and are prepared for the final packing. Specially designed trolleys hold complete sets of 25 cycle parts and are made up at one end of the packing department for use by the case assemblers. A very complete and well equipped woodworking section makes all the cases, which are built up section by section as each layer of parts is stowed and secured.

At Marsh Lane the main works covers an area of some 13 acres (sic), and at present employs about 400 workers. Labour is not easy to obtain in Barton-on-Humber and another 100 employees could be absorbed with ease if materials were available.

Partly because of their situation away from the manufacturing Midlands and partly due to the fact that they have always made as much of their machines as they can, Elswick-Hopper are self-contained to a very high degree and produce many of the individual components that other manufacturers obtain from outside suppliers. During the war the works was engaged mainly on government contracts and in spite of its closeness to much-bombed Hull, it suffered no damage from enemy action.

The works has its own powerhouse where three large diesel-driven generating sets can supply the complete power necessary. Mains power, however, is used to supply the motorized machines in the works that require AC. Owing to the necessity for as much economy as possible with power, there is a certain amount of staggering of labour in some departments, although apart from this the factory works the normal five-day week. Every department is heated by overhead hot-water radiators fed from a central boiler house.

In many ways the heart of the works is the machine shop, an up-to-date department with all machines individually driven and no overhead shafting. Among the machines here is a large Wickman automatic which is used on small brake parts and can be tooled-up to produce seven different articles from bar up to $1^3/_8$ in diameter. As an example, it will produce eye bolts for the brake complete in five seconds, the operations including turning, drilling, and threading. A new machine for bar to 1¼in is to be installed alongside it.

Fig. 6.4 The tool room in 1949.

*Fig. 6.5   The Marsh Lane tube shop, where sheet metal was cut, formed and welded to make frame parts such as seat and chain stays and fork legs.*
*Fig. 6.6   Frame shop in the early 1950s. Harry Haddock had recently started using a jig (bottom left).*

Another machine noticed was a four spindle radial used for drilling cranks, while millers were in use for facing the cranks two at a time. In this department the firm produces its own hubs from the rough casting, small brake parts, chain wheels and cranks from the rough stampings and forgings, all tools in the shop being new since approximately the middle of the war. A well-equipped tool room works in conjunction with the machine shop, to produce tools, jigs, and fixtures and has its own case-hardening plant (Fig. 6.4). A new case-hardening plant of the gas-fed electrically-controlled type is in process of installation for production work, adjacent to the machine shop.

Seat and chain stays and fork blades are other components that are made by Elswick-Hopper themselves. For these, strip steel is cut to size, bent and formed to shape and the joints are gas welded in jigs (Fig. 6.5). The standard of welding is very high, and is done largely by girl operators.

In the frame building shop (Fig. 6.6) the parts are jigged and tack welded, or in other cases, such as when 531 tubing is used, jig built and pinned before the brazing operation. Brazing is done by the dip method, the frames being fed two at a time to the three brazing furnaces by overhead gantries. After brazing the frames are trued before passing to the rough grinding department. Front forks are built up, and shaped in a special bending machine, being jigged after bending before the crown is fitted. Elswick fork crowns are machined forgings while the Hopper crowns are machined castings or fabricated.

In the rough grinding shop, where each machine has its own extraction plant, surplus spelter is ground off before bonderizing. After rough grinding two large shot-blast cabinets give the frames and other parts a final clean up before bonderizing, the bonderizing process being done in tanks in the usual manner.

Mudguards are also made complete at Barton, and here again another new department is being fitted up for this purpose. The present department, which is rather congested, has several machines which will produce a mudguard complete from steel strip, with the rolling, shaping and beading done in a single operation. One machine produces Vee-type guards for the Indian market.

Chromium plate on all bright parts is standard on both Elswick and Hopper machines again and the plating department handles both nickel and chrome. Among the polishing machines was an automatic for dealing with plated chainwheels.

The press shop is another busy section for here are produced many brake parts, crown covers, lamp brackets, mudguard stays and other components that the company makes for itself without relying on outside contractors. Crown covers are produced from the strip on a fully automatic press.

Before the final finish is applied all parts are dried in a gas-fired oven. Two large Carrier enamelling ovens of the oil-burning type deal with the black parts, one of these ovens normally acting as a spare. Total time for a part to pass through from the enamel dip to the dry end is 75 minutes. A separate shop, the colour shop, deals with other types of finish. Plain coloured frames are handled in dipping tanks, while the polychromatic finishes are sprayed in fan-backed booths. After dipping or spraying they are dried in gas-fired stoves which are electrically controlled.

From the colour shop or the enamelling oven the frames go to the lining and transfer shop. Gold lining is done by hand with brushes in the old-time craftsman's manner, to match up with the previously applied transfers.

Final assembly of bicycles is done on the floor of the main assembly building round the gallery of which such subassemblies as handlebars, brakes and other components are built up. The various machines seen assembled or partially assembled here included examples of the standard Elswick and Hopper ranges as well as several special export orders such as a quantity of machines for the Argentine, which had a chromium-plated front tube, and some with completely chromium plated frames for Cyprus. Every machine after assembly is given a careful final check, and although I have not mentioned inspection before, this takes place at every stage of manufacture or assembly throughout the works.

Several other subsidiary departments were visited, such as the one in which handlebars are bent to the various curves required by different markets, the wheel building department, where girls lace and partially tighten the wheels, leaving the final truing to skilled men operators, hub assembly and so on.

Adjoining the main offices is a well arranged showroom where all current Elswick and Hopper models are displayed under fluorescent lighting. This has already been visited by many of the company's dealers from overseas.

A firm that is situated in a small town like Barton-on-Humber, where it is the largest employer of labour usually assumes certain social obligations towards its employees and Elswick-Hopper set a high standard in this respect. There is a works social club in the town with several billiards tables, club rooms and other amenities, and a works canteen at the Marsh Lane factory.

Reference has already been made to the chairman Arthur Stow, who is one of the longest serving employees, and who has the satisfaction of seeing his son Peter with him in the firm. Mr Stow was elected to the board in 1930 (sic), became managing director in 1935 (sic) and chairman in 1944 (sic). Talking of the future outlook he pointed out that he had plenty of confidence that their export demands could be met providing that raw materials were made available. Under his guidance his firm has maintained a steady and conservative policy, and while no immediate plans have been made for large-scale extensions, should these be required there would be no difficulty in carrying them out. Ample space and facilities are already available for this at Marsh Lane.

## Arthur Stow Dies

Just over two years after Ayton's article appeared Arthur Stow (Fig. 6.7) died at the age of 59, on 2 June 1951. As president of Barton on Humber Agricultural Society he had been talking with officials at the annual gymkhana in Baysgarth Park when he collapsed and died almost immediately. From the age of 13 as an office boy we have seen him appointed export manager during the First World War, made a director in 1931, appointed managing director in 1936 and finally chairman in 1943. [These dates differ from those in the Ayton article and are taken from company archives.] There is no doubt that he had been the main driving force for many years and effectively ran the company on similar lines to Fred Hopper – firm but fair in his dealings, though inevitably lacking the hands-on expertise and understanding of the hardware of his mentor that can only come from learning the business on the shop floor.

George Clarke (Fig. 6.8) took over from Stow as general manager at Barton and ran the business until 1955. It appears that his fellow directors were not happy with the performance of the

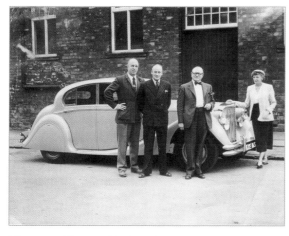 

*Fig. 6.7   Taken outside the Brigg Road packing shop, from left to right: Hans Ohrt, an American customer from California, Harold Crook, Arthur Stow and (presumably) Mrs Ohrt.*

*Fig. 6.8   George Clarke (fourth from right) presenting Grimsby born Brenda Fisher with an Elswick bicycle on 15 January 1952. This was in recognition of her record swim across the English Channel on 16 August 1951. Her time of 12 hours 42 min stood until 1958.*

company during that year and he was duly appointed scapegoat. According to his wife Betty he was very bitter at this treatment and as the company was sold just three years after his departure it would seem that the 'absentee' directors had little idea of how to run a bicycle manufacturing company. Although George Clarke had no previous experience of the industry he did have an excellent management track record from a very early age. An obvious problem was that Hopper and Stow had been too much in command and had failed to develop successors.

Harry Heselton took over the reins from George Clarke, having joined the company in 1954. His previous experience was certainly varied, including an engineering apprenticeship with Ericsson Telephones of Beeston, Nottingham, study at Nottingham that yielded a degree in economics, commerce and administration and jobs with Rudge-Whitworth, Raleigh and Hercules. During the war he was involved in the conversion of Rudge-Whitworth to the production of Oerlikon gun production. In photographs he is always well dressed and invariably wearing spats. He hailed from Hutton Cranswick, between Beverley and Driffield and no more than 25 miles from Barton on Humber.[3] Heselton's appointment came at a time when the industry was starting to face rising costs, increased competition from imports and a move to smaller and cheaper motor vehicles. The mighty Raleigh was not immune to such factors and their net profits peaked in 1955, but just three years later had fallen back by 71%.

## Export Boom, Bust and Boom

Export orders poured in from all over the world, from pre-war customers starved of supplies during most of the conflict. G Atherton & Co (Eastern) Ltd, with a head office on Water St, Liverpool, ordered frame sets for delivery to their Bombay depot with model names such as 'Fort', 'Race', 'Quick March', 'Royal Brilliant' and 'Atlas', as well as Hopper Advance and Phoenix models and Elswicks. Literally thousands were ordered in 1949 alone, and strangely, all with 24" frames. The Indian Post Office was supplied with all black models and the police with Police Model khaki enamelled cycles. Phoenix roadsters and racers, both ladies' and gents', were dispatched to Buenos Aires and Rosario through the offices of Oswald Behrens Bros Ltd of St Dunstan's Hill, London, and the Anglo-African Shipping

*Fig. 6.9  A brightly lit Brigg Road office after refurbishment in 1952. From The National Journal December 1952.*

Co (SA) Ltd imported Hopper cycles through Beira. The list goes on: Canada, USA, West Indies, Switzerland, Cyprus, Syria, Singapore, Dutch East Indies, Denmark, Australia, New Zealand, Egypt, etc. Two interesting enquiries came from the West Indies, indicating a strong racing interest. One from St Lucia was for Special Path Racers equipped with Major Taylor bars and Constrictor wood rim wheels and Dunlop sprint tyres, in three frame sizes. The second was an order for a Hopper Hawk racer and an enquiry for a special lightweight bicycle with a 23" frame to weigh between 15 and 18 pounds. The equipment specified was top of the range but it is highly unlikely that the finished machine would have come in at less than 21 pounds.

The boom for Elswick-Hopper lasted until 1952, when overseas orders fell sharply. By June 1952 two thirds of the employees had been put on a 40 hour week – normal hours were 44. The company hoped to return to normal working and blamed the problem on overbuying in two important export markets – India and Malaya.[4] At the time there was virtually no unemployment in Barton, with just 24 registered out of a population of 4,000.[5]

Export manager Harold Crook was dispatched to drum up fresh business. He recorded his memories of his epic trip on tape for his three sons, to whom I am indebted for the opportunity to reproduce them. This transcript provides a unique insight into the problems faced by a UK exporting company at the end of Empire, and the difficulties faced by Harold Crook in his efforts to procure orders. It also describes a few of the problems faced by many countries in 1952, many still unresolved.

After the war there was a pent up demand for bicycles all over the world. It was decided by the trade that 75% of one's output should go overseas and 25% to the home market[6]. Materials were in short supply and were rationed. Raw material allocations were based on what one could export. Any one country at that time could have absorbed the entire output of the factory and that applied to any factory in the country. In the immediate years after the war they all built up their outputs and they even went to the extent of placing factories in India and South Africa and other countries to meet the demand, not seeing it was a short term demand. Once the immediate demand had been met there would be a gradual fall off – not entirely due to the lack of demand but due to the lack of wherewithal to pay for them. It was a very difficult world to be in. At one moment you could have an order book closed – too full to cope with – and overnight some country would put an embargo on the import of British bicycles and you were left with nothing. Whether or not Britain contributed to its own downfall by encouraging overproduction, not only here, but overseas, I can't say. By the time the 1950s had arrived the writing was on the wall, the recession had started.

Before the war the company would send out to various countries a representative to visit the markets and contact the people there. When one looks back on it, everyone they sent abroad before the war either died on the journey or died when they came home, the strain was too much for them! There was only one survived any length of time and that was Fred Armstrong, but he left the firm and went south. However I'd always pressed to visit the customers overseas and in September of 1952 they decided to send me on a mission to the Middle and Far East. This was a bit of a rush job and was a job I would never have undertaken if I had had more experience. The whole journey was far too ambitious and the timing not propitious, if it was tangible results they wanted. As a goodwill mission it was a success, but, having gone at the beginning of a recession when every country was short of money and their warehouses stacked to the roof or there were restrictions on trade. I booked through Thomas Cook and gave them a list of all the places I wanted to visit. They drew up a comprehensive ticket and booked me in all the various hotels and I was due to leave London early in December. When they handed me the ticket they said, 'It's a lovely journey if your health will only stand it. It's a bit of a killer!' I went down to London on Saturday, 6 December. It was slightly foggy when I set off and eventually got to London in the smog. There was hardly a taxi to be seen. I got one of the few that was available, which took me from Kings Cross to the BOAC terminal in Buckingham Palace Road. It was done at walking pace and he said, 'I am not going any further tonight.' When I got to the terminal they said there was no chance whatever of flying off to Baghdad that night which was the first official stop and they put me into the Grosvenor Hotel and told me to report back in the morning. I reported back but it was still smoggy and there was no possibility of flying that day. They booked me into the Strand Palace Hotel. All I had with me was my airway's bag as my main luggage was in BOAC's possession. I travelled on the Underground as it was the only form of travel available. It was afternoon; I came out at Charing Cross Station and just couldn't remember whether the Strand Palace was up or down. You couldn't see more than a yard in front. There was not a soul in sight. There wasn't a taxi, bus, bicycle or pedestrian. Never have I seen the Strand so empty. I strolled up one side of the street, walked across the road and down the other side without meeting anyone until I found the hotel. To illustrate how bad it was the Smithfield Show was on and the cattle were dying from the effects of the smog. The people in London were going about with facemasks on. It killed quite a few people. On the Monday morning I spoke to BOAC and they said they would fly from Herne, near Bournemouth and would send a vehicle to take us to Paddington Station and on to Herne. After a night there they decided the fog had gone and we could set off. We took off on a cold and sunny day and the first stop was Rome. This is a beautiful city, very interesting, full of history; traffic that is quiet, but a vast place. I was lucky to make the acquaintance of a Major General seconded to the Jordanian Army. We all stayed at the same hotel and we went for a walk round Rome. He was quite humorous and knew Rome quite well and showed me around. The following day we set off in the early hours for a place called Mafrac in Jordan, which was a landing strip in the desert, because we were not allowed to fly over, or land on, Israeli territory (Fig. 6.10). If we had, the Arabs wouldn't have had us. This was the destination of the Major General. He was picked up from one of the tents there.

*Fig. 6.10 Taken around the time of Harold Crook's trip this shows tool maker Arthur Such in Mafraq during his National Service. He was delighted to discover a Barton-made bicycle there.*

After refuelling we set off for Baghdad. It was late at night when we arrived there and it is a very peculiar feeling to land in a town in a strange country where one doesn't know anyone at all or even the language. There were Arabs there in their National dress and as I stepped out of the arrival lounge a small Indian girl stepped forward and mentioned my name. She had been delegated to meet me as she spoke better English and could act as interpreter. She took me over to four Arabs who were customers of our firm and introduced us. Then we got in a car and they took me along to my hotel, which was the Sinbad on the banks of the Tigris in Raschid Street. We woke, or disturbed, the guard behind the iron gate of the hotel. He looked to be a huge Indian in a turban and with a big stick. We were let in and they wished me a good night and said they would meet me in the morning. I should mention that before I left London we had heard of the troubles in Baghdad – anti-British riots brought about by some incident. The first trouble was a policeman had shot at a student and the students had retaliated by hacking the policemen to bits and anyway they declared a curfew and it was called the anti-British riots. I suggested that this was a place that should be omitted, but the so-called general manager said, 'No, carry on.' So there I was in a hostile land, with a curfew in place from 11pm to 6am, and rioting. I never realised what hatred was until I saw the attitude of the Arabs to the Jews and the Jews to the Arabs. It was brought home to me most vividly during my stay in Iraq. We had for years sold bicycles to both groups and on my list of calls were the Arabs who had met me and who I went with the following day. Now, in the Moslem world Friday is the religious day. Saturday is the Jewish religious day and Sunday the Christian. It meant there were only four days where one had unrestricted access. The Arabs looked after me, but on the Friday I thought this is the day to see the Jewish customer, not knowing the hard feelings. So I went to see this Jewish firm. It is customary in all Eastern countries to offer to a visitor a drink as soon as they step in and it is incumbent on the visitor to accept. When this ceremony is over they are bound to protect you while in their company. When walking in the streets in Baghdad you would meet Arabs of immense stature, 6ft 4in seemed common. They also had a habit of chewing Betel nuts and when they saw anyone who looked like an Englishman coming along they would spit at his feet. There was nothing you could do about it. On the Friday I thought it would be a good day to see my friend Mr Haqhaq. I found his premises in a little back street and climbed up to see him. He was very shabby when I got there. He was an old man and was terrified I had gone to see him. He said, 'You shouldn't have come to see me, they will kill me! You don't understand what it is like, all my family have gone and I can't go and if I go I can't take any money so please go!' So there was nothing for it but to leave. Anyway I got back to the hotel and had a meal. The next day my Arab friends came for me and they told me very straight, where I had been and who I had seen. I said, 'Yes, I have been there, he used to buy thousands of bicycles from us years ago but hadn't bought any lately.' They said 'He never will, the Jews are finished in this country, you want to do business with us or have anything to do with us you mustn't have anything to do with the Jews.' I said that was what he had told me: we could no longer do business. Anyway we patched it up and they took me round Baghdad; one day to Hillah and then to the oldest city in the world, Babylon, which they have to periodically dig out of the sand. The streets are visible and certain ruins of houses are there. There is the statue on a plinth of a lion and woman, which dominates the Babylonian city. I sent a postcard back to the office from there of 'The Loin of Babelon', which no doubt caused some amusement. They promised to take me round the old market, which is one of the sights of Baghdad. But they couldn't do it until things had quietened down a bit and would try to do it before I left. One night they took me out to dinner and this was in a cabaret. All over the East there are cabarets where you can get a meal and they generally have entertainment with artists and this one I think was the Abdullah. It had a small stage surrounded by tables. We had a table by the side of the stage, on which was a small band with a lady crooner. In the course of our meal she sang a song, which, being in a foreign language, I didn't understand. There was a soldier sat at one of the tables in front of the stage, and he picked up a chair and slung it at her. The lights went out, the band went out, and the crooner went out. There was some scuffling and the soldier was removed. The lights came on, the band came back, so did the lady crooner. Whether or not her repertoire was extremely small – she started to sing the same song – and what the bouncers hadn't realised was that there were some of his friends left in and one of them picked up a chair and slung it at her. The lights went out again and the band and girl departed. There was a scuffle, a man was being carried out and when the lights came on there was a trail of blood, which would indicate that something serious had happened to him. I asked my companion what would happen to him. 'Oh! Throw him in the Tigris!' 'Don't you think it's time we were going home?' I asked. 'Oh no, you will be quite alright with us!' So we stayed on a bit longer at their insistence. I was introduced to a radio star and she seemed to think that I might be interested in her. She kept saying to me, 'Do you love me, do you love me?' I said, 'Of course!', and pretended not to know what she meant. Anyway she eventually went away and I said to the Arabs, 'Don't they get well paid on the radio that they have got to come round like this?' 'Oh, every woman has her price!' They thought nothing of it. Eventually the last day came and they assembled all their friends and relatives and we went to the old market. I was in the middle of this large number of friends and we started at one end of the market and I was rushed through. I could hardly pause anywhere, they were so frightened of repercussions from the people there, but it was to enable me to say I had seen something of the old market. I would like to have seen more of it.

My next stop was Basra and there I got a surprise. I was stuck near a hut on the aerodrome when a very handsome Arab spoke to me. He was in full Arab dress and I was surprised because he even mentioned my name. Apparently he was the Hercules representative. The bush telegraph in these so-called backward countries was really amazing. I was now beginning to realise how boring air travel was. Sitting for hours with nothing to do but think; too noisy to sleep and the ungodly hours that one had to rise to catch particular planes. I was now on my way to Bahrain, my schedule completely haywire. In those days Bahrain was noted for pearl diving, not oil, as it is today. It is a series of islands connected by causeways and it was not very friendly towards the English. There were no hotels, just a government rest house and I had been booked in there. But when I arrived in Bahrain there was no possibility of me staying in the rest house as there was no room free, due to the delays. Furthermore there was only one flight out every 10 days to Karachi where I was going next. It was suggested that I did my business quickly and get out, which I was glad to do as one does not like an unfriendly atmosphere. The people I had to see were Indians, and after hunting round I found their premises, which was a workshop where they made bedsteads. I got through my business and managed to catch the plane to Karachi. Bahrain is one of the hottest places imaginable. Here it was literally possible to fry an egg on the pavement or on the bonnet of a car. One could not touch the car handle without a glove, as the heat would have burned. I duly arrived at Karachi and stayed at the Great Eastern Hotel. It is a fine city showing distinct traces of the British Empire, wide streets and interesting buildings, and these streets were filled with all sorts of transport and people. Many people seemed to live and sleep in the streets. The beggars were pitiful; some of course were professionals. The transport was amazing. One could see pedestrians, cyclists – though rickshaws had been banned – donkeys, camels, oxen, ox carts, camels drawing carts, elephants, cars, anything that was capable of being moved was there. My arrival in Pakistan was not long after partition and this had not been too friendly. There are no accurate figures of how many were killed during the transition period, both sides claimed literally thousands. I received a cable while I was in Karachi, instructing me to break my journey and travel on to Agra. This was going to throw my schedule out, and I had only just got back on it, so I had to book on Indian Airways, because on interior flights BOAC passengers had to use Indian Airways. This was a bit of a shock to me because after travelling on the big Argonauts with 4 engines I was confronted by a small Dakota type plane to travel from Karachi to Delhi. I got stung very heavily as I was carrying more baggage than I should have been.

In Delhi I contracted dysentery, which made it very inconvenient and my Pakistani friend who was travelling with me took me to a doctors. Again this was a new experience. His surgery was out in the open street and his dispensing room was a little tent behind. However I got some medicine, had a disturbed night and the following day we set off by train for Agra. It was a most interesting ride despite feeling off colour. We travelled in an air-conditioned carriage, but this did not prevent the dust coming in and settling all over us. I set off with a clean pair of shoes and they were white over in no time. The countryside was interesting in places, just barren in others. When we arrived in Agra a small boy came into the carriage and wanted to clean our shoes. We agreed and he cleaned both our pairs of shoes between Agra and Agra Cantonment where we disembarked. I was met by a welcoming committee and was garlanded as being the guest of honour. This all took place on the station amidst crowds. The purpose of my visit was to attend a conference at the Popular Cycle Works and to inspect a disused goat meat factory, because the Agawalla family in Agra had got the idea of turning it into a cycle manufacturing plant. I was inspecting it on behalf of the firm. The Agawallas treated me royally; we had an open air meal with all the family – so many generations. I was taken to see the factory and later was escorted round the Taj Mahal, both in daylight and in moonlight. Its architectural splendour, built in marble with inlaid gems.., but in a way it left me cold because when all is said and done it is a tomb, and a lot of the beautiful work that was done on it was by labour procured from all over the world, particularly from China. I enjoyed my little stay there and we returned to Delhi and from there I went on to Calcutta. The scheduled itinerary was way out. On our way to Calcutta we passed at a distance Mt Everest. It was a wonderful sight, flying at 20,000 ft. I forgot to mention that on our way from Karachi to Delhi we put down at two strange principalities, Jaipur and Jodhpur. These were intensely security conscious and were still ruled by the Maharajahs. We eventually arrived in Calcutta where our agents were waiting to have a discussion with us on the future of trade in India. By way of background I should explain that between the two world wars the bicycle trade had adjusted itself in a very convenient way. In the summer the trade was all in the home market while in the winter months it was all overseas, which was very convenient for us. This was due to the monsoon period in our principal markets. During the war, while we did export a small quantity to permitted countries, the bulk of the production was going to airfields in the country. When the war was over material was allocated to us on the basis of past exports. For us that was on the basis of 75% for export and 25% for the home market. With the pent up demand of virtually no supplies overseas for years every bicycle manufacturer was chock-a-block with orders. They were working long hours, all of them trying to achieve greater output. Some were getting new factories or enlarging existing ones, some even went so far as to build factories overseas. But what they didn't realise was that it was only a temporary boom and soon turned into the beginning of a recession. All economies had been upset by the war and few had really got built up. Most countries were virtually bankrupt. India, when the war finished, had a pent up demand of millions of bicycles, but it wasn't many years, probably 1951, when they stopped all imports of British bicycles and it was done overnight. We could have had a million bicycles on

*Fig. 6.11 Harold Crook with Lieng Heng in Bangkok*

order one day and virtually nil the next, and they brought into use a word that I had not heard before that is now commonplace. The word is indigenous. This was laced throughout all the rules and regulations issued. So I was moving through the world in the aftermath of war in very uncertain times, both politically and financially.

Back to Calcutta, I had my meeting and then caught the same plane on my way to Rangoon. Here was a city very much depressed by the war and showing little sign of recovery at that time. We landed at the airport but we were hustled away as the bandits of the day had a distressful habit of firing at the plane or the passengers. I was taken to the hotel, the Strand, and then had the job of finding the various people that were on our books. Some had disappeared forever, some told the same old story – they hadn't any money. Rangoon is a town of many Buddhist temples and I saw the biggest rat I have ever seen in my life there. It was going along one of the monsoon drains, which are very deep gutters at the side of all the streets in the Far East. In flying in and out of Rangoon I got an idea of the terrible terrain on which our soldiers had had to fight in the last war. Most people think of jungle as a flat mass of green but this is not so. There are hills and valleys and ravines, rocks and trees.

Anyway, I had to move on after a few days to Bangkok, with visits arranged to two dealers, Lieng Heng (Fig. 6.11) and Seng Guan Hong. This is a city again by the side of water. It is built on the Bangkok River and the hotel where I stayed, the Oriental, was right on the riverbank and from the balcony of my hotel room I could watch the boats plying backwards and forwards, mostly propelled by the women, who did a sort of a walking scull. Christmas Day in 1952 occurred when I was staying at the Oriental. The hotel threw a party for all the guests, but I was unable to attend as I had been invited to a party by Chinese and Siamese friends. The hotel left me a present in the bedroom, a very nice cigarette lighter. On Christmas Day we started this Chinese party at about 6.30 and we were still eating at 10.30. It was an education in itself. Each course had to be toasted in brandy, or something as strong, and the courses seemed to be interminable. At 11pm I was feeling very woozy and the host was intending to go to a dance room above the restaurant, but I made the excuse that I had had too much to drink and had better get back to the hotel, which I did, otherwise I don't know what might have happened to me. There are literally hundreds of trishaws in this city. There did not appear to be many motor vehicles. I suppose this was due to the poverty but nearly everyone moved around in trishaws. We went to look at all the various pagodas, of which there seemed to be hundreds. There was one there that was gold; it had generations of gold leaf pasted on it. There were shops leading to these temples that sold various things, including gold leaf and we purchased a small sheet of leaf and climbed on the pagoda and put our share of gold on it. It was a most interesting place, but I could not stay very long.

At the end of a week I moved on to Hong Kong. The landing in those days had to be done in daylight. If this was not done the plane usually went on to the Philippines. When one was approaching the landing ground it was a bit frightening. Originally, Hong Kong, like Singapore had been a flying boat base and to land an aeroplane one came over the sea over the masts of the shipping and on to what looked like a narrow strip at the side of a mountain with another mountain at the other end. However we got safely down and transferred to the island of Hong Kong. Here I stayed at the Gloucester Hotel. Hong Kong is a very beautiful island, very overcrowded, but outside the city itself, in amongst the mountains, it really is beautiful, with lovely bays and beaches. The city itself is colourful, full of interesting shops, and I was met by Mr Butong Chung and Mr Mok who looked after me while I was there. We explored the island and saw the last station on the Trans-Siberian Railway. We went on the island ferry to Kowloon and then on to the mandated territories as far as the village of Lulong, and to within rifle shot of the Chinese border. We had a huge advert near the border advertising Hopper bicycles. We went closer so I could inspect it and there were many bullet holes all over it. It looked as though the Chinese used it as target practice. The village had only very narrow streets between the stalls, not sufficiently wide to take any vehicle, other than a bicycle. There were what were called taxi bicycles that had a big carrier on the back and if the ladies wanted to go shopping down the narrow streets they sat side saddle and were carried along. Very picturesque, as they all wore huge hats like a standard lamp shade. When I was in Hong Kong there was a water shortage, with water only available for a few hours every day, so baths were at a premium. The two gentlemen I was dealing with were domiciled in Macao. It had been my intention to go over to Macao, but as they had come to Hong Kong I didn't bother, though I imagine it would have been very interesting, as it had been the haunt of many pirates and other rogues. The land of Hong Kong could not possibly handle all the thousands of bicycles that were imported into it, so it was obvious that they were smuggled into China and the extent to which this was happening made one think that the Chinese looked in the opposite direction when they saw the smugglers coming. The Chinese have some extraordinary customs. Mr Butong Chung had in the previous year lost his father, and in memory of the old gentleman he was growing one single hair on his throat. How he managed to shave without cutting it was a wonder. I went on the usual round of Chinese parties and then I moved on to Singapore, which was really my prime target.

I had caught up with my schedule and so was able to stay at the hotel I was booked at, which was the Raffles. In a way I was a bit disappointed after all I had read about it. But then it had an atmosphere, perhaps decaying and decadent but there was something there. The lizards ran happily up the walls across the windows, and were very useful for keeping the flies down. I did not have an especially cold room, one of the ones with a fan in the ceiling. The suite was quite a nice one. I was met by the twins, Khoo Soo Gee and Khoo Soo Gin, owners of the Guan Hoe company. These venerable gentlemen during the war had managed to escape up into the hills to a Buddhist monastery and became Buddhist priests. The families, as one could expect, were very united. One of these brothers was unable to have children so the other brother gave him one of his and he was brought up as that man's son and they all lived very happily. The younger members of the family took me in hand and once business was finished they took me to the Happy World restaurant. They had games of chance, as the Chinese are very fond of gambling. They had Chinese theatre, a Chinese dancehall, which was a novelty in itself. The girls stood in the middle and the men did not take partners with them, they hired these girls, who were called taxi dancers, by the dance or by the hour. They hired the one for our table and expected me to dance every dance, which in the heat of Singapore was not possible, so they had to pay her off. I did the usual gambling and managed to win far more cigarettes than I could ever smoke and which I gave away and lost. Another feature of Singapore, in fact of most of Malaya, there were all-night restaurants in the open air where you could get a really good meal. I was also taken to the Tiger Gardens, which is a feature of Singapore. One of the so-called entertainments is a journey round hell as conjured up by the Chinese. It is horrifying and very realistic. I was also taken to the House of Jade. It is a house full of absolutely priceless jade from the floor to the ceiling and has to be seen to be believed. All these things, such as the Tiger House of Jade, and the Tiger Gardens were given by the Chinese millionaire who invented Tiger Balm, a remedy for practically every ailment you can think of. He also owned the Tiger newspaper and Tiger beer, but he was apparently very generous with it.

After exploring Singapore I had to take in the rest of the principal places in Malaya. Now before I left England I had to insure myself, and one of the provisos was any travelling outside Singapore had to be done by air not by road. To do what I had to do and to fit in with my Chinese friends meant that I could not abide by this agreement. I explained the situation to my friends, who said, 'We must go by road, you will be alright, you will sit in the back with us and the driver will not stop for anything and he will go flat out.' The car they used was a big Buick and the driver did exactly what he was expected to. If anyone tried to stop us he would just keep on going and we would have to duck down to the floor of the car. I could understand this when I saw how easy it would be to hide whole armies amongst the rubber plantation trees, as they made great cover for jungle warfare. But I think they must also have had a good knowledge of the rebels. At that time Malaya was torn by the rebels, who were ravaging and terrorising the countryside. It was one of the mistakes of our government after the war ended in not treating these people properly. Most of the so-called rebels were remnants of the army that had been organised to fight the Japanese and they had sort of been sacked overnight without a bounty or anything and it cost us dear for being so mean. However I got through to Kuala Lumpur, where I had promised to meet a friend who was in the cycle trade and who I had seen in the lounge of the Raffles Hotel. I had gone up to him and said, 'Don't I know you?' He said, 'I don't think so.' I said, 'Aren't you Eric Hazel?' To which he said, 'Yes, but I don't know you.' I said, 'You used to work for the same firm

that I do. You are with BSA now.' We had quite an interesting time. We made arrangements to meet in KL for a chat and a drink. He was not there, and later, when I got back to England and made enquiries through his firm I learned that he was still out in Malaya, having suffered a heart attack. He was kept out there for six months in hospital before coming home. I think he eventually came home by sea. KL is a very interesting spot. The railway station looked like some Sultan's house in the Middle East; it had a Moorish look about it. I think it was either in KL or Penang that I first saw civilians openly carrying revolvers. We took side trips to customers at Port Swettenham and Klang before arriving at KL. Eventually, after staying a few days in KL (Fig. 6.12) I went on to Penang, which is an extremely beautiful island. I stayed in Georgetown at the P and O and was made extremely welcome.

Trade in Malaya was at a virtual standstill. I went round the various dealers, their godowns, or warehouses, were full to the doors and they would show me a heap of bills they were unable to pay. So it would have been folly to ship more stuff to them. I attended a number of meetings and dinners given in my honour but business was not obtainable. They were quite honest about it. The amount of stuff that could be imported was governed by what they could export and the trouble with the rebels and the troops trying to quell the rebels, played havoc with their production of rubber, copper and tin. So all I could do was create goodwill and hope for better things to come. We made our way back to Singapore without incident. We stopped at some very small villages for food but we met no trouble. So it was back to the Raffles at Singapore and then on to Kuching in Sarawak. Now Kuching is a relatively small place and at that time had no hotels, so I had to stay at the government rest house – shades of the old colonial empire – this was a house on a hillside. Very nice with a veranda and a sort of dormitory with three bedrooms, complete with mosquito nets and a bathroom which consisted of a big tub with a billycan to throw water over oneself. We had only one agent in Sarawak and I went to see him. He was Mr Lim Bab Too of B T Lim and Sons and was very surprised to see me, as he didn't know I was coming. The visit was reported in the Sarawak Tribune on 16 January, as the agent had hurriedly organised a dinner for me to meet some of the local dealers. It was the same story as Malaya and Singapore, no money, too many goods; the manufacturing industry at home was over producing. I thought as I walked round that they were growing an enormous quantity of runner beans. When I remarked on this I was told it was pepper. There were hundreds of acres being grown. In Sarawak there were longhouses housing families. The women walked about bare-breasted, the same as the Malays. I finished my business in Kuching and returned once more to the Raffles in Singapore.

I contacted all my friends to arrange a party and a day or so later was on my way to another place, to Jakarta, in Indonesia. It was originally known as Batavia in the Dutch East Indies. I was booked in at the Hotel des Indies, but when I got there they wouldn't have me as the army had occupied it and there was a very strong sign of hatred to all people of European origin, particularly the Dutch. So Qantas Airways accommodated me at their compound. This was a series of huts like little prison cells behind barred windows, set high in an oblong with something like grass in the centre. At each end of this row of huts there was the bathroom, which comprised a wooden tub full of water and a billycan. The heat was terrific. It seemed hotter than Singapore and the humidity was higher still. We were warned not to go out at night, especially alone, because of people being molested and according to what I was told it was often soldiers, but if it was soldiers you mustn't say so, as you would get a longer stay in prison than you would want. Now Jakarta is full of canals, presumably a relic of the Dutch, and in these canals everything in life goes on. You would see them washing clothes, urinating, defecating, washing the children, bathing in them. At that time there were not many cars or taxis about. I don't think anyone could afford them and practically all travel had to be done by trishaw. If I could have got out the same day I arrived I would have been very pleased, but I had to wait until the next flight to Cairo called there, which was not for some days. It gave me the chance of a good look round and while I was there I wanted to post my reports back to England. I went into the main post office in Jakarta and there were queues at each window. I got in one of the queues and as soon as it came to my turn the window was slammed down. I thought well maybe it was a coincidence so I tried another queue and the same thing happened, as soon as it was my turn, no service. So I went back to the Qantas compound, found one of the native boys, gave him some money and asked him to get some stamps and post. I had to take a chance that he was honest and he must have been as the letters duly arrived. These Indonesians were just feeling their feet, they had just been released from the dominance of the Dutch and anything that they associated with the old regime was abhorrent to them.

The next official call was in Cairo but to go from Jakarta to Cairo was what they called a 24 hour non-stop flight but this could not be, as we had to stop for refuelling. We left Jakarta on a KLM Lockheed on 24 January and stayed overnight in Bangkok and then set out early the following morning, calling at Rangoon, Calcutta and Karachi, before putting down in Cairo. Now in Jakarta it was extremely hot and humid and I had tropical clothes on. There was no way of changing clothes on the plane, so when I arrived in Cairo in the early hours of the morning it was very cold, enough to give anyone the shivers. I was very glad to get to the Metropolitan Hotel. There was a very nice dragoman (interpreter) on the bus and I was very thankful to him later on in the stay. Originally I was scheduled to stay at Sheppard's Hotel, but just before I set off on the tour the Egyptians had attacked this hotel, killing people. Some escaped by hiding in dustbins. So there was a distinct feeling of antagonism from the Egyptians. Anyway I got to bed and the following day was a Sunday and I rang through to Barton.

Unfortunately my visit coincided with the three or six month anniversary of the so called massacre of the Auxiliary Police at Ismalia[7]. It was Saturday when I arrived and I could not get in touch for a while with my French friends who owned the Tractor Engineering Company. Eventually I got them on the phone and they had already made arrangements for that particular night so we arranged to meet the following day for lunch. I had to find out when my next flight for Cyprus would be and this was on the Monday morning. On contact with the airport terminal I was told I must present my documents in person the following morning at Farouk Square, otherwise I would not be allowed to leave Cairo. They said I may have some difficulties getting through as there was a large gathering scheduled to be in this square to be addressed by a man named Neguib. I don't know if he was the president or prime minister, but he was a man who was a real rabble rouser and they said it wouldn't be safe to attempt it[8].

I said I must, as I was behind schedule. So I dressed in a light grey suit, put on a big Homburg hat, horn rimmed glasses and joined the Arabs walking towards this square. In fact they were my guide, as I didn't know where the square was. They kept looking at me, some would say, 'Inglesi?' I took no notice and just strolled gently along until I reached this square. I found the airport office, went in and they were astonished that I had managed to get through. 'You have been very lucky!' – I said I must catch that plane, so I gave them all the details that they wanted and I said that seeing it is so risky I had better stay until the meeting was over. They said I couldn't do that, they would tear the place down if they knew I was there. I said, 'You are sending me out to face that lot?' They said they couldn't do anything else. So I set off to stroll gently back and by the grace of God I got back to the hotel. Here again they didn't want me to stay, so I rang through to my French friends to see what time they estimated they would be with me. They said they couldn't make it; they couldn't get through the streets as they were chock-a-block. They were getting out of the city and the best thing I could do was to find a reliable dragoman and get out to somewhere like Gaza and look at the pyramids and the Sphinx until late evening when they would all have dispersed. Well, I found the dragoman that had looked after me on the coach and arranged for him to find a reliable taxi driver and to accompany me to the pyramids. This all went off very nicely. We got to the end of the metalled road and he hired a donkey and pony and we did the last part of the trip in style, with me on the donkey and him on the pony. We had a look round and had the customary ride on a camel and in the evening he said it would be safe to return. We trotted back to where the taxi was waiting and as he had been such a good chap I let him take me to one of his friends, who ran a fancy goods shop. I let this chap persuade me to buy something on which he would possibly make 10% or more commission. What he didn't realise was that Englishmen at that time could not take out of England unlimited amounts of currency. In sterling we were allowed £5. The rest was in letters of credit. Anyway the next day I got up and went to the airport. The reception was frigid and the delay lengthy. Eventually I was put on an Egyptian plane destined for Cyprus. I think it was a Hastings twin-engine job on which I was supposed to have my breakfast. However, as they had seen my passport there was no breakfast forthcoming, not even a cup of coffee, or a drink of water. Probably just as well as they could have spat in it. I landed at Nicosia airport and was conveyed to the Ledra Palace Hotel. There was one of our customers waiting for me. He must have been studying the flight schedule. This customer was a Greek gentleman. I must explain that in Cyprus the three principle groups of inhabitants are Greeks, Turks and Armenians. There is no love lost between any of them. The Armenians hate the Turks because they are the people that drove them out of Turkey. At least from Thrace, massacred them, and a few escaped and dropped into Cyprus. Their hatred has not lessened with the years. The Greeks and Armenians do not agree, nor do the Turks and the Greeks. I was in the position of having to deal with both, though Greeks principally. Only in a minor way did I have to deal with the Turks. The differences between these two rival customers were very intense. I decided to go for a stroll later in the day to see the Armenian, who was really the principal customer and he was in Lazarus Gate. He owned the Lazarus Garage and he was very concerned that the Greek had got in first, and he invited me to have lunch with him. But I had to steer a careful course and try to share my time between the two factions. I must say that Cyprus is a beautiful and interesting island. While I was there it was on the cool side, like an early spring day in England. Between them they took me all over the island and entertained me very royally. The Greek dealt with the Greek areas such as Famagusta; it is a wonderful town with its walled areas that speak of the Saracens and Crusaders. Practically every religion has had its say there. The Armenian side took me round Nicosia, round the various cabarets and we also went up into the Troodos Mountains and to a castle, I think it was the Illyrian Castle, and to Paphos, Limassol and Larnaka. The sixteen days I spent there were very nice and I was extremely tired. The journey was catching up with me, yet I still had some distance to go.

My next port of call was Beirut in the Lebanon and another beautiful city on the edge of the Mediterranean with boulevards along the sea front and hills behind with snow on them. Skiing was possible on the same day you were sunbathing down on the beach. There were relics of the French occupation – they controlled it for a number of years. The streets were named after Frenchmen. Here I stayed at the Palm Beach Hotel. I was originally going to stay at the Hotel des Georges but due to my schedule being out I stayed at the Palm Beach. One of the customers was a Frenchman and the other I don't know what he was, could have been Lebanese, but it was a very mixed community. The city I understand has now been absolutely devastated, but when I was there it was reasonably peaceful. As long as one walked in the light and kept clear of the dubious areas one was alright. It was another lovely city in an interesting country.

Then to Istanbul in Turkey and this was the last one for business purposes. Here was another lovely city in a lovely setting on the Bosphorous and with the Golden Horn and bridge. The hotel was on a sort of island; I think it was called the Terra Palm Hotel or some such name. One could sit in the dining room and watch the traffic on the Bosphorous. There were regular services flitting from Istanbul and the river was used like a bus service. My friends took me on one of the ferries and we could get off at a remote place for a drink or a meal and then come back to the city. The hotel seemed to be the centre of a fair amount of intrigue, the black market in currency seemed to be on the go there. I was able to get more money for my letters of credit than the official rate. Here again was a city full of history. We looked at the old Sultan's palace on the Bosphorous where he housed his many wives and concubines. When he was summarily removed a lot of his female companions were just turned loose on the streets and from what I heard some were still operating while I was there. They would be getting a bit long in the tooth. In the days I was there you could see what they called porters, men with a harness on their shoulders and a head strap and they were carrying colossal loads and would run with them. The streets were not flat; they were hilly and were of stone setts. I could have enjoyed being there longer. Apart from the Sultan's palace I would think the next largest building was the German Embassy.

By now it was the second week of February; I had finished my itinerary and was due to head for home. I was getting very edgy and unfortunately the plane was delayed and we had to wait for it to be repaired. We took off late and as I had a date with my wife in London at the airport at 1030 I could see I would not make it. We had to call at Frankfurt in Germany and the journey seemed endless. I did eventually reach London Airport. My wife had given it up as a bad job and gone back to the hotel. Well, I found a taxi and set off for the Regent Palace, where she was staying. I had been lucky and had got through Customs without a search. It had been a marvellous experience but it left me ill and very tired. I dropped into bed at 2am and it was the middle of the afternoon before I woke up. My wife and I decided to go to a show and by amazing luck managed to find two stalls at Agatha Christie's play 'The Mousetrap'. My wife enjoyed it very much but I never saw a thing, I saw and heard the overture; when the lights went down I fell asleep, when they came on at the interval I woke up and as soon as they went out I was fast asleep again. My wife woke me up to tell me it was all over and we went home. I was given two days to recover and it was back to work. From there on I have been subject to bronchitis and of course it has become gradually chronic bronchitis. All the places I visited had been torn by strife, though I don't attribute any of this to myself, but it is human nature, being nationalistic, greedy, unforgiving and grabbing. What I did for the company was wasted because they changed management and threw away their overseas market on the word of a small progress chaser imported from Birmingham, because he had the gift of the gab and they believed what they wanted to hear.

Harold Crook's marathon trip had lasted two months. Iraq yielded an order from M T Irani of Baghdad, for which they were given the sole agency for the Hopper brand until the end of 1953. As the company had many other registered export brand names he was able to quote other customers in Iraq for brands including 'Rimau', 'Wolf Dog Brand', 'Buffalo', 'Sun & Lion', 'President' and 'Portland'. Iraq had been a big market for the company, with nine dealers in Baghdad alone. In Kuwait M T Irani also gave Crook an order and this was again on the basis of exclusive supply of Hopper cycles. In Burma he granted the Burmani Cycle Store a sole agency for Elswick sales in Rangoon to the end of June 1954. Though no fault of his own his efforts yielded few orders, and the directors needed a scapegoat. He was dismissed and went on to run his own grocery shop in the High Street.

As often happens in the cycle industry it was not long before the market improved. On 15 June 1953 the *Scunthorpe Evening Telegraph* ran an article headlined: 'Factory, once on short-time, wants labour.' Business with the USA and Canada had grown dramatically and after eight months of short-time working the company was hoping to hire 50 additional workers. Though the company could not guarantee full production it stated that a long-term business arrangement had been reached in the USA and that there was an appreciable backlog of orders. From the archives it would seem that the biggest customer between 1953 and 1955 was the Skaggs Payless Drug Stores. There were 125 customers listed throughout the country. While some 'old hands' were persuaded back it proved difficult to attract new employees as it was a time when the Scunthorpe steelworks was expanding and recruiting from the local area, with bus transport laid on to solve the transport problem.

*Fig. 6.13 No 258 Jack Tighe Hopper mounted at Quibell Park track, Scunthorpe, during 1952.*

## Sponsorship

Grass track racing during the summer months had long been popular in Lincolnshire and a cheap way for young riders to enter the sport. The early 1950s saw three North Lincolnshire lads do well at the sport – Jack Tighe, Neville Tong and Peter Brotherton.[9] Although the company had always assisted youngsters with the odd component, when Harry Heselton joined in 1954 he saw the advantages of competitive local riders using local bikes, and though cash was available for some expenses, the main contribution was a machine or two, boldly carrying the name HOPPER. Jack Tighe joined Scunthorpe Wheelers (later Scunthorpe Polytechnic) in the late 1940s, a club now sponsored by his industrial painting company, and recalls that Elswick-Hopper became much more generous when Heselton joined and he was duly provided with two hand built track bikes (Fig. 6.13). He had many successes both in the UK and abroad and was selected for the Helsinki Olympics, though a few months of ill health put paid to this opportunity. Peter Brotherton started his racing career with Barton Wheelers and also worked for a while for Elswick-Hopper as a carpenter, though he managed to get ample time off for training on pay. He made a speciality of pursuit and was selected for both Helsinki (as a reserve) (Fig. 6.14) and Melbourne. So smitten was he with Australia that he sent for his wife Daisy, Nev Tong's sister, and continued his racing 'down under'. Nev Tong also rode with the Wheelers and spent most summers attending the various weekend racing events, often taking unpaid time off work if it interfered with his racing. His 1958 Empire Games appearance in the 1,000m time trial saw him setting a new Games record of 1m 12.1s. This was on his Hopper Lincoln Imp (Fig. 6.15) pushing a 90" gear.

Fig. 6.14 1952 British Olympics cycling team. Peter Brotherton is the tall man standing centrally at the back.
Fig. 6.15 Neville Tong taking Gold in the 1000m time trial during the 1958 Cardiff Commonwealth Games. The bike was supplied by Hoppers.

## An Attempt at Innovation – The Convincible

Ben Oldridge was born in Barton in 1898, one of 10 children of 'Barton Bill' Oldridge, captain of a sea-going barque.[10] After serving an apprenticeship at Marsh Lane he worked for a while in the motorcycle erection department and then followed two older brothers into the army, serving in France with the Royal Fusiliers, where he fell ill and was not expected to pull through. The authorities were rather precipitate informing his parents that he had died, a fact that he eventually disputed by sending them a 'whiz-bang'. This was the slang term for a special tick-box postcard informing one's nearest and dearest that one was still alive. During the war the Oldridge family left Barton for Hull and it was in Newland Avenue that Ben eventually started a business in partnership with a Mr Barry, repairing cars, motorcycles, cycles and radios. Despite losing his shop and equipment during an air raid in the next war, which resulted in him being sent to Lincoln to work on Lancaster bombers, he found new premises, again on Newland Avenue. He held a Raleigh and Humber agency, but spent increasing amounts of time looking for ways to improve the bicycle. It is believed that he built five prototypes, including one in the Museum of Street Life, in Hull (Fig. 6.16). He tried out several ideas incorporating a back pedal brake, shaft drive and a gearbox within the bottom bracket. He also believed that a short wheelbase was a way to improve rider performance. The design innovation that could incorporate these ideas was a twin down and seat tube frame with a wide bottom bracket. He also tried to solve the problem of chain alignment using derailleur gears by building an inboard sliding chain wheel, automatically aligned with the chosen rear sprocket. A patent was applied for in 1947 and awarded in 1950, No 640,683.[11] Raleigh turned down the opportunity to use the design, due to tooling costs and eventually Elswick-Hopper took up the challenge in late 1954, perhaps thinking that the novel design would find a new market. The resulting machine was shown at the November 1955 Earls Court Show, as the Hopper Vampire Convincible or Elswick Avenger Convincible, along with a glass case containing a working model of the drive mechanism. Although described in later years as 'the last hurrah of the British obsession with chain alignment',[12] the bicycles were described in *Cycling* at the time as the 'sensation of the show'.

Two factors conspired to ensure that the Convincible would be a commercial failure. Firstly, in the years since Ben Oldridge had first applied for a patent, the French and Italians had developed chains that were far more flexible and so less likely to unship when changing gear. Secondly, the price of £38 17s 5d did not compare well with £28 16s 8d for the standard model. The Convincible was

*Fig. 6.16 One of Ben Oldridge's prototypes.*
*Fig. 6.17 Peter Brown's prototype Convincible.*

a very difficult machine to build, as confirmed by the toolmakers who were involved assembling a small number of prototypes. One of these, serial number 002, was loaned to Jack Tighe and he recalls that the wide bottom bracket took a bit of getting used to, but the main problem was caused by the plain bearing carrying the sliding chain. It tended to stick due to road dirt. This particular machine was handed back to the factory in the 1970s – actually to Ernie Clements, who appears in the next chapter, and was running Falcon Cycles at the time. Ernie eventually took it back to Shropshire, sold it to a collector in Manchester, who passed it on to a fellow V-CC member in North East Lincolnshire, Peter Brown. Peter, and his highly skilled bike mechanic friend Roy Wilkinson, meticulously rebuilt it with contemporary parts, making others that were missing and unique to the design (Fig.6.17). This challenging task confirmed the complexity of assembly. It is probable that the design would have been rejected had not Arthur Stow died prematurely. In 1955 the novelty was probably the attraction to the management, struggling as they were at the time with a shrinking market. The model was listed through 1956 and 1957 but failed to sell in any quantity. During a stock take in the summer of 1956 there were 951 'No 2491 Vampire Convincible' and 950 'No 2492 Avenger Convincible' transfers listed. If we assume that 1000 were originally ordered it would indicate a maximum of 50 machines had been made, based on transfers both sides of the down tubes. Initial assessments that just a mere handful had been manufactured have indeed proved incorrect, following the discovery of a pristine machine in New York that had been supplied through Hans Ohrt's Beverley Hills bike shop. The photograph of the chain wheel area shows that a strip spring protected device (Fig. 6.18), similar to that used for many years by Cyclo Benelux for their rear derailleurs had been used on the chain wheel positioner, and the sliding chain wheel bearing appears to be better protected than the prototype. The number of machines produced and sold remains a mystery, but the fact that the Convincible remained in the catalogues for two years indicates that it did find some sort of market, though it must have proved an expensive diversion and was clear evidence that management had lost touch with the practicalities of cycle manufacture. Two long service Hopper employees remain convinced that no production models were made at Marsh Lane, so it is also possible that the ones that were made were subcontracted. Apart from the complete New York Convincible a second 'production' frame has been found and is in the hands of an enthusiastic restorer in Essex. The 1956 stock records note that the working model was loaned to Jordan & Co, a major customer based in Hull.

*Fig. 6.18 The chain wheel arrangement on the New York Convincible.*

## Tricycle for Children with Cerebral Palsy

The *Lincolnshire Chronicle* reported a new development on 7 March 1958:

> A North Lincolnshire invention may mean thousands of severely handicapped children all over the world can at last get around on their own. The invention is a specially constructed tricycle developed by the Elswick-Hopper Cycle and Motor Co Ltd, Barton on Humber, in co-operation with the senior staff of the Hesley Hall School for Severely Handicapped Children at Tickhill, near Doncaster. Work has gone on in the drawing office for months to build the machine which is thought to be the only one of its kind in the world.
>
> The most difficult engineering problem was to rotate the pedals without allowing the child's heels to drop. Both feet have to remain parallel to the ground throughout the pedalling, for if the heels were allowed to drop, the child would have difficulty contracting the leg muscles again. The obstacle was overcome by devising a special foot-length pedal that remains horizontal and operates on an ingenious cross-over drive. Ski-type heels are fitted to the pedals for ankle support, also toe straps. To counter the typical scissor gait of spastic paraplegia paralysis of the lower body the extended saddle has vertically adjustable knee guides, which to prevent chafing the child's limbs are of polished wood. A fully supporting back rest with a retaining strap keeps the child upright and a lengthened handlebar stem ensures that he can maintain an erect posture in comfort. A coupled brake lever can be fitted for use with both hands.
>
> The first models of the tricycle are now in daily use and have proved a great success.

The tricycle was also featured in an article in *Hospital Equipment News*, May 1958, accompanied by a similar article. Apprentice tool maker Eddie Gaunt recalls the job of making it was the best he ever did. 'It was brilliant because you literally did everything. We used to think how much better they were than a battery powered one, because if you had any mobility left you got the exercise. Imagine a tricycle that has a back frame so you can strap the child in. The pedals, if they press, the foot just collapses, so we had a double crank linked by chain and a plate across so that the foot was always held flat. There were drawings supplied and so far as I know it was a Hopper design. I don't know whether they charged for them and we only made maybe one or two a year.' It seems they were never seriously marketed and that only a handful were made. In March 1959, after an eight week stay at the Western Hospital in Fulham, the new managing director, Maurice Moss, presented the hospital Superintendent, Dr Kelleher, with one of the £60 tricycles as a token of appreciation for the care he had received. The doctor and his staff were 'delighted with the gift and impressed with its potentialities'.[13]

## 1958 – A Turning Point

On 1 February 1958 *The Lincolnshire Times* reported a 'sudden upward trend' in the shares of Elswick-Hopper. In Barton the question on everyone's lips was 'Who is buying Hopper's shares to such an extent that the value of a 5s share has risen from 2s 10d to 4s 1½d in about one month?' Director Harry Heselton had no explanation to offer and remarked that 'After all, they are 5s shares. I bought mine at 5s 7½d, so I am pleased they are moving up, but so far as I am concerned there will be nothing to regard as startling until they reach 15s.' In view of the consistently poor results over the previous few years and the interest shown by a group of investors, of which Heselton was undoubtedly aware, he was being somewhat disingenuous as we shall see in the next chapter. The board of directors at this time was chaired by Lt Col Richard Lowther Broad MC and his fellow directors were Henry Ernest Spry, James Howe Bruce, William Anthony Kevin Igoe and Harry Heselton. Spry's wife was Constance, well known for her books on flower arranging and cookery. Broad was a war hero who had completed many missions with the SOE in France and whose exploits have been recorded by Rex Woods in his book *A Talent to Survive*. In line with the misguided practice of so many public companies in the UK Heselton was the only director with industry experience.

The Conservative governments of the 1950s did little to help industry, with the advent of 'Stop-Go' business cycles and the decision not to join the newly-created Common Market. However, it is also clear that the Elswick-Hopper board had little interest in addressing the problems of an Edwardian production system that had seen little real investment since well before the war. Even at a local level they did little to advertise their bicycles – the *Scunthorpe Evening Telegraph* of 2 March 1958 carried a full page of advertisements from local bicycle dealers, with the title 'Easter is Cyclists' Dress Rehearsal for Summer Holidays'. All 10 participating dealers were agents of the Nottingham stable of Raleigh, Humber, Rudge and Triumph. Not that a bit of local advertising could revitalise the company, and Raleigh itself was struggling at the time. G H Bowden in his *Story of the Raleigh Cycle* observes:

> ..British manufacturers had failed to keep abreast of public opinion: that by 1958 they were no longer really making the sort of bicycle that the public wanted. People had perhaps grown a little tired of the traditional roadsters and were looking for machines with lighter fittings and derailleur gears. In short, more and more people were beginning to want something that looked as though it was capable of being ridden in the Tour de France! As this was not readily available, the cycling movement lost many potential enthusiasts, since teenagers and others were beginning to drift away from bicycling.

Bowden also comments on the growing respectability of hire purchase and consequent finance for wider car ownership. The country had indeed moved on from post war austerity and recovery to relative prosperity and people did aspire to motorised transport. In the two wheeled category this often meant one of the many mopeds, which had become so popular in Europe. *Cycling* featured a review of 63 assorted mopeds in the 7 November 1957 edition, including the Mobylette, Heinkel, Lambretta, NSU Quickly, Norman Nippy, Phillips Gadabout and Zundapp; the vast majority were imported. Elswick-Hopper had been offered the chance to enter the market as early as 1953 in partnership with the Bradford company Trojan, but after some development work had backed out. An entry into the market had to wait for new management. This was not a long wait as the old board of directors had decided to sell their controlling shares.

## Endnotes

1       *Cycling* 17 November 1948.

2       *The Bicycle* 26 October 1949.

3       *The National Journal* December 1957.

4       *Scunthorpe Evening Telegraph* 16 June 1952.

5       Ibid.

6       It was Government, rather than the industry, that set export targets in its efforts to earn foreign currency.

7       It was actually the first anniversary of the attack by British troops on the Ismalia police station in which 50 police were killed and 100 wounded.

8       General Mohammed Neguib had seized power through a military coup on 23 July 1952. He became president on 18 June 1953. It is an indication of the British disdain for such events that Harold was so ill-informed of the political situation in Egypt and, indeed, in all the countries he visited. Walking into the lion's den springs to mind.

9       To be precise, Tighe was born in Todmorden and Peter Brotherton near Boston, Lincolnshire.

10      I am indebted to Mrs Janet Mathias of Melbourne, Australia, for information on her father, Ben Oldridge.

11      Bachelier of France produced a similar design in the late 1920s – the Intégrale, but it was not a success.

12      *The Dancing Chain* Frank Berto p 187.

13      *Kensington News* 27 March 1959.

# CHAPTER 7

## THE TURNER YEARS 1958 - 1987

The title of this chapter acknowledges the important part played by James Livingston Turner in the history of Elswick-Hopper. It is second only to that of the founder, given that he took control at a time when the industry was struggling. He stuck with bicycles through numerous downturns, but also developed a large and profitable diversification into agriculture, following a path taken by Fred Hopper, father and son.

### New Management

After a slow post-war recovery many people in Britain were enjoying greater prosperity by the end of the 1950s. Coal, the last resource to be subject to austerity rationing, became freely available in 1958. The provision of a National Health Service released some of the historic pressure to 'save for a rainy day' and unemployment was far lower than in the interwar period. Increased prosperity did not result in another golden age for the bicycle industry, however, as motorcycles and cars became more affordable and were no longer the preserve of the middle and upper classes. Car prices were falling, as new models, like the Mini, were designed for mass production and high volume sales. Raleigh's management even claimed that bicycle sales were affected by the 'introduction of so many forms of advertised domestic appliances.'[1] Cars, motorcycles, fridges and televisions were supplanting bicycles on the list of priorities. An obvious outcome was a marked decline in bicycle manufacture and profitability. The British Cycle and Motor Cycle Industries' Association made strong representations to the government concerning the unfavourable treatment of bicycles with respect to purchase tax, for in 1958 it was 30% compared to 15% for such 'necessities' as garden furniture and sporting trophies. The Association pointed out that production was barely at 50% of capacity and that exports in 1957 were 25% down on 1956. Domestically the number of bicycles manufactured fell to less than 1 million in 1957 compared with 1.25 million in 1938.

In this climate Elswick-Hopper's profits fell again in 1957 from £10,211 to £6,243, though the Director's report for the December AGM of that year blamed a steady increase in the cost of materials and further wage rises. The directors had clearly run out of ideas and claimed that the fall in profits was:

> ...almost entirely due to factors beyond the control of management and does not reflect any falling off in efficiency of the factory or the slackening off of the efforts of the sales organisation.

Clearly the management board was in denial, though shareholders were probably mollified by the maintenance of a 5% dividend on ordinary shares, met, in a cavalier fashion, almost entirely out of reserves. However, towards the end of 1957 W A K 'Bill' Igoe, the stockbroker director of Elswick-Hopper with a holding of about 20% of shares, decided to sell up. Luckily for him this decision coincided with a search for a new business by Maurice Moss, a 50-year old Lloyd's underwriter, who had made his money in the Manchester textile industry. His accountants were Turner and Easdale, a relatively new London accounting firm set up by Jim Turner, with business partner Hamish Easdale. Born in 1924 Turner's accounting career started in 1940 but was halted by the war when he joined the RAF, training as a pilot. He completed his studies in 1949 and had already developed an interest in business turnarounds, gaining practical experience in this field. Significantly, Hamish Easdale was the rare combination of qualified engineer and chartered accountant. Jim Turner relates the next steps in the story:

> Maurice was interested in acquiring a stake in a publicly quoted company which he could use as a vehicle for his future business activities. I did a lot of research for him on this and eventually came up with Elswick-Hopper as a possibility....Maurice and I, and possibly Hamish, arranged to go up

to Barton, meet Heselton and look round the factory. We were staggered to see this vast area of old buildings and people working in very poor conditions and almost everything done by hand. Despite the fact that the cycle industry was declining, and finding it difficult to make worthwhile profits, Maurice decided to buy Igoe's shares. I recall two factors which influenced him. First he thought he could bring his textile design skills to revolutionise the bicycle and second he thought there was potential in redeveloping or selling unused buildings. So there was a change in the directorate with Maurice, myself and Hamish becoming directors and the Igoe interests resigning. We were very pleased to be able to work with Leslie Green as company secretary.

As none of us knew anything about the manufacture of bicycles we were on a rapid learning curve! Jim's observations concerning the condition of the buildings and the amount of hand-crafting involved were probably coloured by comparison with Moss's heavily automated textile companies. However, we know that little money had been spent on the buildings for over 50 years and not much on equipment, apart from during the Second World War.

M Moss and J B Yearsley were elected directors of Elswick-Hopper 1 April 1958 and S Moore was appointed alternate director to Mr W A K Igoe. Moss was appointed managing director 1 July 1958 and Turner and Easdale joined the board at the same time. The *Yorkshire Post* of 5 April welcomed the news that: 'an all out effort is to be made to expand the cycle manufacturing branch of the business. This news will be welcomed by shareholders who have watched with growing anxiety the decline of earnings since 1955.'

In a move to enable diversification the cycle business at Barton became Elswick-Hopper Cycle and Motor Co (Manufacturing) Ltd, reporting to the parent Elswick-Hopper Company. This change took place at the end of the trading year, in August 1958, but it took several years for diversification to begin in earnest. Harry Heselton was appointed chairman and managing director of the new subsidiary company, relinquishing his place on the parent board. Reginald Arthur McKenna arrived from Manchester quite soon as deputy to Heselton. Appointed by Moss to look after his interests he had worked for him in his Manchester textile business. Bill Igoe resigned from the main board at the end of August, completing the transfer of power.

The new management team rapidly made its presence felt and was not averse to spending money to gain market share. A thorough appraisal of all aspects of the business was first on the agenda and a raft of fresh initiatives was introduced. These included race team sponsorship, redesign of the bicycle range and re-entry into the motorised two-wheeler business. To fund these plans the company created 50,000 Ordinary 5/- shares 'as a prelude to embarking upon a policy of vigorous expansion of the cycle manufacturing business.'[2]

One of the first innovations was a new advertising campaign conducted by Henderson-Luckin Advertising Ltd. F H Radford was appointed public relations consultant at the same time. The peak period for cycle sales of mid May was set for the start and space was booked in the popular press, such as the *Daily Express*, *Daily Mirror*, Sunday editions, and in provincial evening newspapers throughout the country.[3] Interestingly, the campaign promoted just three of the many models manufactured: the Lincoln Imp, the Tour Anglais de Luxe and the Lincoln Tourist (also sold as the Elswick Escort Tourist). Advertising in the national press was quite a break from tradition and clearly recognised the need to appeal to people who were not already cyclists, and so attract new buyers.

Henderson-Luckin also designed a national children's competition, called the '£1,000 Flying Start'. Participants had to state how they would use the £250 first prize to make sure of a flying start in life. They also had to spot the mistakes in a 'what's wrong' problem picture, requiring a knowledge of road safety. There were several lower value prizes to make up the total to £1,000. To get the backing of schools the company also ran a special 'Improve Your School' competition alongside the Flying Start, and £50 was awarded to the class making the best suggestion for improvements. Entry forms were available from all Elswick-Hopper dealers holding stocks of the Lincoln Imp, and to ensure that the children actually looked at the bike they had to write the serial number, colour and number of gears of the display model on the form. The competition was very successful with 25,000 children participating,[4] and the awards were made on 11 July at the Waldorf Hotel, London. A highly qualified team of judges was appointed, comprising Brigg MP Lance Mallalieu QC, as chairman, tennis star Angela Buxton, Jill Day, film and TV star, Eileen Sheridan, cycling champion, Harry England, editor of *Cycling* and Reg Shaw, secretary of the CTC. Roderick Scriven, age 12½, of Chard took the first prize and a local Grimsby school won the £50 prize. Roderick's flying start scheme was to 'purchase two poultry houses costing £87 for two and spend £125 on hens. This would leave me with £38 for initial feeding. The profit I would re-invest in the business until finally I should own a large poultry business.' He also won a Lincoln Imp and was presented with his cheque by the Mayor of Chard. Hamish Easdale represented the company.

One theme of the suggestions for improving school facilities was to provide cycle repair sheds where pupils could be taught basic maintenance skills. Jim Turner was so taken with this idea that he passed it on to both the Minister of Transport and the Minister of Education. The response was predictably that it would be 'in the first place a matter for consideration by the school authorities.' It is clear that management saw children as the key to the future success of the company and school factory visits were actively encouraged so that pupils could view the complete manufacturing process.

No opportunities were lost to promote the products and *Cycle Sport* of 16 July 1958 carried a photograph of several young women in swimming costumes riding the latest models at the opening of the annual Soho Fair. The bicycles, on loan from Elswick-Hopper, carried banners bearing the exhortation: 'Have fun on a Bike!'

Was all the publicity worth the money? According to F H Radford, the public relations consultant, over 22 million people had heard of Elswick-Hopper as a result of the campaign. There is no mention of how this number was calculated, or what effect it had on sales.

## Purchase Tax and the SITA Contract

The Students International Travel Association (SITA) was formed in the USA during the early 1930s. Elswick-Hopper first supplied bicycles to SITA World Travel Inc before the war. It was never a huge order, being determined by the number of American students with enough money to take part in organised tours of Europe riding light roadsters. The arrangement was for the bicycles to be taken home by the students at the end of the tour and so the whole consignment was considered as export and therefore not liable to purchase tax. In 1958 the Treasury bizarrely decided there was a risk that the machines could be disposed of within the UK, thus avoiding purchase tax at 30%, and that the manufacturer should be held responsible for the tax.[5] At the time it was possible for visitors to buy a car in the UK, tour for a few weeks and export it with no payment of tax. According to the Treasury this was acceptable as cars were difficult to dispose of illegally. The impact for Elswick-Hopper was that the SITA contract for 1958, valued at £2,000 for 225 light roadsters, was in jeopardy and likely to go to Germany. The editor of *Cycling* suggested in the 21 April 1958 edition that it was a matter for the whole of the cycle industry to devise a foolproof scheme for submission to the Chancellor of the Exchequer, assuring him that such delayed exports would be controlled at the port of departure. According to the *Nottingham Evening Post* of 17 April 1958 Gerald Nabarro told the cycle trade to try to present to the Treasury a scheme that would enable purchase tax to be waived in such cases without being open to abuse. 'British cycles are a very useful dollar earner. We should be trying to increase rather than decrease the sale of our machines to American tourists.' Purchase tax continued to be a thorn in the side of the industry for some years and is just another example of the lack of Government understanding of the importance of a UK manufacturing industry.

## Tried and Tested Techniques

One aspect of the company that did not change immediately was the production methods used to build the bicycles. An article for the house magazine of paint manufacturers Pinchin, Johnson & Co described the process in detail, and included a photograph of liner Jack Austin (Fig. 7.1), detailing a Lincoln Imp frame. Although undated, the first part of this article appeared on 24 May 1958 in *Motor Cycle and Cycle Trader*, written by Harry Heselton.

> Since the war there has been a far greater demand for colour on cycles and the Elswick-Hopper Company has doubly justified its slogan of 'Famous for Finish' by the use of P J synthetics for practically the whole of its range of cycles.
>
> One of the oldest and certainly the largest of the independent cycle companies, Elswick-Hopper have always aimed to be ahead of competitors. Long years of experience have given them infinite faith in their own products and they are ever ready to try out new ideas – many of which have now become part and parcel of universal cycle manufacture.
>
> The firm's factory at Barton on Humber is well planned and equipped with every modern device to ensure that the utmost advantage is taken of the latest engineering techniques.
>
> The company makes its own chain stays, seat stays and fork blades and uses purchased tubing for the frame diamond only. The frames are jig built to ensure accuracy and consistency and are then liquid brazed. The residue left on the tubes and joints after dipping in molten brass is removed in a debrassing plant. The frames are then shot blasted; the seat lug is machined to allow for tightening of the seat pillar; the head is machined to receive the ball race seatings and the bottom bracket is reamed as a datum point for setting the frame completely in line.
>
> The frames and forks are fastidiously inspected and polished; then Bonderized to ensure that the following coat of superior quality enamel is keyed to the bonded metal to prevent corrosion and chipping. Both under and finishing coats are applied by complete immersion, dipping into deep tanks containing several hundred gallons of the particular enamel, after which the various components are suspended on special jigs and, by means of an overhead conveyor, carried into a convector oven for baking at a thermostatically controlled heat of 450 degrees Fahrenheit. Full use is made of the great variety of P J colours in shades to satisfy the most exacting demands, for which both they and we have become famous in the last few years. Next, the hand lining is applied by experienced liners with sword lining brushes and the transfers are fixed. The frames are then given a final coat of clear varnish.

In the assembly shops, metal head badges are fitted and the seat tube is reamed, so that the seat pillar is adjustable. The reamed bottom bracket is tapped with right and left hand threads, and the ball cups are screwed to accept the bottom bracket axle.

After loose ball race seatings have been pressed into the head tube at the top and bottom to house the head ball races, the front fork and then the bottom bracket unit – consisting of one fast ball race on the chain wheel side and one adjustable ball race on the left hand side – are assembled into the frame; the fast race is screwed in and locked tight to prevent movement and the ball bearings – 22 in all, 11 on each side – are inserted. The left hand adjustable ball race is screwed into position and a lock ring is screwed on to the adjustable ball race to lock it.

The fixed crown ball race is then fitted to the forks and driven tight on to a seating on the base of the steering column. After this, the top lower race is filled with grease and ball bearings and fitted over the crown race, completing the lower bearing. The fork and bottom bearing assembly is then introduced into the head of the frame in an upside-down position; the upper ball race assembly is applied, using a loose ball race and a screw ball race. The last named screws on to the threaded steering column and tightens the whole mechanism to the required degree.

The final operation of frame assembly is the fitting of the chain wheel and cranks, cotter pins, and washers and nuts. After careful inspection, the frame assembly is passed to the final assemblers, for the ultimate touches.

Elswick-Hopper has never accepted the conventional mass production practices of cycle erection, and each assembler takes the frame fitted with fork and a chain wheel and cranks, and completes the machine from that stage.

As for the colours, visitors to the factory stand enthralled as they watch the application of these new-look finishes to the machines. One in particular ('Hopper Marble') is most intriguing to watch. Deftly handling a feather plucked from a local rooster a girl operator can apply this finish to a frame in about 15 seconds. For mudguards and forks a lighted taper is used.

Each component in turn is lifted out from a mobile rack, then skilfully moved through the thin streamer of rising black smoke. As soon as each has gained an attractive black marble effect over its silver blue finish, it is replaced in the rack for fixing by varnish. The 'Marble' cycles, ranging from adult lightweight machines to junior cycles, are part of an order from a country in the Middle East, one of the 75 countries throughout the world to whom Elswick-Hopper supply their cycles each year. Value of the company's exports in their last financial year was £300,000.

It is five years since the company moved on from traditional decorative schemes (black and green were long-standing favourites) to the gay hues of its now famous 'peaked' effect. The change immediately delighted English youngsters and sent home sales soaring overnight....

## Elswick-Hopper Racing Team

Road racing in England had never reached the levels of popularity achieved in mainland Europe, to some extent due to the antipathy of the police that virtually closed down the sport by the end of the 1890s. Worried that competition would be driven off the roads altogether, the governing body, the National Cyclists Union, opted for subterfuge rather than confrontation. This led to the development of the peculiarly British sport of time trials, where riders set off at minute intervals and 'drafting' (taking shelter behind the lead rider) is banned. After many futile attempts to persuade the NCU to recommence open road racing, a breakaway organisation was set up in 1942, the British League of Racing Cyclists. Often riven by political in-fighting the League nevertheless succeeded in re-establishing road racing as a domestic sport. It was an odd time to sponsor a new team, bearing in mind that the big factory teams such as Hercules, Viking and BSA had not contributed much to the profitability of those companies, despite the popularity of major races like the Tour of Britain. However, as we saw in the last chapter Elswick-Hopper had helped local riders for many years, with equipment and support, so an interest in racing had been well established by the time they decided to sponsor a team in early 1958, with a plan to compete in over 60 of the season's major road events.[6] J F (Jim) Wilson, an ex-racer who ran a bike shop in City Road, Sheffield, was appointed manager and the bicycles were, of course, Lincoln Imps. They were claimed to be standard production models with just sufficient adjustments to meet road racing conditions and regulations, and were finished in one of the standard colour schemes of cherry red and pearl green. Red and white were chosen for the team jerseys. Based on discussions with Jim Wilson's son, Nigel, who now runs the family business, and team member Frank Clements, it is very likely that the bike frames were actually made by Jim Wilson. Jim had raced professionally, including in the Tour of Britain, and had managed successful racing teams since 1954; he was also an accomplished frame builder, who had sold many frames to European riders.[7] Five top independent riders were recruited:

Ron Coe of Sheffield – team captain,
Sidney Wilson of Sheffield,
Frank Clements of Dawley,
Alan Bladon of Birmingham,
Harry Reynolds of Birmingham, who was just completing his Army National Service.

The independent category of rider was intended to be a half-way house between amateurs and professionals. They were paid on results, and usually held a day job.

Coe had won both British road racing titles in 1957, but all team members were capable of winning major events. Sid Wilson was, of course, Jim's brother. (Fig. 7.2)

Fig. 7.2    From right to left, Sid Wilson, Ron Coe and Alan Bladon out training. Bladon and Wilson are riding Lincoln Imps, and all three jerseys are of different design, so probably taken in early 1958.

The first year's results were certainly impressive, with Coe personally winning 33 races and also competing in the Tour de France, though retiring at stage 6. In the first team outing in early April at the Bournemouth Olympic Three Day Race Coe took first place, with Reynolds second and Wilson seventh. Coe won four stages in the Tour of Britain, though riding riding for England, and was placed seventh overall, one place above Reynolds, who was part of the ACU team. Later in the season Coe won the BCF road race championship for the second year running. Some publicity was certainly gained by the sponsorship, at least for Maurice Moss, who was interviewed on the popular 'In Town Tonight' radio programme. This was after Sid Wilson won the Welsh National Trophy on 14 May and Alan Bladon took the Cader Idris Trophy the following day, when, with Coe third and Wilson fifth, Elswick-Hopper also took the team award. The end of the season was celebrated in fine style at the British Professional and Independent Racing Men's Association race at Swanwick near Derby, where the team took the first three places. Elswick-Hopper riders amassed 55 individual and 23 team wins during the season, both all time records (Fig. 7.3, 7.4 & 7.6).

The company made the most of its team's racing success through advertisements and even ran a series of footnote style adverts in the BLRC magazine *The Leaguer*, where the final footnote read, 'Lincoln Imp for <u>real</u> cycling enthusiasts!'

*Fig. 7.3    Ron Coe with the Mayor of Bournemouth after winning the 223 mile 1958 Three Day Race in early April. The most interesting feature is the J F Wilson bike that Ron is holding – Sheffield built, not Barton! Harry Reynolds was runner-up.*

*Fig. 7.4    Ron Coe with an 'official' Lincoln Imp, made in Barton.*

*Fig. 7.5    Ron Coe leading Frank Clements, race unknown, but a good action shot.*

*Fig. 7.6    Harry Reynolds receiving his cup for winning the 1958 Tour of the Lakes. He is flanked by Sid and Jim Wilson to the left of the photograph and team captain Ron Coe to the right.*

## The Scoo-Ped debacle and the Earls Court Show of November 1958

The Elswick-Hopper stand covered 2,000 sq ft in a prominent position in the main aisle. Ron Coe and Harry Reynolds were pressed into service and the rest of the team attended part time. The new Vogue Modèle, competitively priced at £19 17s 6d, occupied pride of place on a revolving centre stand in the new coffee and cream colour scheme. This bicycle was described as 'the new town and country model, designed to appeal to all women especially the younger housewives, secretaries and the smarter set generally'.[8] Coe's Lincoln Imp racing bike was on display, also a selection of photographs showing the team in action during the year. The involvement of the successful racing team in the annual cycle show is proof of a strategy aimed at keeping the two brands in the public eye, thereby maintaining and hopefully increasing market share. Raleigh had, of course, been capitalising on the success of Reg Harris for many years, but the scope of the Elswick-Hopper revitalisation campaign was intended to go far beyond racing.

The *East Anglian Daily Times* captured the spirit of the times in its 14 November report of the Earls Court Show:

> Bicycles for 1959 have gone gay. The new models to be seen at Earls Court have burst into every imaginable colour scheme and some thoroughly pleasing effects result. There is still little enough of colour in every day things and this development on the part of the cycle makers helps to make our day brighter and more cheerful.

During an interview with the *Scunthorpe Evening Telegraph*, published on 27 October, Jim Turner had promised 'a machine of revolutionary design' to be launched at the November International Cycle and Motor Cycle Show, and indeed the Scoo-Ped was 'different', but it was mainly an excellent example of how it is impossible to design a new bicycle with no experience of what bicycle riders actually want. The Scoo-ped was devised by Maurice Moss and looked like a moped, and indeed it may have been a good one had it not lacked an engine. It was designed to keep the cyclist dry and clean and comprised a complex moulded fibreglass cover over a steel backbone frame (Fig. 7.7). The project was completed in great secrecy and on a fast track to make the planned launch at a special press conference at the Show on 6 November. Some early road testing had been done by the office girls at 'Top Hoppers', the local name for the head office on the corner of Brigg Road. The girls identified handling difficulties in strong crosswinds, though this was probably discounted, given its perceived role as primarily town transport.

*Fig. 7.7   A surviving museum-based Scoo-ped in all its fibreglass folly.*

The machine was given the very best of starts, with Lady Lewisham (Katie Boyle) christening it with champagne at the press launch. This was followed by a cocktail party at the Dorchester Hotel hosted by the newly-formed Scoo-Ped Ltd and attended by over 700 guests, including several hundred Elswick-Hopper dealers and their spouses. Maurice Moss took the opportunity to tell his guests that sales were up by 16%, thanks to extensive advertising, compared to a national fall of 22%. He also told them that the fleet of delivery vans had been repainted with a bold caption along each side, which had been taken from the national advertising campaign: 'Cycle-logically, your choice must be an Elswick-Hopper'. The front of each van carried the Lincoln Imp motif.

Fig. 7.8    *From the company sales brochure, casting a wide net.*

For dealers unable to attend the launch Hamish Easdale designed a mobile showroom, comprising a trailer covered with a Perspex box, which could be towed around the country by the sales reps, while the January 1959 *Elswick-Hopper News Letter* clearly stated the objective of widening the appeal of the bicycle:

> The Scoo-Ped is not intended to replace the ordinary cycle, our aim in introducing the Scoo-Ped was to bring into dealers' shops people who have never previously bought cycles and to whom a cycle on classic lines has never had any appeal at all.

The article goes on to identify the businessman and the housewife as potential customers (Fig. 7.8).

> Even housewives lucky enough to have their own car will find such a machine handy in main shopping areas where parking is a very real problem.

Press comment actually seems to have been quite positive, probably because it was a real attempt to be innovative at a time when people were wide open to new ideas as prosperity grew and memories of rationing and post-war shortages faded. The dealers' comments in the March 1959 *Newsletter* were positive and illustrative of the times. Mr F A Wagstaff, of A Williams & Co in Cheltenham remarked that the recent recession in cycle sales was due to the conservatism of the dealers:

> The trade as a whole cannot afford to continue in the belief that the bicycle as such is unalterable and can't progress. It is essential to realise that the market is changing. People are always looking for something new, something different. It is therefore absolutely imperative when something as novel as the Scoo-Ped comes on the market that every effort is made to sell it and sell it impressively.

Prophetic words. The *Newsletter* also featured a photograph of Mr Eric 'Guv' Stow, sitting on a Scoo-Ped outside his shop in Slough. He is smartly dressed in a dark suit and coat and a Homburg hat, looking rather like a middle-aged Winston Churchill. He had been running his business since 1927 and thought that a major advantage of the new machine was that it could be ridden in best dress in all weathers. He thought it would:

> ..sell well to folk such as insurance agents, who want to look neat and tidy yet have to call on numerous houses in a single road. This makes the car not only an uneconomical proposition but a time-waster. The Scoo-Ped will meet their needs whereas they probably feel an ordinary cycle a bit unbusinesslike.

A conservative view was recorded by Mr J Cheeseman, of Harwich Radio & Cycle Supplies. Though he liked the Scoo-Ped, he hoped that neither the design nor the colour would be varied for a long time: 'As dealers our main trouble these days is that there is too much variety.' One wonders what he would have made of the almost infinite variety available to the bicycle trade in the early 21st century.

Not content with the potential UK market Maurice Moss flew to New York in February to arrange distribution in the USA and Canada. Floyd Clymer, owner of the US journal *Cycle*, had seen

*Fig. 7.9   Patrick Trench of the Veteran-Cycle Club riding a Scoo-ped around the venerable, and venerated, Herne Hill track on 18 July 2002.*

the Scoo-Ped at Earls Court and made favourable comments to the effect that he hoped to see Moss in Los Angeles. The transport of a sample machine to Heathrow fell to John Stockdale, so he asked two of his tool makers, Barry Wood and Dennis Moody, and a joiner to construct a special crate. They worked through the night and John duly took it to the airport, only to discover that the crate was too large to load. The Scoo-ped made the flight without protection and arrived undamaged. The March *Newsletter* reported that many USA distributors were seeking rights to distribute the new machine.

With so much promise, why did this attempt at innovation fail? Harold Briercliffe called it 'one of the most outstanding of the post-war bicycle designs.'[9] He also noted that only 36 were ever made. The view of the tool makers was that there had been no quality control of the manufacture of the fairings, making their assembly highly labour intensive. According to Barry Wood it took his colleague Peter Warcup a week to assemble the first one. Keith Clark recalls Dennis Moody doing some work on the panels, which were made in Wales, and most of them were so ill-fitting they had to be scrapped. A personal view comes from Scunthorpe bicycle shop owner Tony Baines, who recalls his mother winning one at the local Lysaght's steelworks gala. It was ridden by the family for 12 months and though rather noisy, was fun to ride. The fibre-glass enclosure tended to magnify the normal mechanical sounds and the body fixings caused rattles, but the major drawback was that the police kept pulling him up and telling him he was too young to ride a moped (Fig. 7.9)! From a marketing perspective it was clearly competing neither with mopeds, as it was human powered, nor with conventional bicycles, and though providing weather protection, the price was harder work turning the pedals of the chunky 47 lb machine. 1959 was also the year of the Mini launch, which lowered the cost of car ownership and brought it within reach of more of those aspiring 'housewives' identified as potential Scoo-ped buyers. As tool maker Eddie Gaunt sums it up: 'The trouble was it cost £33, which was a lot of money and for £40 you could buy a moped. The only time I remember seeing one in a shop was in the window at Hammond's department store in Hull.' So even if the technical problems with the attachment of the panels to the simple loop frame had been overcome it is difficult to imagine that ex-factory prices could ever have yielded a reasonable profit margin. At the AGM on 31 December 1959 it was announced that 'difficulties have been encountered by our fibreglass fairing suppliers in attaining adequate standards of precision commensurate with the necessity of achieving the minimum weight factor.' The company was still confident that problems would be overcome but the plug was eventually pulled and the Scoo-Ped never made it to the market, though at least four have survived, one of which is at the National Museum of Scotland in Edinburgh. It is likely that the 36 that Briercliffe quotes were disposed of in a similar way to the Baines' machine, a disastrous result for a struggling company, considering the large investment in development and promotion. It is interesting to note that motorcycle manufacturers of this era, such as Velocette and Triumph were also fitting fibreglass fairings and 'bathtub' rear enclosures, in the case of Triumph. These were unpopular and often discarded.

Bicycles have always been a magnet to innovators and inventors, who refuse to accept that the simple traditional configuration cannot be radically improved. The Swedish Itera and Sinclair C5 are two of the better known attempts, though the Itera was novel only in material of construction rather than configuration. Only Alex Moulton continued to develop what was the most successful attempt at a 'different' bicycle in the twentieth century. Although no costs for the Scoo-Ped are available there is no doubt that it consumed large amounts of cash, and, more importantly large amounts of management effort, with some ex-employees blaming it for the ensuing financial problems.

In 1965 the company was approached by Dr Joe Ehrlich, a successful Austrian-born two-stroke motorcycle engine designer, who had formed a new company with Bristol Siddeley – Bristol Siddeley Ehrlich Engineering Ltd. As well as developing improved engine scavenging systems for the new company Ehrlich had found time to build a prototype compact cycle using rear wheel quadrant drive connected by arms to treadles. A patent search found two overseas patents based on quadrant propulsion, showing that the idea was not novel. Looking at the whole machine the bicycle company was enthusiastic about one aspect: 'this concerns an anti-locking device, essential to the practicability of the bicycle design as it allows reverse motion. We are in the process of examining the patentable aspects of this anti-locking device.' Fortunately commercial sense prevailed on this occasion, probably due to the recent experience of the Scoo-Ped, (and the equally ill-judged Convincible) and no further action was taken.

The 1958 Show also included a new range of Falcon bicycles designed by 'Ernie Clements'. There were three models: the Black Diamond, the Club Special and the Super Route.

## One year on

The first financial year under new ownership saw a loss of £32,131, five times that for the previous year. Given the mass of initiatives introduced this was a surprisingly good result. On 29 December 1958 Jim Turner spoke at the AGM at Barton, and the following extract from his report is taken from the *Motor Cycle and Cycle Trader* of 20 December. It provides a detailed summary of the challenges facing the new board.

> The 1957/58 season was indeed an unfortunate one for British cycle manufacturers and, in common with our competitors, our company experienced a further contraction in the export trade both in quantity of orders and prices. This is largely due to the increased establishment of protected local factories in many of our traditional markets and the continued pressure on prices arising from the entry into these markets of our European and Far Eastern competitors. Our company's export trade is now unprofitable but nevertheless makes a small but welcome contribution to our overheads. With the continued imposition of purchase tax and home demand continuing to contract, I view with some apprehension the future profitability of the industry.
>
> When I was appointed to the board, midway through the last financial year, my colleagues and I came to the conclusion that, whereas the name of Elswick-Hopper held a high reputation in the cycle trade and with the older members of the public, this was not the case with the younger generation in this country, to whom the name of our company meant very little, as a result of our defence

production during the war and subsequent concentration on the export trade. With this in mind and in order to endeavour to arrest the continuing decline in profits, it was decided to embark on a national sales campaign directed particularly at the teenager group, which now comprises the largest part of the British cycling public. Most of the expenditure for this campaign was incurred before the end of the last financial year and I am pleased to report that subsequent home sales showed a substantial increase in a period in which the home sales of the industry as a whole showed a considerable decline.

Unlike our principal competitors, we do not have diversified activities in the bicycle field and, indeed, we are dependent on these competitors for supplies of many of our raw materials and components. For this reason, and on account of the relatively unfavourable geographical location of our factory in relation to our source of supplies and to our customers, it is evident that our production costs are a matter of continuing concern.

Although we have maintained a full working week for the production of our bicycles, which continue to exhibit the highest standards of finish and craftsmanship, we are apprehensive of the position which may arise when the full potential of the new factories of the two large groups is brought to bear on the home market.[10]

Nevertheless, your board are sparing no efforts to take the fullest advantage of the 80-year-old goodwill of our company by bringing our marques into the forefront of the cycling community. The reconstructed board, including three executive directors, have taken steps to reorganise the administrative and selling structure of your company. It has been found necessary to arrange for the installation of a system of material control, budgetary control and standard costing. Strenuous steps are being taken to reduce the level of stocks held by the company, but a permanently lower level is difficult to achieve without reduction of the full range which it is necessary to keep in our dealers' shops. A survey has been undertaken of obsolete and obsolescent stocks of raw materials and components and a sum exceeding £7,000 has been written off the stock in this connection.

As a step towards diversification, negotiations are in a final stage for the purchase of a business in the Midlands, which should also make a small contribution towards future profits.[11] Further steps in this direction are, however, limited by capital considerations.

....From 1 August last, the bicycle activities of the company have been carried on by a wholly-owned subsidiary company, The Elswick-Hopper Cycle and Motor Co. (Manufacturing) Ltd. The parent company is now, therefore, a holding company.

Shareholders will no doubt appreciate the inability of the board to recommend the payment of a dividend on the Ordinary shares for the year to 31 July last.

The AGM was followed by a party for 400 employees on the floor of the main assembly department, the 1911 Elswick building. Turner and Moss made brief speeches and presentations were made to two employees who had retired after 60 years service.

The management control systems referred to by Jim Turner were the result of a study undertaken by Newton, Armstrong & Co, whose consultants discovered several areas requiring improvement. Many other aspects of the business were also under investigation at this time, including discussions with Cecil Le May on the possible use of Araldite adhesives to replace traditional liquid brazing techniques. A letter to Le May dated March 18 1960 shows that several destructive tests were made on brazed and glued frames. While brazing withstood higher loads, the use of Araldite appears to have yielded acceptable strength. However, the benefit gained by the use of glue was the time saved in cleaning frames after liquid brazing. As absolute cleanliness is necessary when using adhesives it would seem that there was no net benefit in production costs. It was another 29 years before a bonded frame was produced commercially by Raleigh. The Dyna-Tech bonded range was, however, prone to failure and the process was dropped in the mid 1990s. Other projects under consideration at this time included relocation of production shops to allow for conveyor movement, automatic plating equipment, new polishing equipment etc. The costs involved in such improvements quickly showed them to be unjustifiable.

Organisational changes on the sales side were announced in January 1959.[12] Bert Crofts, who had worked in the cycle industry since his discharge from the Royal Flying Corps at the end of the 1914/18 war, was promoted from sales manager to group sales controller. He had joined Elswick-Hopper in 1934 as a representative and was promoted to sales manager in 1939. As sales controller Bert was directly responsible to the board for all bicycle sales, including the new Scoo-Ped. Barton born Walter Foster was appointed home sales manager, having worked for the company from the age of 14, with experience in every department. The third appointment was of a second generation Hopper employee, Peter Stow, as export sales manager. Peter was the son of Arthur Stow, and joined the company in 1948 after service in the armed forces during the war. The company was also strengthening the sales force in the field and succeeded in attracting George Fleming as sales representative for the south-east.[13] George had experience in the Birmingham bicycle trade and of the retail business. He had been a renowned time triallist and road racer, becoming National 25 mile champion in 1937 and the first Englishman to beat the hour for 25 miles with a time of 57m 56s in 1938, though not recognised by the record books as it took place in Ireland and was not done under the auspices of the Road Time Trials Council.[14] He was also the first Briton to break the two hour barrier for 50 miles, with a time of 1h 59m 14s, also in 1938. That was a great year for George as he also broke the French indoor hour record with a distance of 27 miles. After the war he won the Paris to London road race, held in 1947. On ceasing competitive cycling he made a contribution to the sport in team management and led the English Olympic road and track team at the Helsinki Games in 1952.

The 'Comment' article in the *Motor Cycle and Cycle Trader* of 27 February 1959 mentioned another plea by Maurice Moss at the Reading National Association dinner for a review of purchase tax. He warned that even the complete removal of purchase tax would not solve the trade's problems. What is more relevant to our understanding of the situation in 1959 is the analysis of the current conditions contained in the article.

> Every year there are 750,000 children attaining the age of grammar or secondary modern schooling; every year an equal number leaves school at 15 years of age or more and these 1½ millions, with longer journeys to school or to work, provide the best market for the bicycle trade. Older people may replace their bicycles from time to time; there is the enthusiastic quarter million of touring and racing cyclists; but the greatest market today is among youngsters of between 12 and 19 and the industry and retail trade is well aware of the fact.
>
> Where the home cycle-business as a whole has failed in the 1950s is in its underestimation of the strength of the rival claims on public (especially youthful) spending money and its limited public counter-challenge to these. Unlike the 1930s – when 'the pictures', field sports and dancing were possibly the main alternatives – the young people of today are faced with a bewildering choice of appeals for their spare money. Earlier marriages, Continental travel, 'pop' discs, tape recorders and more expensive clothes are among the competitive forces that now face the cycle trade.

Anyone who was a teenager in the late 1950s can identify with the problems facing the cycle industry at that time. The next decade was even tougher, with 16 year olds aspiring to motorcycles or scooters, and young adults to the affordable Mini. However, Elswick-Hopper management stuck to its belief that modernisation of its range would boost sales and sought help from Italy, a source of design talent that had already made an impact on the car industry and was making serious inroads into the British cycle component market through the quality products supplied by companies such as Campagnolo and Cinelli.

The February 1959 *Motor Cycle and Cycle Trader* also reported a recent Elswick-Hopper sales conference attended by all sales representatives and advertising agents. The company emphasised the importance of advertising and cooperation with dealers to further increase market share. The need to push the Scoo-Ped was also stressed. A public relations speaker suggested that dealers could help by bold window dressing, by contact with local cycling and youth clubs and by co-ordination of local advertising with national schemes. A weakness was identified of not capitalising on brand names such as Lincoln Imp, Vogue Modèle and Scoo-Ped, around which a national campaign could be built. The importance of advertising was demonstrated by the appointment in April 1959 of D T Chadwick as the first ever marketing and sales promotion manager, based at Barton.[15]

A G M Grassick was appointed general manager in June 1959, succeeding Heselton. Born in Aberdeen Grassick was 49 when he took on the job, having worked as an industrial management consultant for 8 years. His background was in engineering with both Rolls Royce in Glasgow and Coventry Gauge and Tool at Clydebank.[16] In a letter dated 7 April Turner had explained the roles of the three executive directors.

Moss:            overall supervision, selling and distribution.
Turner:          finance, costing, public relations, advertising, secretarial and road racing team.
Easdale:         production, buying, Midland Motor Company.

Also in June suggestion boxes were placed in all parts of the works for improvement ideas on any topic, including techniques, conditions, bicycle names and colour schemes.[17] This was followed in the same month by the setting up of a Design Committee, with a remit from Turner to 'keep under constant review the styling, design and technical specification of our current models in order that improvements can be made and ideas for next season's models be well considered.' The first meeting was chaired by D Elias, with Moss, Fleming, Crofts, and Plumtree (buyer) appointed as permanent members. At the first meeting the new 1960 range was reviewed as to colour selection and components, including saddles, carriers and pumps. Bert Crofts was asked to explore the market potential for a cheap sports roadster and it was agreed that the popular Lincoln Imp should be continued but that the traditional box lining should be deleted.

Business was fairly brisk in the second quarter of 1959. 23,498 bicycles were ordered and 20,172 despatched. This equates to 1,566 orders and 1,345 despatches each week.

Further appointments within the manufacturing subsidiary followed in August.[18] Local man Leslie W Green started his career with F Hopper & Co Ltd in 1909 as an office boy, a common method of entry into the firm for bright boys in those days. He worked through most departments before his appointment as company secretary in 1953. He was appointed director in August 1959. Another local man, George Franklin, was promoted from works manager to works director, having been in charge of the works since 1925. Crofts received his second change of job title during the year when he was made sales director and Grassick became executive director. These moves were due to the company's 'continuing expansion'. It is commendable that despite its difficulties the company decided in mid 1959 to improve training opportunities for its 16 apprentices. This entailed the provision of day release at Scunthorpe Technical College, evening classes one evening per week with fees paid and free transport provided.[19]

Optimistic expansion plans were also demonstrated by the opening of two new depots to serve the dealers in Cheshire and East Anglia. The Cheshire depot, at Stockport, was intended to have an ultimate capacity of 1,000 machines, handling scooters and mopeds as well as bicycles. The London area had been served by a local company, G F Co Ltd based in NW5. In September the company opened its own depot and distribution centre in Hounslow. At the end of 1959 a review of transport was made, at which time the company owned four pantechnicons, a Ford Luton van and a Morris 15 cwt van. In addition three vehicles were on hire.

## More Racing

Jim Wilson was supplanted by Benny Foster as team manager for the 1959 season. Foster had a long career in team management, including at National level and according to associates was something of an ebullient and controversial character. The Elswick-Hopper team comprised Ron Coe, Frank Clements

Fig. 7.10   *The 1959 team at Barton with one of the erectors, Mr Foster. From left to right the team members are Owen Blower, Harry Reynolds, John Geddes, Ron Coe and Frank Clements.*

Fig. 7.11   *The new team support vehicle at Barton, with new manager Benny Foster wearing the suit. From left to right: Arthur Such, Dennis Moody, Benny, Barry Wood and Peter Warcup.*

and Harry Reynolds from the previous year, and newcomers Owen Blower and John Geddes. Though the team appeared in a photograph with an Elswick-Hopper employee at Marsh Lane (Fig. 7.10), according to Frank Clements the actual new season racing frames were made in the Manchester area. The previous section on racing also mentioned this odd question of origin – one that was not unique to Elswick-Hopper and that continues to this day. The whole point of supporting racing teams is to sell bikes, but the star riders have always had their own ideas on which frame builder will be best for them. The team was also equipped with a new van, seen at Marsh Lane in Fig. 7.11.

Early season success saw Coe winning the Ovaltine Spring Classic and Reynolds the Bournemouth Olympic Easter three-day race. John Geddes won the 90 mile Langsett road race with Blower, Coe and Reynolds making it a first four place win for the team. Clements won the Welsh National with Blower in third place, Coe won the Tour of the Cotswolds and Geddes the Hull Corporation 100 mile race. However, the big event was the Tour of Britain.

Serious controversy arose in June during the 1959 Tour of Britain. This seventh tour was the first run under the newly formed British Cycling Federation banner, marking the end of both the BLRC and NCU, which had been at loggerheads ever since the BLRC was formed. It was also the last that incorporated trade team riders into regional and national teams, a practice that inevitably resulted in split loyalties. Coe and Reynolds were riding for England, Clements was leader of the Central Division, Blower was part of the East Midlands team and Geddes was riding for the Army Cycling Union. Frank Clements remembers that Foster followed the race in the Elswick-Hopper team car, accompanied by team masseur Bill Shillibeer. Whether this was allowed by the organisers because of Foster's long association with the event is unclear. What is clear is that he directly influenced the way that his Elswick-Hopper independents rode the stages, even though they were not riding for that team. At the end of stage 8 Bill Bradley, an amateur riding for England, was in the lead and should have been able to rely on Coe and Reynolds to help control breakaways over the last three road stages. However, he did not take into account Foster's desire for the final winner to be one of 'his boys'. Foster told Clements after stage eight that it was bad publicity to have an amateur beating a sponsored semi-pro and that either Ron or Harry must take the yellow jersey. Frank was told to sit on Bradley's wheel the next day to make sure he got no help chasing breakaways. Reynolds and Coe duly made a break with six other riders while Clements just stuck to Bradley's back wheel as instructed.  Foster's plans backfired dramatically when Gordon Thomas, the England manager, withdrew both Coe and Reynolds for riding contrary to his instructions. Reynolds, who was understandably distraught at the decision, claimed that he had decided to ignore the instruction not to attack when he realised that neither of his team mates, Ron Coe and Bill Bradley, were able to do so. The leading group finished eight minutes up and it is probable that Reynolds would have won the Tour had he not been disqualified. From being in first place England had been reduced to one man and forfeited the team prize. Bradley went on to win the event with a lead of nearly 11m 57s over Geddes in second place. According to the Daily Mirror of June 4 Jim Turner said: 'As far as we are concerned our riders were competing exclusively for their regional or national teams. They have instructions to this effect. **They are not being paid by us for taking part in this race.**' Frank Clements version is supported by Peter Clifford in his *History of the Tour of Britain*, where he states: 'It appeared that Reynolds and Coe, both from the same team, did not want to see an amateur win the race, and were not prepared to assist him.' According to contemporary sources, such as Frank Clements and Dave Orford the disqualification incident severely damaged the independent category, which had served to ease the path of so many amateurs into the professional ranks.

Ron Coe won his third BCF Road Race Championship at Wolverhampton in July 1959, the first ever three in a row. The event was also a tremendous achievement for the Elswick-Hopper team, which took the first five places in a sprint finish; new team members Owen Blower and John Geddes took second and third places respectively, with Reynolds fourth and Clements out-sprinting the bunch to take fifth place. After the race Coe paid tribute to his team mates with the statement that, 'Nowhere in the world and in no other sport can there be the *esprit de corps* which exists in this team. I am proud to ride with them.'[20] On Sunday 18 November Owen Blower added to the reputation of his team by beating the Cardiff to London time by 35 minutes. He had endured several weeks of contrary winds to finally take the Road Racing Association record in 6 hours 26 minutes 55 seconds on his Lincoln Imp, equipped with Cyclo gears, Milremo tyres, Brampton chain and GB brakes. His 50 mile time was an impressive 1-58-53 and the 100 took 3-57-47.[21]

Despite another successful year Jim Turner decided not to support a full Elswick-Hopper team in 1960, as he could see no benefit in terms of increased sales. In the climate of the early 1960s it was a good decision. The team went in different directions. Reynolds and Clements joined Falcon, and Coe and Geddes contracted with Andre Bertin's French team. A small racing presence did continue, however, through what appears to have been an ad hoc Hopper-Milremo professional team. Milremo was the brand name for Harrogate based Ron Kitching's imported components, some of which were used on the new Continentale racing cycle. The team competed in at least one professional road race, the 100 mile 1960 Manx Premier, run over the Clypse Circuit. Won by Darrigade, Hopper-Milremo riders included Brian Robinson, Ron Coe, John Geddes and Bernard Pusey. Robinson was first home of the four, in tenth place, 44 seconds down. An advert for Elswick-Hopper and Milremo appeared in *Cycling* on 3 August 1960, just over a month after the race. It referred to the 'immaculate MILREMO equipped HOPPER cycles used by the team.' In the event it would appear that the new team was short lived, as most of the members were busy riding in Continental races.

## A Long Distance Ride

The drive for higher public awareness of the company's bicycles worked to the advantage of two Polish engineers, Marian Kay (40) and Kazimierz Izmajlowicz (22). Living in Gloucestershire they had decided to team up for an 18,000 mile expedition to Australia. They were duly presented with two Lincoln Imp machines by Jim Turner, who saw them off from Australia House in July 1959.[22] Kazimierz got as far as the Turkish border before turning back due to visa problems. After five weeks he was forced to sell his bicycle and hitch-hiked back to England. Marian Kay continued alone to Australia, calling in at agents W & A Adler Frères in Istanbul. Mr Adler commented:

We thought we would have to cope with a badly damaged bicycle after the shocking road conditions

Mr Kay encountered on the way to Istanbul, but when we saw the cycle it looked practically as if it had come from the factory. Not only the frame, the wheels and all the parts were in excellent condition, but the finish was still good despite the heavy luggage.[23]

## Italian Styling – Coppi and Bertolini

Following the expensive failure of the Scoo-Ped attention was focussed on modernising the range of conventional bicycles and in August 1959 it was announced that the 'up and coming' Italian engineering and industrial designer, Enrico Bertolini of Milan, had been hired to create revolutionary new styles and colour schemes for the 1960 season.[24] In October 1959 an announcement was made that could have had a significant impact on the fortunes of the company: the great Italian rider Fausto Coppi had signed up as a technical adviser and stylist.[25] He was to work in close collaboration with Bertolini on the design of a new bicycle called the Coppi, which would undoubtedly have displaced the Imp as the top racing model. Coppi had little time to work on the new project as he left Paris in December 1959 for a high altitude training and safari trip to Burkina Faso, West Africa. He contracted malaria and died at home in Italy on 2 January 1960, just 40 years old. There is still, to this day, speculation as to exactly what happened, but ill-luck continued to dog the family, his brother Serse dying after a crash in the 1951 Tour of Piedmont, just 28 years old. Such was the stature of Fausto Coppi in the world of cycling that racing cycles are still made bearing his name 50 years after his death.

Moss visited the Bertolini studio and in September 1959 the designer was quoted as saying that he would make no attempt to improve on the strength and durability of traditional British bicycles: 'I am tremendously excited at being invited to style bicycles for Britain. My designs for the Elswick-Hopper fashion bicycles and the new club machine are nearly complete and I hope they will become as popular as the Italian line in fashions, furniture and cars.'[26]

The Bertolini range was attractively styled and Moss had asked for particular emphasis on ladies' models, getting involved personally in the colour combinations and design of transfers. Until then, there was little to distinguish gents' and ladies' bicycles, apart from the frame configuration. The Italian stamp was given to the new model names as well as to the hardware. The range fell into 5 categories: Ladies Fashion Tourist, Ladies Italian Fashion, Tourist, Juvenile and Sports. Apart from bread and butter names like Light Roadster, the only models carried over from 1959 were the Lincoln Imp (Fig. 7.12), Tour Anglais and Vogue, though the venerable Tour Anglais had become Prima, rather than de Luxe. The Fashion Range was the biggest break with convention with colours such as baby mink, violet and sylvan green, and special detachable shopping baskets and carriers available at extra cost. The purchaser's initials were also included in the price, for the lucky lady to affix in a special panel on the

*Fig. 7.12   1960 Lincoln Imp with new Italian styling.*

*Fig. 7.13   Taken at the Brigg Road showroom this is the 1960 Fiora, priced at £20 19s.*

chain guard. Names were Fiora (Fig. 7.13), Florentina, Forget Me Not, Itala, Rosebud and Violetta. These really were pretty, yet serviceable bicycles with the usual durable bonderised treatment under the paint finish. The star of the juvenile range was the Jetstream, designed specifically for the 12 to 15 age group. The frame was finished in a silver-blue colour with bright transfers, with a 19½ inch frame and 26 inch wheels. The saddle and saddle-bag were in TWA red, following an agreement with the airline company to reflect the colour of their Jetstream airliners. A special feature was the bell, shaped like a jet engine and painted in TWA red, silver and white.[27] Trans World Airlines gave over a main window in their Piccadilly showrooms for a display of the Jetstream to promote a competition run during September and October in the *Lion* and *Schoolfriend* children's magazines. There were 59 bicycles won from 27,000 entries. The price of a Jetstream shows that purchase tax was almost identical to VAT in 2007 at 17.3%. The bike sold to the trade for £10 9s 6d and retailed at £14 8s 11d. With tax at £2 10s 7d the full retail price was £16 19s 6d. This bicycle found favour with a reporter for the *Scottish Miner* in November 1959:

> It isn't often we women fall in love with a bicycle, but I've done just that. I was passing by when some young men were organising the photography of a new teenage bicycle.
> The bicycle was not like any I've ever seen. Known as the Elswick-Hopper Jetstream, it is brightly coloured on the lines of the sleek Jetstream airliners, whose predominant colour is brilliant red. This is certainly a change from the dreary bikes we used to have. Already I'm saving up for one for my favourite niece. I shall have hire purchase round my neck, but it'll be worth it to give her such pleasure. Price of the Jetstream? £16 19s 6d.

Other innovative junior models included the Olympic Orb, also available in TWA red frame with peacock blue trim and white mudguards, and the Black Beauty, with 18in frame and 24in wheels. The boy's model had a black frame with flamboyant orange trim and orange mudguards, whilst the girl's came with a peacock-blue trim and mudguards.[28] To the Sports models were added the Milano Maestro and the brand new top of the range Continentale, presumably with the final 'e' pronounced Italian style. This was the racer that would have borne the Coppi name.

A letter from Maurice Moss on 1 September 1959 to Newton, Armstrong & Co shows that the search for a profitable manufacturing strategy was uppermost in the minds of the new management team. A point of disagreement centred on the cost of exporting and Moss argued that this was higher than the consultants had estimated and, moreover, that sales effort should be concentrated on the domestic market by giving the sales team incentives to bring more retailers into the Elswick-Hopper fold. Moss handed control of the bicycle business to Jim Turner at the end of September 1959 and made mention of 'moving from the mausoleum back into the factory.' Reading between the lines it would appear that Moss was not happy dealing with personnel issues and described the problems he was experiencing in getting Bert Crofts out into the field with his sales team. Apart from this the Scoo-Ped disaster must have convinced him that textiles were, perhaps, a little different from bicycles. Moss appears to have taken little further interest in Elswick-Hopper and sometime in 1961 Jim Turner persuaded him to resign from the board – he had been extremely upset when Moss used company funds for a convalescence visit to the USA after a bout of typhoid in early 1959. Moss eventually moved to southern France, where he was murdered at his home sometime in the 1970s. Bert Crofts did not make it to retirement with Elswick-Hopper and left the company in early 1962, moving to a cycle firm in Birmingham. He died on 3 December 1962 while on a sales trip to Southampton.

## A Return to Petrol Power

Just 40 years after the last motorcycle left St Mary's Works Elswick-Hopper again entered the motorised market. Some of the information in this section has been supplied by Mark Daniels, who has written several articles for *Buzzing*, the appropriately named magazine of the National Autocycle and

Cyclemotor Club. The growth of the scooter and moped market in the 1950s saw the industry develop far beyond the old style 'bolt-on' engine-assisted bicycles. Typically, it was left to foreign companies to fill the gap between demand and supply and to capture the imagination of the young buyers with their French and Italian styling. Records show that UK makers supplied 83% of the domestic market for scooters in 1953 but this proportion had dropped to 38% by 1957.[29] Neither Phillips nor Raleigh showed interest in this lightweight end of the motorcycle market until the end of the decade when demand for mopeds took off, with Raleigh finally jumping in to take a large slice of the market.[30]

Fig. 7.14   The prototype Elswick-Trojan, built in 1952.

Elswick-Hopper had been approached by Trojan of Croydon as early as 1952 for the construction of a frame to test a new 2-speed moped motor.[31] This machine (Fig. 7.14) was registered 19 January 1953 with Lincolnshire number JFW 601, but it seems that Elswick-Hopper management were not impressed with the gearbox. Trojan persevered for a few months and their sales manager, George M Denton, competed in the ACU 24 hour rally in July 1953, taking a bronze medal with a distance of 303 miles. A lost opportunity to enter a new market, but moped production was not considered again until 1958 when, under the new management team, a programme of engine evaluation commenced. Bernard Hopfinger acted as consultant on this project, and the work was carried out in the Marsh Lane tool room. A prototype with a Dunkley engine was registered in July 1958 and covered many miles before failing at Skegness with a broken pushrod. Tool maker Barry Wood pushed it into Skegness and rang the works manager – 'a guy called Morton, a little guy – he used to shout a lot. He asked me what the hell I was doing in effing Skegness? I said I had been up all them hills in the Wolds, and had just got topped up with a gallon of petrol. Anyway they wouldn't let me on the train unless I emptied the fuel, and so the guard got a gallon of fuel. They picked me up from Brigg, I think.' So Barry was not at all impressed with the reliability of the British engine with its slender $1/8''$ diameter failure-prone push rods. Better results were achieved using a French Auto-Vap type 57 engine and a testing and development programme followed. Keith Clarke got to spend a few weeks at the ex-Heinz Scootamatic premises in Nottingham at the request of John Stockdale: "I happened to walk in the shop one afternoon and he said, 'Ah, Keith, you have a motor bike don't you? Mr Moss wants us to send somebody down to this place in Nottingham for two or three weeks. We want you to get one of the Auto-Vap engines and strip every little bit.' There were three models, the Standard, Deluxe and Super Deluxe, and my job was to strip every model down, every little piece had to be laid on a big bench with a white sheet and they put a catalogue number on each piece as part of making their own parts catalogue in English. They were a lovely little engine." The preparation of prototypes took some time to complete due

*Fig. 7.15  On the MIRA test track. From right to left: Alan Manchester, Dennis Moody, Peter Warcup, Keith Clark, Barry Wood and John Stockdale.*

*Fig. 7.16  Harold Hunsley and Barry Wood reunited with the two Earl Court Lynx mopeds at a gathering in Barton during 1993.*

to delivery problems from the French factory and culminated in six machines being taken to the MIRA proving ground at Nuneaton in July 1959. Five toolmakers – Barry Wood, Dennis Moody, Keith Clark, Peter Warcup and Alan Manchester – enjoyed a break from routine work, riding on the test circuits and foreman John Stockdale supervised the operation with Bernard Hopfinger (Fig. 7.15). They discovered that the ground had been booked by Hercules a week earlier and that their frames failed after just two days on the notorious pavé section. Just one of the Elswick prototypes experienced a failure – of a fork brake anchor. The prototypes used Hopper frames, forks and handlebars, with bought in wheels and petrol tank.

By August the company was getting close to an official announcement and Sales Controller Bert Crofts told a visiting group of dealers from Liverpool that he had been 'thrilled to bits' with the performance of the prototype moped he had ridden at MIRA. Apart from telling them that it would have a Continental engine and that he hoped they would be on sale from March or April the following year, Bert gave out no more details. Pressure was now on to finalise the production model in time for the November Earls Court Show. The purposeful looking bicycle frame derived prototype was hidden by a pair of hand beaten panels and the tank relocated beneath the saddle. A two-tone blue colour scheme was selected and the Lynx name sign written on the front panels and rear mudguards by one of the highly skilled liners, Harold Hunsley (Fig. 7.16). The two show models were fitted with 20″ wheels, in-house leading link front forks and Miller lighting. Both machines were 'rescued' by local enthusiasts and one was sold to Mark Daniels in 2002. It needed considerable work before it was roadworthy, but Mark succeeded in restoring it to its former glory and was quite impressed by the crisp performance of the Vap engine, which he found gave a pleasant cruising speed of 25 mph.

In October 1959 it was announced that Scootamatic Ltd (the renamed Scoo-Ped Ltd) had become the UK concessionaires for a range of three Vap engined French mopeds with single control automatic clutch.[32] They were to be marketed from the Nottingham premises, at Glaisdale Drive, Aspley, and new depots had been opened at London Airport, Manchester and Wolverhampton. The models were to be known as the Standard, De Luxe and Super De Luxe, and dealers were expected to be fully trained to handle servicing, with specialist expertise provided by a force of Scootamatic service engineers. Import of the Italian lightweight Capri scooter, with associated service and spare parts

Fig. 7.17   A leaflet for the Agrati Capri scooter sold by Scootamatic.

Fig. 7.18   The Auto-Vap 48.5cc Caravelle as it appeared in the 1960 riding and maintenance instruction booklet.

facilities, was announced at the same time (Fig. 7.17). This deal was with the manufacturers, Agrati, and was based on selling 10,000 scooters per year.

It is fairly clear that the decision to import Auto-Vap mopeds (Fig. 7.18) must have been made well before the November Earls Court Show. Perhaps there were no Auto-Vap machines available, though a party of dealers was shown the new moped during a visit to Barton in November, eliciting comments that it was a delightful machine to handle, owing particularly to the simplicity of the controls and the quietness of the engine.[33] In any event, on stand 83 Scootamatic displayed the two Lynx models in all their Show-prepared glory, though alongside machines from Auto-Vap, Capri, Honda and Laverda. A major factor in the decision to become concessionaires was that the estimated production cost of £58 did not exactly compare well with a selling price of £56 13s for the equivalent Auto-Vap. Even so the *Investors' Chronicle* of November 1959 recorded that Scootamatic was planning to introduce its own British moped of an advanced design in 1960. Given the costings this plan was wisely shelved, so perhaps something had been learned from the Scoo-ped debacle, and Auto-Vaps were imported from France until 1963.

The French connection gave John Stockdale and Barry Wood the opportunity to visit the factory in Paris and Barry was given the job of writing the English manuals with the assistance of an interpreter. It was the first time either had been abroad and John didn't like the flight in the turbo prop Viscount at all. Barry spent a solid eight hours a day asking questions, but at least they had the opportunity to visit the Eiffel Tower and Palace of Versailles.

As we have seen Elswick-Hopper was not alone in wanting a slice of moped profits and at an industry dinner in Nottingham in early 1960 A E Cave of Raleigh exhorted the retail trade to take in the moped business: 'Only the fortunate cycle trader can nowadays turn his back on the moped sales that are coming along. The rising standard of living has meant that many people were now looking for a cheap form of powered personal transport.' Scootamatic commenced a major sales drive, with nine salesmen employed during the quarter to 31 March 1961. Based on their commissions sales were 26% Auto-Vap, 10% Laverda and 64% Capri. During the period 2,290 Capri scooters had been sold, surely an indication of where the potential lay. Other imports included the Laverda mini-scooter,[34] but more significantly, Scootamatic turned down the opportunity in June 1961 to import the Honda 50:

No Hondas from Scootamatic

Scootamatic Ltd of Glaisdale Drive West, Aspley, Nottingham, announces that following comprehensive tests of the Japanese Honda 50 lightweight motor cycle and investigations into its market potential, the company will not act as concessionaire for the machine in Great Britain.[35]

According to the NACC the first imports of the Honda 50 did not start until November 1962. It has to be wondered what the contribution would have been to future profitability had the 'comprehensive tests' yielded more positive results. However, it is likely that management were concerned at the level of investment required and the risks involved in such a venture. By late-1963 Honda had opened a factory in Belgium aimed specifically at the 50cc moped market. At the time Honda had been in business for just 15 years. Starting with £1,000 capital, Soichiro Honda was the son of a blacksmith.[36] A deal with Honda would, in hindsight, have been a fantastic opportunity for the company, but they failed to grasp it. As for the comprehensive tests it is doubtful that any took place, as employees simply recall a Honda lurking in a corner of the factory for a few months.

In January 1960 Scootamatic had 3415 machines on dealer consignment and 3387 at the depots, which numbered seven at that time. It is not surprising that the return to motorised transport did little for company profits and diverted resources that would have been more usefully applied to selling bicycles. It is clear that the company was committed to the import business, and to cater for the north-west of the country even opened a new depot in Urmston, near Manchester. Near the main railway line the depot had space for thousands of mopeds, scooters and bicycles and meant that 'Auto-Vaps and Capri scooters, after being loaded at the French and Italian factories, only have to be unloaded at the door of the new depot in perfect ex-factory condition.'[37] Auto-Vaps and Capris did sell, but not in the numbers necessary to support the new subsidiary. Scootamatic sputtered along for a few months, relocating from Nottingham to St Mary's Works, Barton in early 1962,[38] and ceased trading the following year, though some machines and spares were handled by the parent company until 1970. Looking at the advertising coverage for the Auto-Vap during 1960 it is clear that the company did its best to promote sales. The adverts are interesting in that there was no attempt to leverage the Elswick-Hopper name, unlike other British cycle makers entering the market. It is almost as if Scootamatic was left to sink or swim. The separation of mopeds from bicycles also loaded the new venture with its own management, sales and service staff, with associated overheads. Perhaps the growth in UK moped sales led management to believe that Scootamatic could not fail. *Cycling* of 16 October 1960 reported a moped boom with 10,774 registrations in August compared with 6,874 the previous year. There is no doubt that the moped market was ignored by UK cycle manufacturers for far too long. This was especially the case with Elswick-Hopper and the Auto-Vap had to compete against machines that had already become established, and were being sold under well known brand names.

## AGM 31 December 1959

An astonishing amount had happened in less than two years and in a further break with traditions the 1959 AGM was held at the new Scootamatic headquarters in Nottingham. Jim Turner thought that this would be a more convenient venue for shareholders and would give those attending the opportunity to visit the new premises. Times were changing and Jim confirmed that the last 12 months had seen a reorganisation of virtually every facet of the company's activities. As a result of the advertising campaign, and an expanded sales force, home sales had increased substantially and now accounted for 75% of turnover. The order book was full but 'production had been somewhat retarded by shortages of labour and supplies. The recruitment of satisfactory local labour is proving difficult and the existing factory layout is not conducive to modern productive methods.' Turner went on to warn that heavy capital expenditure would be necessary if the company aspired to a place in the forefront of the cycle industry.

The new production and cost control systems that had been announced a year before were almost in place and were providing reliable interim trading figures. Purchasing arrangements had also been reorganised to reduce reliance on components from competitor bicycle manufacturers, through a search for new UK and European suppliers. Turner assured shareholders that the losses of the past two years had been arrested, though full benefits would only come through at the end of the next financial year. He concluded with positive news on Midland Motor Company seven months into the acquisition, but advised that it was necessary to raise additional capital to finance current expansion plans.

Following the formation of the Elswick-Hopper Cycle and Motor Co (Manufacturing) Ltd in 1958 there had been a transfer of the net assets of the parent organisation to the new company at the end of the next financial year in July 1959 in exchange for 382,900 shares of £1 each. This action was reported in the *Motor Cycle and Cycle Trader* on 1 January 1960:

> Unfortunately, this deprives the consolidated accounts of the comparative figures for the previous year but the group loss for the period under review was £38,190 and, after a transfer of £40,000 from general reserve, the carry forward is down to £6,440. Needless to say there is no dividend recommended on the Ordinary capital although net current assets are £234,596, largely made up of stock and work in progress and debtors.

The November *Investors' Chronicle* offered the following advice to a potential investor:

> Elswick-Hopper shares were well regarded a few years back, but sentiment changed following the decline in earnings which set in around 1952-3 and which culminated in a trading loss being sustained for 1957-8. But conditions now appear to be improving, assisted by the diversification of interests. Besides the manufacture of the usual range of bicycles a new subsidiary, Scoo-Ped, has been formed to market a new all-weather fibre-glass covered bicycle which has already met with a favourable response. In April Midland Motor Company was acquired, which carries on business as hirers for commercial vehicles. A more recent development is the formation of a further subsidiary, Scootamatic, to arrange the distribution of the French Auto-Vap, a moped with a single twist-grip control which eliminates gear changing. Scootamatic is planning to introduce its own British moped of an advanced design in 1960. It is evident that the board of Elswick-Hopper is sparing no efforts to take the fullest advantage of the 80-year goodwill of the company. It is possible, therefore, that the net loss of £29,000 recorded for the year to July 31, 1958, when the dividend was passed, might well be turned into a profit when the results for the past year are made available later in the month. We regard the 5s shares now 4s 3d as a long shot, but, provided you are willing to speculate, we would not stop you buying a few.

It appears that the company had not made public its decision to drop the Lynx moped, but there was no further development in that direction. As for taking the fullest advantage of 80 years of goodwill, the creation of a new company put paid to that idea.

## A Big Anniversary

The start of the new decade was declared as the 80th anniversary of the company. Happily this coincided with the introduction of the Italian range, including the new top-of-the-range Continentale. The racing team took to the road to demonstrate the new bicycle, along with team manager Benny Foster. Tour de France rider Brian Robinson had joined the team at the end of the season and accompanied Benny, Ron Coe, Owen Blower and John Geddes. Ron Coe commented that, 'We're really enjoying ourselves. Selling is quite a change from racing though it's just as tough!'[39] Within a few days they learned that the team did not have a future in 1960.

A special 80th anniversary model was the Gay Sixties. This was a lady's bicycle in black with primrose trim, primrose saddle and kitbag, both trimmed with black and primrose handlegrips and brake cables. With carrier and basket it retailed at £19 19s 0d, also known in those days as 19 guineas. The Continentale was described in the 15 January 1960 *Motor Cycle and Cycle Trader* as the 'pièce de résistance'. It retailed at £33 12s 0d and 'into this machine Elswick-Hopper has put all its accumulated

*Fig. 7.19   1960 Vogue Modèle, selected by Hollywood.*

knowledge and experience of bicycle design and manufacture combined with the contemporary inspiration of the firm's Italian designer.' The result was a bicycle with a Continental feature-cut lug set and crown, chrome plated top and bottom head lugs and continental pedals. Frame sizes were 21½″, 22½″ and 23½″.

Despite a 50% hike in import duty in 1955 the American market was still important to Elswick-Hopper and Jim Turner was pictured in the *Motor Cycle & Cycle Export Trader* of March 1960 with W L Wilde and K W Hunt of the Hunt-Wilde Corporation of Dayton Ohio, grouped around a new Rosebud model. Further US exposure came from the selection of a Vogue Modèle (Fig. 7.19) for the Columbia Pictures film 'Our Man in Havana'. This was ridden by Jo Morrow, who played the part of Milly, the daughter of the Alec Guinness character, Jim Wormold. Photographs of her on the bicycle were displayed in cinema foyers where the film was showing. In some cinemas local dealers even supplied the real thing to gain publicity.

Glamour was again enlisted for the Easter Parade held in Battersea Park, where the Elswick-Hopper display featured 12 Tiller Girls riding the latest fashion cycles. Vespa and Lambretta were also represented in the parade.[40]

The growing influence of television advertising was reported in the *Motor Cycle and Cycle Trader* of 17 June 1960, with an article by Elswick-Hopper group sales controller E R Sulley. This covered the Granada TV programme 'Talking Shop', which had featured the Scootamatic range of Auto-Vap mopeds. As a first venture into TV the trial was confined to a single area so that its impact could be better measured. Sulley was delighted with the results, especially where dealers had followed up with local newspaper adverts.

Elswick-Hopper participated again in the annual York Rally with a display of the Continentale, Lincoln Imp, Tour Anglais and Milano Maestro. Bert Crofts represented the company and was a popular rally personality.[41] The final of the Yorkshire children's cycling proficiency championships was held at the rally with the winner receiving a Jetstream bicycle.

The mid-year forward production plan was produced by George Franklin on the basis of producing 1,750 machines per week. Over a 50-week production year this gave a works capacity of 87,500 bicycles a year. At this time Elswick-Hopper was not advertising on a routine basis. During 1960 adverts were placed in only 10 issues of the weekly *Cycling* magazine; just two in *Motor Cycle and Cycle Trader* and two in the *National Journal*.

The loss of Fausto Coppi did not deter the company from searching for another cycling star and in the middle of the year Brian Robinson signed a long-term contract as a technical and design consultant for sports bicycles. Brian had been one of the most successful English riders on the Continent and was the first to win a stage of the Tour de France, the seventh of the 1959 Tour. He capped this achievement by also winning the 20th stage by more than 20 minutes. He had already ridden with the short-lived Hopper-Milremo team and had appeared in full page adverts for the new Continentale, but according to a *Cycling* report of 27 July 1960 his first task was to advise the company's designers on the styling and specification of a new lightweight that would carry his name. It was supposed to be ready for the November Earls Court Show.[42] Brian recalls visiting Barton on occasions between Continental races during 1960 and remained on the books as 'team manager' until 1961, also appearing in company advertisements – 'Robinson leads….on Elswick-Hopper.'[43] Although transfers were designed and printed they never graced a Barton-built bike; the coming downturn put such developments firmly on the back-burner.

*Fig. 7.20   Yahaya Bin Bahari with his Hopper bicycle at its 'birthplace'. From left to right with Yahaya: A J M Grassick, George Franklin and Peter Stow.*

*Fig. 7.21   A Malaysian customer with Elswick-Hopper management, from left to right:*

*Henry Cole, George Franklin, Leslie Marshall, Harry Heselton, Bert Crofts, Leslie Green and Peter Stow. Location is the Elswick building.*

## More Long Distance Rides

Marian Kay's ride to Australia was eclipsed by Malaysian cyclist Yahaya Bin Bahari. The 31-year old visited the factory in Barton on Humber in 1960, where he met executive director A G M Grassick, works director George Franklin and export manager Peter Stow (Fig. 7.20). They took him on a tour of the factory, gave him a donation of £10 towards expenses and sent him off to the London offices to meet Jim Turner, who gave him a further £25. His Hopper export 'Special' roadster had been delivered to a dealer in Ipoh in 1957 and he started his round the world ride in March 1959. Over the following 16 months he had covered 40,000 miles and visited 30 countries, riding through Thailand, India,

Pakistan, Iran, Syria, Lebanon, Jordan and Egypt, before arriving in Europe. The journey had presented many challenges, with sand storms, torrential rain, insect attacks and at one stage a wind so strong that he and his machine were blown into the sea! Despite this and heavy luggage of 100lb the bicycle had been trouble free, requiring just new rear tyres every 10,000 miles and front tyres every 20,000. After a few weeks in the UK Yahaya planned to cycle through the USA, with Ottawa, Canada as his ultimate destination. The ex-soldier and trapeze artist had done some hard training rides in the year before leaving Malaysia to prove the machine and had been confident that it would carry him round the world with no trouble.[44] Malaysian dealers continued to be loyal customers of the company and Fig. 7.21 shows a visit from a buyer from the peninsular.

## Another Downturn

The buoyant mood at the start of the decade did not last long, but public statements were necessarily upbeat in order to maintain public confidence in the company. Around the middle of 1960 an undated report by Jim Turner marked 'Strictly Private and Confidential' shows that a plan to liquidate the manufacturing assets at Barton was being considered. Stocks and work in progress were valued at £335,000, plant and machinery at £32,000 and land and buildings at £40,000, a total of £407,000. Of this, 10,000 finished bicycles were valued at £96,000, the majority in the form of consignment stock. This method of selling had long been a bone of contention between manufacturers and retailers as it gave too little incentive to the retailer to move stock. Turner proposed breaking ranks with the BCMCIA membership by giving dealers an extra 10% discount by way of an advertising allowance, for purchasing stock outright and that the same discount should apply to future sales. This applied to the 350 dealers selling 25 or more bicycles per year. Distributors were to be given six months notice, after which dealers would be approached directly. Depot stocks were to be cleared and their cycle sections closed, after which deliveries would be made directly from Barton to the 350 main dealers. Henry Coles was to be appointed materials and production controller charged with buying in any components still made in-house. The result would be the closure of the following sections:

> Machine Shop
> Case Hardening
> Press Shop
> Tube Making
> Polishing-rough, smooth and buffing
> Gearcase Department
> Mudguard Department
> Plating – nickel and chrome
> Handlebar and Brake Assembly
> Canteen
> Tool Room (part)

Once this had been achieved the factory was to become an assembly operation comprising the following sections:

> Frame and Fork Building
> Painting
> Frame Assembly
> Wheel Building
> Machine Erection
> Tool Room (part)

Surplus plant and machinery were to be offered to overseas buyers setting up domestic factories, and enquiries had already been received from Iran and Peru. Scootamatic Ltd spares were to be relocated from Nottingham to Barton utilising redundant labour and space. Finally remaining redundant space was to be sold or let.

These proposals were revealed to senior managers only and they were instructed to maintain secrecy in an effort to prevent rumours that the company was going out of business and to allow an orderly and controlled redundancy of labour.

Publicly Jim Turner remained optimistic but was worried by the recent merger of Raleigh and the TI companies. His concern was that the newly-formed giant would dominate both home and export markets due to economies of scale and availability of cash for sales campaigns and dealer incentives. However he believed that Elswick-Hopper, as the largest of the cycle companies outside the Raleigh TI group, had competitive advantages that stemmed from:

> ...originality harnessed to experience; great pride in our products and a 'know-how' and personal attention to detail in the production of our bicycles unrivalled by anyone in the industry.

The creation of Raleigh TI was, of course, a response to a declining market and gave the new company 90% of UK exports and 70% of home sales.[45] It was also a response to intensified competition from Europe and Asia for Raleigh's traditional export markets and the growing trend to domestic manufacture in these countries, with India as a notable example.[46] Although still the largest independent bicycle maker in the country Elswick-Hopper did not have the cash to grow by merger, could not afford to modernise its Edwardian factory and so had to search for alternative survival strategies.

In a progress report written by A G M Grassick dated September 1960 it was reported that 64,658 cycles and frame sets had been sold in the previous 12 months, of which 25,590 were export sales. Labour levels had been trimmed by reducing overtime, an action that had 'induced personnel to seek employment elsewhere.' After consultation with the trade union representative 20 married women had been 'suspended and a number of full time employees had been told that they would lose their jobs by the middle of the month. These actions were aimed at reducing employee numbers by 70. Finished bicycle stocks had been cut to 8,700. Rumours had been rife, as would be expected in a small community like Barton, and a statement was made to the press on September 9 to 'refute the rumour that the company is closing down.' Grassick blamed hire purchase restrictions for a cut in sales, as the previous year, before the restrictions, the factory could not meet demand.

On 3 February 1961 Turner wrote a very troubled letter to Maurice Moss. He reported that the workforce had been cut by about 130 and that the sales force comprised just four men – Crofts, Linley, Young and Fleming. However, the bicycle operation was apparently the least of his worries – all was not well at Scootamatic. Raleigh had decided to sell only the Mobylette, and to clear 23,000 Corvettes, Pandas and Nippys, had slashed retail prices by £10 to £14, also giving dealers £10 credit notes for each machine in stock. In response Scootamatic had offered consignment stock to selected dealers with a sliding scale rebate and had managed to clear about 350 Auto-Vaps on that basis. However, this left a whopping stock of 2,900 machines. Of these, 500 single seaters were being converted at Barton to dual seat models. But, in Turner's words:

> Trade is still terrible – the public not buying and everyone overstocked. We are still owed a lot of money despite writs, etc.

The situation with Capri scooters was the same: 1250 70cc and 1600 80cc in stock and more in transit. The Laverda scooter concession was a little different in that the supplier was insisting on firm orders. Agreement was reached after a price reduction and lowering of delivery charges. In summary Jim Turner wrote that:

> Pervading all our thoughts is the financial position. Total bank borrowing is £480,000 and we cannot go beyond. Capri/Scootamatic is £350,000 of this and where the trouble lies. With nearly 6,000 machines in stock and hundreds of thousands of pounds owed to us by the trade, it is not surprising. We have had to take many drastic steps. I have seen Agrati (Capri scooters) who has agreed to defer maturity on some of his bills. We have cut the sales force considerably and are closing Hounslow and Urmston, going back

to central distribution. I am afraid that these depots have been good examples of Parkinson's Law in respect of staff as well as tempting dealers to rely on them for stocking instead of ordering.

Despite these frank admissions Turner ended on a characteristically optimistic note:

If we can hold on financially for the next six months I have every confidence in the future of the company and can see no reason why your shares should not be worth 12/6d in two years time.

This ambitious share price was never realised but by 1963 Moss had already sold his interest. The ironic twist was that history had repeated itself, as it has a nasty habit of doing. What seemed like a natural diversification into motorised transport had not been backed by sufficient financial resources to support consequential cash flow problems, and had struck almost a mortal blow to the company, just as it had in 1913. But, like Fred Hopper, Jim Turner was not about to give up the fight.

The early 1960s was not entirely gloom and doom for the industry as proved by the launch of Alex Moulton's small wheeled bicycle at the 1962 Earls Court Cycle and Motor Cycle Show. It was so well received by the public that Moulton doubled the size of his factory on the strength of orders from the Show.[47] Elswick-Hopper eventually responded with the 20" wheel Continentale, but not until 1965, a year when the majority of UK makers woke up to the fact that this market was too large to ignore.

## Survival

Despite all the set backs Elswick-Hopper continued limited production at Barton for quite a few more years, though it is perhaps surprising that Jim Turner was so reluctant to give up on the company's traditional product. It was not until the early 1970s that he began to diversify in earnest. As we have seen there were serious moves to cut overheads, a major step taking place in 1961, when the registered office moved to St Mary's Works. The impressive offices on Brigg Road, built in 1905, and referred to by Moss as 'the mausoleum', were no longer needed and the two packing shops and sawmill were also closed, consolidating the whole operation on to the main factory site. The grand office building was used as a snooker hall for some years, then as an engineering drawing office, and eventually as a second-hand furniture store. The condition gradually deteriorated until finally, in 2005, a bold scheme was devised by Barry Smith of Copperfield Developments to construct luxury apartments.

Part of the plot housing the export packing shop and saw mill buildings on the south side of Castledyke South was leased to Birds Eye Frozen Foods in June 1966 for £1300 pa, for Brussels sprout preparation. This lease continued until September 1970. Three other buildings on the site were used by Cliff Beedham for car bodywork repairs. Eventually the site was inevitably sold for housing some 20 years later. While excavating the foundations human remains were found and work on the development was held up for several months while a Saxon burial ground was uncovered.

Elswick-Hopper had been for many years an excellent company in which to learn a trade, especially for those fortunate enough to go through the tool room apprenticeship scheme. Unfortunately, Fred Hopper's realisation that he could produce components cheaper than the big companies in the Midlands no longer applied in 1961 and so, at a stroke, the machine shop became surplus to requirements, and with it, much of the function of the tool makers. There were many sales of machine tools throughout 1961, and the sad end of the Elswick-Hopper apprenticeship scheme was announced in the *Lincolnshire Times* of 26 February 1961. In reality component manufacture had been uneconomic for some time. The same newspaper featured an article on 11 March on the industrial deterioration of Barton in which Councillor Ben Sharpe pointed out that employment for 500 men had disappeared during the past 20 or 25 years and this had been emphasised in recent months by decreased production at the local cycle works (where he had once worked). 'The reason, of course, in an age of mopeds, motorcycles and cars, there is a decreasing demand for cycles.' Miss Handsley added to the nostalgia for past industries in the *Lincolnshire Times* on 25 March, providing an interesting perspective on the boom employment years when Barton provided so much employment:

Gone from our midst: a once prosperous cement works, three whiting mills, a tannery, boot and shoe factory, a small candle house, brickyards, a chalk quarry, gas works, corn grinding mills, lime kilns, several blacksmiths, carriers, milk dairies, coal depots employing men with drays and horses, a small pottery where plant pots were made, a small cod liver oil works, a sail loft for making and repairing of sloop and keel sails, and lastly, many sloops and keels employing two men each for sailing purposes, needing wheelers, whippers, and stowage hands for the loading and unloading of the many and varied cargoes which came into and went out of Barton to Hull, Grimsby, up the canals and rivers Ouse, Trent and Ancholme going as far as York, Leeds, Newark, and Gainsborough with the picturesque three-masted schooners loading bricks, tiles, drainpipes etc for London and Aberdeen.

Amidst all the gloom substantial orders were still being captured, and in September 1961 W H Smith & Son Ltd ordered 500 cycles for their paperboys. These were to be built to a precise specification for delivery to New Fetter Lane, London, and other destinations advised by Smiths. Price was £12 15s 0d delivered, colour black, chrome bars and levers and no pump, pump pegs or bell. The long term requirements were fixed by the number of machines removed from the pool each month and Smiths kept a stock of 130 bicycles in London for immediate requirements. This contract continued at least until 1966. However, given the general business climate a loss of £1372 was posted for 1961.

A link with the Edwardian years was broken in 1962 when works director George Franklin died in April, still working at the age of 69. George had started working for Fred Hopper as an office boy in 1905 and had served for 56 years. George's brothers had also made a career in the industry, but in the retail trade, with a shop in George Street, later relocating to the Market Place. Franklin Brothers was unusual in that it sold both Elswick and Hopper models, probably due to being the hometown agent. Lack of adequate pension schemes meant that long service, well past normal retirement, was not at all unusual as illustrated by a report in the *Lincolnshire Times* on 18 August 1962, relating the career of Walter Jennings. Walter also joined Hopper's in 1905 as a 14 year old to train as a machinist. He saw army service in France where he survived a poison gas attack and was still working as timekeeper in 1962 at the age of 72.

There were five sales areas in England and Wales in 1964 with Ireland and Scotland covered by agents. The unit sales cover the period 1 October 1963 to 30 September 1964.

| Area Designation | Territory | Representative/ (Dealers) | Cycles/Frames Sold |
|---|---|---|---|
| A1 | Ireland | J H Gass Belfast | 284 |
| A2 | Scotland | Alex Cheyne Ltd | 1364 |
| 5 | Miscellaneous | ★ | 721/4313 |
| B1 | Lancs, Tamworth, Market Drayton, Cheshire, Wolverhampton, Newport | J K Hogan/(337) | 5238 |
| B2 | Yorks, Lincs, Derby, Northumberland, Leics, Notts, Durham | J Benson/(264) | 6822 |
| B3 | London, Hants, Kent, Sussex | G H Fleming/(246) | 8633 |
| B4 | Norfolk, Suffolk, Middx, Beds, Northants, Essex, Bucks, Cambs. | B J Young/(228) | 8310 |
| B5 | Warwicks, Oxford, Dorset, Wales, Worcs, Gloucs. | W S Howells/(171) | 2737 |
| | **Total** | | **34109/4313** |

* The miscellaneous category was reserved for direct customers, such as Brown Brothers, the East Midlands Gas Board (204) and W H Smiths (238). It also included the two Barton bike shops, Franklin Bros (68) and Ellerby's (82), and SITA World Travel (38). All 4313 frame sets listed under miscellaneous were for Browns, confirming the continuing importance of this customer. The six representatives covered a total of 1246 cycle dealers and sold 31,740 cycles, or an average of 25 per shop. Selling was clearly a tough business, with Fleming and Young the most successful, averaging 35 and 36 cycles per shop over the year. They did, of course, have the advantage of the two most densely populated areas. A typical salary was £840 pa + £200 commission.

October 1964 saw the end of retail price maintenance under Harold Wilson's new Labour government, to be followed in 1965 by his Prices and Incomes Board. April 1965 saw the sales team equipped with new technology in the shape of a case of slides and a stereoscopic viewer. This device presumably saved carting around too many samples.

In February 1965 McKenna, who had taken over from Grassick as managing director, decided that there was sufficient wheel building capacity to supply dealers with their replacement wheel requirements. This has always been a large market in the UK, due in part to the propensity of children to ride up kerbs and in part to the ravages caused by salted winter roads, and is one still served from Barton by Target Wheel Products Ltd. He instructed the four area salesmen – by this date Linley and Crofts had retired and been replaced by Rackley and Benson – to offer a total of 200 pairs per week. The specification was for 26" x 1$^3/_8$" wheels, built with Rigida rims and Raleigh hubs. Once import duty surcharge was reduced he would prefer to buy Pelissier hubs, provided they were supplied with Imperial sized nuts. The French component manufacturer already supplied hubs for the Sports Light Roadster, but had initially used metric nuts – presumably to the consternation of pre-metric buyers, though European components had been imported for many years before this date, and were very popular with enthusiasts. Christmas drinks were an inducement to buy wheels later that year. In addition to a 4% discount for payment within ten days, and avoidance of a price rise in January, gin, vodka and whisky were on offer – one bottle with 30 wheels, three with 75 and 5 with 100.

Fleming decided to leave Elswick-Hopper early in 1965 to run his own business. Ever the gentleman he stayed on for some weeks so that his replacement could be trained and was also offered consignment stock. In making the offer McKenna was quite persuasive, stating that: 'It may mean only the sale of half a dozen bicycles for us during the year, but it would help to keep you in touch with the business in which you have steeped yourself for most of your life.' He was due to leave at the end of April, but it seems that the company valued his services too much to let him go. In July 1965 he received written confirmation from Jim Turner of his appointment as field sales manager at a salary of £1,500 per annum and a commission of £150 plus 0.05% of any increase in turnover over the previous years figure of £344,574. His appointment entailed moving to Barton, for which an allowance of £50 was offered.

Comparing employee numbers for 1966 with 1965 it is clear that Jim Turner's plan for liquidating the cycle company assets had not been put into effect:

| Job | 1965 employees | 1966 employees |
|---|---|---|
| Van drivers, loading and despatch | 3 | 6 |
| Rough polishing | 3 | 4 |
| Tool room and plant maintenance | 1 | 2 |
| Frame building | 31 | 33 |
| Enamelling | 33 | 33 |
| Lining | 6 | 6 |
| Frame erecting | 8 | 8 |
| Machine erecting and export shop | 27 | 26 |
| Wheel building | 15 | 16 |
| Stores | 3 | 2 |
| Mudguard | 3 | 2 |

| | | |
|---|---:|---:|
| Gearcase | 3 | 4 |
| Press | 4 | 4 |
| Electrical | 1 | 1 |
| Engines and boilers | 2 | 2 |
| Repair | 1 | 1 |
| Time office | 1 | 1 |
| Machine shop | 2 | 2 |
| Wrapping | 5 | 6 |
| Toys and Auto-Vap | 2 | 3 |
| **TOTAL** | **154** | **162** |

*Fig. 7.22   Nigel Haddock with his Scout Trailblazer bicycle outside George Fleming's house on Caistor Road.*

The company was still searching for ways to boost sales as shown in a memo from George Fleming to R A McKenna in May 1966. A new range of scout bikes was planned to be launched in June – the Trailblazer and smaller Trailblazer Cub, both in Scout green and gold mudguards and chainguard, and the Venturer in Scout red. The idea of a special Scout and Guide range had first surfaced in 1960 but co-ordination with the Boy Scouts and Girl Guides Associations for the production of special transfers took time to arrange. Finally, a seven year agreement was reached and the launch took place during the Fathers' Day event at Scout Headquarters in Gilwell Park, near Chingford, Essex – still the home of the movement. Fig. 7.22 shows a young Nigel Haddock in his Barton Scout uniform outside George Fleming's house on Caistor Road, with one of the new bicycles. The company was also considering building some police models for Southend police, who were contemplating a return to two wheeled transport in response to 'enormous parking problems'. They sent in an enquiry for six police bicycles to be built with 24"frames and 28" wheels. The choice between motorised and bicycle transport for the police has been debated for many years since then. Despite these developments Fleming was disappointed at the state of trade, and wrote that 'it is quite a long time since I have known of such a general recession in trade.'

The first purchases of Japanese components date from 1964, when chains were bought from the Meisei Trading Company. Despite 16% import duty and a surcharge of 15% introduced in 1964 the cost of a 104 link chain was 2s 8½d compared to 3s 6½d from Perry. These are 1966 prices, and heralded the death knell of British cycle component manufacture. In that year discussions also took place with Queensmead Components Ltd for the supply of Japanese bottom bracket and chain wheel sets.

The industrial unrest of the period did not help the company in its efforts to expand its remaining export markets. After trying for some time to re-enter the Irish market a small order had been won for 50 bicycles to be delivered to Walker's of Dublin in early May. Due to the threat of a seamen's strike the order was rushed through the factory, packed and loaded on a train at Barton station, where the company was told that the four cases would be in Holyhead ready for shipment within two to three days. In follow up to a letter from the customer, asking what had happened to the bicycles, McKenna wrote to the British Railways area sales officer in Grimsby:

We are frustrated, and so is our customer....

On Monday, 23 May we received a letter from the customer in Dublin advising us that they had no information that the goods were in Dublin and would we find out what had happened to them. Our local station could not help us; all they knew was that the four cases had been forwarded. We got in touch by telephone with the Missing and Tracing Goods Department at Doncaster, and they advised us that it would take two/three days to find out what had happened. On Wednesday lunchtime they telephoned to tell us that the wagon holding the goods had not arrived at Holyhead early enough to catch the last sailing on 15 May to Dublin, and the goods were now at Holyhead waiting for the seamen's strike to settle. Nine days from lifting the goods at Barton on Humber to the quayside at Holyhead.

We have had to write to our customer today to explain the situation (as best we can) and hope that the seamen's strike terminates quickly to allow the goods to go forward.

In view of the unfortunate balance of payments position it seems a pity that our efforts to introduce our goods into a new market should be thwarted by such an extraordinary period of time for carriage.

McKenna concluded by asking for the reason for the delay and learned that it had been caused by a strike of British Railways guards in the Manchester area, the effect of which was to lock in the Barton consignment. The strike, which resulted in a State of Emergency being declared, lasted until 29 June, no doubt adding to the frustration of both McKenna and customer. According to Walker's, the strike had given Raleigh the opportunity to push their Irish factory bicycles. This was the year when the RSW 16 was introduced and had the advantage of being a home-produced alternative to the Elswick-Hopper models.

In June 1966 McKenna wrote to all representatives to give them his view of prospects for the year, knowing that 'at this time of year you must be feeling despondent about the general prospects.' In fact sales for the first four months of the financial year from 1 February were up on the two previous years. This was primarily due to the introduction of the Boy Scout range, the impact of the Continentale shopper (far removed from the racing machine of the same name), and the new Lincoln Imp. He saw no reason why the rest of the year should not be at least up to the level of the last three, with a good build-up to the Christmas rush. However, he also acknowledged the impact of the restrictive purchasing practices imposed by the government, which were achieving the aim of delaying spending by the public. He was referring to the impact of the prices and incomes controls imposed by the Department of Economic Affairs set up by the Labour government in 1964, which placed a six month freeze on prices and wages after the re-election of Labour in March 1966, and to the increased cost of imported components caused by a 15% surcharge. These measures were intended to head off a growing balance of payments crisis. In the event a run on sterling began, leading to eventual devaluation in November 1967.[48]

In this climate the board decided once again not to exhibit at Earls Court in 1966, though it did participate in the York Rally that year. While costs may have been a major consideration it would seem that Jim Turner had other issues on his mind as will be explained shortly. L L Roberts, President of the

British Cycle & Motor Cycle Industries Association (BCMCIA), wrote to Turner on 21 June in an effort to change his mind. It describes the seriousness of the situation within the industry:

> ...I believe it will be doubtfully advisable to proceed with the Cycle and Motor Cycle Show if your own Company, Dawes, Coventry-Eagle, Viking and Wearwell were not to participate. It might be preferable to call it a Motor Cycle Exhibition and leave it at that. If this were to happen I would regard it as little less than a tragedy, since it must surely reflect an image of an Industry that no longer has sufficient faith in its present, nor confidence in its future. The Earls Court Show is the Industry's shop window in which it presents its products to the World. The home market requires this stimulus and as an industry we must play our part in contributing to the National economy by achieving a fair quota of exports....

For some years, of course, bicycles had played second fiddle to their motorised cousins at the annual show and it was inevitable that the combined historic format would need to change. The BCMCIA eventually split into the Bicycle Association and Motor Cycle Association in 1973. Turner also decided in July 1966 that membership of the Association no longer warranted the payment of £750 pa, and wrote to H M Palin withdrawing from 'our long association' and expressing great regret. Cost cutting had for some time been very much on McKenna's mind, with concern over water, gas and electrical consumption. One sunny day in 1965 he had taken issue with employees for leaving lights on, and had complained about excessive consumption of file handles and shot blast material.

During September 1966 the company decided to withdraw from Scotland following the closure of the main distributor, Alex Cheyne Ltd, of Glasgow. Though some sales were still being made in Aberdeen and Dundee McKenna decided that the high cost of transport meant that economically they were not worth the effort. The lack of interest from other distributors in Scotland in taking on the Cheyne business was a strong sign of the low point that the industry had reached.[49]

A further insight can be gained from a survey sent out by the BCMCIA in December 1966. They had been collecting regular statistics on imports and exports, and the national figures for November 1966 give an import value of £190,792 and export of £742,649. This has to be put in the context of falling sales, with UK sales falling from 728,000 machines in 1965 to 590,000 in 1967.[50] The largest export market in the month of November was the USA, followed by Nigeria and Zambia. 57% of imports were shared almost equally by France and Germany, with Italy at just under 1%, the same figure as Japan, just at the start of the latter's rise to dominance of the industry. Even Elswick-Hopper had managed to hold on to a few of its old export markets and a total of 1,923 bicycles were dispatched to 21 different companies. The biggest customer was Malaya, followed by Surinam, Cyprus, Eire and Iraq. It would appear that the seamen's strike had not quite killed off the Irish market.

George Fleming continued trying to make the best of things, however, and he informed dealers at the end of 1966 of a new promotion to be run in February and March 1967. This was the Bata Wayfinders Tracking Competition and was featured in 20 giant advertisements in the boys' magazines of the day, such as *Eagle*, *Hotspur*, *Victor*, *Lion*, *Champion* and *Boy's Own Paper*. The prizes were 25 Elswick-Hopper cycles, presumably all boy's models. Prize winners received their machines at the dealer's shop and Elswick-Hopper promised assistance to obtain 'the utmost publicity from these presentations.'

At the end of August Henry Cole retired from his job as works manager. He was one of the last of the young office boys hired in the first decade of the century and had steadily progressed through the ranks. The position was taken by Steve Johnson.

During the 1966 Christmas break the Marsh Lane factory converted to AC electricity, thereby avoiding the capital cost of replacing the aging Ruston & Hornsby diesel generators. Instead an AC/DC rectifier was installed to provide national grid power to the plating shops.

At some stage in late 1966 or early 1967 Jim Turner developed a survival strategy that he hoped would cut costs, maintain a position in the industry, and finally allow him to gain some revenue from the Marsh Lane buildings. He planned to achieve all this by subcontracting production of the majority of the Elswick-Hopper range to Raleigh. Cost savings would, of course, come from a drastic cut in employee levels. Turner and Fleming negotiated the details of the contract, which within a couple of years entailed the replacement of all but one model of Barton built bicycles with Raleigh equivalents, augmented by a few models imported from Austria and Hungary. Elswick fork crowns replaced the unmistakeable Raleigh tubular design, and Elswick-Hopper transfers completed the transformation. There were some tell-tale signs of the true origins of these machines, such as a Raleigh heron stamped into the handlebars. A popular model from this range was the Elswick Safeway, made with both ladies' and gents' frames. The supply contract may have started in a small way during 1967 but was definitely in place with several models for the 1968 season, including the Safeway. Establishing an exact date for the start of the Raleigh contract has so far proved difficult as, for obvious reasons, it was not an event that received publicity. However, the 1968 range was substantially different from that for 1967, and an archive letter from Raleigh sets the credit limit available to Elswick-Hopper at £20,000. It is dated November 1 1966 and was sent to Jim Turner from A M A McLarty, a director of Raleigh Industries Ltd. It concludes with the sentence: "I look forward to receiving a copy of the Balance Sheet of your Cycle Company that you promised to send me during our recent meeting.' This letter was clearly not referring to negotiations for a small supply contract. November has always been a key month for the cycle industry when the next year's models are introduced, so it is likely that some 1967 models were outsourced. There had been a long term relationship with Raleigh on hire purchase agreements with Raleigh receiving 15s per bicycle. In 1959 Jim Turner negotiated a new agreement based on a sliding scale. For the first 7,500 hire purchase sales payment was £1, between 7,501 and 20,000 15s and between 20,001 and 30,000 just 10s. Sales in excess of 30,000 would be charged at 7s. This must have made HP sales very attractive to the company. Employment figures also indicate that 1968 saw the main switch in production to Raleigh, though from evidence of employees, the threat of redundancies in that month encouraged many to leave, especially when Coventry-Eagle arrived on the scene.

The contract was mutually beneficial as it enabled Raleigh to fill up spare production capacity, and Elswick-Hopper to avoid spending money on long overdue modernisation. It was not without problems and there are several letters on file complaining about component quality issues. Production did continue at Barton so that the company could retain its tax efficient status of manufacturer, and building 41, the old press shop, was retained for the production of the attractive looking Continentale shopper. Nine years after Moss had first mentioned the possibility, the company could at last offer a large slice of the Marsh Lane properties for sale or lease. An announcement to that effect was made in the *Scunthorpe Evening Telegraph* of 26 July 1967:

> After nearly three years of working at a loss, the Elswick-Hopper Cycle and Motor Co has decided to cash in on its most valuable asset – the £200,000 worth of property it holds at Barton on Humber.
> The firm said today that a substantial proportion of its holdings will be up for sale and explained: 'The space utilised for bicycle manufacture is far in excess of requirements.'
> The managing director, Mr R A McKenna, said that negotiations with any purchaser will include arrangements for the present bicycle manufacturing structure to continue in space more suited to its needs.
> It was the board's intention to continue with the manufacture and sale of bicycles.
> Mr McKenna said he could not foresee any plans to cut back production or make redundancies....

Just one month later, on 31 August, R A McKenna died at the manager's residence, Elm Tree House, aged 55. His place was taken by Leslie Wilson Green, appointed on 9 October 1967. It was another difficult year for businesses nationally with continued industrial unrest and an eight week London dock strike that ended on 27 November. A week earlier the bank rate had been raised to 8%, and in the same month Wilson's government devalued the pound, thereby giving a theoretical advantage in the export market. On 24 October the *Scunthorpe Evening Telegraph* reported the latest figures for the company:

> Elswick-Hopper, the cycle firm, last paid an ordinary dividend 10 years ago and has turned in a bigger loss.
>
> Yesterday the chairman, Mr Jim Turner, reported that last year's loss was £58,063 against £35,876. Chief culprit for this state of affairs was the road haulage side, which has since been sold. Elswick are also passing the preference dividend, which is now in arrears since 1960.

So, first Scootamatic and then Midland were blamed for the continued downward slide. The manufacture of bicycles incurred a trading loss of £2,492 during the year, and, to make matters worse, continued to lose money through the final years of the decade, despite outsourcing; pre-tax losses were £28,103 in 1968 rising to £35,889 in 1969. In 1968 the total number of employees was just 190. Ten years on from acquisition Jim Turner must have entertained some doubts as to his initial assessment of the potential of the company for wealth creation. However, the decision to make money from the Marsh Lane buildings quickly bore fruit when Coventry-Eagle moved to Barton from Smethwick in 1968, occupying the Elswick building, situated along Marsh Lane, the 'aerodrome' and other smaller buildings.

The end of an extraordinarily difficult decade provided a crumb of comfort to Jim Turner, as the manufacturing subsidiary made a trading profit of £10,516.

Between 1966 and 1974 the number of manufacturing subsidiary employees fell dramatically:

| Date | Factory | Admin/Clerical | Sales | Total |
|------|---------|----------------|-------|-------|
| January 1966 | 162 | 34 | 6 | 202 |
| December 1966 | 153 | 32 | 6 | 191 |
| January 1967 | 149 | 32 | 6 | 187 |
| January 1968 | 156 | 28 | 6 | 190 |
| May 1968 | 11 | 17 | 5 | 33 |
| January 1969 | 14 | 18 | 5 | 37 |
| January 1970 | 21 | 16 | 5 | 42 |
| January 1971 | 26 | 14 | 4 | 44 |
| January 1972 | 31 | 15 | 4 | 50 |
| January 1973 | 39 | 20 | 4 | 63 |
| January 1974 | 30 | 18 | 6 | 54 |

Frame building on a small scale continued until at least 1978 and assembly through to the early 1980s.

## Coventry-Eagle Moves to St Mary's Works

Much of the following story was provided by Mrs Mary Mayo, widow of Douglas Mayo, managing director of Coventry-Eagle, and by Mr and Mrs Ernest Clements. The exception is the detail of the strike and this material was gleaned from local newspapers.

The venerable Coventry-Eagle Cycle and Motor Co Ltd dates from 1890 as a partnership between Edmund Mayo, Richard Hotchkiss and John Meek. Its history mirrors that of Hopper in the early days, with motorcycle production starting in 1904, though Coventry-Eagle continued with this market through the inter-war period, outselling BSA in some years. The original factory was in Hill Cross, Coventry, and when it was unable to meet demand a new factory was built in Lincoln Street, Coventry. The blitz destroyed not only the factory but also that of their steel suppliers, Rubery Owen, and production was essentially halted. Relocation followed to an ex-MOD factory in Tile Hill, Coventry, and then in 1957 they moved to Birmingham. According to an unidentified newspaper clipping quoting Douglas Mayo: 'the sole reason for the move is the difficulty of training sufficient local labour to cope with expanding sales.' Mayo also stated that workers had already been commuting from Birmingham and raw materials were also brought in from that city. The new premises were in Harford Street, Hockley and, interestingly, Mayo stated that he hoped to buy a larger factory near the new one to satisfy growing demand. This factory was owned by Roberts Cycle Industries (RCI) of Smethwick, where

Ernest Clements had found work, following the failure of his Dawley, Shropshire, business in 1955. After his move to Smethwick, in late 1955 or early 1956, he soon convinced RCI management that they should venture into the lightweight end of the market. They were already well established as makers for own-label dealers and had never sold under their own name. Frank Clements was also working for RCI at the time and relates how his brother was looking for a name for the new lightweights when Frank discovered a collection of 'Falcon' decals in the attic of the stores. The name seemed appropriate and the Falcon brand is still thriving as one of the largest in the UK 50 years later. Ernest became works manager for RCI and retained that position when the company was acquired by Coventry-Eagle in 1957. He was later made a director of that company. One of the best sellers was the Falcon San Remo range, born in 1960, and named after the classic Italian Milan-San Remo race.

Ernest Clements did an excellent job promoting the racing side of cycling and his Falcon teams spanned the years from 1960 to 1991, the last being Banana-Falcon, many years after he had left the company. He was also the first to recognise the potential of Majorca for early season training, running the first training camp there in 1966. Tommy Godwin was the manager appointed for the six week camp, where groups came and returned at intervals. Brian Robinson and Billy Holmes were involved and Tom Simpson put in an appearance, though a foot in plaster following a skiing accident kept him off the bikes.

In 1968 Coventry-Eagle again faced a move though redevelopment plans for their factory site, and accepted the offer of redundant buildings and offices at Barton on Humber, freed up, as we have seen, by the Raleigh contract. This arrangement certainly worked in favour of the employees and many joined the new company. Douglas Mayo was injured in a car crash shortly after the relocation and never fully recovered. He retired in 1971, at which point Clements took over the reins, though Mayo stayed on for a year as a consultant, before retiring to Shropshire.

Coventry-Eagle's sixth move does not appear to have affected sales, though labour shortages became acute during January 1969. Clements appealed to local racing enthusiasts to join Falcon as trainees, complaining that production of specialised racing cycles was at a virtual standstill.[51] He claimed that sales over the previous month had been the best for 15 years and that production of standard cycles was running at 800 per week. The export potential was also mentioned, with reference to the USA and South Africa. He was looking to recruit at least 20 men to produce frames, with potentially a further 50 jobs being created within 6 months. His immediate objective was to recruit three enthusiasts, possibly from the local Scunthorpe Polytechnic Club, to train for racing production, believing they would bring an enthusiastic atmosphere into the workshop.

Just a year later Coventry-Eagle faced the longest strike in Barton's history. The occasion was the Milk Race, when stage 6 was set off from the town's Baysgarth Park to Skegness at lunchtime on 29 May 1970 by the chairman of Barton UDC, Councillor Ted Appleyard. Management had agreed to extend the lunch break by an hour to enable the workforce to be at the start. Unfortunately there was a misunderstanding over payment for the extra hour and the shop steward tried to sort out the situation with Ernest Clements on behalf of her fellow General and Municipal Workers' Union members. She was summarily dismissed, because, according to the *Scunthorpe Evening Telegraph* report the following day, 'of her manner'. The 120 members duly walked out. They received a letter from Douglas Mayo pointing out that finished stocks had been building for some time; there were more than 8,000 cycles unsold in dealers' depots; there was hardly room to move in the wheel shop and frames were piling up alarmingly. He blamed the financial squeeze for the situation and said that the walkout had 'solved the problem'. He also asked anyone who wanted to continue working to come in. On 1 June the strikers were demanding the steward's reinstatement and the strike was declared official. By 6 June another 12 workers had been dismissed, including another shop steward and this number had grown to 48 a week later. The GMWU had requested the convenors at Raleigh Industries to 'black' cycle components destined for the firm and the handling of Coventry-Eagle products at airports and docks. Clements was quoted as saying, 'We can go on for months and we are prepared to do so.' On 2 July the *Evening Telegraph* reported a resumption of production earlier that week, with 140 cycles built in three days, 23 strikers having returned to work. Clements foresaw a need for an additional 10 or 12 employees within a month and stated, 'We are going to run our business the way we want to and we are going to employ who we want to.' It wasn't a good time for Coventry-Eagle (or the country) and by 27 July he was reporting to the *Evening Telegraph* that the national dock strike was threatening the shipment of 300 Falcon cycles to the USA and Canada, with a value of £14,000. Two other orders were already trapped at Liverpool docks, one for Canada and one for British Honduras. A state of emergency had been declared by Edward Heath's new government on 16 July and by the time the dockers voted to return to work it had cost the economy between 50 and 100 million pounds. Clements added that he had about 35 employees and they were producing about 300 cycles per week, compared to between 600 and 800 before the strike. Meanwhile a dwindling number of union members continued to picket the Marsh Lane factory. Matters were still not resolved at the end of August, when Coventry-Eagle issued a statement that it was considering issuing a High Court writ against pickets at its factory gates. Douglas Mayo reported that some pickets had been aggressive, while the shop steward dismissed the threat of a writ as ridiculous and stated that 'pickets are meant to cause inconvenience to the firm, otherwise it's no use our picketing.'[52] She noted that there were normally four or five pickets outside the gates every day. They turned away lorries bringing components and called workers who were leaving or entering 'blacklegs'.

The strike was eventually resolved at a meeting almost four months later on Friday 16 October 1970 between a Nottingham GMWU organiser and Coventry-Eagle management. The company promised to recognise the national engineering wages agreement and to allow employees to belong to trade unions of their choice. However, it refused to recognise any one union and was under no commitment to enter into agreements with any one union.[53] The pickets had dwindled to around 29 by this time and few of these were regularly outside the factory. A number asked to be reinstated but Ernest Clements was adamant that an offer of jobs would depend on who they were and what vacancies existed. In a typical upbeat statement he remarked, 'We have got a very efficient workforce now and a very happy one. The last few months have been very successful and the company has a bright future because we have some wonderful orders.' The company had significantly scaled back its workforce and avoided redundancies, but had Coventry-Eagle fostered the strike at a time when production was far outstripping sales? Certainly the workers were naive in striking when they had plenty of visible evidence that the company was awash with stock, and were up against a very experienced adversary in Ernest Clements. Perhaps they had been sucked into the idea of striking because at that time it was what so many workers were doing? Sadly it resulted in much bitterness amongst former friends, who finished up on different sides of the picket line and almost 40 years on is still a subject that those involved are reluctant to discuss. As for the steward she said that she would not be applying for her old job, and commented, 'I am going to rearrange my life. I have a few hobbies which I have neglected.'

Clements' predictions of a bright future were accurate and the early 1970s were boom times for Falcon with major sales in the USA and the development of a distribution company to take advantage of the seemingly insatiable appetite of Americans for British sports bicycles. What has been termed 'The Great American Bike Boom' lasted from 1971 to 1973. At the peak in 1973 more than 15 million bicycles were sold, of which over 5 million were imported.[54] These were without doubt the most successful years of Ernest Clements' long career in bicycles and he made the most of it, buying professional golfer Tony Jacklin's house in Elsham and several upmarket cars.

The old Edwardian 'Elswick' building became Falcon's main production shop, though it was far from ideal (Fig. 7.23). Very little money had been spent on the infrastructure of the whole site for many years. Clements started exploring the hinterland for a more suitable location, eventually, in late

*Fig. 7.23 The Falcon assembly shop in October 1970.*

1976, settling on the empty Corah factory in Brigg and commenced negotiations. Corah was a textile manufacturer supplying underwear to companies such as Marks and Spencer, and had closed the Brigg factory in 1975 in response to a clothing recession, though they retained the factory in nearby Scunthorpe. Closure had involved the loss of 350 jobs and was a major blow to the small market town. The *Scunthorpe Telegraph* of 21 February 1977 reported that the 58,000 sq ft factory had been taken over by Falcon as a satellite for their operations in Barton. Clements hoped to relocate production during April with plans to eventually employ 140 people. He acknowledged that the recession in the USA, triggered by the 1973-74 Arab oil embargo, had cut exports, but claimed that: 'Everyone else is crying out for bicycles, especially the kind we make. I think in three years time, providing the demand is there we should be making about 40,000 a year in Brigg. Just over two years ago we had this fire in Barton and we have never been really organised since, because of the lack of space. We will get Brigg organised on a flow basis and that will enable us to organise Barton better.' The lease was signed on 3 June 1977 and on 27 June the *Scunthorpe Evening Telegraph* reported that the company had now moved in staff and machinery and was making its first bicycles there.

Clements' optimism was borne out at the Milan International Cycling Exhibition later in 1977 when his general manager, Peter Brix, announced orders worth £350,000 had been placed by new agents, dealers and distributors across Europe.[55] Ernest Clements was also at Milan and from there flew to Majorca to finalise plans for the annual training camp. By now it had developed into a six-week event catering for 200 riders and also included a dealers' convention – an opportunity to entertain customers and take orders.

## The Long Awaited Diversification – into Farming and Construction

Although a tentative, and unsuccessful, diversification had started with the acquisition of the Midland Motor Company in 1959, it was another 11 years before Jim Turner identified what he believed was a major area of potential earnings growth – agricultural equipment and services. In 1971 John Williams was appointed a director of the parent company to bring on board some expertise. He was a farmer, and more significantly, director of the Holderness Plough Co Ltd. Money for diversification was raised following approval at an EGM held at Winchester House, London in 1972 and at the same meeting the company name was shortened to Elswick-Hopper Ltd, in recognition of the declining role of the bicycle and the lack of a motor related business. Pre-tax losses for the year were held at just £1,132.

Ryehill Farm Service Ltd was formed in 1969, based in East Yorkshire and was acquired by

Elswick-Hopper in April 1972. This was followed by toolmaker Picador Engineering Co Ltd., bought from Crittall-Hope for £283,000 in the same month. Holderness Plough was eventually bought in January 1973, followed by Richardson and Calvert of Quernhow, Thirsk, in January 1974 for £300,000 through an allotment of 268,041 shares. Joint owner George Calvert joined the main board, which now comprised Jim Turner, Hamish Easdale, Leslie Green, John Williams and George Calvert. This set the company firmly in the direction of supplying machinery and services to the farming industry.

Further diversification followed in 1974 with the purchase of Purdue Construction Co Ltd on 1 April for 460,528 ordinary shares and a cash consideration of £35,000. This included subsidiary Cost-Wright Erection and Cladding Co Ltd. The directors were clearly convinced of the success of the new strategy and declared a final dividend for the year ending 31 January 1976 that provided a theoretical yield of 15.6%. To fund further expansion it was proposed to increase share capital from £600,000 to £1.2 million by the creation of 12 million shares at 5p each. This was passed at an EGM in June 1976, when it was also announced that an international business was being set up to develop agricultural markets in the Middle East and North Africa, involving the supply of know-how, livestock and equipment. This new company was known as FarmKey Ltd. In December 1976 Paul Seward & Co was acquired, bringing an International Harvester agency to the group.

A link with the glory days of bicycle manufacture was broken at the end of January 1977 when Leslie Green resigned as company secretary and was replaced by Michael Goodall. Green was responsible for ensuring that the company archives did not receive the same treatment as those of many long established organisations – consigned to the skip – and were given to the local archives office, making this book much easier to write.

*Fig. 7.24 Elswick-Hopper's response to the Raleigh Chopper, the Bronco, imported from Hungary, © David Lee.*

Expansion and reorganisation of assets continued unabated through the 1970s, for example, at the end of 1977 the 75% interest in FarmKey Ltd was sold to Universal Livestock Services (Holdings) Ltd with the agreement of partner BP Nutrition Ltd. The holding was exchanged for shares in ULS. Just a month later the share capital of B H Brown Ltd was acquired from the Carr-Ellison Estates in exchange for 2 million shares. Sir Ralph Carr-Ellison was appointed a director at the same time; he already served on the boards of Tyne Tees Television and the Northumbrian Water Authority. Following a well-established pattern an EGM was called in July 1978 to agree a rights issue of just under 5.5 million shares at 14.5p/share. Reasons given were the acquisitions of Paul Seward, B H

Brown, (agricultural machinery distributor), the formation of Elswick-Becker, to distribute the German company's range of cultivation equipment, and the formation of Elswick Livestock Systems.

*Fig. 7.25   Gordon Linley and Cyril Haddock loading a pantechnicon at Marsh Lane.*

## Bicycles Again

In contrast to the gloomy end of the 1960s the early years of the next decade saw a slow revival in the fortunes of the cycle division led by a positive contribution to profits of just £5,700 in 1970, reversing a loss of £10,200 in 1969, and a profit of almost £7,000 in the 1971 financial year, though this was overshadowed by £12,452 in rental from the 20 or so companies that had moved to the Marsh Lane site. However, the profit trend was in the right direction, assisted by such events as the 1973 oil crisis, which triggered a sustained rise in the cost of oil products, and also by an increasing interest in fitness and all forms of sport. Exports were also healthy – led, as for Coventry-Eagle, by the US 'bicycle boom'. Young people were offered a completely different bicycle experience when Raleigh introduced the Chopper in 1970, quickly copied by many rival companies – including Pannonia of Hungary. Elswick-Hopper marketed the Pannonia sourced Bronco in 1971, though it was an ugly machine when compared with the Poppy, marketed under Pannonia's own name (Fig.7.24).

The whole industry benefited from the renewed popularity of bicycles. In 1973 Reynolds Tube Company celebrated its 75th year and an article in *Cycling* of 31 March 1973 observed that the company was enjoying boom times due to US demand, and that this was in marked contrast to the mid 1960s when demand had been so slow that there were thoughts of abandoning cycle-tube production entirely.

In September 1978 Elswick-Hopper employed eight UK sales area representatives, a marked contrast to the situation in 1961. Each sales area was identified by a coloured sales ticket, affixed to each bicycle to facilitate loading of the transport lorries. Nigel Haddock related how he spent many Saturday mornings helping his father Cyril to load his pantechnicon ready for the Monday morning start. These lorries had been fitted with timber supports to allow double stacking of machines. Delivery to dealers was often followed by a journey to Nottingham to collect Raleigh Elswicks for delivery to Barton (Fig. 7.25).

While the Raleigh supply contract continued to sustain the Elswick-Hopper marque, bicycles were not the only asset to come from that source; Richard Blundell joined the company from Raleigh as General Manager in February 1972. Richard had been with Raleigh since 1953, apart from two years National Service and was appointed regional sales manager to Scotland in 1963. By 1971 he was Raleigh product manager responsible for introducing a new range of prams and pushchairs, and looking for a fresh challenge. He certainly brought much needed industry experience to the bicycle division. One of his first goals was to strengthen the management team and in time-honoured fashion he tempted Phillip Bradley from his old employer in May 1972. Phillip had been with Raleigh for 16 years and, as a sales representative with a large area, could see few opportunities to progress. I am indebted to him for much of the material in this section. Also to Peter Sweetman, Falcon's financial director, who had previously worked as the auditor of Elswick-Hopper's accounts while employed by Fawley, Judge and Easton, and had worked for Elswick-Hopper directly from 1979, and finally to Stan Havercroft, who served his apprenticeship as a toolmaker with Elswick-Hopper from 1940 to 1945 and was enticed back to bicycle manufacture by Richard Blundell in 1974.

By the time Richard Blundell moved to Barton the Raleigh supply contract was in full swing and the redundant Marsh Lane buildings had become a small industrial estate leased to steel fabricators, machining companies and a variety of other organisations, mainly involved in the growing South Humberside oil and chemical industries. As already mentioned Elswick-Hopper retained a foot in manufacturing by making the Continentale shopper virtually by hand. The chrome shop, paint shop, warehousing, office accommodation and a sizeable wheel building section were still in operation; the wheel shop mainly supplying the large domestic replacement market. The bicycle division was selling between 20,000 and 40,000 bicycles per year, the majority supplied by Raleigh.

Fred Hopper, son of the founder, died 20 October 1973, leaving no family. Although he had little involvement in his father's firm since the war he remained a respected figure in Barton. His preference for farming over bicycles had no doubt been fostered by his father's purchase of Park Farm in 1917 and for many years he had worked in partnership with a local farmer.

Richard Blundell and Phillip Bradley both saw opportunities to build up the export market and trips were made to Scandinavia and Ireland. Business was good in Denmark, where Elswick models ironically gained a better reputation than their Raleigh counterparts, despite coming off the same assembly lines. The fact that they were priced to undercut Raleigh was a major factor in their success, and must have been a great source of annoyance to Raleigh sales staff.

Sales to Denmark were primarily of the roadster full oil bath type and averaged 2,000 per year through a Copenhagen importer, via an agent. As soon as Barton management decided to get more directly involved sales were significantly increased and eventually a Hopper agency was established as a way to avoid upsetting the existing Elswick importer. It was easy money for Elswick-Hopper as Raleigh even dispatched some containers direct to the customer, so all the Barton office had to do was raise the invoice and process the payment to Raleigh. Other sales were trucked up to the Barton warehouse, following an outward consignment of wheels. The contract with Raleigh lasted until 1979, which was the earliest date it could be terminated by the supplier. It was clear that reliance on Raleigh to produce profits for a competitor was not a sustainable long-term strategy from the supplier's viewpoint, and so the opportunity was taken to buy a new factory, as the option of developing Marsh Lane was no longer available. Along with the factory premises in Shropshire the old Wearwell name was acquired. The fact that Jim Turner still had faith in bicycle manufacture is perhaps surprising, given all the years of financial losses. Was it the pull of history, or his unshakeable optimism that kept the company in bicycles? Perhaps a bit of both.

## Manufacturing at Alveley

Wearwell Cycles, founded in Wolverhampton in 1890, could claim as long a cycle manufacturing history as Hopper's. Production had recently moved from Wolverhampton as part of the redevelopment of the old site, to a grass-roots facility in Alveley, Shropshire. This had been built by Bridgnorth Rural District Council to attract manufacturing companies in an effort to provide jobs for redundant miners. The National Coal Board had expanded the Alveley colliery in the early 1960s, based on a predicted 50 year life, employing 1,000 miners at the peak. Sadly the predictions proved optimistic when a geological fault forced closure at the end of January 1969. Wearwell had taken a lease on the factory buildings in March 1971, but could not make a go of it due to acute liquidity problems and poor management. They sold out to Elswick-Hopper in November 1974 for £32,000. One of the attractions of Wearwell was a large contract to supply bicycles to the Post Office, though the main objective was to acquire a modern factory with modern equipment. For a time the factory continued to produce Wearwell branded bicycles, many of them low end mail order machines, but gradually a new Elswick range was developed to supplement those sourced from Raleigh. From the 1975 annual report:

> In recent years the company has had most of its bicycles produced on a contracted out basis to designs and specifications provided by Elswick-Hopper. With the acquisition of the manufacturing facilities of Wearwell Cycles Co Ltd, it is anticipated that some 40% of bicycles will now be produced in the Group's own factories.

The new factory was not expected to contribute to earnings for the year, but following a complete management reorganisation was expected to improve profits from the cycle division in the years to come. In 1974 Phillip Bradley was appointed sales manager of Wearwell Cycles, as the Alveley factory was still known, and promoted to general manager of the Alveley Production Unit of Elswick-Hopper Cycles just one year later with responsibility for the reorganisation. He replaced Martin Wells, a pig farmer who had been running the Wearwell company. Factory improvements took much time and effort and Phillip stayed there for four years, assisted by Stan Havercroft, who relocated from North Lincolnshire as factory manager. The workforce unsurprisingly comprised mainly ex-NUM members, now represented by the GMWU. Modern equipment had been installed by Wearwell as part of the move from Wolverhampton, with frame-building jigs and a Muller welding carousel.

Richard Blundell brought in consultants during 1977 to perform a job evaluation study. All jobs were being paid the same flat rate, with variations only based on age and gender. There were 20 identifiable jobs, including 10 in the frame shop and three in assembly. It should be remembered that this was in the days before flexible working became a major driver to improve productivity. Skill requirement, responsibility, physical effort and job conditions were assessed and although a full analysis of jobs is not available it does appear that effort and conditions skewed the results, while skills and responsibility were undervalued.

The new management team eventually improved productivity to a significant extent, cutting jobs and bringing the factory into profit. At the time of the takeover Wearwell employed about 60 and was by far the biggest employer in Alveley. Being the 1970s there were strikes – usually about money, as government controls were imposed on pay rises, but they rarely lasted longer than a day.

As already mentioned old export markets were reopened quite successfully, and the home market was expanded. The Wearwell Post Office contract was rebid and won, accounting for some 3,500 machines per year. These were all made at Alveley to the old unique design. Stan Havercroft recalls suggesting a more modern design, far lighter than the old 'five bar gate job'. It would have been fitted with a 3-speed hub, cable brakes, lighter tubing and a lighter front carrier. Stan even visited Pashley, another small company with a long relationship with the Post Office, to discuss a prototype. There was no response from the customer, although modern Pashley-made Post Office bicycles are much like the design suggested by Stan. Phil Bradley recalled the problem of sourcing parts for the Post Office contract. Designed in the 1920s, almost every part was unique due, no doubt, to mistrust of employees. Martin Wells had bought 3,000 sets of brakes from India, but these did not fit, and were tipped down the old mine shaft. A similar batch of bottom brackets was sold on, and Phil decided to source parts from Japan, where the growing component industry had started supplying the old ex-colonial African bicycle market with roadster components, and was flexible enough to accommodate the idiosyncratic requirements of the unique English Post Office bicycle.

Unfortunately there was little scope for new designs to compete with such innovations as the Raleigh Chopper, except through imports. Radically new designs meant new jigs and special tubing, requiring confidence that a large enough number would be made to cover set-up costs and consume the special tubing that would incur a minimum order. Stan realised that the bicycle division was just too small to carry the risk involved with innovation and concentrated on ensuring that production was as efficient as possible, minimising overtime and other impacts on profitability. An annual model review was made by Blundell, Bradley and Havercroft and towards the end of the decade more frames were being bought in, especially at the lower end of the range, destined for catalogue sales with companies such as Empire and Gratton.

*Fig. 7.26  Jack Dimoline is pictured at Marsh Lane assembling a Merckx bicycle. To his left are Ernie Clements, Ferdinand Kessels, Eddy Merckx and Frank Clements. To his right is believed to be Kessel's personal assistant, © David Lee.*

## Purchase of Falcon Cycles

The proximity of the Coventry-Eagle/Falcon business, renamed Falcon Cycles after Ernest took over control, to the remaining Elswick-Hopper cycle division must have led to discussions on how the two concerns could cut costs by sharing facilities. Indeed, on 1 December 1973 *Cycling* carried the announcement 'FALCON TIE-UP COMPLETED', stating:

> Amalgamation of Elswick-Hopper and Falcon Cycles is now official, but the Barton-upon-Humber firms will continue to operate independently for the next 12 to 18 months.
> Elswick-Hopper sales will still be controlled by Richard Blundell, while Frank Clements continues with Falcon and Eddy Merckx sales. Ernest Clements remains managing director of Falcon Cycles.
> The move means more space for Falcon. Since their move from the Midlands in 1968 sales of Falcon and Coventry-Eagle bicycles have multiplied five times. At present Falcon occupy 60,000 square feet at Barton; with production increasing there could also be expansion abroad for Falcon, with a new distribution centre in Canada a possibility in the near future. Dealer service, now top priority, will be maintained by the combined pantechnicon fleets operating from the Barton factory area in which both firms are quartered...'

While it is likely that transport was amalgamated (though no firm evidence has been discovered) this was the extent of the 'amalgamation'. The report does, however, give an indication of Clements' expansion plans. The Eddy Merckx sales mentioned in *Cycling* referred to a range of Falcon machines adorned with Merckx transfers. A deal had been struck with Merckx by Frank Clements on the basis of 35,000 machines per year, based on a reasoned assessment of demand and capacity. On his return to Barton his brother Ernest decided that he would travel to Belgium himself to finalise the contract. On his return he announced that he had increased the contract to 70,000 per year. At a cost of £1 per set it was good business for Merckx, but despite later using some of the capacity at the Clements' Cycle Producers Ltd factory at Northwich, Ernest's ambitious target was never met. Frank recalls that the best year was about 23,000 machines. The Merckx range was announced in *Cycling* on 24 November 1973 and the following year Eddy visited Barton. He was accompanied by Ferdinand Kessels, a fellow Belgian and a specialist bike builder who had supplied all Eddy's personal racing frames. The range continued until the early 1980s, based on catalogue evidence, and Frank recalls that Merckx was very satisfied with the quality of frames being produced in Barton at the time of his visit (Fig. 7.26).

The Merckx deal was a good example of Ernest Clements' main strength that was also a weakness – an optimism and self-belief that, while essential for a career as a road racer, could lead to poor business decisions. There is no doubt that the work involved in moving production to Brigg caused financial problems for Falcon, especially as the US export boom had run its course. So in January 1978 Clements sold out to his Barton landlord. The agreement reached by Elswick-Hopper was to acquire from him, his wife Rosemary, and his brother Walter, the entire share capital of Cycle Producers Ltd and 75% of Falcon Cycles for £100,000 in cash and 1,388,888 Elswick-Hopper shares. Ever the entrepreneur he also negotiated a performance bonus, whereby in the event that Falcon profits exceeded £110,000 pre-tax for the year ended 28 February 1978, an additional payment of £3 for every additional £1 of profit would be paid, up to a maximum of £270,000. Two-thirds of the payment was to be in cash with the balance in shares. Clements agreed to serve as an executive director until the end of January 1983 at an annual salary of £11,500. The full bonus was paid in due course.[56]

Cycle Producers Ltd had been set up by the four Clements brothers in 1975. Based in Northwich it was run by Roy Clements, a talented engineer who left a good position in industry to set up the new company. According to Frank Clements his brother Roy had proposed acquiring a Northwich factory in partnership with his brothers as a base to deal in heavy plant. Ernest had other ideas and the new company would make frames for Falcon and, later, produce a second range of 'British Eagle' bicycles.

The takeover of Falcon changed at a stroke the position of the parent group in the pecking order of British bicycle manufacturers at a time when diversification was in full swing. Falcon brought with it a successful export business, a long and successful racing pedigree, and a high volume of production from the partly occupied Brigg factory and the leased Marsh Lane buildings. The sting in the tail was that it also brought a separate management team, most definitely not working to the same agenda as the parent. Ernest Clements did not change his style from that of a flamboyant risk-taking entrepreneur to that of a main board director of a diversified public quoted company. The expensive cars remained, he ran Falcon as his own business, and resentment started to build, especially when attempts were eventually made to merge the two bicycle businesses. With hindsight conflict was inevitable and the interplay between an individualistic ex-bike rider and a major corporation makes this part of the Elswick-Hopper story the most complex since receivership in 1913. The first step towards bringing the two organisations together was to appoint Richard Blundell to the Falcon board and Ernest Clements to the Elswick-Hopper Mfg board.

## Consolidation

The late 1970s and early 1980s were busy times for the board of directors as they continued to look for productivity improvements at Alveley, boost exports and grapple with the opportunities presented by the Falcon acquisition. Roger Denniss was appointed company secretary in April 1978, replacing Leslie Green on his retirement. The decision was taken to drop the Hopper name from the Elswick-Hopper bicycle brand, a decision that had already been implemented for the export market. So after 88 years the Hopper name disappeared as a marque and future bicycles only carried 'Elswick' transfers. For the first time ever Elswick-Hopper exhibited at the Cologne Cycle Show that year, courtesy of Ernest Clements, who agreed that one or two models could be accommodated. Discussions also started on how to leverage the combined buying power of the two organisations and how to set up common systems for stock records. The figures for income and expenditure for the seven months ended 31 January 1978 show that economies were essential with a small loss of £9,300 resulting from a sales income of £1.8 million. By August 1978 sales had started to improve and the Harrogate Cycle Show resulted in far better orders than the previous year, with firm orders for 2,187 machines compared to fewer than 400 in 1977. Elswick-Hopper also raised its industry profile by sponsoring the Grand Prix des Gentlemen run during the Show.

Exports were seen as key to sales growth and after several trips by Philip Bradley an order for 851 machines was received from the Dublin distributor. Discussions were also underway with a Danish wholesaler for own transfer bicycles, showing in some ways how little the industry had changed over the years. The decline of British manufacturing was demonstrated by Elswick's search for cheaper tyres outside the UK during 1978, which concluded that it was likely that there would be a move away from British tyres and tubes almost entirely.

When George Fleming's duties were changed in 1978 to that of service manager he was essentially running what remained of the Marsh Lane factory at Barton, including the production of 2,300 wheels per week, with one third destined for the Alveley Post Office bicycle contract. The situation with cycle building at St Mary's is graphically described by Fleming's report to the board, dated 30 August 1978:

> Production is averaging 86 per week, which must be raised to a minimum of 100. The paint shop can produce this number but there will have to be some small adjustment to the staff in assembly to enable this figure to be achieved. The current staff consists of one full-timer age 69, one part-timer age 72 and one full-timer, plus two young girls who fit the small items.

Fleming suggested transferring the oldest man to wheel despatch and general cleaning duties, replacing him with a full-time assembler. In reality Barton had become a centre for small model runs where production line techniques did not add value, and many of the frames at this time were being imported from the Japanese Marui company, better known for its Tioga brand name. They were of excellent quality.

Performance was improving at Alveley and Blundell stated in his review for the six months ending 31 July 1978:

> At 31 July 1977 we were showing an adverse production variance of £19,687 at Alveley. After six months this year the figure is only £3,256, which with the assistance of £20,250 TES (Temporary Employment Subsidy) puts this part of the operation comfortably in the black for the first time ever.

The forecast for the 1978 year end was upbeat with unit sales expected to exceed 50,000 at a total value exceeding £2,500,000 yielding pre tax profits of £200,000. Just two months later home sales were on target but exports were disappointing, leading to the idea of sharing a full time export sales executive with Falcon. Actual results for 1978 were a turnover of £2,856,930 with a pre tax profit of £160,217. Exports were just £171,401.

Alveley production had been hit during the year by a work to rule that lasted three weeks, badly affecting the production of sports frames. The issue was a claim for a minimum basic wage and a fixed flat rate for holidays. This was in the days of the Callaghan government's pay code and the employer responded that the union's claim broke the code, especially in view of the Post Office contract and the TES payments. The work to rule ended with no gain for the union and Hamish Easdale commented that he felt it would be a permanent situation the company would have to live with in the Alveley area. He had not, of course, foreseen the impact of the 1979 election results. Falcon and another supplier had met the production short fall, leading to a decision to buy in these frames so that Alveley production could be focussed just on Cosmopolitan and Post Office frames. Blundell remarked that this action would result in several jobs becoming redundant in the frame shop. The decision was enacted immediately and seven frame shop operatives lost their jobs. Stan Havercroft reported that the dispute had cost the company 750 machines, 1,200 wheels, 600 frame sets and 150 forks and that morale was not particularly good, though measures were being taken to improve communications, and to create a better industrial relations atmosphere generally. He also noted that the 350 sports frames from Falcon 'proved disappointing.' Stan was appointed a director of Elswick-Hopper Cycles on 26 October 1979.

In November Philip Bradley reported that a merchant house had been appointed as the agent for the Caribbean Islands, and that sample cycles were being dispatched to the Danish distributors. Sales to Ireland were healthy and a further contract had been received for 2,400 Post Office bikes at a value of £147,600. In November 1978 Richard Blundell submitted an outline budget to Jim Turner in which he asked for clearer direction from the parent board. He suggested two alternative paths:

> ...either continue to seek out a larger market share (currently 5%) and accept poor levels of trading profit, or consolidate our position, and by tightening up on overhead expenditure and gross profit margins produce a much more acceptable return.

Jim Turner was happy to leave such decisions to Blundell, though it must have been clear that the two options were not mutually exclusive – to simply 'batten down the hatches' and ignore opportunities to find new customers would have been business suicide.

The budget for the 1979 financial year, February through January 1980, called for 55,000 home sale units and 5,000 export. The profit on sales of £3,284,000 was forecast at nearly 20% before deducting overheads and just 4.8% after deduction. Productivity was certainly a major issue for bicycle makers in the late 1970s. The Far East was flexing its production muscles and labour costs were being driven up in the UK by high inflation and poor labour relations.

The Raleigh contract was still going strong and was fixed at 2,000 units per month for the first quarter of 1979. At the November board meeting Phil Bradley reported the poor quality of the Falcon sports models and Clements stated that it was the first he had heard of it, and would look into the matter.

The consolidation issue was raised by Ernest Clements at the November board meeting when he asked if Elswick-Hopper would be interested in the idea of the professional 'Falcon' team becoming the 'Elswick-Falcon' team. He had designed new racing jerseys and also asked if there could be a joint Elswick-Falcon training camp in Majorca in 1979. Richard Blundell asked for time to consider this offer, but when asked by Bradley if there were any immediate plans to unite the two organisations administratively, said there were no such plans. However, business information was being exchanged and Bradley relayed details of Alveley rates of pay and the cost of production for two of the main range bicycles to Clements later in the month. At that time Alveley jobs grades had been cut to four with pay varying only by 7.5p/hr from top to bottom – the top rate being £1.075. The cost breakdowns were for the S42 Mistral and F43 Cosmopolitan. In response Ernest promised to provide similar information and asked if Phil would like him to look for anything during his tour of the Far East and North America, scheduled for April 1979.

The clear opportunities to improve earnings through consolidation of the two companies were laid out by Bradley in respect of wheel building. He noted in late December 1978 that wheels were being produced at four sites. Falcon was building wheels at both Barton and Brigg and Elswick-Hopper at Barton and Alveley. He proposed a single site on the basis of lower stocks and more efficient use of machinery. At the time 50,000 wheels per year were coming from Alveley, 120,000 from Barton, with similar combined numbers from Falcon; the proposal was for a single operation to build 350,000 wheels per year.

The year end report stated that sales were up in the home market 34% by volume and 54% by value, but again down for exports. Total sales value was up 45%. An indication of the inflation of these years is that Raleigh notified an increase in prices to Elswick of 7% from February 1979. A new racing model was planned for the spring to retail at around £140 with a main triangle of Reynolds 531 tubing, and it had been agreed to purchase 3,000 sports machines from Falcon. Approaching the start of the Thatcher years prospects were bright for the enlarged cycle company. With a target of 50,000 bicycles it was believed that Alveley and Barton combined production could be maintained at 25,000. Raleigh had confirmed their willingness to increase supplies to 27,000, more than filling the production gap. Although assembly was going well problems remained with sourcing frames, mainly due to the 1978 disputes at Alveley. Townsend Cycles had been meeting some of the shortfall but a quality problem meant that some remedial work had to be carried out by Falcon at Brigg, increasing production costs.

Phil Bradley was appointed to the board of Elswick-Hopper Cycles in 1977, and as well as having responsibilities for Alveley was in charge of exports and purchasing. While unit exports had improved by 20% in 1978 it was believed that the figure of 3,883 bicycles sold during the 1978 calendar year could be boosted to 5,000. Bradley planned to visit Dublin, Copenhagen and the Channel Islands, where the burgeoning rental market looked attractive. The list of countries to be targeted also included the USA, Norway, Sweden and Denmark, Western Europe, Greece, Libya, Australia and the Caribbean Islands.  Canada had also been on the list but was deleted due to high import duties.

In March 1979 Stan Havercroft's daughter Jane Jordan, who was Elswick-Hopper's sales director, was concerned that exports were still down on target, though the home market was up, and seven models had been selected by Empire Stores for their winter catalogue, and four by Gratton. She also noted the benefits of regular low-priced limited edition models to 'open the order books'. March also saw Phil Bradley selling in Jersey and Guernsey. Jersey yielded several orders and most potential customers were impressed with the pricing of the Elswick-Hopper range. However, many had already placed their orders for the year. Typical of the hirers was Pitcher's Garage in St Helier, which carried around 200 cycles for hire. It seems that the growth in the hire business was due to increasing numbers of French tourists. Sales were also achieved in Guernsey, though Phil noted that it was far less commercialised than Jersey and that signposts were a rarity. He also noted that the island supported five cycle shops, three of which were 100% Raleigh. All potential customers were again very impressed with Elswick-Hopper prices, which were substantially lower than Raleigh. The conclusion was to concentrate on supplying the hire market, which could yield sales of 300 units per year, with 3-speed versions of the Safeway, Rimini and Cosmopolitan models being the most suitable. Phil returned to the mainland with orders for 53 machines for immediate delivery.

Jane Jordan attended the Falcon training camp in Majorca in the spring of 1979 to look for opportunities for Elswick-Hopper participation. She was impressed with the organisation of the third event since its inception and noted the commonality of many of the dealers present at the camp. Interestingly she noted that 'with more guidance and discipline the racing team could portray a more desirable image of the professional sportsman to so many very keen and promising youngsters'. However, she recommended against future participation by Elswick-Hopper as the majority of their dealers had little or no interest in racing and it would do nothing to enhance the very important Falcon racing image.

By the end of the first quarter Richard Blundell was upbeat, believing that production levels would need to increase to keep pace with sales – Alveley was set to reach 650 machines per week by the end of the year. He noted that 'the increasing availability of our own production at lower costs plus the interesting opportunities for purchasing from existing suppliers, ie Raleigh, Comrade and Pannonia

all mean that we can concentrate once again on the fact that we are a marketing oriented company.' Success had even been met in Scotland, where Jane Jordan had noted an absence of dealers compared with Falcon and 250 traders had been identified. Sales visits had shown a good potential and the board approved the appointment of a sales representative for Scotland; the situation north of the border had clearly changed somewhat since 1966. After just two weeks sales of 500 units were achieved and so a similar drive was planned for Eire and Ulster.

Peter Sweetman started work on 1 May 1979 to take up the accounting work left when R A Denniss assumed the role of company secretary of Falcon, in addition to that of Elswick-Hopper. The company 'centenary' was due in 1980, and it was decided to spread the events over the full year rather than pick a specific month. Jane Jordan and Richard Blundell were charged with coming up with some commemorative ideas. One of these was to produce a 'Sovereign' range, bearing a distinctive gold coloured head tube transfer and 'Sovereign' transfers on both sides of the seat tubes, down tubes and chain stays. There were five models; gent's sports and tourist models, a lady's mixte tourist, a junior sports and a Cosmopolitan shopper. All were finished in 'Celebration Champagne Metallic' livery, priced at under £100,[57] and were on sale for a limited period. At the other end of the range was the Elswick Monarch, which received a good review in *Cycling* on 9 February 1980, as an out and out racer. 'Elswick, celebrating their centenary in 1980, have not been very active on the racing and lightweight side in recent years. But you wouldn't know it from the sleek appearance and big-name specification of the Monarch.' The article went on to record that this was one of the machines that could be bought from a dealer and immediately raced as it stood; it warned that the average racing man had his own ideas and prejudices – which was, after all, the basis for the multitude of specialist lightweight frame builders. The £350 price tag was also a barrier, given the lack of a racing pedigree.

Cost reduction was still vital for the maintenance of profits, given increasing Far Eastern competition and the depressed domestic economy, and Richard Blundell set out the principles of integration in June 1979. He emphasised that internally a new Elswick-Falcon identity had to be forged, but that externally the two separate identities must be strengthened. Not surprisingly the proposed merger created serious morale problems with Falcon employees, and their concerns were discussed at an unofficial Falcon board meeting in September 1979. It was attended by Ernest Clements and his wife Rosemary, Walter Clements, Richard Blundell, PKJ Brix (Purchasing), Bill Holmes (Sales) (Fig. 7.27) and GN Guest (Personnel and Admin). Mrs Clements stated that she felt that Falcon as a company was

Fig. 7.28  Programme cover for the 1980 Elswick Centennial road race.
Fig. 7.29  A pile of scrap following a bad fire at Marsh Lane, © David Lee.

rapidly losing its identity, that Mr E A Clements was being made to look ridiculous by not being advised of changes being made, and that integration was being taken as a walk-in situation. The first tangible issue discussed was the continued provision of transport from Barton to Brigg, which had been agreed by Clements when Falcon first moved production there, just prior to the take-over. Many individual grievances were aired and it is clear that the Falcon directors just wanted to continue as they had under Ernest Clements' ownership – a situation that Blundell could not countenance. There does seem to have been an impression that Falcon and Elswick-Hopper had 'merged', but the deal was simply that a majority of the Falcon business had been acquired for cash and shares, with Clements becoming a main board director – a good move for him, but with unavoidable consequences for Falcon staff. The meeting finished with agreement to suspend further moves of staff between Brigg and Barton and that all directors should submit their ideas for organisational changes.

Rosemary Clements duly responded in writing in October and listed several instances where changes had been instituted without consultation. She asked for Falcon sales and service sections to remain in Brigg, that transport to and from Barton should continue, and that the management structure be completely reorganised. Failing this she suggested that Ernest should be freed from his obligations and allowed, with Walter, to run Falcon independently. Walter Clements stated that he wished to control production at all three factories and expressed concern that Falcon had 'suddenly developed into a Raleigh organisation from a small private family company.' (Clearly a comment directed at Richard Blundell.) Many other suggestions and pleas were made, mainly, and understandably, aimed at safeguarding the jobs of the incumbents. In October 1979 Jim Turner, who must have been regretting his decision to buy Falcon, set up a new Elswick-Falcon Ltd board to co-ordinate the merger. Members were:

J L Turner, chairman, R T Blundell, P J Bradley, E A Clements, W R Clements, R A Denniss, secretary, W Holmes, J Jordan.

Jim Turner attended the following meeting of the Elswick-Hopper Cycles Ltd Board on 26 October and stressed that the commitment to merge was still there, but, due to conflicts, had been postponed.

A new board of Elswick-Hopper Cycles was also appointed late in 1979 with Blundell as chairman and managing director, Jane Jordan as marketing director, Stan Havercroft as manufacturing director, Phil Bradley as purchasing director, R A Denniss as financial director and company secretary. Jim Turner and Ernest Clements remained non-executive directors. The year ending 31 January 1980 saw Elswick bicycle sales at £4,060,658 and pre tax profit at £329,169. Exports for the year were £180,539, just in excess of 1978. During 1980 two more directors were appointed: George Fleming, who was due to retire within six months, and Barry J Young (later founder of the Factory Cycle Shop chain), both in November.

The most significant event to mark the 1980 100th 'anniversary' of the company was the promotion of an Easter Bank Holiday road race. This Elswick Centennial Tour was a major event of 441 miles over four days between Harlow and Glasgow open to both professional and amateur riders (Fig. 7.28). The second stage from King's Lynn to Barton on Humber included a sprint for points outside the Falcon factory in Brigg. The fourth and final stage started in Newcastle, the city where Elswick Cycles began. The overall winner was Ian Hallam of the KP Crisps-Viscount team, with Barry Hoban the first Elswick-Falcon rider home, in third place just 25 seconds down. It was not lack of training that prevented the 'home' team from winning as the fourth Falcon training camp at Puerto de Pollensa had occupied most of March.

In spite of a major fire at Falcon's warehouse in Barton, which resulted in the loss of 10,000 frames, Jim Turner gave an upbeat interview to Harold Briercliffe at the Harrogate Show at the end of June 1980 (Fig. 7.29).[58] His confidence in the future of the Elswick, Falcon, Coventry-Eagle and Eddy Merckx cycles was born out by plans to make investments in both the manufacturing and warehousing facilities. The Elswick stand at Harrogate had received praise from *Cycling's* correspondent in the 5 July edition, especially for the Maestro racing bike, for sale at £189.95, at a time when, 'a racing bike for under £200 just doesn't exist these days.' To encourage dealers to visit the stand the company ran a competition with first prize a Sovereign holiday for two in the Bahamas, two holidays in Paris for the runners-up and bottles of champagne as consolation prizes.

## Coventry-Eagle sets up in Wales

Just how Clements managed to persuade the main board of the business logic is a matter of speculation, but in early 1981 Elswick-Hopper opened a new Coventry-Eagle factory in the Mochdre development area of Newtown, Powys, to manufacture a new range of high grade bicycles.[59] According to Barry Hoban the main incentive was the 60% grant for all plant and three years free of rent and rates as the area was supported by grants through the Welsh Development Agency. This is borne out by the announcement in *Cycling* 20 December 1980 that Elswick-Hopper intended boosting the group's share of the growing bicycle market by establishing a production and distribution base away from existing centres at Brigg and Barton, though oddly there was no mention of Alveley. The company added that the move had been helped by the Development Board for Rural Wales, which provided the factory. So, a free factory and concessions on rates etc made sense if all production was to be shifted to Wales, but creating a third plant just because it was not close to Lincolnshire made no sense, unless Clements was planning for his own future. The *Cycling* article added that the factory would initially provide 20 jobs, increasing to 120 within three years. It was intended that frame building, wheel building, painting, assembly, storage and distribution would all take place at Newtown. *Cycling* also mentions that Elswick-Hopper was finding it difficult to obtain orders and attributed the down-turn to a high level of retail stocks. Whatever the rationale for the new factory, production of a new Coventry-Eagle range, complemented by 'Ernie Clements' and 'Barry Hoban' models, was transferred to Wales. The Ernie Clements cycles were the first to bear his name since the Shropshire days and the Hoban name was expected to appeal to aspiring racing types. Clements was successful in persuading a few Brigg employees to relocate, and several others did spend some time there setting up, including his brother Walter. One couple made the move to Wales, having been with Ernest since the Smethwick days. Barry Hoban joined the new venture as a sales executive. He had been a rare long-term British success on the Continental cycling scene for 19 years and completed twelve Tours de France, notching up eight stage wins. Barry had announced his retirement from the sport at the end of 1979, but Ernest persuaded him to join the Elswick-Falcon team for a final and 18th year as a professional rider with a job waiting for him at the end of the season. Ernest kept his word as Barry records in his autobiography, *Watching the Wheels Go Round*.

On leaving Falcon in 1975 Frank Clements set up JHF Cycle Distributors Ltd with Harry Quinn, using Harry's Liverpool premises as an office base and built up a successful business importing components from Europe and Taiwan. A few years later, when Harry decided to retire, Frank bought the business and built up trade both within the UK and abroad. While on a business trip to Brigg Ernest asked him if he would consider selling both businesses to Falcon. While suspicious of the motives, Frank was attracted by an offer where he would still be in control, while receiving a secure salary. One of Ernest's motives was that stock control at Brigg was in a mess and he wanted Frank back on board to sort it out. When the deal was made in 1981 Ernest immediately closed the old Harry Quinn business.

## Update on Diversification

While Elswick-Hopper Ltd had become a large and diverse conglomerate, with turnover increasing from £1 million in 1973 to £22 million in 1980, it was not immune to the periodic downturns that had always characterised the cycle division. Profits for the group had increased from £106,741 in 1973 to £1,311,008 in 1980, vindicating the strategies adopted by the board. However, 1979 saw the first fall in profits for seven years due to recession in the agricultural machinery market. Taking the longer view the company continued to expand into agricultural machinery and a circular in February 1979 announced the purchase of Turner International (Engineering) Ltd and EW Downs & Sons Ltd. Turner manufactured flail mowers for agricultural and industrial users, and was a market leader for motorway, verge and hedge cutting machinery. Downs produced potato handling and grading equipment. Anthony Leonard Turner, based at Kings Coughton, Alcester joined the board, and was appointed joint managing director responsible for the Engineering Division, now comprising Turner, Picador and Downs, but no longer the cycle companies. Although the 1980 AGM report stated that no further acquisitions were in the pipeline it did reveal the setting up of Elswick Special Vehicles Ltd to manufacture a unique car for the disabled as a joint development with the National Research Development Corporation.

Conglomerates must operate a disposal policy to weed out bad performers and Elswick-Becker was sold in 1980, along with the 25% stake in FarmKey. Poor sales were cited for both disposals. The July 1981 AGM report also recorded that farm income had continued to drop, with less money available for new equipment, though Ryehill continued to excel with its crop spraying and drainage business. Typically with new acquisitions there were problems with both Turner International and Downs. The former had been hit by local authority spending curbs, imposed by Margaret Thatcher's new government, the latter by poor potato prices and declining sales.

The following year, reported in July 1982, saw agricultural sales up from £8.8 million to £10.5 million as a result of improving farm incomes and the need to replace equipment after years of making do. The need to appoint a divisional chief executive was recognised and Paul Seward, who had been a director since 1976, was given this position. At this time the total employment of the company was 675, a post Fred Hopper record, and a tribute to Jim Turner's diversification strategy.

1982/83 was a further record year for Ryehill and there were improvements in Engineering turnover. Relocation of the corporate head office to Alcester led to the resignation of Mike Goodall as financial director, with M K Dyer appointed to the role in April 1983.

Although agricultural sales bounded upwards in 1984 to a £14.1 million turnover, profits fell, due to increased competition and farmers' nervousness about the effect of the impending Common Agricultural Policy reforms. Engineering performed well that year with Turner International achieving record results, buoyed by high sales at the USA subsidiary, based in Georgia.

## Flight of the Eagle

Peter Sweetman's account of the attempts to merge the two cycle producers is based on first hand observations and gives valuable insights into a difficult situation. His comments have been used liberally and woven into other first-hand accounts.

Clements had run Falcon since taking control from Douglas Mayo as his personal domain, and the decision to sell to Elswick-Hopper must have been difficult. The theory that Falcon had been over-extended financially by the Corah factory purchase seems the most likely explanation as significant extensions and modifications were necessary to create a bicycle factory from one designed to produce underwear. The dates are significant:

| | |
|---|---|
| Falcon purchase of Brigg site | June 1977 |
| Falcon sale to Elswick-Hopper | January 1978 |
| Move to Brigg completed | during 1979 |

Whatever the reasons, Clements became a director of a publicly quoted company and became seriously wealthy, if only on paper. According to the 1978 Annual Report he held the largest number of shares with 7%, with George Calvert holding 6.6% and Sir Ralph Carr-Ellison 5.9%. The market value of Clements' shares would have been around £276,000. It must have been difficult for him to come to terms with the financial restraints expected from public company directors but his four company cars and an employee to keep them all clean did not sit well with Richard Blundell, the very 'correct' Raleigh trained executive. Had the move to Brigg been prior to the take-over the cars would not have been quite so visible to the Elswick-Hopper manager, but the two were totally incompatible. Both had valuable strengths and both were strongly sales oriented. It seemed at the start that the main board was unsure which one to back – they had forced together two disparate organisations with two strong leaders and neither would give ground.

Eventually Ernest had had enough and negotiated an exit deal, in which he left the company before his contract had expired, in June 1982, without dumping shares on the market. He took the Coventry-Eagle brand and the Newtown factory, as well as some of the Falcon management team with him. Sadly, the combined experience of Clements and Hoban did not prevent Newtown going into receivership in December 1989, finally drawing a curtain on Ernest Clements' long career in cycle manufacture.

The cycling world is a small one, as demonstrated by the fact that the Newtown business was bought from the receivers by Townsend Cycles, which eventually became part of Tandem, the eventual owners of Falcon, thus reuniting this family branch – but we have not yet reached that part of the story.

The departure of Ernest Clements gave Jim Turner the opportunity to finally merge the two cycle producers. In the July 1982 chairman's report he stated that a major reorganisation was underway 'that involved the disposal of the Coventry-Eagle company, which had made losses since it was re-established in Newtown, and also the disposal of a small cycle accessory importing business which had also been making losses.'

## Tiger Sports and Leisure & Nigel Dean Cycles

Ernest Clements had not yet finished with Barton and in 1983 set up a manufacturing facility in Marsh Lane through a company that he first registered in October 1979 as Tiger Sports and Leisure. A range of Clements branded racing cycles was produced until 1988 and marketed through the Newtown factory. One of Falcon's ex-racing cyclists, Nigel Dean, was hired to work for the new company as sales manager in 1986, becoming a director in August of that year. He had bought Stan Miles' St Albans bike shop only the year before, but must have seen a greater potential working for Clements once more. Nigel started racing professionally in 1971 and first rode for Falcon in 1978. Clements' teams had many names during these years and Nigel's last season with him was in the 1982 Falcon-Campagnolo team. Just a year into the job, Nigel and his wife Roberta were given the opportunity to buy out Clements' 100% holding in Tiger Sports and Leisure. A deal was struck and the business, trading as Nigel Dean Cycles, enjoyed a few good years, with production peaking at 40 frames per week, though Dean's target was 100. Unfortunately Nigel was one of the many racing cyclists who did not succeed in transforming from sportsman to businessman. He brought in Ben Blow, an experienced engineer who had managed companies in Hull, to run the production side, and Ben's wife Beverley to run the business side, but to no avail. Volumes were just too low to allow components and materials to be bought at a sufficient discount to provide an adequate profit margin, and there was insufficient cash to boost production by building stocks for the main selling season. The company went into voluntary liquidation in 1992, with debts of £243,000, and Nigel took himself off to Zimbabwe with a new wife. Ben Blow and the workforce raised the funds to buy the physical assets at auction, using mainly their own savings, and turned the business into a co-operative, still trading under the Nigel Dean name. Sadly, and despite good reviews of their machines, the organisation still lacked the financial resources to survive in the tough competitive world of bike building and was wound up in 1995.

## Productivity and Expansion

The range of products was gradually switched to Alveley-made Elswick models, so that by the time the Raleigh contract ended the factory was able to supply the needs of the customers. However, it soon became clear that more radical changes were necessary to ensure the long-term survival of the cycle division. Investment was one key to unlocking productivity improvements, and after a visit to Italy Stan Havercroft persuaded the board to buy a Marchetti and Lange frame production carousel. This consisted of five operator stations on a chain driven turntable, each operator responsible for hand brazing one joint of the frame. The fifth operator removed the completed frame from the machine. There was no time-consuming drilling and pinning involved and, according to Stan, output was quite good. Paint productivity was also improved through investment in a new powder coating plant. Transportation was streamlined by the use of freestanding containers that were pre-loaded so that a lorry tractor unit could be turned around in no more than 15 minutes. The factory was almost self-contained, though some wheels were still supplied from Barton.

In addition to capital investment several improvement studies were made by Urwick Orr and Partners Ltd, the first being an audit of systems and procedures. This was commissioned by Richard Blundell in March 1980 and the scope was wide, including financial and management accounting systems, order to sales invoicing, purchase and stock control, debt, credit and cash control, costing and management information, and production scheduling and control. It was pointed out that the existing systems had been required to cope with significant growth and that further growth was anticipated. At this time a standard costing system was used and the consultants saw scope for improvement, mainly in terms of data accuracy and the way in which financial information could be used to improve management decisions.

Stock control improvements were recommended, in view of the £1 million of stock being carried at that time. This equated to between two and four months sales, depending on the time of year, and the report indicated scope for either stock reduction or an improvement in customer service. Warehousing was criticised in that 'storage areas are widely dispersed and separated over the site at Barton, and at peak times you have to use additional premises away from your main site.' Space was considered inadequate at peak times leading to accidental damage and slow handling. In some locations lack of racking meant that cycles and wheels had to be stacked in heaps. To a large extent this was, of course, the result of hanging on to the Barton site and its Edwardian layout, rather than moving to new premises, or replacing the old buildings with new.

However, perhaps the most significant recommendation was to provide monthly gross profit information that differentiated between bought-in products and own-produced models, so that rational 'make or buy' decisions could be made.

Another indication of lack of investment, this time in systems, is the reference to an earlier report on 'The use of Computers at Elswick-Hopper Cycles'. This had indicated the possible advantages of using a microcomputer to cover sales ledger, purchase ledger and nominal ledger work. At this time, 1979, the purchase ledger was in the traditional form of separate daybooks and ledgers. The report comments on the relatively low base salaries and high commission for field sales staff, and that Barton office staff pay was low, a situation that could give problems once the Humber Bridge was opened (two years later).

One finding from the study calculated the cost of an Alveley built frame set at £7 compared with £3 for a bought in item. Clearly, continued frame production was not viable, a fact of life that was being discovered across the industry.

A second survey by Urwick, Orr was carried out in April 1980 into manufacturing at Alveley, suggesting improvements to the incentive system, a better layout to minimise work in progress and improved production information. Lack of information with respect to quantities of substandard items, scrap and rectifications, was identified as a major hindrance to the production supervisors' ability to manage production. This report also provides a snapshot of the situation at Alveley in early 1980:

- Production had increased from averages of 200 to 700 bicycles per week since 1974.
- In April 1980 850 cycles and 2,000 wheels had been produced.
- Total number of employees was down to 56, of whom 36 were production operatives:
  - frame and fork production, 14
  - painting and transfer application, 7
  - wheel building, 6
  - final assembly, 9

The remaining 20 employees were employed in: receipt and storage of components and materials, stock control, warehousing finished components and despatch, packing, calculation and payment of hourly wages, procurement of consumables and general administration. At this time 18 basic specifications were in place, with additional colour and component variations. However, analysis showed that two models had not been produced for 50 weeks, three specifications accounted for 54% of production and six for 77%. The GPO contract filled just 8% of production capacity.

By mid-1980 a new and even more ambitious strategy was developed for Alveley and Barton involving the following steps:

- Alveley to become a 1,000 cycle per week manufacturing unit and to provide depot storage facilities. Wheel manufacture to be phased out.
- Barton to be developed so that 500 cycles per week could be assembled. This would require eight operatives. Top of the range models to be built at Barton. Wheel building facilities to be extended to supply Alveley.
- Marketing to be strengthened by the appointment of a product development manager, and marketing statistics to be improved by assigning the role to a clerk.
- Manual systems and control information to be set up prior to a transition to a computerised system.

This work was to be co-ordinated by Richard Blundell from Barton with assistance from Urwick Orr at Alveley. Their study made several recommendations including work analysis and measurement to support a new bonus scheme, a new stores system to support the production programme, preparation of full engineering specifications for bought in components, and a change in the reporting structure to make the quality inspectors independent of line management.

By August the manufacturing and storage targets had been refined somewhat, based on operating plans for the 1981/82 financial year. Urwick Orr prepared a fixed fee for the work entailed in making recommendations for changes to enable Alveley to meet the new targets. Unit production stayed at 1,000 per week with an annual target of 46,000. These comprised three model groups: sports 7,500; tourist and junior 35,000; post office roadsters 3,500. Storage for raw materials and components was to be sized for 10,000 equivalent cycles and finished storage for 3,500 cycles. Results for the year ended 31 January 1981 showed there was still a mountain to climb. Turnover was up at £4,441,025 but profits were slashed to £37,515.

Studies continued through 1982 and included advice to Stan Havercroft on setting up the new frame brazing equipment bought from Marchetti and Lange. Inevitably, Urwick Orr's cost analysis of own frame costs versus buying in quickly led to the closure of the frame shop at Alveley and procurement of all frames from the Far East.

## The Far East

As noted earlier frames and components had been procured from Japan since the late-1970s, initially through Marui, which operated as an export house for many other Japanese manufacturers. Nationally the trend was to import components, as British suppliers progressively priced themselves out of the market. Phil Bradley visited the Far East on several occasions and his trip reports read like a *Who's Who* of the Japanese and Taiwanese cycle industry. Falcon had already been dealing with many of the suppliers visited by Phil in August 1980, when he covered 21 companies in 15 days. The Japanese industry was already operating in a very different league to that in Europe, with predicted home sales of six million bicycles and a further one million for export. Marui, based in Kobe, had been expanding into the USA and Western Europe for some years and received an enquiry from Phil for 23,000 completely knocked down (CKD) bicycles to be delivered for the 1981 season. Over half of these were for the model S64 'Turbo 12' 12-speed racing models. The advantage of shipping bicycles in their component parts was the beneficial import tax on components compared to assembled bicycles – 8% as against 17½%, provided that containers comprising a complete order were shipped separately. The next visit was to Miki Industrial Co Ltd in Osaka. With a reputation for building the best quality frames in Japan the company could produce 3,000 frames per week at a factory employing 30, with electrostatic painting carried out at a second factory with 28 employees. Component manufacturers visited included Tange, Shimano, Arai, Showa, and Sakae Ringyo (SR). The latter company was, at the time, the largest manufacturer of alloy chain wheels, stems, seat pillars and pedals in Japan, producing 10,000 double chain wheel sets per day from their Tokyo factory. Their sights were firmly set on the European market, which was taking 60% of production. Phil learned that George Hooley, Raleigh's purchasing manager had recently visited SR and placed a three year order for one million stems per year.

In Taiwan 13 companies were visited in the search for competitive frames and components. At the time there were 30 frame manufacturers, with the larger being: Giant, Dodsun, Fairly, Steel Master, Asai, Merida and EE. Fairly, based in Taipei, were already supplying frames to Falcon and were a major supplier to Raleigh Industries of America (RIA), with eight RIA models displayed in its showroom. Giant, also based in Taipei were producing 350,000 bicycles per year, mainly sports and BMX models. As their frame capacity exceeded cycle production they were selling frames to Schwinn in the USA and to Falcon in Brigg. Executive vice president Tony Lo told Phil that a second factory was under construction to increase production to 750,000 bicycles per year. Continuous investment has made Giant one of the top bicycle manufacturers into the 21st century. However, not all Taiwanese companies were up to scratch, and Phil was horrified at the conditions in one factory near Taipei. It had dirt flooring and a totally unsatisfactory brazing shop. A swift telex to Alveley had Stan Havercroft cutting up a frame for inspection and finding it perfect – the order had fortunately been subcontracted to another supplier.

Such visits sometimes yielded unexpected benefits, such as the time when Phil was sitting in a meeting room at the EE Company when someone walked past the window carrying what appeared to be a Raleigh 20. It was confirmed as such a model, made for Raleigh Australia. He requested a frame set to take back to Barton and this became the new Elswick Cosmopolitan, replacing the one previously made in Alveley.

A second visit took place in September 1981, during a mild recession caused by lower demand from the USA. It would appear that not all Japanese sourced components were of adequate quality as some brake pull rods for the Elswick post office contract had failed. Ahead of fashion, Marui were pushing their streamlined Aero models. Phil's view was that whilst they would catch on eventually such models would not be the answer in the short term. Other quality problems were resolved during a visit to Shimano, which had supplied over 5,000 Selecta chain wheels in late-1980/early-1981. When offered replacement parts Phil pointed out that the problem had been overcome by fitting SR components and that the Selecta model was not acceptable to the UK market – other companies had also met with problems. Shimano promised to send their quality control inspector to Barton and to consider a claim for £20,000.

The situation in Taiwan was gloomy, due to the general turndown in demand for bicycles and the considerable damage caused by four summer typhoons. Schwinn had cancelled 250,000 bicycles from Giant, and Raleigh America 27,000 from Merida. One result was the closure of the Giant factory for 45 days from 28 September. However, Pacific Cycles Inc, based in Taipei, were more upbeat, having just opened a new factory producing 1,000 frames per week, though capable of almost 6,000. Pacific

Fig. 7.30  Advertisement for the Elswick Envoy.

had been set up by the EE Company, specifically to manufacture bicycles for export, and primarily with an eye on the US and German markets.

In 1982/83 the Taiwanese Giant company supplied large numbers of all chrome BMX bicycles to Falcon and was owed $1 million. Phil Bradley recalls taking Giant's Tony Lo out for a meal during a UK visit and reassuring him that he would get paid, which he did. Lo became chairman of Giant and so probably the most influential man in the world-wide cycle trade. The long-standing Hopper 'Little Giant' trade mark was transferred to Giant at this time.

## Elswick Envoy

Elswick Special Vehicles Division was set up in 1980 specifically to take over the rights to a new type of car for the disabled developed by GKN Sankey and the National Research Development Corporation. I am grateful to Envoy owner Nick Davenport for supplying information on the car and for putting me on to the 'unofficial Austin Rover website', austin-rover.co.uk, in which the full history of the vehicle is recorded by Aspoèe Simelli, and on which this section is based. Given the company's previous failures in road transport it is clearly true that hope dies hard in the human heart. In fact the Elswick Envoy was a well thought out and attractive car that allowed rear door wheelchair access. The gestation period for the Envoy was a long one, as the car from which it had been derived was first seen at the 1973 Motor Show British Leyland Motor Corporation stand and had been designed by William Towns, better known for his Aston Martin DBS. The Townscar was ahead of its time, being tall and short, rather like the compact cars of the early 21st century, but had typical sharp 1970 lines. It was originally conceived as a Mini replacement, using the A-series engine and automatic gearbox and could still carry four passengers despite being 75cm shorter. The negative feature was that access was through the single rear door, and this proved a major sticking point for the government safety approval authorities. However, BLMC were sufficiently interested to patent the design and renamed it Minissima. Bearing in mind the problems the company was facing at the time it is not surprising that the popular Mini continued to be produced and the Minissima was quietly withdrawn from the shows after a couple of years, never having made it beyond the prototype stage.

GKN Sankey eventually bought the design and solved the single door problem by adding one on the nearside. After further development a prototype that featured ramp access and a central location for the wheelchair driver won a Design Council award in 1978. As ever with British innovations there were further delays until Elswick finally took on the challenge in 1980 to produce a market version, using the Metro one litre engine. The standard version had provisions to automatically lock the driver's wheelchair to the floor. Two inward facing seats were provided in the rear, hinged and spring loaded to fold away for chair access. However, alternative configurations were available, for example a right or left hand drive position for non-disabled drivers with rear accommodation for the wheelchair occupant. Elswick publicity advised that production was due to start in September 1981 at a cost of around £5,500 + VAT + Vehicle Excise Duty, with enquirers directed to call Tony Turner at the Alcester base. Unfortunately the addition of taxes pushed the price to a hefty £7,000, beyond the reach of many potential customers. Production delays were announced at the 1982 AGM held on 14 July, though the first units were to be delivered 'shortly'. The fibreglass bodies were sourced from Reliant, based just on the other side of Birmingham at Tamworth.

A year later to the day it was announced that delivery problems had been overcome and, though UK sales had been slow, there had been some promising export orders from the USA, Canada and France. A price cut of £813 was tried during 1983, but the on-road price still came to £6598.92 (Fig. 7.30). On 12 July 1984 sales of the Envoy were reported as 'disappointing'. Clearance to market in the USA was still awaited from the authorities. Production ceased before the next AGM, according to the August 1985 report, due to insufficient volume demand at acceptable price levels. According to Simelli the design was just too dated and too expensive. Furthermore, she states that Gowrings Mobility had brought out the Metro Chairman, which also incorporated rear ramp access and, significantly, was supported by the Austin-Rover dealers' network.

A brave effort or a foolhardy mistake? Given the can-do attitudes of the decade it is perhaps not too surprising that a grass cutting machinery manufacturer saw no problems entering a new car-based market. But why did it take so long to find a company willing to invest, and why did a car manufacturer not enter the market? Established car companies would have recognised it as a small and specialised niche market, and one that could never be profitable. The Envoy can still be seen on the roads in the UK and Europe, and is now quite cheap to buy. The cost of the venture to Elswick-Hopper is not recorded, but must have been substantial. According to internet sources just 200 were made and two exported to the USA, though Jim Turner remembers the number as more like 20 to 30. Based on the quantity that come up for sale 200 is probably closer than 20. However, this quirky looking car did inspire a short film that received wide acclaim – 'Elegy for the Elswick Envoy' was made by disabled artist Nancy Willis during her quest for a home for her aging but much loved Envoy. In many ways the Envoy is yet another example of the ability of the UK to innovate but then fail to develop a market, or to innovate without first establishing a need. The Envoy could have been the basis for a very energy efficient 'Smart' type car for general use, but this idea was left for Mercedes to develop.

## The Overdue Merger

In the 1982 *International Cycling Guide* Harold Briercliffe reported falling sales, increased competition from overseas, and the more general use on 'British' bicycles of fittings made elsewhere.[60] He also noted the recent American import of bicycle motocross and that a leading importer had picked up an order for £100,000 BMX related items at the Harrogate Show. Raleigh was also suffering from competition from the Far East with sales falling from 2 million cycles in 1978 to half that number by 1986.[61]

With Ernest Clements out of the equation and the pressure on profit margins the Elswick/Falcon integration problem had to be resolved. Jim Turner announced a major reorganisation at the 1981 AGM, stating that:

> ...following a consultant's report we are concentrating our production facilities at Brigg and Alveley, which are both modern factories, and are in the process of closing the company's factories at Barton on Humber, where the company originally started over 100 years ago. This will eventually release the Barton site for disposal.
>
> The Brigg and Alveley factories will be operated under central control and will serve the marketing companies, Elswick and Falcon, which will retain their separate identities. A new company, Astra Cycles, has recently been started to market bicycles purchased from outside sources.

Clearly disappointed with the failure of his managers to sort themselves out, Turner brought in Peter Morris from the 3i investment group, and it was his report that was cited in the announcement. Casting further doubts on Richard Blundell's ability to pull things together Jim Turner also announced the recent appointment of Morris as chief executive of the Cycle Division, though Blundell remained as managing director. Morris had been very successful in his management career and was not far from retirement. According to Phil Bradley, Morris was seen by the incumbent management as a 'hatchet man'. He certainly had doubts concerning Phil Bradley's efforts in the Far East and decided to take his place during a visit in late-1982, accompanied by his wife, and Phil dutifully prepared a recommended itinerary for the visit. Whatever Morris discovered on the trip – no report was circulated – Phil survived his return. Stan Havercroft and Jane Jordan were made redundant as part of the merger, though Richard Blundell remained.

On 25 February 1983 the Elswick-Hopper Cycle Co Ltd was re-registered with Companies House as Elswick-Falcon Cycle Co Ltd, thereby finally severing the Hopper connection, though the Elswick name itself had but three years to run.

At the July 1983 AGM it was reported that Peter Morris had stepped down and Blundell was appointed divisional chief executive. Results for the 1982/83 financial year had been encouraging with sales of over £9 million and an operating profit, despite merger costs of £241,000. Management expressed the hope that the fall in sterling would make cycle production competitive with imports. Things did not work out that way, and Jim Turner expressed disappointment with results in his July 1984 report. He laid the blame on difficulties and problems encountered with the reorganised Cycle Division and had decided that he needed to take over the role of Chief Executive. This he did in October 1983. Richard Blundell was made redundant, presumably due to a disagreement with the board, and founded Target Cycles, initially based on the St Mary's site and now, as a large wheel building operation, at the Falkland Way Industrial Estate. He died in May 1989 after a protracted fight with cancer, having built a successful new company from scratch. His support for cycling in his adopted hometown is commemorated by the annual presentation by Barton Wheelers of the Richard Blundell trophy, based on a season-long time trial points competition.

Phil Bradley and Bill Holmes attended the 24th International Cycle Show in New York in February 1983. The 20" BMX was still selling well, with a gradual increase in the popularity of the 24" model – the peak for BMX sales occurring in 1984. Phil made an interesting observation in his trip report concerning the West Coast newcomer, the 'mountain bike'. 'To date there has been little sign of popularity for this type of cycle on the East Coast and I believe there is only minimal interest in Europe and Australia at the moment. As far as the UK is concerned I believe that the requirement for this type of bicycle could be fairly small.' Well, everyone makes mistakes, and to be fair the market did not take off until 1987, but after that it was unstoppable. Not surprisingly many of the companies represented at the show were from Japan and Taiwan.

## Retrenchment

With a large factory at Brigg, and increasing imports from the Far East, there was little point in keeping Alveley open. It duly closed in January 1984, with a few key people transferring to Brigg. The closure was announced by Jim Turner at a board meeting, and was accepted, to his surprise, without dissent. Though the objective was to minimise production costs by running a single production factory it was still intended to market the Falcon and Elswick brands through separate sales teams. However, it proved impossible to run two sales teams from the same premises with a single back office and retain a unique identity. In Peter Sweetman's experience it had not worked at other companies, as 'dealers are not that stupid'.

The Barton St Mary's site retained the Elswick building as a warehouse until 1986, with an office from which the sale of the industrial buildings was handled by the group financial controller, Fred Northgraves. The major part of the St Mary's site was eventually sold to Meldan Fabrications, a locally owned steel fabrication business, with petrochemical contracts along the Humber Bank. The site has seen planning applications for housing development, but in 2010 is still primarily an industrial estate. The old 1911 Elswick building, under separate ownership, received planning permission in 2005 for conversion to apartments. Thus ended 106 years of Hopper involvement in Barton on Humber, though even when the factory site is eventually demolished there is still a terrace of single bedroom bungalows built into the old roadside machine shop on Marsh Lane, the still to be developed Elswick apartments and the conversion of the remarkable Brigg Road office building to luxury apartments to remind people of the town's industrial past; not to mention the many houses erected in the Edwardian years to house the bicycle builders of Barton. It is perhaps fitting, given the national obsession with homes, that Fred Hopper's main legacy to his home town is housing.

## Bill Cross Takes the Reins

The mid-1980s saw the group in recession in the midst of general industrial turmoil – the decisive defeat of the miners, the start of Margaret Thatcher's privatisation programme, and the first-ever peacetime deficit in the balance of trade in manufactured goods in 1986.[62] For Elswick-Hopper plc sales and margins declined dramatically and the financial pressures were enormous. The accounts for year ended 31 January 1984 reported a turnover of £28 million and an operating pre-tax profit of £331,000. Interest on borrowing turned this nominal profit into a loss of £217,000. Jim Turner lay the blame on a variety of factors, including the impact of the prolonged drought on the performance of the grass cutting machinery subsidiary, highly competitive conditions for agricultural machinery, and the impact of the new British Standard for bicycles, which had led to disposal of old stock at poor margins. Decisive action was called for and was announced by Jim at an EGM on October 29 1984:

> Over recent years, as shareholders will be aware, all divisions of the Company and its subsidiaries have encountered difficult trading conditions and the steps taken to offset these problems have not been as successful as your board had hoped. Consequently, results have been disappointing and losses have been incurred, and have continued in the six months ended 31 July 1984. Reorganisation has been undertaken, especially in the Cycle Division….the associated costs have been substantial…borrowings remain unacceptably high and the interest costs of these borrowings is an additional burden on the Company's results.
>
> Recognising the need to strengthen the management of the Company, an approach was made to Mr HW Cross, the chairman of Brent Chemicals International plc with a view to Mr Cross joining the Board.

HW (Bill) Cross was 62 when he joined the Elswick-Hopper plc board as executive chairman. He had been running Brent Chemicals for 14 years and brought in his son, David, as deputy managing director. David had been financial director of the Cleansing Service Group Ltd and took particular responsibility for the Agricultural and Engineering Divisions. According to Phil Bradley, he was the most intelligent man he had ever met, having an instant grasp of new information.

Other new main board members were brought in, including Paul Hill as financial director, though Jim Turner remained managing director, with particular responsibility for the cycle business. The EGM also sought approval for a rights issue to raise £925,000, initially to be applied to the reduction of bank indebtedness.

The Cross management team brought in new management strategies, philosophies and techniques, backed by money, experience and fresh expertise. So far as the bicycle division was concerned Norman Court was promoted from sales and marketing director to managing director of Elswick-Falcon in February 1985. He had joined the company from Humbrol, the Hull-based paint manufacturer, replacing Jane Jordan, and had wide marketing expertise.

At his first AGM in August 1985 Cross reported group sales up 4.4% to £29.4 million, with an overall loss for the year of £1.192 million, almost double that of the previous 12 months. He went on:

> The cycle industry normally experiences a rapid upsurge of business in the final months of the year as stockists buy in for the Christmas season. In 1984 this trend was much less marked with demand for BMX bicycles being particularly weak, and the Cycle Division's sales along with those of its main competitors, were much lower than expected, leaving much higher stocks of finished cycles, work in progress and components than planned. The financial burden resulting from excessive stocks was exacerbated by the sharp and considerable rise in interest rates, which took place soon afterwards.
>
> Core problem with cycles has been excessively high stocks of finished products and components and its long and inflexible supply line. Components were traditionally sourced mainly from overseas, especially Far East and Japan, causing a very lengthy supply line and heavy exposure to currency fluctuations. An intensive resourcing programme replacing distant suppliers by UK or Continental suppliers has been introduced with the following objectives:
> • greater flexibility to respond to market changes

- requirement for much lower stock levels
- reduced currency exposure

Manufacturing and assembly methods have been reorganised and the Brigg factory is now capable of producing bicycles of outstanding design, quality and reliability at competitive cost levels.

A thorough strategic review has led to the conclusion that the Cycles Division, as a quality supplier, is capable of becoming profitable within a reasonable period, building on its position as the UK's second largest cycle company.

The reconstructed board has set in motion a recovery programme to improve cash flow, substantially reduce overall borrowings, stemming losses and creating a firm base from which to launch a profitable expansion of the business.

The Brigg factory reorganisation had resulted from a new business plan drawn up by Norman Court. It involved significant investment in frame brazing equipment, chemical pre-treatment plant and a new electrostatic paint plant.

It took less than a year for the new chief's rosy view of the bicycle business to turn to more of a shade of grey and for him to realise that it was not as easy to foresee the future of the market for bikes as for bulk chemicals. In hindsight it seems incredible that the Cycle Division believed it could manage its business only through UK and European suppliers, and the loss of senior managers with cycle industry experience must have been a major factor in the adoption of the new strategies.

At the end of 1985 Hamish Easdale retired after 27 years service as a director and in February the following year David Cross took over the role of group managing director, with Turner acting as deputy chairman. By the next AGM in August 1986 the Hopper link had finally been erased and the company was renamed Elswick plc – much more in tune with the snappy 80s. Despite high interest rates improved performance had been achieved in all operations except bicycles, which saw a 30% fall in sales and a loss of £288,000. This was blamed on a severe downturn in demand for BMX bikes and the generally poor weather during 1985. Nationally sales were indeed down, by 26%, but both 1984 and 1983 had been skewed by the BMX boom.[63] Early in 1986 Elswick disappeared from the Cycle Division's name, becoming Falcon Cycles Ltd, complete with a new corporate identity and redesigned range of bicycles. To catch a growing USA market a special range was launched at the New York trade show in March 1986 under the name 'Falcon of England'. An office was also opened in New York with a stated strategy 'to capture a small but profitable niche in this very large market for quality sports cycles'. British Olympic cyclist Karl Barton was appointed to run the operation and to advise the factory on American specifications. Although dealers were appointed and orders obtained the quality provided was not good enough and eventually the project was abandoned, despite great efforts from Turner, Barton, and Court, on both sides of the Atlantic.[64]

By August 1986 all surplus property at Barton had been sold. Philip Bradley took redundancy in 1986, following a period of ill health, though he was asked to stay on for a few months and was eventually replaced by David Duffield, another ex-Raleigh employee, and latterly a well-known cycle racing commentator. Philip used his hard won knowledge of the industry to start a successful component and frame import business in Barton on Humber – Philby Enterprises.

## 1987 The End of an Era

Jim Turner's final year proved to be something of an epic one, not least because it saw the Cycles Division return to profit for the year ending 31 January 1987. His last financial year was also a good one overall with the first dividend payment for six years. It also heralded a new diversification strategy into packaging through the acquisition of Macleans, and away from agriculture with the disposal of Seward Agricultural Machinery of York and B H Brown of Alnwick. Engineering was also slimmed down when Picador Engineering was sold in February 1987. This was all in line with the new corporate strategy: to intensify the search for suitable acquisition opportunities, especially in the packaging industry and to offset the marked seasonal pattern and cash flows that existed in bicycle sales and, of course, in agriculture.

Macleans was a London based supplier of flexible decorative packaging for the food, confectionary, pharmaceutical and novelty product markets, using aluminium foil and laminated substrates. 1986 turnover was £2.4 million with 50 employees. The company was to act as a nucleus around which a significant Elswick presence could be built in the industry. Just six months later an EGM was held to seek approval for a rights issue to fund the acquisition of a second company involved in the new industry. This was Labeltech, a supplier of multicolour printed labels, mainly to food, confectionary, chemicals and toiletries businesses. Compound growth of 30% per year had been recorded for several years and this perhaps justified the £6 million purchase price.

Another link with the old regime disappeared in 1987 when the Elswick cycle brand was dropped. It had been relegated to the shopper range and Norman Court could not see any reason to retain the name at the expense of the more marketable Falcon brand.

The Cycles Division received a major boost with the acquisition of the Holdsworthy business, reported to shareholders as follows:

> The acquisition in March 1987 of the Holdsworthy business, including the prestigious brand names 'Claud Butler' and 'Holdsworth', has reinforced Falcon's position as the second largest supplier to the UK cycles market. Integration of the business into Falcon Cycles Ltd is proceeding smoothly and most of the production has been transferred from the Holdsworthy factory at Darlaston, currently occupied on short-term rental, to the Falcon factory at Brigg. The Darlsaton factory will be vacated in the near future but certain skilled operatives have been retained by Falcon and a specialist light-weight frame building facility will be set up on a small leased site in the Darlaston area.
>
> Capital equipment costing over £800,000 is to be installed during the current financial year at the Brigg factory to increase capacity, improve production methods and enable the appearance and finish of the products to reach the highest standards of the industry worldwide.
>
> The small Astra Cycles company, selling a range of budget-priced products, also had a profitable year and is expected to make steady continuing progress.

Holdsworthy was founded in 1939 by W F Holdsworth, a builder of lightweight cycles since the late 1920s. He bought the rights to the name of a contemporary builder, Claud Butler, in 1958. The company had been a major player in the corporate and mail order business with its high volume Comrade brand. The rationale was to absorb the Comrade volume, but the reality was that Holdsworthy had been building these bikes at close to cost, though the Claud Butler trademark was in time built back to a profitable line.

In the second half of 1987 the new paint plant at Brigg was experiencing start-up problems. As a result of a greater customer demand for a wide variety of paint colours and finishes, coupled with a financial demand for lower stocks, there was an almost overnight demand for shorter production runs in the factory. As the new plant had been designed for longer runs this caused a serious problem in meeting customer delivery requirements. By September these problems were compounded by a fire in the new paint plant, which led to a substantial insurance claim, with arguments over the level of consequential loss. Despite all these problems Falcon Cycles made a healthy operating profit of over £700,000 during 1987.

Yet another company was bought in October, this time within the Engineering Division – Bomford and Evershed another manufacturer and distributor of professional grass cutting equipment.

Jim Turner retired on 31 December 1987. He had been in the driving seat for almost 30 years and had seen Elswick-Hopper transformed from a failing bicycle manufacturer into an international conglomerate. Many challenges faced him over the years but his buoyant personality and, perhaps, his early training as a Spitfire pilot had clearly equipped him well for the challenge. One of his final jobs was to try to divest Elswick of its 'troublesome' cycle division and in his own words, 'I flew out to Taiwan for a meeting with Tony Lo, head of Giant, as I had heard that Giant was about to enter the UK market. I had previously met Lo in Taiwan with Philip Bradley and later in Brigg. The visit was unsuccessful, however, as Giant wanted to supply the UK from their own factory.' In terms of his influence on the history of Elswick-Hopper Jim Turner was clearly second only to the founder himself. Strangely, both made fruitless ventures into motorised transport. Where Jim could have taught Fred some serious lessons was in the field of financial management. So they probably deserve equal recognition, especially as Jim remained convinced, to the end of his tenure, of the value of the cycle division. Fred Hopper would have approved. Jim retained a link with the industry through his role as vice president of the Bicycle Association. His final year saw a 20% growth in Falcon sales – constrained due to supply problems – a first year record profit from Macleans, and a return to an Elswick plc dividend payment for the first time in six years. It had been a good year to retire.

## Endnotes

1       *Raleigh and the British Bicycle Industry*, Lloyd-Jones and Lewis, Ashgate 2000, p 244.
2       *The Times* April 15 1958.
3       *Motor Cycle and Cycle Trader* March 1958.
4       *Motor Cycle and Cycle Trader* July 1958.
5       *Cycling* 23 April 1958 p 408.
6       *The National Journal* May 1958.
7       *The Star* 8 October 1954 (Sheffield).
8       *Elswick-Hopper Newsletter* January 1959.
9       *Bicycle and Bicycling* H Briercliffe 1985.
10      Turner is referring to Raleigh and the British Cycle Corporation.
11      The Midlands business mentioned in the report was the Midland Motor Company, a commercial vehicle hire business acquired at the end of 1958.
12      *The National Journal* January 1959.
13      Ibid.
14      *Alpaca to Skinsuit* Bernard Thompson,Geerings of Ashford p 11.
15      *Motor Cycle and Cycle Trader* May 1959.
16      *Scunthorpe Evening Telegraph* 12 June 1959.
17      *Grimsby Evening Telegraph* 19 June 1959.
18      *Scunthorpe Evening Telegraph* 3 September 1959.
19      *Industrial Welfare* July 1959.
20      *Motor Cycle and Cycle Trader* July 1959.
21      *Cycling and Mopeds* 22 October 1959.
22      *The National Journal* July 1959.
23      *Motor Cycle and Cycle Export Trader* June 1960.
24      *The National Journal* August 1959.
25      *Cycling and Mopeds* 28 October 1959.
26      *Scunthorpe Evening Telegraph* 14 September1959.

27      *Motor Cycle and Cycle Export Trader* December 1959.

28      *Motor Cycle and Cycle Trader* 6 November 1959.

29      *Raleigh and the British Bicycle Industry* Lloyd-Jones and Lewis 2000 page 211.

30      Ibid page 213.

31      *Buzzing* volume 22 no 1 February 2003, The Lynx Project Mark Daniels p 21.

32      *Power and Pedal* October 1959 p 556.

33      *The National Journal* November 1959.

34      *Power and Pedal with The Scooter* June 1961 p 323.

35      Ibid.

36      *Cycling* 2 Oct 1963.

37      *The National Journal* July 1960.

38      *Power and Pedal with The Scooter* March 1962 p 153.

39      *The National Journal* January 1960.

40      *Motor Cycle and Cycle Trader* 8 April 1960.

41      *Motor Cycle and Cycle Trader* 26 August 1960.

42      *CTC Gazette* July 1960.

43      *CTC Handbook* 1961 page 27.

44      *Motor Cycle & Cycle Export Trader* September 1960.

45      *Raleigh and the British Bicycle Industry* Lloyd-Jones and Lewis 2000 p 218.

46      Ibid.

47      *The Moulton Bicycle* Tony Hadland 1981 p 29.

48      *20th Century Britain Economic, Social and Cultural Change* Paul Johnson 1994 pp 328-334.

49      Letter from McKenna to Fleming 26 Sept1966 North East Lincolnshire Archives.

50      *Framing Production* Paul Rosen 2002 p 120.

51      *Lincolnshire Times* 10 January 1969.

52      *Scunthorpe Evening Telegraph* 27 August 1970, front page.

53      Ibid 22 October 1970 p 14.

54      *The Dancing Chain* 2005 Frank Berto p 219.

55      *Scunthorpe Evening Telegraph* 19 December 1977.

56      The information in this section has been taken from Companies House records.

57      *Cycling* 21 June 1980.

58      *Cycling* 12 July 1980.

59      Elswick-Hopper chairman's report 23 July 1981 Companies House.

60      *International Cycling Guide* 1982 p 86 Tantivy Press.

61      *Framing Production* Paul Rosen 2002 p 111.

62      *20th Century Britain Economic, Social and Cultural Change* Paul Johnson 1994 pp 502-503.

63      *Framing Production* Paul Rosen 2002 p 120.

64      Statement from Jim Turner.

# CHAPTER 8

## ELSWICK PLC RIP

My thanks again to Peter Sweetman for much of the information in this chapter, which bridges the gap between Elswick-Falcon and Falcon under Casket/Tandem ownership. Another major source of information was company reports filed with Companies House.

The 1980s and 90s were a tumultuous time, with many companies searching for the holy grail of growth through acquisition and the creation of so-called 'conglomerates'. Under Cross management the company was steered firmly into printing and packaging, despite the steady and consistent results provided by Ryehill Farm Service Ltd, one of Jim Turner's early diversifications.

### 1987 Results

As recorded in the last chapter 1987 had been a good year to mark Jim Turner's departure. Published in April 1988 the final results were an increase in sales from £27.9 million to £29.2 million and a profit before tax of £1.6 million compared with a loss of £0.7 million in 1986. Sales were split 41% cycles, 40% equipment & services (mowers and Ryehill Farm Service), and 19% print and packaging. Even the £1.1 million bank overdraft had been paid off and turned into a cash credit of £1.5 million. In July 1987 Neil Eades joined the organisation as deputy chief executive. A Harvard Business School graduate, his business experience had been gained in the paint industry. Paul Hill was another executive recruited as financial director in November. Politically 1987 had also marked the start of the third and final term of Margaret Thatcher and was a period of unrestrained growth for many UK companies, accompanied by rising share prices as people built diversified portfolios on the back of popular privatisation issues. Even the dramatic stock market crash on 19 October, known as 'Black Monday', failed to obliterate the gains in Elswick plc shares and they had more than doubled in value by year end. An interesting note from the company records is that since 1985 the number of shareholders in the company had grown from 3,000 to over 20,000, with 75% in private hands.

### Newsletter

New management often feels the need to improve communications with employees and shareholders, and February 1988 saw the publication of Issue 1 of the *Chief Executive's Newsletter,* with a 'warm welcome' from David Cross. The cover page gave details of the component companies and a map to show their location. As a status report on where Elswick plc stood in 1988 it was neat and concise.

### WHO WE ARE AND WHAT WE DO

| Subsidiary | Location | Business |
|---|---|---|
| Falcon Cycles Ltd | Brigg & Scunthorpe | Manufacture and sale of bicycles. |
| Astra Cycles Ltd | Scunthorpe | Sales of bicycles. |
| Bike Rack Ltd | Wednesbury | Sale of bicycle spares and accessories. |
| Macleans Printed Packaging Ltd | London | Aluminium foil for biscuits, confectionery and Christmas markets. |
| Labeltech Ltd | Witham, Essex | Self-adhesive, multi-coloured labels for food, toiletries and other products. |
| Turner International (Engineering) Ltd | Alcester | Grass, scrub and hedge cutting equipment for use particularly by public authorities. |
| Bomford & Evershed Ltd | Salford Priors | Grass, scrub and hedge cutting equipment and agricultural machinery. |

| Agri-Projects International Ltd | St Peter Port, Guernsey | Grass, scrub and hedge cutting equipment and agricultural machinery. |
| Ryehill Farm Service Ltd | Malton and Burstwick | Supply of agro-chemicals and agricultural services. |

Two overseas subsidiaries were also listed:

Turner International (Engineering) Ltd, Conyers, Georgia, USA.

Turner Coughton (Victoria) Pty Ltd, Dandenong, Victoria, Australia.

Employees numbered 680.

Bike Rack was a new company set up to handle the component and accessory side of the cycle business, which had previously been part of Falcon Cycles. David Duffield was appointed general manager.

The remainder of this first newsletter was taken up with a history of Falcon, back to the early days in 1880, followed by an update on the business by Norman Court. This mentioned the almost £1 million investment in the Brigg factory, as well as acknowledging the challenges presented by the UK market, supplied as it was by 63 companies competing for the 1.5 million bicycles sold each year.

## Princess Diana Visits Brigg, Norman Court Departs

The new factory extension was opened by HRH the Princess of Wales with much fanfare on 29 March 1988. The event was recorded in Issue 2 of the *Chief Executive's Newsletter*. Bill Cross, his son and daughter-in-law, and Norman Court were the hosts and after the formal opening the Princess toured the factory and met the workforce, even trying her hand at paint spraying. Simon Weston, the Welsh Guardsman who had been severely burned when aboard HMS Sir Galahad during the Falklands War, was there with the bike he had ridden for charity along the west coast of the USA. The Princess was, predictably, given two Falcon bicycles to take home for William and Edward.

As the year progressed the industry entered another of its periodic downturns, compounded for Falcon by further operational problems with the new pre-treatment and paint plant at Brigg. Just when these problems seemed to be resolved a serious fire broke out in the pre-treatment plant in September, at the time of the year when production should have been getting into gear for the start of the Christmas sales peak. A substantial claim was made for consequential loss and appeared in the accounts. Consideration was also given to suing the suppliers for losses due to delayed start-up. As had happened with George Clarke and Harold Crook in the early 1950s a scapegoat was demanded, rather than a rational explanation of the problem, and Norman Court departed in July 1988, to be replaced by Neil Eades. His remit was to sort out what was being regarded by the main board as the corporate 'problem child' when compared with the new printing companies, which were demanding money for investment, and reliable old performers such as Ryehill.

Eades' solution was to cut back the business to its Falcon core. Astra and Bike Rack were sold, and the USA business transferred to a single large distributor. Emphasis was also placed on specialist dealers and a new style of promotion was offered where a mobile showroom was created in a double-decker bus. 1988 was something of a turning point for the industry as it was the year when the All Terrain Bicycle (also known as ATB, MTB and Mountain Bike) started to come into fashion, creating a massive opportunity for imports, including from mainland China, and requiring a major change in the model range. A new strategy was developed to invest heavily in quality systems in an effort to rebuild customer confidence. Eades insisted on 100% inspection at the end of every line. He tried to cut costs by deleting non-essential overheads, and also instituted an aggressive and expensive marketing campaign. A new range was launched for 1989 with a new style of catalogue, available from dealers, but also from W H Smith.

# A Return to Racing and more Acquisitions

The new strategy did not restore profitability and a loss of £487,000 was made on sales of £8.8 million. On a brighter note a professional racing team, PMS Falcon, had arrived on the scene after a two year gap, thanks to Norman Court, and appeared in an episode of 'Boon', a long running TV series starring Michael Elphick. Keith Lambert was appointed team manager, with Australian Shane Sutton team captain. Channel 4 had just started its love affair with road racing and captured many viewers with its coverage of city centre races, as well as its excellent Tour de France coverage.

Elsewhere in Elswick plc growth continued. Spark Industrial Electronics had been acquired in July 1988 for £380,000, yet another move into labels and print. Based in Northallerton, Sparkprint, as it was known, supplied self-adhesive labels to the food industry, and so was in the same business as Labeltech, though with a different customer base. International business expanded with the purchase of Dandl Manufacturing for $1.890 million. Based in California Dandl manufactured orchard mowers and crop shredders, a profitable niche business. Dandl and Turner International at Conyers were regrouped under a new subsidiary, Elswick Inc, in February 1989 and Locke Mowers Inc, a supplier of domestic lawn mowers, was added to the portfolio of US companies for $400,000 just three months later. Anthony Turner, head of the Engineering and Equipment Division since 1979, retired from the main board at the end of January 1989. In 2010 he was listed as chairman of GreenMech Ltd, still based at Kings Coughton, Alcester. This company was set up in 1993 to develop, manufacture and market a range of wood chippers and green waste shredders.

Overall the 1988 results were impressive, with the loss at Falcon offset by profits of £1.6 million on equipment and services and £1.1 million from print and packaging. The new division's performance was on sales of £10.6 million, half that for equipment and services, which was seen as ample justification for the new direction.

Financially the good times continued through 1989. Sales rose to £47.2 million and group profits by 34% to £2.4 million. Two more print companies were acquired: Rotatec in August 1989, makers of self-adhesive labels and, in January 1990, Blue Ribbon Label Co, makers of printed and woven clothing labels. Blue Ribbon cost was a substantial £6.4 million, requiring a large share issue. Bomford and Evershed and Turner International were brought together as a business entity, Bomford and Turner. Overseas sales in the sector outgrew domestic with 53% of the total. Falcon's problems continued from the production disruptions caused by the fire, and management effort was taken up rebuilding customer confidence.

For 1990 racing continued under the Team Banana Falcon name, Falcon having replaced Raleigh as partner of the Banana Group, the UK representative of the industry. Keith Lambert remained as manager, Shane Sutton as captain, with Dave Rayner, Chris Walker, Glenn Clarke, Rob Holden and Chris Lillywhite completing the line-up. With echoes of 1958 the team attended the March 1990 Cyclex Exhibition at Olympia, where they were officially 'launched'. New model ranges were on show for Falcon, Holdsworth and Claud Butler and included a Falcon Team Banana replica. It was a good year for the team, again echoing 1958, especially in the prestigious 12 day, 1,150 mile Milk Race, in which Sutton was overall winner and Rob Holden second. Banana Falcon also won the team prize. By the end of the season they had notched up a creditable 41 victories. Of course, with mountain bikes taking an ever larger share of the market and professional teams incurring ever higher costs it was difficult to justify on a cost benefit basis, though Falcon Banana did survive for a final season in 1991. Another successful Falcon team event in 1990 was the 58 mile London to Brighton charity ride, when a team of nine raised more than £2,000 for the British Heart Foundation. Neil Eades set an example by completing the course and Tim Higgins celebrated Falcon's heritage by riding a 1938 Elswick tandem, with Andy Preskey as stoker.

# Recession

Bill Cross gave an upbeat interim report on the half year's results in October 1990, in which he recorded Falcon's return to profit from May of that year. A note of caution was voiced over the growing recession. This was a consequence of Chancellor Lawson's 1988 boom, not helped by interest rates at 8%, though this was a welcomed drop of 2% compared to the year before. The *Financial Times* published a clinical analysis of the results on 16 October, but the *Daily Mirror*, the following day, was far more fun, with the headline 'Elswick ride high':

> Elswick, the cycles firm, are glad they got on their bikes and moved into the print and packaging business, specialising in labels, for this is where the big money is. Half-year profits soared by 133% to £1.5 million. Chairman Bill Cross reveals: 'Now we want to buy a private company, which would fit in with this important side of our operation.' Elswick's heavy-duty, grass-cutting machinery business is also growing. Only the poor old bikes, which the firm started 110 years ago, are showing a loss. But Bill Cross insists he has no plans to close them down.

Cross was telling the truth, why close down a saleable subsidiary?

The *Chief Executive's Newsletter* reached issue 11 in November 1990 and recorded continuing success for Bomford Turner's grass cutting machinery, despite two years of drought and virtually no grass growth in many parts of Europe. Labeltech was also featured, having developed and patented a new re-sealable leaflet system that was selling throughout Europe and was set for launch in the USA.

The 1990 results reported a 23% increase in sales and a 21% profit improvement. Despite the recession print and packaging had improved by 50% in both sales and profit. Equipment and Services had experienced another unusually dry year, not good for grass cutting sales, though Ryehill Farm Service (RFS) had maintained its consistent profitable growth, with further expansion of the technical sales and service organisation. Cycles had been doing well until the end of 1990, when consumers finally responded to the recession by keeping their credit cards in their wallets. Strong efforts to reposition Falcon as a supplier of quality bicycles at the upper end of the market, where higher average selling prices could be set, had not worked. Losses were building and accumulating on the Falcon balance sheet, making it more difficult to obtain credit terms from foreign suppliers. In 1991 Elswick plc decided to engineer an asset swap with RFS. As a supplier of chemicals and services to farms, and no manufacturing costs, RFS did not need a strong balance sheet, so Falcon Cycles acquired the undertakings and assets of RFS, and RFS acquired the undertakings and assets of Falcon Cycles. When this swap had been completed the names of the companies were changed, to return things to normal. All that was required was a change of company registration number, and a change in letter headings. Although this move restored Falcon's financial position it did not change the basic situation that bicycle manufacture was no longer consistent with the aims of the parent company. A buyer had to be found.

Paul Vicary joined Falcon in 1991, with experience at Richardson Vick and Samsung, and took responsibility for the marketing of the Falcon, Claud Butler and Holdsworth ranges. It was not a good year for Falcon with losses of £1 million and Elswick plc finally decided that the company was a lost cause. Falcon was sold to the Casket Group in December 1991 for around £600,000, marking the end of the long relationship of the Elswick name with bicycles.

There were positive signs that the restructuring of the previous two years was working, but the recession was still biting and competition from overseas manufacturers depressed prices. Management's mindset was that continued manufacture of bicycles would place an unsustainable drain on the financial resources of the company. The alternative strategy to achieve more substantial profit margins for Elswick plc was an expansion of the packaging businesses. The results for the year ending 31 January 1991 give a clear indication of the new direction for the company and the figures for the cycle division explain the reasoning behind the new strategy:

| | 1991 £ | 1990 £ | % Change +(-) |
|---|---|---|---|
| Sales | | | |
| Print & packaging | 24,288,000 | 15,765,000 | 54 |
| Equipment & services | 24,531,000 | 22,628,000 | 8 |
| Cycles | 9,368,000 | 9,030,000 | 4 |
| Total | 58,187,000 | 47,423,000 | 23 |
| | | | |
| Operating profit | | | |
| Print & packaging | 2,607,000 | 1,747,000 | 49 |
| Equipment & services | 1,519,000 | 1,869,000 | (19) |
| Cycles | (215,000) | (394,000) | 45 |
| Total | 3,911,000 | 3,222,000 | 21 |

## The End

Elswick plc followed its withdrawal from the bicycle industry with the sale of Locke Mowers. These disposals gave rise to an extraordinary item of £3.656 million on the balance sheet and in 1993 an application was made to the High Court for capital reconstruction. Bill Cross stepped down on 22 July 1993 at the AGM and handed the chair to Lord Lane of Horsell. The latter had joined Elswick plc as Sir Peter Lane in 1984, having, like Bill Cross, also acted as chairman of Brent Chemicals. At his first AGM he announced the disposal of Bomford Turner 'at a satisfactory price', and recorded that Ryehill was still doing well. The year had seen the group focussed on two core activities, specialised print and packaging, and marketing of agrochemicals. Surprisingly employees were recorded at 741 in 1993. On 13 September 1994 the whole of the issued share capital of Elswick plc was acquired by Ferguson International Holdings plc in what has been termed a reverse takeover. Lord Lane, Bill Cross and Prof Farmer resigned from the board on 7 October 1994, followed by Paul Hill in December and David Cross on 29 March 1995. A loss of £2.295 million was reported for 1995 compared to a profit of £2.777 million the year before. On 28 February 1995 the trade and assets of Elswick plc were transferred to Ferguson UK Ltd.

Ryehill Farm Service finally broke free from this mess on 28 April 1995 and Elswick reported a profit for the year of £1.7 million. In 1996 there were six employees and a loss was incurred of £15.7 million. The last entry with Companies House is dated 1997. 'Zero employees. Holding Company.' The various Elswick companies registered with Companies House were dissolved in 2000.

## Epilogue

The machinations of large corporations are a mystery to the majority of the population and I am grateful to 'DC' of London for asking the 'thisismoney' website the following question in April 2000:

> You recently published my question asking what happened to the company Elswick plc and said Elswick had been taken over by Ferguson International Holdings. I can't find a listing for Ferguson. What has happened to them?

The question was answered by Jeremy Batstone of NatWest Stockbrokers:

> Elswick was a bicycle manufacturer which sold itself to Ferguson International in September 1994. Elswick shareholders got one Ferguson share and £1.75 in cash for every 29.2 Elswick shares. But bad news! Ferguson International went into liquidation at the end of January and liquidators are currently selling the remaining assets. Its shares have been removed from the market.

Fred Hopper would not have been amused.

# CHAPTER 9

# MODERN TIMES

Although not strictly part of the Elswick-Hopper story bicycles had been such an integral part of the company for so many years that it would be remiss not to record what happened to Falcon Cycles after its sale and to end the story in the second millenium. I am once again indebted to Peter Sweetman and to Falcon Cycles for their assistance.

## Exit Elswick, enter Casket

The Elswick connection with the bicycle industry ended in December 1991, after a span of 111 years. A deal was struck with the Casket Group, run by chief executive Joe Smith, for £600,000. Casket's cycle division managing director, Steven Walsh, had been keeping a speculative eye on Falcon for a number of years. He had already turned round Townsend Cycles, which had bought Ernie Clements' failed Newtown company, British Eagle, including the Coventry Eagle brand, from the receivers in February 1990 for £182,500. Townsend was located at Leigh, Lancashire, where it ran a small scale manufacturing facility with annual sales of around 300,000 cycles, of which 250,000 were imported. British Eagle had been competing directly with Falcon, though on a smaller scale, so the additional production capacity at Brigg and the reputation of the Falcon brand were seen as valuable assets in the quest for increased market share. Casket's original business had been in clothing, including ownership of the Pakamak plastic raincoat brand. Steven Walsh's recommendation was vindicated by a dramatic turn round in the fortunes of Falcon, providing yet another example of the cyclic nature of the business. At the end of the first six months under new ownership Falcon turned in a profit of £600,000, a remarkably short repayment period of the purchase price, enhancing Walsh's reputation within the Casket organisation. The company was already doing well as shown by the results for the year to 31 March 1992. Earnings per share jumped from 0.4p to 1.9p, debt was reduced by 38% and pre-tax profits had risen to £2.1 million from £212,000. Joe Smith stated that 'although markets are still difficult for us, I am confident we will continue to make good progress this year.'

A return was made in 1992 to the junior market, including junior All Terrain Bicycles, which were just becoming popular, and the profit for the year from the bicycle division hit £1 million, an astonishing reversal of the previous year's results. This was a major contribution to the company's overall pre-tax profit as the clothing division was in decline; it was indeed a novel experience for the ex-Elswick managers to be cast as the good guys. The report for the year ended 30 September stated that:

> The success of the group's bicycle operations continued with a further substantial increase in turnover and profitability. Sales of the group's UK manufactured mountain bikes have been particularly strong. The integration of Falcon Cycles has gone especially well and this business made a significant contribution to the division's results in the period. Casket's share of the UK bicycle market now exceeds 20% and continues to grow through strong brands – Claud Butler, Falcon, British Eagle and Townsend – and the group is well positioned for the important Christmas sales period.

## Expansion

1992 continued in an upbeat note with a report in the *Financial Times* of 11 November that pre-tax profits had increased by 79% for the six months to 30 September. On the back of these results further expansion was planned, following the well-established, but often illusory belief, that good times follow good times. This invoked feelings of déjà-vu amongst the more experienced managers. New investment in the Brigg factory included additional stores, new automatic wheel building equipment and modifications to the paint shop. These improvements increased manufacturing capacity by 35% and allowed the production of the new junior range in-house. Simultaneously it was decided to build a grass-roots manufacturing plant at Leigh for Townsend production at a cost of £6.5 million, based on the belief that what worked for Falcon would work for Townsend. Up to that time Townsend had been a low capital operation yielding a return on capital that exceeded Falcon's.

By the end of March 1993 Joe Smith was able to announce an increase in turnover of 34% from £71.93 million to £96.48 million and an operating profit up by 38%. Investment in clothing continued with the acquisition of Yates (Leicestrella) Ltd, which produced a range of own label children's wear. The big news for the cycle industry was an agreement with Lotus Engineering to manufacture and distribute a range of seven bicycles under the LotusSport range including both road and mountain bikes (MTBs) and of carbon fibre as well as conventional materials. The bicycle division now held 25% of the UK Market and turnover and profit had increased by 70% and 77% respectively; this was despite a poor level of Christmas sales throughout the industry.

In 1993 Falcon made a record operating profit of more than £2 million and Casket results for the six months to 30 September reported significant progress despite the weak recovery in the UK economy. The manufacturing scene had changed dramatically, in a way that would appear unimaginable just 10 years later. From the report:

> The bicycle operations have undergone a period of considerable change with a major shift from imports to own assembly being achieved. This limited the turnover increase to 4.3% but 60% of bicycle sales was represented by UK assembled product against 37% in the corresponding period of last years. This shift will benefit margins in the coming months. Export sales of bicycles increased by approximately 100% over the corresponding period, while accessory sales grew by some 47%.[1]

It was also stated that the increase in assembly capacity at Brigg had been successfully completed and that the construction of the new assembly, warehouse and administration facility at Leigh was due to be ready for occupation in February 1994.

## The German Misadventure

The potential for acquisition of bicycle-based companies in the UK was limited, so Casket management turned its attention to mainland Europe and saw possibilities in the well-established German manufacturer, Heidemann Fahrrad. Based at Einbeck, near Hanover, the company ranked tenth in the German bicycle manufacturing league and a deal was struck for £1.3 million on 25 November 1993. This investment was backed by Walsh, based on a belief that Heidemann's reputation for quality could be leveraged to increase market share. It was also felt that ownership of a German company would promote sales of UK produced bicycles to the German market. The Heidemann subsidiary made a positive contribution during the current accounting period and 'a more significant impact in next year's results was anticipated'. These words were prophetic, though not as the statement intended. The £1 million expansion at Brigg was completed in November 1993 and in March 1994 Townsend Cycles moved to the purpose built, 230,000 square foot facility at Leigh, Lancashire.

Interim results for the six months ended 30 September 1994 were downbeat, with a profit before tax of £1.032 million, a reduction of 51.5% compared to the previous year. A slow demand in the UK market and an operating loss in Germany were blamed. Clothing had done much better with a 167% increase in operating profit for the 'value for money' businesses of £972,000. Taxation charges increased to 33% because losses at Heidemann could not be offset against UK profits. In the UK the company faced a dilemma:

> Although overall unit sales increased by 2% to over 310,000 bicycles, the market's move to cheaper bicycles resulted in a 6% fall in sales value to £24.5 million.....Casket's manufacturing capability continues to increase following the major capital expenditure programme undertaken last year and 80% of the bicycles sold in the period were assembled in the UK as compared to 60% in the corresponding period. However, the combination of the move to cheaper models and the slower than anticipated build up in both demand and assembly capability had a negative effect on margins and

operating profits reduced by some 23% to £1.99 million.[2]

The Heidemann acquisition was proving to be a disappointment with an operating loss of £607,000 for the six months. The German market had:

> ..suffered an unexpectedly sharp decline of approximately 20% to an estimated 4.7 million bicycles in 1994 and has led to short time working throughout the industry. This market position adversely affected the launch of the new 'Boss Bikes' range and highlighted the weakness of the Heidemann sales distribution channels as a result of the company's poor 1993 delivery record. It has taken longer than anticipated to redress this situation and unit sales in the first six months of the financial year were below the corresponding period in the previous year.[3]

Actions planned to re-establish the growth of recent years included an increase in UK manufacturing capacity and the re-establishment of Heidemann distribution channels. However, Casket management had seriously underestimated the difficulties in running a foreign subsidiary, with a different culture and different trading conditions, while also attempting a significant expansion of its UK manufacturing plants. After a mere eight months running the German company it was clear that Casket could not afford the continuing drain on its financial resources. The clothing division was now in decline and the new plant at Leigh was hitting major problems. The challenge of going from 50,000 to 300,000 cycles a year had been underestimated on all fronts. The computer system, cloned from Falcon, was not working, and planning, purchasing and production problems were rife. Casket made a corporate loss in 1994 of £12.3 million, on the heels of 'darling of the City' status just a year earlier. Falcon contributed a profit of just under £2 million as the investments started to pay out.

According to the September 1994 issue of *Cycle Industry*, Joe Smith believed that Townsend had further potential for earnings growth and replaced managing director Gary Grey with Paul Vicary. Paul had been in charge of Falcon for just a year and his new job was to run both organisations. He had been sales and marketing director for Falcon under 12 months when promoted to managing director, but before that had earned his spurs during five years running the sales and marketing operation of Samsung UK. The previous month Casket had announced that it was in preliminary discussions with another listed company regarding a possible merger. Market value stood at £9 million, based on share price, but Smith warned that further sackings were to be expected, as Townsend management structure needed tightening to reduce overhead losses. Other moves saw Steven Walsh returning from Germany to run British Eagle and the Townsend accessory division and Robert Pollard moving from Newtown to Leigh to become the Townsend commercial director.

Casket's trading statement of 15 February 1995 announced that pre-tax profits for the year ending 31 March were expected to be positive, though substantially below brokers' current forecasts. Heidemann had not achieved the hoped for improvement in performance and would incur a significant loss after accounting for the cost of clearing surplus stocks. On a positive note, it had won approved supplier status with major stores for the 1995 season and profitable trading was anticipated if the German market made its predicted recovery.

Christmas 1994 had been disappointing for the UK business also, with both reduced volumes and selling prices. Unit sales for the whole of 1994 had fallen to 1.9 million from 2.1 million in 1993. Casket's share of the home market had, however, increased by 3% to 29 % (in second place to Raleigh) and forward orders for the 1995 season were breaking previous records, thanks to the increased capacity at Leigh. The company strategy was still to grow the bicycle businesses and to reduce exposure to the textile market.

The Heidemann debacle came to a head on 6 July 1995 when shares in Casket were suspended due to the insolvency of the German subsidiary.[4] The problem was that Casket had guaranteed debts to the German banks and its recently negotiated UK banking facilities were insufficient to cover Heidemann liabilities. Finance director Ian Butcher denied that Casket's survival was at stake, but acknowledged that the group faced an uncertain time. Shares had been suspended at 10½p, compared to 56p in May 1994. The reasons put forward for the failure were stated to be a misreading of the German market (bicycle sales fell by 20% during 1994), the depth of the recession there and the extent of Heidemann's internal problems. A major problem appeared to be the failure of the previous management to prepare for the 1994 season. Ian Butcher was quoted as saying that: 'We've come unstuck, there's no question about that. Our priority now is to stabilise the UK business.'

On 26 July 1995 Casket's share listing was restored. In the company statement of that date, the preliminary results for the year ended 31 March were announced:

- UK turnover £87.67 million (1994: £85.38 million)
- UK operating profits £3.1 million (1994: £5.7 million)
- Heidemann operating losses £2.8 million (1994 profit £395,000)
- Estimated losses from Heidemann insolvency £7.4 million.
- Loss before taxation £12.3 million (1994 profit £3.6 million)
- No final dividend.
- UK bicycle sales 620,000 – 28.5% market share.
- 83% of bicycle sales now assembled in UK.
- Clothing exports 44% of on-going clothing sales.

## Tandem Merger

Chairman Graham Waldron announced that the immediate focus was the profitable development of the UK bicycle business and a reduction of the central cost base. As a first step the head office in Horsforth, Leeds, was to be closed and relocated to the Townsend facility at Leigh. Despite all the gloom Falcon continued to prosper and produced a record 175,000 bicycles in the year to 31 March 1995. Part of the subsequent restructuring of Casket involved the formation of a new company, Casket Leisure Products, CLP, created to consolidate the profits made by the bicycle manufacturing entities, such as British Eagle and Falcon. These companies acted as agents of CLP, which meant that sensitive production and earnings information was hidden from competitors, as well as from the City. This arrangement continues to this day with Falcon listed as a non-trading company.

On 23 August 1995 the *Yorkshire Post* recorded that 'Rescuer may ride in to save Casket cycles group.' The clothing business was already up for sale by this time and Graham Waldron cautioned that a premium on the current share price of 9.25p was unlikely, valuing the company at about £9 million. *The Times* of the same day made the odd observation that: 'Analysts were in agreement yesterday that Casket needed a financial and managerial sugar daddy.' The predicted sale was finally announced to Casket staff on 25 October 1995. This involved a merger with the Economic Forestry Group, EFG plc, to be effected by an offer for the whole of the issued ordinary share capital of Casket. The *Financial Times* article announcing the deal on 26 October stated that:

> The future of the UK's second largest bicycle maker was assured yesterday when Casket, which has been struggling with losses and heavy debts, announced plans to merge with EFG, the cash-rich horticultural products group.
>
> Under the terms of the agreed deal, shareholders will be offered one new EFG share for every two Casket, valuing the bicycle and clothing company at £8 million, or 8½p a share – a 21 per cent premium to yesterday's opening price.
>
> The combined group – to be known as Tandem Group – will have turnover of £88 million, net assets of £18 million and debts of £9.1 million on a pro forma basis.
>
> Mr Robin Garland, EFG's chief executive who will take over a similar role at Tandem, said the new group would focus solely on bicycle manufacture and assembly.

Peterborough based EFG plc had been sitting on a cash pile since the disposal of its World's End Garden Centre business and had used the code name 'Tandem' for its takeover plans. The name fitted remarkably well with its new two-wheeled venture. The ownership change brought about a major restructuring of the business. Steven Walsh resigned and set up Concept Cycles, based in Oldham and destined to become a very successful company. The bankers insisted that the huge overdraft inherited from Casket should be reduced. In the meanwhile losses were mounting at Leigh, while Falcon turned in a sturdy profit in excess of £1.5 million for the ten months to 31 January 1995. For the second time in four years Falcon's future had been ensured by the ability of soil-based businesses to generate cash.

## Project Fusion Derailed by Horses

In 1996 the ex-Ernie Clements British Eagle Newtown works closed as part of a rationalisation of the division and production moved to the new Leigh factory. The remaining clothing interests were sold and a new chief executive, Robin Bromley-Martin, was appointed specifically to resolve the continuing problems at Leigh. Falcon managed to return a profit for the year ending 31 January 1997 of £1.7 million. Bromley-Martin's strategy was entitled 'Project Fusion', which sought to close Leigh and build a grass-roots plant at Brigg. In addition to a huge investment in infrastructure the distribution systems were to be contracted out, thus saving on the need for a new warehouse. Management at Brigg was sceptical, believing the new factory would not be large enough for combined production and that there was little or no margin for error in the estimates. Paul Vicary moved back to Brigg and operating profits grew to £2.1 million for the year ending 31 January 1998. Exports were boosted by a large order from Europe, but Project Fusion finally crashed when a 'concert party'[5] of 20 per cent of the shareholders decided that horse racing offered more potential for higher profits than bicycles. This concert party already owned Doncaster Race Course and a sizeable stable of racehorses, and planned to generate a cash surplus by selling the cycle companies, which had managed to reduce the overdraft and to achieve a valuation of £12 million. The new strategy was rejected by the board of directors but approved by a majority of shareholders at an EGM held on 30 June 1998. Bromley-Martin resigned from the board and Paul Vicary instigated discussions with venture capitalists with the objective of a management buy-out of Falcon Cycles. Discussions continued during 1998, with the MBO team the only prospective buyer of Falcon and no takers for the Townsend business. Losses continued to build at Leigh, while Falcon made £1.3 million profit for 1998. Finally, on 4 March 1999, the racehorse strategy was abandoned, the concert party bought out and Graham Waldron appointed as chairman of Tandem.

## Rationalisation

It was soon decided that Leigh would never be profitable in the face of competition from imports and from the rival Concept Cycles. The scale of the problem is explained by a single example. Townsend had been making cycles for Halfords, until the latter had discovered they could buy equivalents from China for an incredible US$2 each. The Townsend and British Eagle businesses were transferred to Brigg and the Leigh premises sold to reduce debt, making Brigg the sole operating company in the group. Paul Vicary joined the Tandem board, the banks wrote off £839,000 of debt and Tandem returned to profit with a contribution from Falcon of £800,000 for 1999.

In the second half of 2000 Tandem diversified into the home pool and snooker market through the acquisition of Pot Black, a manufacturer and distributor of leisure equipment.[6] In the same period the core bicycle business was strengthened with the purchase of Two Wheel Trading, a distributor of bicycle accessories. Falcon continued to improve financially with a profit contribution for the year of £850,000.

Steve Bell took on the top job at Falcon in January 2001, while Tandem seized the opportunity to purchase Dawes Cycles in June of that year for an initial consideration of £231,000. Dawes, first established in 1926, was best known for its reliable and popular Galaxy touring cycles and, appropriately, for its tandem range. As the lease had run out on the Dawes factory production was moved to a new line at Brigg, though a separate marketing operation was retained. Tandem's results for the six months ending 31 July 2001 included an operating profit up by 125% and turnover increased by 43% compared to the same period in 2000. In view of the wet spring and the catastrophic effect of the foot and mouth epidemic on outdoor activities, this was a remarkable achievement. Graham Waldron remarked that Falcon, Tandem's largest subsidiary, continued to make solid progress and to achieve margin growth in a highly competitive market. By the end of 2001 production was in excess of 1200 bicycles per day, of which 800 were Falcon and the rest Claud Butler, Dawes etc. Falcon's contribution for the year had grown to £2.1 million.

Following the decision by Raleigh to import all their bicycles fully assembled from November 2002, Tandem became for a short while the sole UK company engaged in high volume assembly. However, despite a good year in 2003, with pre-tax profits for the year to 31 January 2004 rising to £609,000 from £234,000 the previous year, it was clear that Brigg could not compete with the Far East at the lower end. The decision was taken to shut down two of the three production lines in July 2004 with assembly remaining only of Falcon, Dawes and Shogun models selling at £250+. Steven Bell also withdrew membership of the Bicycle Association of Great Britain because 'I couldn't justify the membership fee when I was about to make 51 people redundant.'[7]

It was soon clear that outsourcing assembly was the only logical route and Graham Waldron announced that:

> With our reputation for product design and service our customer base continues to grow, from which we should benefit as the retail environment improves.....Production at the Group's manufacturing facilities in the UK has been reducing over the last few years and has been concentrating on the higher value bikes. This will cease in the summer of 2006 as production is moved abroad. Overhead savings will be made, which, together with a reduction in working capital, should lead to increased profitability.

Brigg remains the head office of Falcon, of course, but the old Corah factory is no longer the hive of activity it once was.

And so the tangled history of Elswick-Hopper and Falcon comes to an end – on a high note, as Tandem brought the Elswick name back into its 2010 range. This has been a roller-coaster story, recalling the challenges faced by British manufacturers over more than a century. I hope it will be a suitable memorial to the Elswick-Hopper Company, its people, and especially to its founder, Fred Hopper.

But there remains one more chapter – the testimony of those who worked at Hopper's.

### Endnotes

1    Casket plc interim results to 30 September 1993.
2    Casket plc news release for six months to 30 September 1994.
3    Ibid.
4    *Yorkshire Post* 6 July 1995.
5    A concert party is a group of people acting together to take control of a target company.
6    Peel Hunt plc report 26 July 2001.
7    Bike Biz website 10 May 2004.

# CHAPTER 10

## WORKING FOR HOPPER'S

The overriding impression from talking to ex-employees is that it was a good place to work. From the early days Fred Hopper and Henry Wilson had been enlightened employers and Fred's careful planning of the St Mary's Works was a tribute to his intimate knowledge of all aspects of bicycle manufacture.

*Fig. 10.1 An early photograph of the Barton Cycle Works Silver Band.*

## Barton Cycle Works Silver Band

Fred Hopper, like many late Victorian employers, believed in encouraging his workers to spend their leisure time in constructive endeavours, and preferably ones that kept them out of the many public houses in town. Sponsorship of the two cycling clubs has already been covered, but the first direct involvement of the company in forming a group for a leisure activity appears to have been the setting up of the Barton Cycle Works Silver Band (Fig. 10.1). This was formed around 1899,[1] as, according to an obituary provided by his great-grandson, that was the year when John Furniss left the brick works where he had worked from the age of nine, to join the cycle works. He was 43 years old by then and was given an office job and asked to form a works band. He had been a pioneer of cycling in the area and was often to be seen on his 'penny farthing' in the company of Fred Hopper and Robert Hill.[2] Another Hopper employee, Morwood Thompson, was an early member of the Band and in the *Hull Times* of 22 March 1941 he recalled playing at Belle Vue, Manchester, where the very first brass band contest had been held in 1853, and at the Crystal Palace. *Bicycling News and Motor Review* of 16 July 1902 recorded that the Band was to appear at Belle Vue later that year – see chapter 2. Thompson went on to form the Barton Prize Town Band in 1915, the year in which the Cycle Works instruments were valued at £285. It is assumed that this was after an incident recalled in Barton folk memory when the band performed at the Ritz Hotel whilst intoxicated. Fred Hopper, it is said, immediately withdrew his support and burned the uniforms.

Hopper appears with cornet in hand in some photographs, so it is possible that he took an active role. He certainly hired workers from far afield on the basis of musical talent and the Band did very well in competition. An employment contract has survived dated 1 June 1910 and spells out that in addition to a weekly wage of 25 shillings per week for 55½ hours work, the employee 'will also become a member of the Barton Cycle Works Band and will play any instrument therein which the Bandmaster for the time being shall direct and will regularly attend all practices, rehearsals and engagements of the said Band.' It was also spelled out that the employer was not liable to pay any wages in the event of illness or accident, though as National Insurance had been brought in during 1908 there would have been money available from the State.

The *Lincolnshire and Lindsey Star* of 7 September 1907 records:

The Annual Brass Band contest took place in the Pier Gardens, Cleethorpes, on Saturday afternoon, eleven bands entering the contest. The contest was divided in two parts, a quick step contest, choice of music being left to the band and a selection contest, the set piece being an arrangement of themes from Verdi's Il Trovatore. In addition to the monetary prizes there were medals for the best solo cornet, horn, euphonium and best trio of trombones, while the Lincolnshire Silver Challenge Shield awaited the Lincolnshire band coming first in the judging.

Unfortunately a heavy rainstorm in the afternoon militated against the attendance and made matters uncomfortable for everyone concerned. The playing all round was of an unusual standard of excellence and Mr T A Greenwood of Birkenhead, the judge, had a difficult task to perform. His placing, however, appeared to give the crowd considerable satisfaction, the awards being received with loud applause.

Selection Contest:
1. Barton Cycle Works Silver Band, conductor Mr George White.
2. Holme Brass band, Huddersfield.
3. Lincoln Malleable Iron and Steel Alloy Works Band.
Quickstep Contest: Barton second to Holme Brass Band.
By their success the Barton band retained the Lincolnshire Shield, which they held last year, while they also secured the euphonium medal.

The 1912 Hopper catalogue included a photograph of the Silver Band and lists its achievements as 24 first prizes, 9 second, 11 third and 5 fourth. The Band also won the East Yorkshire and North Lincs Amateur Band Association Championship Cup in 1905, 1906 and 1907 and won the Lincolnshire County Championship Baton in 1909.

The Band also took on local engagements, such as one recorded in May 1913 regarding the annual Barton Fair:

The welcome change in the weather was the cause of a record attendance at the fair in the Market Place and the George Hotel Paddock, the venue of attraction. Amusements were numerous. On Sunday night the annual church parade of the Territorials took place. The National Reserve men, of whom there are about 40 in the town, were invited, but only about six responded, Captain H G Wilson [son of Henry] and Lieut Fieldsend were the officers in command. The company was headed by the Cycle Works Band. The band did not attend church. The preacher was the Rev W E Varah, the vicar, and at the close the men paraded the town and were dismissed at the Drill Hall.

## The Barton Cycle Works Recreation Club and Institute Ltd.

The first statutory meeting of the new club was held on Tuesday 6 March 1906.[3] Fred Hopper was elected president and his partner, Henry Wilson, vice-president. R Todd was elected secretary, with H Flowers as his deputy, and C H Atkinson as treasurer. A further nine employees were elected to the committee by ballot, including the company secretary Herbert Bell. At the meeting Hopper threw a challenge to Wilson: if he would give a prize for a whist match, Hopper promised a prize for billiards. In accepting the challenge Wilson said that anything that drew employers and employees together was worthy of support. He also told the meeting that it was the intention of Mrs Wilson and himself, in celebration of their silver wedding, to entertain all their workpeople to supper or dinner (Fig. 2.20). While the partners' approach could be termed paternalistic, in many ways it was simply good management – look after your people and they will produce the goods, sadly a principle that seems to be rediscovered and lost with each generation. At the first AGM on 5 February 1907 there were 100 members attending and Mr W Welsh was recorded as the librarian.[4] Hopper's club, as it was known, spawned many local events, such as dances at the Assembly Rooms and the first ever Barton Rose Show in August 1908. A newspaper report dated Christmas 1908 reported that billiards, bagatelle, ping-pong, whist, dominoes and darts were all popular and for the first five named pastimes a series of 'Christmas flying handicaps had been arranged. Over 300 entries had been received and everyone would receive a prize. The prizes will smack of Christmas cheer, from turkey and other luxurious substances down to probably one ounce of tobacco.' An earlier darts tournament had seen H Gammidge win a gold Albert and gold medal, contributed by Mr Hopper JP. Whist was a popular card game across the town and in 1909 the Barton Whist League comprised the Cycle Works Club, Liberal Club, Constitutional Club, the Church Institute and the Territorials.

Henry Wilson's commitment to employee welfare had not waned with the years and he was reported in *The Star* of 25 February 1911 as saying at the adjournment of the Club AGM that he was pleased to know that there was plenty of employment at the Cycle Works. The welfare of Barton depended to a great measure upon the Cycle Works and he hoped the present flourishing conditions would continue. They did not intend to stand still but to make it the finest company of its kind in England.

For most of its existence the club was based at the rear of Laurel House in Whitecross Street, with the house itself being used as accommodation for the club steward and visiting customers. The property was acquired in 1907 and a plan filed with the UDC for the construction of new outbuildings in 1908. Following conversion and enlargement the facilities eventually included a .22 rifle range in the basement,[5] a reading room, billiard tables, a lounge bar area and baths. The latter were a very important and well-used facility, given that few houses had bathrooms or hot running water, and that much of the work was inevitably dirty – the employees, or at least the sand blasters, weren't called 'Hopper's Black Angels' for nothing. The Club made its first 'public' appearance in the 1913 Hopper catalogue, which pictured the billiard and reading rooms (Fig. 10.2). Ownership of the clubhouse is unclear, however, as the property is not listed in the 1924 asset list, so it is assumed that it was owned by the Club from the start.

Fig. 10.2 The Cycle Works Club reading room, from the 1912 catalogue.
Fig. 10.3 The Cycle Works Club second shooting team: Back row l-r Stanley Anderson (?) Frank Barratt, Jack Robinson, Norman Cook. Front Row Icky Brown and (?).

The objectives are recorded as 'to carry out the business of a club by providing for the use of its members and for such Associates of the Working Men's Club and Institute Union Ltd as are admitted to honorary membership, the means of social intercourse, mutual helpfulness and moral improvement, rational recreation and other advantages of a club'. It thrived for many years and became something of a local institution. The facilities provided for a great variety of hobbies and sports, and the rifle section fielded at least two competition teams for several years. As late as 1974 there were still four snooker tables in place.

Bob Griffith's father, William Henry, was appointed club steward in 1923 and lived with his family at Laurel House. Bob recalled, "He had come to Barton from the New Hudson Cycle Manufacturing Co Ltd of Birmingham to work as a wheel builder and had been knocked about quite badly in the war, so that mother had to take over some of the duties for many weeks when he wasn't good. They had a rifle team at Hopper's club, and they were deadly. The first team was George Franklin, Charles Else (Barton surveyor) Henry Cole, Sidney Ashton, Jack Bacon and Bert Golland." The second team is shown in Fig. 10.3.

The baths were used into the 1960s and it is said that even Arthur Stow used them as his wife was rather house-proud and did not like their bathroom being 'dirtied' by use! Jack Austin was a regular: "I was a member of the club and we didn't have a bath at our house, so I used to go on a Friday night, put my name down, and give 6d to the barman and his wife used to get the bath ready and keep it clean. Subs were 1d a week and that was stopped out of your pay packet. The shooting club was run by ex-first world war men. They had their own guns and used to get their bullets out from behind the bar. George Franklin was one of the leading lights. You were in a sick club and if you were off ill you would get some money from it, but if you were off too long you would get less and less." Jack Dimoline was also a regular: "Hopper's club was good and after a while I became a committee member. Until the 70s it was a private club, but then we decided to let outsiders in."

Harry Haddock was told of another use of the club. "In the frame shop, before I went there, old Frank Robinson was foreman, a big fat fellow, and he would be up at the club on a Friday night with his gang buying him ale, so they could get the best jobs the following week! That's a true story, and the ones that bought him most got the best jobs, as every frame was a different price. It was a regular thing that, on a Friday night." Bob Blackburn thought it was the best club in Barton. "It certainly had the best billiard hall. At the time I was a member Freddie Hopper was the president. He came to every AGM and any member that was in the club he bought them a drink. I think he was pretty well thought of, young Freddie."

Sadly, by 1975 Laurel House was empty and the committee was considering options such as conversion to flats or offices. Late in 1975 a decision was taken to sell. Lack of interest saw the price drop to £6,500 in 1977, though it was not until the end of 1978 that a buyer, Dr Warwick Rodwell, was found brave enough to undertake a long overdue major renovation project, though he paid a much reduced price of £4,250. As leader of the archaeological team that excavated the internal burial chambers of St Peter's Church he was well-equipped to deal with an old building. It was built in the 1650s with the addition of a new three-storey red brick facade in 1768. Once the home of Isaac Pitman, a teacher in Barton during the 1830s, it is now a Grade II* listed building.

The club continued to operate throughout the 1970s, though problems of noise and late night disturbances were becoming a problem, culminating in a police raid on 21 January 1977. The rifle range was still in use by members and in early 1978 the local Army Cadet Force started to use it. Following various complaints from local residents, falling membership, rising debts, and failures of management, the club closed in 1982. Dr Rodwell reunited the land occupied by the clubhouse and the buildings with the house, though all that remains of the former is the Edwardian billiard room.

## F Hopper & Company's Girls' Institute Ltd.

Not until the end of 1926, a full year after the death of the founder, were the social needs of the female workers of Elswick-Hopper catered for in the form of a Girls' Institute, with headquarters in the reading rooms on Chapel Lane. It was open to employees aged 16 and over, who were allowed to bring one female friend. Each friend was only to be introduced once per quarter, unless she was from Barton, in which case the restriction was just twice a year! The objectives were 'to provide the means of social intercourse, mutual helpfulness, mental and moral improvement, rational recreation and other advantages of a club for women, including instructions in dressmaking, home-craft, sick nursing and other subjects, and also for organised concerts and such quiet games as may conveniently be played on the club premises, and to provide a reading room with circulating and reference libraries for the use of the members.' The sale of intoxicating liquors was, of course, prohibited. Given its title it could be imagined that an upper age limit pertained, or a bar to membership upon marriage (more likely), but neither is mentioned in the rule book.

## F Hopper & Co Ltd Sick and Dividend Society for Girls

This organisation is known from a document published on its formation in 1933, and would have been formed to fill the gap in health insurance in the 1911 National Insurance Act that left women living at home unable to claim sick pay, a situation that lasted until 1946. The President was Miss E A Jackson, Fred Hopper's sister-in-law, who for many years ran the office typing pool. The purpose was to be 'for the benefit of those members who may become unable through sickness or accident to follow their employment.' The Society met each Friday evening at 8pm at the Cycle Works Recreation Club on Whitecross Street to receive subscriptions, and 'no money shall be paid after 9 o'clock', with all moneys received to be paid into the bank the following day. The minimum age for membership was 14 and subscriptions were 6d per week (2.5p). Benefits were 10s a week for 13 weeks, then 6s for the next 13 weeks, with a limit of 26 weeks sick pay in a year.

## Getting Started

Employment at Hopper's was often a family affair and Chris Cox discovered from the 1911 census that his great grandfather, Albert Cox, was working as a cycle cleaner, with four sons employed as a polisher, a liner, an enameller, and the youngest, aged 14, as a varnisher. Boys with parents who could afford to indenture them could always try for an apprenticeship, but they typically started as errand boys, moving parts from shop to shop on a variety of wooden barrows specially designed to suit the component. For girls a job at 'Top Hopper's', the Brigg Road offices, was the best opportunity, but most found jobs at 'Bottom Hopper's' – St Mary's Works. Since the upheavals of the First World War Hopper's had employed women in many departments and increasingly in the machine shop as machine tool operators. To modern eyes the age of employment appears young, but large families and the lack of state support meant that children's earnings were a vital boost to the household economy. The Elementary Education Act (Mundella's Act) of 1880 made attendance at school compulsory for all children to the age of 10. In 1893 the age for school leavers rose to 11 and in 1899 to 12. The next review took place in 1918 when a further two years were added; 14 was the school leaving age up to 1944, when it became 15, and the last hike was to 16 in 1972. These quite radical changes in attitude to education may explain the interest that Fred Hopper took in the management of the Church School, in the provision of a reading room at the Work's Club.

The earliest record of an apprenticeship was found in the Lincolnshire Archives in the form of a handwritten note: 'Charles Frederick Robinson son of Tom Robinson, twine spinner of Barton on Humber, apprentice to Fred Hopper and Henry Wilson, Cycle Manuf. of Barton on Humber from 5 May 1902 for 6 years, the sum of 8s per week for the first, second and third years and 10s for the fourth, fifth and sixth years.' Clearly Tom thought that bicycles had a better future than ropes for his son. The trade is unfortunately not specified in the note. A formal indenture for a tool maker apprentice has survived, in the name of Cyril Hopper. It was also for a period of six years, with 8s per week for the first year, rising in increments of 2s to a full £1 in the final year, so a major increase compared to 16 years previously. Cyril was the oldest of a family of four boys and one girl, and all of the boys started at Hopper's, with brother Alan becoming foreman of the main machine shop (Fig. 10.4).

Queenie Dixon left Church School at 14 on the first of March and on the first of April Hopper's sent word that there was a job for her. She thought, 'April Fool's Day.' She went, and stayed for just over 53 years, building wheels all the time, the first being a pair of wood rim racing wheels. The photograph shown in Fig. 10.5 is clearly Edwardian and shows just three female workers employed on wheel building.

Audrey Peck also started at Hopper's at 14 and was initially on 2d an hour. In those days children were considered available for work on their actual birthday, and by chance Audrey was 14 on the day of Fred Hopper's funeral on Christmas Eve 1925, a Thursday, and so enjoyed four days off before entering the factory gates the following Tuesday, Monday being a Bank Holiday. "I can remember seeing that funeral going down King Street and up towards the church. I didn't know he was an important man." Her initial impressions were that they didn't know what to do with her, but after a few jobs she settled in as a storekeeper. She also helped Nurse King as a first-aider, though it rankled that she didn't get extra payment. Her parents lived in the house adjoining the Masonic Lodge and as well as looking after the building were responsible for catering. This link did not mean that she was treated any better than anyone else and Audrey eventually decided it was time to ask for a rise. "I was only on about 2½d an hour I think. I asked for more money as I was doing first-aid and a stores job and one day I asked for more money and although George Franklin and Henry Cole ran the factory everything had to go through Arthur Stow. Anyway, one day they sent for me and going down to the office from my department George Franklin told me I would get the sack. I said I didn't mind – I'd rather *do* nothing than *work* for nothing. Anyway, I was sworn to secrecy that if they gave me another three ha'pence an hour that I wasn't to tell anybody. You see they all came to Masonic and my mother used to cook for these folk and Arthur Stow said, 'If war comes, as we do think it might do, would you take another job and train some of the workers in first-aid?' I belonged to the British Red Cross Society in those days. I said I wouldn't, you won't see my heels for dust if war started, and of course it did."

*Fig. 10.4 Main machine shop – foreman Alan Hopper is on the left right at the back. Note the predominance of women.*

*Fig. 10.5 Edwardian wheel builders. The young lads would be employed fetching materials for the builders and taking finished wheels to the store.*

Jack Austin recalled that when you left school there wasn't a lot of choice. Hopper's, of course, and the Ropery; the Maltkilns were for the older men and the brickyards were mostly men (and seasonal). "Families tended to stick with the same firm. You just used to go for a job and I was fortunate that I got the job I did. I started off as an errand boy and finished up as a liner. I also got spraying later on after the war. You didn't normally move around – you just got better at what you were doing and got more money because you were on piece work. I suppose if you got fed up, and there was a vacancy, you could have moved. Some of the work was at a day work rate but piecework got the work through quicker. A frame, fork and mudguards with double lining were 4¼d. I could do that alright and could make money from it. Albert Wall was the foreman and you had to be careful. If he saw you doing something wrong he would just look at you; didn't say anything. So I was 14 on the Friday and I started work on the Monday. It was 2d an hour to start with for a 48 hour week; 8s and if you were lucky you could work to a quarter to six and that brought your money up to about 10s. As soon as Mr Wall said to line two sets I booked that as piece work. I got 6d a gross for varnishing transfers on these orders for Kay Lee San and Guang Hoe [Malay Peninsular], I think there were 14 transfers on a bike, so 10 bikes and I got a gross. The transfers all came down from Brigg Road."

Jack Dimoline started the same time as Jack Austin at Easter 1934, though in the brake department with Fred Green. His first job was as department errand lad, delivering parts to the plating and enamelling shops for their protective coatings to be applied and collecting finished parts for assembly. "The handlebars were made at a different part of the factory where all the welding was done. This was looked after by Charlie Altoft and they used to build the bars; then they went to the polishing shop and then to plating and finally to the big Elswick erecting department run by Thompson. I was fetching brakes and all the components for the girls working there. I was there until 1939, when I was called up. Fred Green used to tell me what they were short of, or the girls would, and I would go to the stores for the parts that were needed. Or take parts to plating or enamelling, whatever was needed to keep them going. I used to start at 6 in the morning and come home for breakfast at 8 o'clock. Go back at half past. Come home at 5, sometimes at 6; used to work 12 hours a day quite often, it was normal really. The little barrow I used to pull about – I've often made people laugh about this – a donkey wouldn't have pulled it sometimes! When I joined the Army I only weighed 8 stone something. So you can tell what I was like when I left school. It was slave labour, 7/6d a week, two pence an hour. I had been there six months and asked the foreman for a rise. I remember I got half a penny an hour more. Most of the foremen in those days were on contract. Fred Green, my foreman, got so much money for the job and he used to pay his workers out of it, so the less he paid you the more he got. It was still on the go when I went into the war and I guess it stopped then. It was all contract in those days, at least in assembly in the Elswick, where I spent most of my time. All the balcony came under Fred Green. He had both the handlebars and the brakes and all that was upstairs. We used to assemble the hubs in the brake department as well, putting in the spindles and the ball bearings. There were two girls did that. Yet the wheel shop was at the far end of the factory so you had to carry everything across on barrows. I remember one day I got a load of stuff and it lifted me off the ground. But I loved working there. I was there 54 years, but I wasn't the longest serving – that was Bob Barratt, or maybe Fred Green. Fred was there from being a kid until he was 76 or 77."

In the late 1920s Maud Hildred was also 14 when she started at the Brigg Road English packing shop next to the offices, joining her three sisters and worked there until she married at 23. "I got the job after the boss had asked my sister, 'Have you anybody else leaving school?' She said: 'Yes, we've one leaving in a fortnight.' 'Oh,' he said, 'bring her up.' I got 3 ha'pence an hour. So by the time it was the weekend it was about 5s; it wasn't much money. My mum had to have it all for our keep, and she used to give us a shilling back, just pocket money. The work was alright, we were always friendly, you see. There were about three wooden stands. We used to lift the bikes on them to wrap, and my sister Gladys used to do the wrapping of the handles, and I did the back stays. Then we took them through to another place to be packed. There was a man packing them and we did all the English and up there [on the south side of Castledyke South] was all the foreign stuff." Proving the strength of family tradition, Maud's grandfather, Thomas Fletcher, worked for Fred Hopper in the very early days of the business.

Walter (Bunny) Horne finished school on a Friday in 1932 and started work at Hopper's the following Monday. His wife Joan followed two years later at the age of 14. "I was supposed to take an apprenticeship and there were two going; you could either be a tool maker apprentice or a cabinet maker and I wanted a cabinet maker's job. They used to make three wheel cycles with a big box on for ice cream companies and things like that. They had just set one on, and they said if another apprenticeship came up I could take it but I never bothered. I just carried on with what I was doing. I started in the press shop at 2d an hour. They were on hand presses then. The foreman was George Bell – they put you on a press, and showed you what to do and told you not to trap your fingers. On hand presses there were no guards, but when you went on to machine presses they were usually well guarded. There was no trial period, I just started in the morning and George Bell took me to a press, gave me a job and showed me how to work it – it was a hand press, you just swung it round. He told you to watch your fingers and maybe came back a bit later to see how you were getting on. You still had your short trousers on when you started and put your overalls on top. But it was a normal thing and nobody took much notice. It was just normal. I lived down Waterside Road then, in the row opposite the shipyard. I had a bike; we used to find all old pieces to make a bike, more or less, in those days. The Popular was 8s 6d, I think, and that was a lot of money then. Most people went to work on bikes. Nearly everybody had a bike, though very few were new. Joan's was, and she had it 'done up' after a few years. It was worn out so she sent it through the repair shop and it came back like a new one again." Joan remembers starting in the brake department and her first wage was 6s a week. Walter's was 8s 4d for working from 6am to 5.45pm.

Harry Haddock started on 8 January 1934, on his 14th birthday on 2d an hour. "It was just after Christmas and I said to my dad I'd start work on the Wednesday [3 January] and I was helping a woman who was painting frames with enamel – there were no sprays in those days, and Steve Atkin – he was the man out of the office, he came to me and said, 'Are you 14 yet Harry?' I said, 'No, not while Monday, Mr Atkin.' He said, 'Well I'm afraid you'll have to go home while Monday.' But I got 9 hours pay and it was 1s 6d in old money. The next Monday I went back, and as you went into Hopper's there was a time office and you got a time sheet. The window used to be open, and all the time sheets were laid out and the time keeper gave you your time sheet. I started off in the handle bar department as a labourer. That was on the balcony that used to run the full length of the Elswick building."

Bob Griffiths also started in 1934 as a 14 year old. "They had a joiners shop and I wanted to be an apprentice joiner, so I signed on there. The main job at that time was making box carriers. Not many for ice cream – most were for bakers, butchers, fishmongers, all kinds of trades. That wasn't a bad job, it was nice and steady. We also had the maintenance of the factory and the property owned by Hopper's. It was a lot of Marsh Lane, Pasture Road, Beck Hill, and there were some down Queen's Avenue. A lot of my time was spent replacing windows, because there were a lot of smashed windows – kids used to pelt them. The box carrier trade flourished for a while, mainly due to the volume of business with Brown Brothers, but by the late 1930s it had tailed right off."

Ray Pettit wanted to go to Trinity House but his father advised that it was too rough a life. "So eventually I decided I wanted to be an electrician, and I applied at Hopper's as one of the main employers in those days, but there was a long waiting list. I should have left school in the September of 1937 but had to stay on until there was a vacancy in '38. John Stockdale knew about this and told my mother there was a vacancy coming up for an apprentice in his department and that is how I got into the tool room. I remember the interior of the Brigg Road offices as I had to go there to sign my indentures. 'Father must keep me in food and drink' and all that stuff. Les Green was a signatory and my father was the other. My first wage was 6s a week, progressing annually to 9s, 13s, 18s and 24s in my last year, and then 1s 3d an hour as a journeyman, which went up to 1s 6d when you were 21. Of course the war intervened, so all wage structures went out the door. Out of the 6s there were 5d stoppages. There was 2d for health, 2d for unemployment benefit and 1d for the Hull and East Riding Sickness Club. In 1938/39, I started going over to Hull Technical College three evenings a week with all my own fares to pay and books to buy, everything to pay for, as I got no help from Hopper's. After my first year's results, Freddie Hopper sent for me and said, 'I'm not interested in this. You've only got 80%. That's not good enough. If you don't do better than that, you won't go another year.' It was all my own initiative and I was the only one from the tool room that went. It was all evenings but I used to leave work a little bit early. I think I left at 5 o'clock those nights instead of half past to catch the half past five train. I had to rush home, get a quick wash, get changed, grab a sandwich, and off to Hull and I came back on the last ferry at 10 o'clock. So I suppose it was all about the half hour off on Mondays, Wednesdays and Fridays. Weekends I was doing homework as well. Then when the war came in '39 they stopped all the river traffic at night time so I got into contact with the college along with Roy Winship, who was apprenticed to Grassby's in Barton. He and I decided to come over all day on a Tuesday and I got day release for that and we did all the subjects in one day. But we weren't getting the attention we would have got on the evening schedule. I did the full year and then decided to take a correspondence course with the National Institute of Engineering in draughtsmanship. I took another one through the Union but I never got far enough to take exams. I think I got courting at that time and the school became of secondary importance."

Stan Havercroft joined Elswick-Hopper on 1 April 1940 as an apprentice in the roadside machine shop. In 1940 bicycles were still being made for the RAF, sprayed in matt khaki and matt blue. Bikes were also supplied to munitions workers, such as the export Phoenix model with an Eadie coaster brake, probably due to having a large stock and no export market. Harry Pond was the tool room foreman and Stan left the machine shop to train as a toolmaker, once there was a 'vacant vice', which occurred after eight months. In 1942/43 the tool room moved into the old powerhouse on Beck Hill, and he worked on getting it ready, scrapping the two gas engine driven generators and installing several new machine tools. The new power house near the Marsh Lane entrance contained three Ruston diesel generators, two six cylinder ex-submarine sets and one new one.

When Bob Blackburn was taken on it was through his grandfather, Jack Curtis, who had been with Hopper's since the early days and was responsible for the electrical generators: "It was 1943 when I started. I went originally to be an apprentice, but never got signed up. I went as a lad of 14 into the big machine shop and the foreman there was Alan Hopper. Most of the older men were away in the Forces and all the machines were manned by women. I moved on to other departments – you had about six months in a department. I was in the tool room for a while and then I moved into the tube department. When I started in the machine shop most machines were line shaft driven and a lot of the practices wouldn't be allowed today. Tubes were made from blanks cut off on the guillotine. They went on to a power press where they made a 'U' bend and then they could finally close them on a press and that would leave a seam down the middle and those girls that were sitting there used to seam weld them using gas (Fig. 6.5). A bit antiquated but that's how they made tubes. They used to buy in the main frame tubes from Birmingham, but we made all the fork blades, chain stays and seat stays. That is Eva Dove working on the press. I stayed in the tube shop until I was called up to the REME in 1947."

Bill Carter started his electrical engineering apprenticeship at Hopper's on his birthday, 22 June 1945. "I was called up for National Service on 25 July 1947 and finished 17 October 1949. Fortunately I was able to continue my trade and so the time counted towards the five years, which duly completed on 21 June 1950. I was not able to get a reserved position because that would have entailed study at Scunthorpe Technical College. With no available transport this was impossible. This affected the majority of people in Barton as there were no buses running at that time. My first weekly wage post apprenticeship was £5 0s 3d a week." Bill actually started work with Cliff Barraclough in industrial wiring. Cliff had a contract with the Ropery and also the Maltkilns. These companies had lost their own staff to the war effort, but after 1945 started hiring again. His parents directed him towards Hopper's and he started there under Stan Franks, foreman of the Electrical Department, who had come to Barton from Sheffield to work at the East Acridge generating station.

Arthur Such echoed Jack Austin's comments on the lack of choice for school leavers. "There was the Farmers' Company, but I didn't want to go down there as a lad. There was the Ropery and I didn't fancy it either, though they had a fitting department so I could have served an apprenticeship there. But I was interested in precision. I knew Hopper's made their own hubs, axles, spindles, mudguards from sheet steel, did their own chroming and enamelling. They even made the old rod brakes; they made the lot, apart from screws. Built all their own wheels too. It was kept pretty well for a big factory – a clean place and I liked it. I started in 1948 as a tool making, fitting and turning apprentice. I was one of the last call-ups. I got my full five years in and then got called up."

Charles Watkinson remembered his dad coming home from work to say, "There's a big order come in from India." He continued: "They used to make these enormous bikes for one of the Sikh customers, but my first recollections as a child were that I used to pinch a ride on one of the horses and carts that were getting coal from the siding off Marsh Lane at Pottery Gates. The driver was Gerry Killick and as he came along Marsh Lane we would run along behind and he would say, 'Up you get' and we would get a ride through Pottery Gates and into the siding. The carts had high sides, because coke is a light material. Other carts were taking cycles in crates to the railway siding at the station. I believe my mother worked in the packing shop on Castledyke. There was a man called Shucksmith who rode about the town looking very important with a nicely polished leather satchel, and he took the truck numbers and the trucking details of all the cycles and everything that came for Hopper's by rail. He looked after all the administration side of what came in and what went out. My father worked there and he used to come in sometimes and say, 'We've all been stood off.' He was there as a boy, from Barrow Haven, and he joined the Territorials. Like all the others dad had to find alternative work when laid off from Hopper's. It was either walk to Immingham for a pit prop ship or work for my grandfather in the brick yard for a while. He did the work of aligning the back stays and chain stays – they had to be knocked in and trued." Being a bright lad Charles stayed at school until he was 16 and then took a job at 'Top Hopper's' with Barton Cycles Ltd. "The manager of that enterprise was Philip Booker. Ken Cox also worked there and Barton Cycles occupied all the offices on the top floor. The purpose was to provide finance for the hire purchase of cycles. There was very considerable paperwork involved, and at that time in 1936 they had two very efficient ladies with big comptometers. Clunk, bang. The system was that people would go to a dealer, buy a cycle on hire purchase and the payments would come in to Barton Cycles – presumably they paid the dealer. There was a young man named Such, Harold Elloughton and me. Each account was on a card and it was our function to take these cards, examine them and, using a simplified slide rule, calculate any arrears, and if the arrears were getting out of hand we just initialled the card with a note as to the type of letter to be sent, from a mild reminder to a stern warning. The kind of thing that you now get churned out by computer. The X and X2 letters were quite strong. These letters were typed and sent off to the individuals, but I can't say arrears were a major problem. On a £5 bike, if you were 10 bob down you got a letter. Edwards' of Camberwell and Bennett's of Plaistow had hundreds of customers all buying cycles. It was good business. There were many, many others. There was so much paper involved that all paperwork was dealt with daily; it was bundled up, put into cases and went down to the bottom floor, where there was a big fireproof safe like a room and it all went in there each night. The next morning we boys would attend and there was a little electric hoist at the top of that building. We would swing it over, lower it down. Everything was put in baskets and we would distribute it around the office. At night we didn't use the motor. We just hooked it on, took a turn round the guard rail and let it go. Ken Cox remembered my work there because at the outbreak of war I was working in a brick yard. Ken had taken up the post of check weigh man at the new meat distribution centre, and he came to our house to ask me if I wanted to go as clerk to the manager. I took the job and earned a darn sight more there than I had at Hopper's. I also used to get extra for humping beef. Carrying a quarter carcase up some steps was nothing. As for Hopper's they were never high payers. In my opinion Fred Hopper's successors never paid enough and never invested enough."

Gladys Hedley recalled starting at Hopper's and then going to the Ropery for about 18 months. "Then I went back to Hopper's. I didn't like the Ropery, you could wash your hair and it still smelled. I remember we worked 6 to 6 at Hopper's. I lived at 3 Soutergate, and I had to run like the blazes. Bread and jam in your hand for breakfast. They don't know they're born today. It was just dashing to work before the buzzer went. The time keeper's place was just on the right." Herbert Hedley remembered a little side door for latecomers, and "they were docked half an hour, which often was me. Just three minutes you were allowed, after that, you were docked." Herbert served a five year apprenticeship followed by two years as an improver, so it took seven years to become a full craftsman. He was one of the first to be lured by better money at Scunthorpe steelworks, leaving in about 1949. "There was no bus then, so I used old motor bikes – talk about getting to Scunthorpe on a wing and a prayer!"

Nora Thompson started in August 1945 at the Brigg Road office. "I would think at that time there would be 50 people working there and to get a job you had to sit a written exam in maths and English and if you were successful you were given a month's trial. My sister had joined the company two years before me and she had gone into the typing pool. It was very good training there. She left school and within six months she was taking down letters in shorthand. This was before the days when shorthand was taught in schools, and she went for shorthand lessons. I think they cost 1s 6d a lesson. Then one of the ladies from the typing pool, Kathleen Smith, started to take a class one afternoon a week and so you got a really good training. I went into the sales department and for the first month I had to learn every part of the bicycle – what a bottom bracket was, what a toggle chain was, what roller lever brakes were, what this type of chain was, different types of mudguards, everything. When a customer wrote in they would say 'I want this part of the thing and that part' and it was out of the question that you sent the wrong part. You just didn't do that. So that's what I did for the first month and my wages were £1 a week for the first month and then £1 5s after that."

Doreen Atkin started in the offices when she left school and cycled daily into work from Wootton, and later from Goxhill, in all weathers. "I think it must have been 1947, in the accounts department under Wilf Dickens dealing with accounts payable. Les Green was in charge of accounts as the cashier and George Clarke was company secretary. I worked there for 13 years until I was expecting my first child. Mr Crofts was the sales manager at the time, Herbert Linley the purchasing man, and Francis Robinson was invoices. Peter Stow was export manager, and his father Arthur Stow was managing director. Nora Bramley was head of the typing pool. Rosalie Wood was on the switch board when I started and then Marjorie Broughton. In the sales department was the office boy who used to run between the works and the offices on a bike – Neville Glover was one. One of my jobs was to order the biscuits and tea from the Huntley and Palmer rep; he used to come to the front entrance. I had to look after the milk and sugar and things as well until I got further ahead. We had one of the best accounting systems I have ever seen for the time. We had ledgers for every letter of the alphabet and we had to balance the books every month without fail, and the figures had to be always accurate for Les Green – not a penny out. It was a wonderful system and all manual, though we did have a comptometer. But we used to run down a column of figures just like that, and of course it was the old system of 12 pence to the shilling and 20 shillings to the pound. We used to go down to the works canteen for lunch."

Ruby Credland remembered Hopper's as being just like one big happy family. Her husband Peter joined in 1946 and left in 1958 for a job at Scunthorpe steelworks. 1958 was also a year of change for Hopper's with the new board of directors. Peter recalls starting work at 14: "I was sent to Brigg Road, round the corner from the offices, where they made the packing cases and packed the cycles. They had a very large timber yard along Castledyke, which is where the wood for the cases was cut. So I started in the saw mill. My jobs were general cleaning up and loading the little railway trucks with timber to bring them up from the sheds to the saw mill. I helped the sawyers because there were really long lengths of timber and he used to cut them into 38", or 40" lengths and I would hold it at the far end, so it didn't drop off and then push it forward. When I first started working there as a boy we used to get two breaks a day with a milk chocolate drink provided by the government. Crawford was the foreman before George Grebby. He used to send me to the Constitutional Club to buy cigarettes, because he was a member. I couldn't leave by the entrance so I used to go down to the timber shed, over the wall through where the Black Bull pub used to be, through there and across to the Cons Club and I had built a stone step on one side so I could get over the wall. The other side was alright because I had a pile of timber lined up. Another job came at 3 o'clock every afternoon. Burkitt's bakery was just round the corner from the office and at the side was a little passage into Hopper's yard. I used to go down that passage, come down to the main gate, have a look to see there was nobody about, run across the road, down the passage, get the sausage rolls, come back, same procedure, and take the sausage rolls to whoever had ordered them. I never went to the shop, always the bake house."

Muriel Peeps worked at the Burkitt's bakery for a year before moving to Hopper's packing shop and it was also her husband Brian's second job: "Pinchbeck's paid me 10s a week when I first worked there, and I got about £2 10s at Hopper's. They always let us take wine or cider on Christmas Eve. We had a bit of a party at about 3 o'clock – we normally finished at 5 (Fig 10.6). George Franklin was the works manager, but we were under the jurisdiction of Brigg Road, of course, and they never seemed to bother us. My mother worked there, in what they called the ice house. As you went through the gateway at the entrance to the saw mill, up at the top was another building, end ways on and that was the ice house. It was a packing shop and that was where my mother started in about 1916. 1/1½d an hour I think she got." Muriel's mum worked in the chrome shop: "They used to send her and my auntie Freda testing rickshaws, because they were both little. They used to ride round the yard. My mum used to pedal and my auntie Freda sat in the wicker basket on the side." Brian's grandfather Robinson worked there and Muriel's father worked in the polishing shop.

Eileen Credland actually started at the Ropery, where her uncle was senior foreman. "I left the Ropery because I got a better job with more money at Hopper's, and it wasn't so dirty. The job wasn't advertised; you just used to go along to see if there were any going. I worked for Arthur Stuffins wiring up in the chrome department. Me and Nora Blackburn went together for a job and both got in. There was a little woman in charge, May Handsley. There was no training – they said this is what you do and that's what you did! Everything for plating had to be wired up on frames. It was one room divided into two. You used to put them on a trolley and then they were wheeled into the vat room. There were no fumes, it was like a big round vat and you had to go up some steps to get to it. Wheels, handlebars, pedal parts, brakes, screws, cotter pins, everything that was chromed went through there. All the wiring was done by women and they used to operate the chroming vat too. I used to go home for my meals – there was a canteen, my sister was a cook there and they did full meals, mainly for people from out of town. We got half and hour for lunch and I would go home on my bike for a quick stand-up lunch and then back again. At the Ropery, if you couldn't lip read you were stuck, it was that noisy, but at Hopper's it was much quieter."

*Fig. 10.6 This is a much earlier Christmas than Brian's but proves that it was a long standing tradition. It is assumed that the main machine shop belt drive shafts had been shut down before hanging the trimmings.*

Keith Clark worked for his father in the blacksmith's shop at South Ferriby for two years before moving to Hopper's. Friends had been telling him to make the move. "I wanted to be with the lads, so I made a break and that was it. I went to Hopper's in 1949 and spent the first five months in the large machine shop; then I went to John Stockdale in the tool shop until I was 21." Keith still has the letter explaining the need for deferment of National Service from 18 to 21, signed by J F Morton, works manager, in 1950. "I wasn't indentured at Ferriby and I wasn't at Hopper's, but they agreed I could serve a full apprenticeship. With Alan Hopper I was working on lathes – all mass production stuff – milling machines, drilling machines, producing head lugs, cranks, bottom brackets. I didn't do piecework as I was still training, but it was mainly piecework. It wasn't too noisy though it was very busy. There were a lot of women working in there. A lot of fun went on – they were a happy bunch of people. I really loved working there – it was a very pleasant place to work due to the majority of people being local, so it was almost like a mining community – everyone knew you."

Barry Wood went to Hopper's to be an apprentice toolmaker in 1949. "I wasn't old enough so they put me in the machine shop for 12 months. After three months I was ready to jack and got a job at the Co-op. Henry Cole then offered me a spell in the welding shop and said it would come in handy if you can weld, and it has! I was there six or seven months and then I went in the tool room.

Why did I go to Hopper's? My father was working there – he was a carrier maker, and I can't remember discussing anything else. My mum worked there as a sprayer – she was Dora Catlin, but that was after I had started. My wife Ida was there as well on back stay welding and then in the spray shop. So all in all it was a bit of a family thing. They had got two Wickman automatic lathes in the machine shop during the war for making rifle bullets. All you did was put the steel in and you had about eight cutters and it was like a turret – it might take a fortnight to set it up, but you just kept feeding it in then. One of my first jobs was preparing the steel bar for these automatics. They used to take 1¼" bar mild steel and the ends had to be turned before being fed in, to protect the tools. I had to fetch these bars from the Elswick store, pull them across the yard – I was only 15 and they weighed almost as much as I did, and there was an old lathe; it was all belt driven and I had to put them in and turn the edge off square, and that was my very first job and it was as much as I could do to lift them in the lathe. The Wickman automatics made the screwed bits, the knurled bits for the headsets and they could turn out 1,000 of them a day. They had never had anything like that at Hopper's before and if it hadn't been for the war they never would have had any. The lathes must have been specially provided for war work.

Eddie Gaunt was a pal of Roger Green, Les Green's son, and an apprentice tool maker. "Roger said to me one day, 'What are you doing when you leave school?' I had no idea, so he said, 'Do you want to come and work in the tool room?' I said 'What's that?', because I had no idea. He said, 'Well you make tools!' 'What, pliers and things like that?' 'Well, all sorts.' So that was it. I started in late 1958 or early 1959 as a barrow boy in the machine shop before starting my apprenticeship in September 1959. They still employed barrow boys at this late stage and it was great because you got to go to all parts of the firm. You got to know all the departments. They were still using the old wooden barrows. In the machine shop they had two very big automatic machines, very advanced, for those days; they would take bars of up to 2" diameter. One of my jobs was to keep them supplied with bars. One of the machines would just take small bars and turn out parts like pump pegs and the other made hub parts." Eddie started his apprenticeship on 23 September 1959 and in his first year took home £2 2s 1d a week, of which £1 went to his mum, 10s in the bank with 12s 1d left over. It had not been the practice to send apprentices to technical school, but suddenly one day they said they had to do day release, which included one evening. This was at Scunthorpe Technical College and Eddie was amazed at how much they didn't know. The college placed them on a City & Guilds machine shop engineering course, and most of them dropped out, but not Eddie. As recorded in Chapter 7 the apprenticeship scheme ceased in 1962, when Eddie transferred to the steelworks.

Norman Broughton's dad knew the tool room foreman, John Stockdale, quite well and he secured an apprenticeship for him. Bernard Gouldthorpe served the same apprenticeship and recalls, "It was one of the best places to serve an apprenticeship. There were all the machines you wanted – universal grinders, surface grinders, millers, shapers, lathes, jig borer, hardening furnaces."

## Working Life

Maud Hildred recalled the early start and late finish during busy times. "Dad would be on the landing – 'Come on, five and twenty past five train just whistled out, time you was getting up!' That was for a 6 o'clock start and when it was wintertime I was really frightened, it was dark mornings and it was snowing and I would walk in between my sisters. I think I was walking in my sleep! We worked while eight o'clock, went home for our breakfast and back by half past eight. Then we used to leave at half past 12 for dinner and then when we had to go back at night we used to leave at half past five but we had to be back by six to start the evening shift. One night we had to go back as there was a special order leaving Immingham at six the next morning and we hadn't quite got them finished during the day. Mr Davies asked us to stop while the order was finished and it got to about 10 o'clock and all the lights went out. The generator had packed in and it was dark, really dark by then, so we had to go home. They said they would fetch us if they got the electric going. Anyway, we just got home and I went to bed and they came back for us. My older sister said, 'Do you want the young 'un?' 'Oh, yes, send 'em all, send 'em all!' We all went toddling up to Brigg Road again, and the bosses went out and fetched us fish and chips and shandy. We finished wrapping them about five o'clock and the boat sailed at six, so we got finished and then we asked, 'What time are we to come back?' They said at six. So we said, 'We aren't bloody coming at six!' So we didn't go back while eight o'clock. And then when it was Friday payday, the man that did the time keeping and wages: 'Why, that lass,' he said, 'she only earned about two bob and she worked all night.' 'Well, give her an extra ha'penny, for now.' And I think I earned about 12 shillings that week, not much! Davies would walk round and one night we had to go back at eight o'clock and we were all working like mad, you know, and I was telling them about a film I'd seen, and one of them said, 'Hey up, there's Davies watching us.' He came over and said to my older sister, 'Your sister's doing a lot of talking, if she hadn't been working, I'd have sent her home!' I was working like mad!" Maud also recalled the work involved when large orders came in for Brown Brothers or Selfridges. "With big orders they used to store the wrapped frames on the top floor of the offices. They would pull them up from the lift well with a hoist and then hang them up on hooks. Mother told us that Mrs Hopper [Hannah Elizabeth] used to wrap frames in the early years, before the business took off." Maud also recalled the story of her grandfather O'Malley being invited to the Wilson's silver wedding, held in the newly built machine shop. Her grandmother was no longer living so he took Maud's mother, who was sufficiently impressed for the event to be remembered almost 100 years later. Maud explained that complete bicycles would arrive at the packing shop by horse drawn rulley. Billy Stow was in charge of the foreign shop and Jack West of the 'English'. The girls would unload the rulley, place each machine on a stand in turn and prepare for wrapping – usually involving turning the bars and removing pedals, depending on the method of transport. Typically, wrapped bicycles would return northwards to the station for loading on the half past five train. "It wasn't really hard work, just steady, but we had to keep on working and we were tired when we finished."

Jack Austin again: "In the enamelling department there were big troughs and they dipped the frames in, hung them up, let them drip, then they put them into ovens. When the enamel was hard I came along with a barrow and wheeled the frames and the forks and the mudguards to the lining shop. It was a wooden barrow and you could get 12 frames on it. I wheeled them down to a store where Dave Dent was waiting to stick tallies in the head tube, and then they would go to the liner, who would line them and apply transfers, depending on the model. The lines were just ordinary paint so they had to be stoved again, and the transfers had to be varnished over. After that they were ready to go to the erecting shop. Once I was given the chance to line a frame I quickly got the hang of it. You can see in the photograph of me lining a Lincoln Imp (Fig. 7.1) how we used to hold a sword pencil. It was the way you held the brush – we called them pencils. After the war we did without the final stoving process as the lines were cellulose and used to dry straight away. I left because it was going down the drain – they had shoved me into the frame filing shop because lining had been dropped and it was just transfers. I left in 1967 to work at the fertiliser plant."

Ray Pettit: "The only investment after the war was when they re-equipped the tool room with new lathes, new shapers and drilling machines. There was also a conveying system put in for the paint shop. We even did some blacksmithing and we hardened our own tools in the forge there until we got the new tool room, which had its own furnace."

Gladys Hedley: "They were all women in roadside machine shop; just the foreman and under-foreman were men. I worked at Hopper's until 1946 when I had my first child. I started at 14, got married at 20, so 8 years I worked there. I didn't go back – there were no baby minders in those days! I just worked on a drilling machine, drilling hubs. I also remember, because cigarettes were rationed, we used to go to the toilet and you couldn't move for smoke – there was a big gang of us. You couldn't smoke in the works. And we used to have a pin on the end of the cigarette to make it last a bit longer. My, we really did have some laughs. Cyril Franklin was our foreman. I wasn't on piece work; I was on about 30 bob a week." Gladys also recalls a tricycle made for Prince Charles – all chrome – but the Palace refused it. "So I said I wanted that bike if they don't want it and I got it. Every piece was chrome. It was beautiful. When my daughter Christine got too big for it we let someone else have it. It was nickel plated first then chrome. I remember when my dad worked in the polishing shop – they didn't have extractor fans in those days, you know. Well, we used to have coal fires and I remember my dad coming home and he took his muffler off – it was a muffler not a scarf –  and it always went round his neck and round his braces and for us kids he used to shake it in front of the fire and there was all sparks came, from all the stuff that was going in my dad's lungs. I think he was about 68 when he died and my mum was 64. They worked and worked."

Eva Such was a wheel builder: "After 1945 the piece work rates were not so good. We got 1¾d for a pair of wheels, and 2¼d if it was a three-speed. You could do about three or four pairs in an hour. That's lacing and tightening and the men did the truing. The foreman used to tell you what sort – six pair, Elswick 26", or such as that. And then you got your rims and hubs and that – you had to collect all the bits yourself, but you soon got to know the different parts you wanted. You had your hub and put your spokes in on one side and then turned it over and built the other side. You crossed your back over four and your front over three. Then the men did the truing. Fred Chappell tried to get me in to truing but I could never seem to fathom it out! When it slackened down they moved me to chrome and I was only in there a fortnight and I got chrome rash and had to come out. I had my arms bandaged from here to here with ulceration. I was only wiring up but I was in the same place as the chrome vats were."

Arthur Such used to take in his own food. "The canteen was used but most people brought their own. We could make tea and eat in the tool room. John Stockdale used to tap the old bell and that was your lunch break and when he tapped it again you got cracking. Harold Altoft worked with me in the tool room and his brother Charlie was foreman in the tube shop. There were some big presses in there. The first one was a big geared machine where they sliced sheet metal for making forks. The press shop was for cutting out all the flat parts, like brake parts, anything that needed holes punching – there were no drills in those shops, anything that needed machining was done in the machine shop. Parts were moved around in hand barrows – there were no fork lifts, but they didn't have far to go; the longest trip was to the Elswick erecting shop. The old aerodrome was used for packing, but at one time they built wheels there as well. Most of the big orders were packed at Brigg Road. All the transport was horse and dray. They used to clip-clop back and forth all day. I believe there were three or four of them. Polishing was a lousy job. The polishing bobs went on a tapered spindle and it had a one sided thread, so you put it on and the more pressure you put on the tighter it got, so there was no chance of it coming off. They didn't wear protection like they would today. Then they had to take them off from time to time to trim them to get the wheel true again. They had trays with glue in them to roll the bobs in and then moved them over to the grit and finally put them in the oven to cure. Different grades of grit and they did their own. They were made of a leathery material all stitched together – layers and layers of it. It used to wear down and the grit got used up. They used a blade to trim it up. From their neck, hanging from a strap, was a sheet metal plate with a lip on the bottom. This was for pushing the piece being polished against the bob."

Things had slackened off in the press shop before the war and Walter Horne spent some time in the repair shop. "Repair work was like a reconditioning service. We used to get a lot of carrier cycles in from different firms to recondition. We would strip them down and send all the components through to different parts of the factory to re-enamel, rechrome, and then we reassembled and they used to come out like a new cycle. When I came back in 1947 I went straight back to the press shop. After four or five weeks on 2d an hour they put you on piece work. Every minute you were stopped you were counting how much money you were losing. It was only pennies or ha'pennies but you made more money on piecework. If you had breakdowns you lost, especially when you went on to the 60 ton machine presses. You see they built all the components in those days, everything. The toolmakers would make the tool, mount them and see to them when they needed tending. Henry Cole set the rates for new jobs. He would come and time you on it. He'd maybe have half an hour with you and then you took your finished components and weighed them. You used to weigh in grosses and got anywhere from a ha'penny a gross to 2d or 3d a gross. Some jobs later on after the war were priced in thousands, so you maybe got 1d a thousand. You got cagey with the rate fixer, you never went flat out at your piecework jobs when Henry was watching you – you took it at a reasonable rate. He didn't time you on every job. If it was a job similar to another one George Bell would say, well it's similar to so and so, we'll give you that price. When the new management came in [1958] the main change was that they started buying components in instead of making them themselves, so my work in the press shop just went down and down and down until there wasn't any work left. They just put us on clearing up and I decided to get out. This was 1962/63 I think. I then got a job down at Farmer's Company on 5s an hour. Joan got finished because she was off when her mother died. "I stayed off work with my dad for a full week because of him grieving, so they finished me. They were cutting down and that's how I finished at Hopper's. It was awful because I wanted to be at work – I wanted to occupy my mind."

*Fig. 10.7 Joseph Small with his team of cycle erectors – probably pre-1914.*

Recalling stories from his dad Harry Haddock related: "The part my dad worked in, on the far side of Elswick, Joe Small was foreman (Fig. 10.7). He was a big churchman and could swear like a trooper – he never used to shout for anyone, he would just whistle. And he was whistling for my dad one day – he would whistle until the person he wanted turned round and then he would wave and my dad never looked round and he came across and said, 'I was whistling for you Haddock!', and my dad said 'When you whistle for me, I aren't a dog!' A lot of the foremen before the war were contractors. They drew the money from Hopper's and they paid you. They were getting all the profits and they just gave us the bare necessities. When I started in the handlebar department I was under a fellow called Jack Thompson and was put on bars for roadsters with rod brakes and my job was to put on the bar knobs. There were two chromed knobs either side where the levers went through. Then they went to another young lad who put the levers in and the brake stops. Then the rods went in and then there was a fellow along the balcony who put the handgrips on, they were celluloid. He used to put them in water to soak them and then slid them on and they stuck, just with cold water. When they built racers we used to put the stems on and tighten them up and put the expander bolts in and then it went to the same fellow at the end and he would put the rubber grips on using a big tin of solution. He would slide them on and they were solid. Finished bars would go into the stores and from there to the erectors on the ground floor for building the finished bicycle. They used to draw all the bits from the stores for whichever model they were making. On the far side under the other balcony was Joe Small's department where they had a machine that tapped bottom brackets; my dad worked on that side. Then they assembled the bracket, fitted the forks and loaded them on to a barrow to go to the erector's store. It was a big place, the Elswick building. After assembling the bike, apart from fitting the saddle (added at Brigg Road) they wheeled it down to the end of the building for a final check before collecting a tally for the next machine. The bikes were all different piece work prices – the old fashioned three-speed with an oil bath would take longer to do than a sports model. The people working there were mostly from Barton and New Holland. A lot biked in from New Holland – the odd one came in on the train. One or two came from Barrow, and the odd one from South Ferriby. Outside Barton it was mainly agricultural work. I left in about 1936 to work for an electrical firm and when that didn't work out I went to work for a fellow who bought a farm at Barrow Haven. That lasted for the best part of a year, and I got 14s a week there. I loved that job, ploughing with three horses on stubble."

Seeing no long term future in agricultural work Harry spent time in one of the brick and tile works along the Humber Bank and then saw service during the war in Burma and Singapore. He returned home in 1946 on loan to the brickyards. Following demob towards the end of 1946 he decided to give Hopper's another go. "I said to my mum I would start work the first Monday in January. I went to the time office and saw Walt Jennings, and he said, 'I'll give Henry Cole a ring to come and see you.' I was 26 by then, past my youth days, and he said, 'It's good money now, it's 1s 8½d an hour.' I asked where they were going to put me. 'We'll see to that on Monday, when you come.' So they set me up in the frame shop. The foreman told me one day in 1949 that the old hands wouldn't use the jig they had built for making diamond frames. They thought it was going to take work off them. So Harry Pownell, who was from Nottingham, said, 'Will you go on that frame jig?' So I said I would if it was more money and he said I would get the same price as the others for frames. They sent this lad to work with me (Fig. 6.6). We would get bundles of tubes, all cut to length and enough for 50 sets. There was a dip brazer at the back of the frame shop. It was a big gas stove lined with bricks and there was a queer shaped pot, really heavy, and it went down into the oven and they put brass in that and borax and it had gas jets blowing on it to melt the brass. After I had finished the 50 frames the brazers collected them up and dipped them. Everything was basic in those days – same length seat tube, same length top tube. I would knock the head set up and the down tube and the lad would drill and pin them. Then I would knock the seat tube and the top tube up and he would drill and pin them. Lastly I would put the bracket on and guide the seat and down tubes into the bracket. We used to pre-drill the brackets and top head lugs. After about three months I was making 250 frames a day and all the old frame builders, there were four, they all went on strike. They could only make 50 or 60 a day by hand. We used to get a 1½d for a diamond, but I had to pay the lad out of that. I used to keep a lad from 16 to 18, and after that I got him on to a man's job. The other frame builders were sent to different departments. One of them was Bill Taylor who had come down with a gang from Newcastle, when Hopper's bought Elswick. They put him in the machine shop, where he was supposed to be head sherang. He didn't speak to me for a lot of years. Bill and Frank Auty were also transferred to the machine shop and there was only me building frames and I was doing enough to keep them all going. Eventually I worked out how to build ladies' frames as well, and utility carriers – they were half a crown each and that was a lot of money, but there was a lot of work in them. If I was making ladies' frames I had to braze them myself, because they couldn't dip them. After making the diamond frames the girls would fit the chain and seat stays. They tacked the stay in place and then they would be dip brazed. In the old days the dip brazing was all done

*Fig. 10.8 This photographs shows how things had changed by the time Harry started jig building frames. These frame builders and filers are pictured in 1913. Note the predominance of waistcoats and jackets – no longer Sunday best, but good enough for work*

in a different department and they would black lead the frames so the brass wouldn't stick. By the time I went back after the war they had a debrassing system and it was all done by electrodes, rods and plates. It would take the brass off the outside but not from the inside. Going back before my time on one side of the frame shop there would be about 15 or 16 filers, filing the excess brass off (Fig 10.8). It was a good job, and I probably had the best paid job in the factory!

When I worked in the handlebar shop, October 1935, I think, I was working with the machine that cut the slot in the handle bar stem. We used a little circular saw. I was doing that and all of a sudden my hand dropped and it took my finger off. I went to see Miss King, the nurse, and she gave me some sal volatile to drink, put a bandage on and I went to see Dr Kirk at his surgery at the top of Marsh Lane. I had to go over to Hull Infirmary to have it taken down to the next joint. I went with my dad on the ferry and I was off work about six weeks. I didn't get paid, but they granted me £18 compensation. When I started at 14 my dad warned me about the road side machine shop, he said 'Don't go into that shop on your own!' So I asked why. He said, 'You don't need to know why, just don't go in.' It was some time before I got to know it was all girls and women in there. When you went in there they had your trousers down and they would slurry oil [cutting oil] all your privates!

Things changed after the war. Before it was 'Mr Franklin' and after it was 'George'. I can see them now, Mr Cole behind his desk and George sat there. 'Now then Harry what are you after?' Oh and Morton, he was the manager after Stow had died – he had come from a radiator firm in Hull. He was only a little chap. I said, 'I feel I can make more. But I don't want you coming and saying we can knock a farthing off this or a ha'penny off that. That's not my way of going on. If you want increased production I'll try and do it, but I don't want to be knocked off pricing.' Henry Cole said, 'We won't do that, if you are making more it is increasing production.' 'Another thing,' I said, 'while I am here, I am paying that lad anything between 7/6 and 10 bob a day. So will you pay him day work and I will boost his wages? The lad is worth that wage but I can't pay him enough without lowering mine.' Henry Cole agreed so the lad got paid his day work rate plus what I paid him. I stayed there until 1962 when I went to work for Reg Harris at Macclesfield. I saw this advert in *Cycling* and went to see Reg. He picked me up at Manchester and took me to Macclesfield. He said, 'Well, I'll pay you £20 a week and we'll see how we go on from there.' I had to give him a demonstration of what I could do. I went as a frame builder for his new company. I only stayed there three months as I was only getting home once a fortnight. I went to see Harold Cox, who had taken over as foreman and he said the fellow who had taken my place wasn't fast enough, so I went straight back to my old job and stayed there until 1967. When Elswick-Hopper had the racing team I built 36 for them, that was six each and they were all hand brazed 531. Ron Coe visited one day and I asked why they needed six each. 'Well, we flog 'em!' he said."

Jack Dimoline went into the machine shop from the brake shop in about 1950. "It was combined with the press shop. We turned bar knobs, hub cups, anything that was needed. It was all piece work. Everything you did was so much a gross. All my life I was on piece work, that's why we did things so fast. Take a chain adjuster as an example. We got the rod from the stores, cut it off and screwed it in the machine shop. Then in the press shop they would take a piece of steel, blank that out and make it into a washer and then a piece of flat steel was blanked and shaped and done in the press shop again. Then it was welded on, taken to the polishing shop and plating shop. There would be about 12 operations on that one part. We made everything there very near. About the only thing we bought in were rims, saddles and pumps. Hubs we used to get as castings but we had to finish them. We made all our own brakes, even calliper brakes. You see, we had a tool room with at least six apprentices and they made all the jigs and tools. We had a good spell after the war working long hours as we had to assemble 300 bikes in a day. I went down to Earls Court two years and the enamel finish on the show bikes was wonderful. Freddie Hopper used to drive Rover cars and some of the bits were taken off and rechromed in the Hopper shop. One night I was talking to him in the Hopper's Club and he said 'How're things going?' I told him not like the old days!"

Bob Blackburn joined the union at 14: "I was told to ask my parents for approval to join. It cost 4d a week and it was called the National Union of General and Municipal Workers back then. As regards pricing Hopper's were very tight – I can remember some of them being called into the office if they had booked too much at piece rate. I think you were allowed at that time 2s 6d a day above day rate and if you went over that the foreman would tell you to watch what you were booking or he would bring the rate fixer in to re-price the job. I enjoyed setting machines. When I put new blades on the guillotine and reset it I had to use feeler gauges, because when you are cutting sheet metal it can become very ragged if you don't set it right. After I had set the machine I had to go to Charlie Altoft and tell him I had set it for shearing whatever metal was on – 16, 18, 22 gauge. 'Right,' he would say, 'I will be along in a minute.' He always used to have a folded newspaper under his arm and he would spread the newspaper out and expected it to cut the paper. He always tested it with a sheet of newspaper. After National Service I went back into the tube shop followed by a short spell in the mudguard shop. I worked under Reg Kent but there were only a couple of people there by then. We had a lot of trouble with the beading on the ends of the mudguards – it was sort of experimental – so I was working on that. We got it right in the end but it took a while. It was a hand press that we used for the beading but the mudguards themselves went through a series of rollers, fed in at one end and out at the other. One job I have never forgotten was for a cycle called a Canadian Humpback. It had a humped cross bar and all the cranks on the tubes were more pronounced than the ordinary ones, and were done on a mandrel. This was an experimental job for about 100 bikes. We made the chain stays and seat stays and then tried using mandrels to crank them. We used a half round mandrel for the 'D' shaped part of the tube and then for the end that went into the bracket we used a short round mandrel. The cranking was so pronounced that it used to burst the metal each time we tried it. So what they came up with was resin. I hated the job – I used to end up with a sore throat and I had to do it in an outbuilding. I had to heat it up to make it molten, then plug one end of the tube with clay, stand all the tubes up in a rack and then fill them with the resin and let it cool off. We would then bring the tubing into the press shop, and after getting the right crank I had to take them back outside to melt out the resin. It would be an order that came in once a year. They couldn't give it to someone on piece work, because you couldn't price it, really. One of the first jobs I did in the machine shop was on rear mudguards for an African order and

I had to drill a series of holes for dress cords, because the African ladies wore long dresses. No 40 drill it was. Everything at that time was line shaft driven, but if a belt broke there was a lightweight Slingsby ladder with two hooks on and I had to go up the ladder and put the belt on at the top and then come down and move the ladder. It was a noisy place, being line shaft driven and no one wore ear protection. Most of us wore boiler suits, or a bib and brace. We had to supply our own, of course."

Bill Carter: "Hopper's generated the majority of its power using three diesel generators. This was just to the right after entering the Marsh Lane gate. The motors at this time were all dc, so there was a lot of work on brush gear. All motors were maintained in house, with 30hp being about the biggest. There were also lots of overhead shaft drives, driven by dc motors. The big machine shop was just having new ac powered lathes installed, with external power supplies, and the old machine shops were shut down. Work was enjoyable, you knew all the people and so it was like a family operation. I met Jean at Hopper's where she started in the mudguard shop under Ned Trout and then went into the gear case shop soldering with Bill Brown. She was just 15 and worked there for one year. They employed a lot of women in the machine shops. My sister Audrey worked in the Elswick shop. Nearly all the employable people in Barton were in work, so it was natural to have a lot of women. Heavy and dirty work tended to be done by men, such as polishing, frame building, handle bar bending, tube bending. Women were thought to be also more dextrous than men. Motors were taken into the shop for overhaul. There was no set preventive maintenance procedure, but every Saturday morning, when the works were shut down, was when you went round and got at the machines. This consisted of cleaning the commutator segments, and setting up or renewing brushes. You had a routine for this as you knew which were the heaviest users. The works was just on five days a week. Two of the main areas for weekend work were the nickel and chrome plating shops. These were a bit unique as, instead of carbon brushes, they used copper wire mesh brushes that gave you a greater surface area for conductivity. The wear was high so they took a lot of maintenance. The people in the plating shops generally looked after their own equipment and cleaned the rods to maintain conductivity. The generation side was the responsibility of the electricians, where there were dc motors driving low voltage generators. That was a job for Saturday mornings. There were four or five dc generators in the nickel plating shop. They had just gone on to ac and they were using ac for the chrome shop – it had just been renewed at the end of the war. The plating vats had rods laid across and the items were hung in the solution. In the chrome shop there was a rotary vat – much more up to date. I used to walk to work – I couldn't afford a bike! But the majority of people had Hopper bikes and when it came time to sound the buzzer at lunch or going home time they used the old air raid siren, mounted on the end of the Elswick building. They sounded the siren at 12 and the number of bicycles coming out of Marsh Lane and going in both directions, you can imagine, no one could go against it, the flow was so strong. I went from Hopper's to Yorkshire Electricity on domestic and industrial wiring. The money was half as much again. One of the main things that kept you in Barton was transport. I lived down Ramsden Avenue when Jean and I got married in 1951 and there was only one car along there at that time. To get to the steel works Mellors ran at least two coaches for each shift, 6 to 2, 2 to 10 and 10 to 6, so something like five or six coaches for day workers – Goxhill to Barton and then to the steelworks."

Nora Thompson: "When I first started in 1945 and for a few years after, they had two horses and carts which used to ferry cycles from the factory. They used to come up Marsh Lane, up the narrow bit, which is now one way, up George Street, turn right up Holydyke and left up Brigg Road to the packing shops. The reason they didn't fit the saddle at Marsh Lane was that the wrappers placed the seat pillar in a special stem so they could spin it round. Paper strips were wrapped round all the stays and the frame. Later on they started using cardboard cloaks that went over the whole cycle. All the wooden crates were made there. They would start with a crate with two or three planks of wood and the bikes going abroad wouldn't be fully assembled, so they would start building up the frames in them, (they had

*Fig. 10.9 As featured in the 1907 catalogue, the ground floor of the Brigg Road office, constructed in 1905.*

all been wrapped) and they would start to build the case up adding wood to the sides as they went. Then they would use stencils for the addresses, India or China, or wherever they were to be sent. The horses and carts would then trundle down to the railway station, or sometimes the railway lorries would come and fetch them. When I first went there they didn't have their own vans, not until the 1950s when they bought the first pantechnicon. Then they got more vans and fewer went by rail. When I first started as the office girl one of my jobs was to deliver the cheques at the end of the month to pay local businesses that had done work for them. We had an office bicycle and it was red with a wire basket on the front and it said 'Elswick-Hopper Cycles' on the plate. I would take a cheque to Stamp's on Burgate; they ran the market boat to Hull. I would go to Standerline's, the blacksmiths that shoed the horses – they had the house next to the Blue Bell and the smithy was through the archway. I used to go to Thompson's, in High Street, opposite where Lidl's is now and he was a carter. At that time there was a rail siding that went up Butts Road and he used to deliver the oil and stuff that came into that siding. Then to Lee's, the chemist on George Street. They had a big warehouse on the other side of the road from where David Lee now has his photography shop and we used to get all our stationery inks from them. They came in big stone jars. At that time we sat at these Charles Dickens desks with these high stools and inkwells, just like it is pictured in the Edwardian catalogues (Fig 10.9). They didn't change that for quite a long time. So Hopper's created a big spin off all over Barton. My father-in-law remembered Queens Avenue being built by Hopper's for the workers and if you look at the houses, the ones on the east side have angels carved over the windows. At the other side they are quite plain. I think the ones that were a bit more elaborate were for those with better jobs, so it was part of the class system! When I returned to Hopper's things had changed a lot. Richard Blundell came from Raleigh and George Fleming worked there too. While an office girl I used to go to the factory to deliver notes. Mostly I had to go to the repair department, where they did a full rebuild. Morwood Thompson was in charge and I married his great nephew. He was also conductor of the Barton Town Band. During the war, when I was at school, there might have been five cars in Barton. When I had to learn the switchboard we had two lines, BOH 2167 and BOH 2168 and that was in 1945, so that gives you an idea of how many telephones there were in the town. I remember the transfer room upstairs with huge wooden drawers. When orders came in from abroad they wanted their own transfers and I remember some with Chinese Sampans and things, and when we got the order we had to get out the transfers and take them to the factory.

When I went back after the children had grown up I used to take the orders and then route all the deliveries for the vans. You could get 150 to 160 cycles on a van, depending on the models. If it was racing bikes the handlebars took up more room, and the last off had to be the first in. They had wooden battens across to stop the load moving so you had to work it all out, taking into account half day closing. So, are they going to be in Tewkesbury on Wednesday, when its half day closing – they wouldn't want to kick their heels there! We had a huge map on the wall with all the dealers marked and it had to be all worked out. All the bikes had a serrated tie-on label and we kept the bottom half. We went to the Cycle Show every November in London at Earls Court. They built the stand on the top floor of the office at Brigg Road to see what it would look like. Quite a few of the staff would go down, and they always stayed at the Regent Palace Hotel. We worked in the office on Saturday mornings till 12 o'clock. All the time I worked in that office I can never remember any of the men calling me by my first name, you were always Miss or Mrs. It was unheard of to call anybody by their first name in an office like that. I was very happy at Hopper's, I worked there 21 years altogether, 10 years the first time. They were all local people, people worked where they lived, there was no public transport, but some of the girls used to bike every day from Wootton or New Holland."

Fred recalled all the sidings at the railway station. "It was so busy, they were bringing coal in, and cycles were going out. There were bricks and tiles going out, and ropes too. There was a siding mainly used by Hopper's for all the oils they used. Blythe's tile works used to ship a lot by rail too before the haulage companies started. I was on shift work at the time and if I was on rest days and they were stuck for a driver I would help out. I used to take a load of bikes out and then call in at Raleigh. This was at the time when Hopper's weren't producing like they used to [1970s]. So we would take a load of bikes out and then call in at Raleigh and bring bicycles back here."

Margaret Rodmell and Doreen Atkins both remember Moira, who came from Leeds to work in accounts. Doreen: "She was a smoker and women weren't allowed to smoke in the offices. She said, 'I did it before and I'll do it here.' This would be 1961 or 1962. Men were allowed to smoke and some never stopped smoking. But we accepted it; it's amazing what you accept, but that was the norm." Doreen recalled the office layout with clarity: "On the ground floor of the office block, on the right of the main entrance, was the board room, where Arthur Stow was, and to the left was the export department. There was a corridor down the middle, and to the left of the export department was George Clarke's office. Then, going round, was the typing pool, and then sales. Upstairs the first office was Francis Robinson, and then Dave Elliott, who did the costing, and then the accounts department. Following round was Les Green's office, and he did all the final accounts. Then there was Herbert Linley, with Gladys and Ron. Then there were the lorry drivers – Gordon Linley and Cyril Haddock. Off the offices was the packing shop and in there was, bless her, Mrs Oldridge. She was a dream and she used to do all the packing of the small parts, all the accessories and we used to go down there to have a natter with her. As a junior you used to have to make the coffee for your bosses and we used condensed milk – I used to eat more than went into the coffee! There was one teaspoon for them and three for me!"

Margaret Rodmell remembers when things started to get slack, "When you looked at the bank balance it was something like £200,000 with a minus, a vast amount of money. I left in 1961 so it would be getting to that time. We moved to St Mary's in the late 1950s before the Brigg Road offices closed. I remember going down there with Nola Stow and Moira Shipstone. The offices were opposite the Marsh Lane entrance, up the iron steps." [Still used by owners Meldan for the same purpose.]

Gordon Linley worked for Bert Crofts, the sales manager, and initially covered sales to the eastern counties – Lincolnshire, Norfolk, Suffolk, Essex, Cambridgeshire, Huntingdonshire, Bedfordshire, Buckinghamshire, and Northants. "When I first started on the road they gave me a list that was pre-war. Some dealers were very faithful and some didn't have time for you, especially if they found better terms from other suppliers, though they weren't supposed to. I went down to London outside the postal areas – so to Enfield, Waltham Cross, Dagenham, round the other side of London to Staines. I did that for several years and then they moved me to Lincolnshire, Yorkshire, Northumberland, Durham, Lancashire, Westmoreland, Cumberland and Cheshire, right up to Berwick, but that was only periodic as there wasn't much up there. There were five of us. The London chap did Kent, another did the South West and lived in Bristol – I was sent down there for three weeks when someone left. Midlands was the other area. There was no one in Scotland as we had three distributors. After the war some dealers had lost interest in Hopper's so we had to find new ones. The amount of advertising was negligible compared to Raleigh and Hercules. Hopper's was the biggest of the small firms and were reputed to do 2,000 a week, but 1500-1700 was more the norm. When you think that Raleigh did 20,000 a week, you would have needed a massive investment to keep up with them. You would keep one copy of the order, give one to the dealer and post the third to the office at the end of the day. Delivery was six or seven weeks and that was one of the problems. I think the factory was limited by production methods. They didn't produce in batches for stock. The best sellers varied dependent on the area, if you were looking at Norfolk generally you were dealing with an agricultural area and you would be selling a sit up and beg bike. There were no set targets, you set your own, trying to do better than you had the week before. There was no bonus incentive or anything like that."

Peter Credland: "I progressed to making the cases as I got older and then I did sawing until I was moved to the packing department. After that I went to the works, packing railway trucks. That would be after I came out of the Army in 1952/53. After that I went into the enamel shop for about four years, starting in what they called the degreasing plant where the steel parts were treated with methylated steam and were then bonderized after drying. Bonderizing left the metal with like a grey paint on them and it was rust proof. There were two vats – one to wash them clean and one to bonderize them. They were then dried in gas ovens – about 30 frames at a time and they would come out warm. The next move was to the enamelling shop. Some frames were sprayed but a lot of them were dipped, all black ones were dipped. They had two tanks, one was a rubbery black solution, which was the first one you used, and then they went through on the conveyor and would come out the other end dry and hardened. They were then put on racks and two girls used to flat them down because you would get little blobs where dust had settled, and then they went through a finishing coat, which was the polish coat. There was an oven half way down the conveyor and so when they came out they were finished. They were allowed to cool down so you could touch them by hand. There was a spraying booth and all the spraying was done by women. From there they went into the lining department. It was a work of art getting the framesets into a 36" box, 25 cycles with the exception of the rims. Rims and tyres went into a rim case, 28" square and 36" high, holding 50 rims and tyres. The wood came from Grimsby docks by lorry, probably two or three loads a week to supply the five people who worked in the saw mill – there was the sawyer, the assistant sawyer, and three case makers. They made either cases or crates, whichever was needed. They were fully employed all day and never had a minute, in fact the case makers were on piece work, so they had to keep going to make their wages. There were eight packers packing frames and rims. They were going all the time but they were never on piece work, I think they were frightened the frames would get damaged. There was just enough room and by the time you put your last set of mudguards in that was the top of the case and you put the boards across. Those double top tube frames were devils to pack because you didn't have the diamonds to put your handlebars in. With that extra tube you had to get the little bend to go over your bottom tube. When we packed CKD [completely knocked down] machines the wheels were also in pieces. We put five tyres in the bottom of the case then 25 rims then four strings and push them down to the half way point, then we put tyres in, in tens, so that was another 20, then five more then another 25 rims and push them right down to the top of the case then we put in the remaining 20 tyres and put saddles down the corner spaces, the bottom one standing point up and the second point down and the same again, so you got four in each corner. To do a case from start to finish took about 35 to 40 minutes. Then you had to nail it all up and put the banding iron round it. Then take it and weigh it and do the stencilling for where it was to go. Some shipments were of partially assembled bikes but they would come up to Brigg Road as if you were going to ride them on the street. You had to take the pedals off, the wheels out, mudguards and brakes off, take the handlebars off, and then as you have the diamond of your frame you put the two wheels in and tied them on, put the handlebars through the spokes at an angle that left it flat and then just tied all the other parts around it. Then you put it in a case and you put six of those together. You put the backs together and then you reversed it, so you didn't take so much space. It's amazing what you can get into small spaces. In the mornings in winter the drayman and I had to carry the coke in the morning through the back way to the offices. It was all in coal bags and we had to carry them down to the furnace and empty them. We used to do that first thing every morning to keep the offices warm."

Dorothy Sobey recalls from her time at Hopper's during the war that the girls in the packing shop used to put their names and addresses in the tool bags of bicycles going for export. She was a wheel builder, but her sister, Hilda had included her name and address in one tool bag and after a few weeks she got a letter from a girl in California, who worked as a riveter in the Douglas aircraft works. They have been in touch since 1944 and have exchanged visits.

Ruby Credland started in 1954. After a spell in packing and being laid off during a slack period around 1958 she spent some time in the big machine shop. "I used to machine the bottom bracket spindles; it was piece work, so much a gross. I was using a lathe with slurry oil running. The shop had glass in the roof and in the winter it was freezing, while in the summer it was like a greenhouse it was so hot. In the winter the slurry oil was so cold when you were taking off a finished piece and you were stood all day from half past seven till five, an hour off for dinner and it was cold, so cold. There was some sort of heating system but I can remember having terrible chilblains at that time. We had a 10 minute break in the morning and a 10 minute break in the afternoon and the main power was stopped during the breaks. Alan Hopper was foreman when I was there. Washers and nuts were all made there. Everything for the bike, even the cranks – they used to come in rough and were finished in the machine shop. Barbara Towle and Freda used to machine the bottom brackets, which also came in rough cast. Saddles were bought in – pedals, brake blocks, pumps and things like that. If you were late they would stop your money. They made you stand outside for 15 minutes waiting for the gate to reopen. The last time I worked there was for Falcon in the Elswick building, wrapping again. Jack Dimoline was our foreman and I worked with them for a few years, until they moved to Brigg, around 1978, because I didn't want to travel. There was always a good sense of friendship. It was so funny when we left at 12 when the buzzer went and at teatime of course. The bikes, a sea of people up Marsh Lane and along High Street – it was a spectacle."

Rick Appleyard was 23 when he joined Hopper's in 1947, just a year after finishing his Army service with the Parachute Regiment. He revealed that the post-war sales boom was not without problems. "I worked for the post office when I was demobbed in 1946, it was a good job but the hours didn't suit me. The lads would be going off to [grass] track meetings on a Saturday and there was me working. I started off in the welding shops, welding and brazing components, such as stay tubes. A girl from Barrow taught me and Teddy Lyons was the foreman. Later on I went in the frame shop and I had a coal gas and compressed air brazing gun, and it was a very soft flame and you couldn't burn the metal. The frame filers used to do the final dressing of the frames after they had been in the debrasser. This equipment should have had a qualified chemist in control so the solution was right, but they were too mean. They had a store down Butts Road, and these two blokes used to go down and mix the debrassing solution[6] in carboys, but whatever they were doing it was hit and miss. It was either too strong, and stripped the brass out altogether from under the lugs, or it didn't remove the surplus. They also had quality problems with the bonderizing process. Cycles were coming back from the Far East with all the paint peeling off. It was the Pyrene Company that supplied the equipment and they sent a rep up, who asked, 'Where are the timers? This is a timed process.' There were timers all over after that. Drying in the ovens had to be timed as well. We took on a lot of contracts to produce bicycles under contract to Triumph, and made a huge number of Triumph cycles. Elswick-Hopper always had contracts with firms such as Brown Brothers, they were the main bread and butter contract. Then there was the foreign side, firms in Malaysia, stacks of them with double top tubes for carrying bags of rice. Mainland China as well, even in those days."

Rick was also witness to problems with the brazing vat. "They were on piece work and there were pyrometers to keep the temperature right for dipping. There was a big cantilever arm that they used to hang two frames on at a time, then turn them round and dip them on the other parts. It was an elliptical brazing bath. They used to put them through, dip the heads, dip the brackets. But instead of hanging them over the bath to warm them up to drive out the cold air they used to whip them in cold and suck the brass in and that's how you got your ringers and things like that[7]. After dip brazing a chap called Pattinson used to put the frame on a spigot through the bracket and check the alignment against a mark at each end of a block. If it went to one side of this mark he used to put a rod through the head and cold set it. They weren't far out. From the frame shop you went through a big pair of double doors to the frame stores and it was like a wind tunnel. With the frame shop being warm it drew the cold air in from the stores and that was where we had trouble with frames snapping above the bottom bracket. The lads on the dipper used to stack them on a rack and as soon as anyone went through the doors the cold draught would chill the hot frames and make them brittle. They were coming back from Lee San in Malaysia and it was one of their technicians who came to Barton and found out why it was happening. They hadn't realised that the cold draughts were hardening the metal and it was breaking at the point up to where they had been dipped. My uncle Bill Appleyard used to work in the machine shop making chain sets. The chain rings were put on to a boss on the cranks and then he had a machine with a counter weight and it used to roll them on. My uncle Jack used to assemble bottom brackets in the aerodrome. I worked in the repair shop for a while with a chap who lived across the road from me on Butts Road. An Elswick lady's had come in. It had been made in Newcastle and needed new dress guards. She actually wanted a complete renovation and we stripped it down and the bearings were like jewels. It belonged to a woman who lived in Newcastle."

Sheila Clark has fond memories of the Hopper horses, as her father Harry Plaskitt took care of them, as well as driving one of the rullies (Fig. 10.10). "In the summer they used to keep the horses down in a field near the potteries. In the summer my dad had the horses in the fields and back in the stables in the winter, and I used to go with him to the stables to help feed the horses. It was 7 o'clock every night in rain, wind, or snow, but I went because I got to stay up a bit later! I used to fetch the buckets, three great big sink buckets and while my dad was feeding the horses I would go to the tap, right at the other side of the field, where they put the rullies, and bring about a quarter bucket at a time

*Fig. 10.10  Harry Plaskitt with rulley, taken at the export packing shop off Brigg Road in 1945.*

and fill the next one up, until I'd got them all filled. Dad would be up at quarter to six every morning to feed them, then come home about half past for breakfast before starting work at half past seven. It was better in the summer months because he would put them out at five o'clock and that was it till next morning. I can see him now coming up Pasture Road on his bike with two horses. My mother's father and uncle used to drive rullies too – George Elm was my grandfather and his brother was Herbert and dad took over from George, becoming head horseman for the works. The three horses, Bonny, Nobby and Dapples were eventually sold to a farm near Birmingham; this would be 1959. When I left school I had no say in where I was going to work. I left school on the Friday and was told where to start on the Monday. Just straight in and that was it. I used to get ribbed – 'Oh! Here comes daddy, daddy's coming!' I worked for George Grebby at the Brigg Road packing shop for about 18 months then I went down to Elswicks. I was wrapping bikes that were to go abroad, to Japan and places like that, and then I went in the old road side machine shop. It was so cold, as there was no heating. I complained and said I couldn't work in those conditions. My brother at the time was taking bikes by lorry all over the country, and my mother worked at Hopper's too, carrying bicycle rims on her arms upstairs to the wheel builders shop."

Richard Holland chose a job at Hopper's rather than the Ropery on leaving school in 1955 and worked for Teddy Lyons in the tube shop. He remembers some of the specialised work done by some of the craftsmen: "Walt Kingswood and Edwin Ayres were carrier makers in the tube shop – the frames that held the baskets on carrier cycles. They had it off to a fine art and didn't tell anyone else how they made them, so when they were off ill no carriers got made! They were made in two pieces and welded together. They had tube inserts to align them for welding and the weld was then ground smooth so you got a perfect top rail and you couldn't see the join after painting. The press shop made all sorts like the shoe that holds the brake blocks. They would get the strip and feed it through and punch them out. They made all the washers – plain washers as well – buckets full. May Handsley was another character - she was the storekeeper in the press shop and she knew everyone. She must have been there 50 years when I started and was so attached to the place. The old timers were like that, you could see it in their work patterns – they had been there in the days when the foreman was in a bowler hat. They would take a new piece of work at 10 to five and the young lads would say, 'Chuck it on the floor and leave it till tomorrow'. Then there was Mr Green with his bull terrier – he was night watchman and used to be stationed in the timekeeper's box. If you went to work at six in the morning you would see him going off. As far as I know he worked seven 12 hour nights a week. He did permanent nights – 12 hours regular. They even made their own pump pegs in the machine shop. When they came out of the machine they were just straight, and were brought to the tube shop where a woman would spend all day bending them. On most of the ordinary bikes they were put on with a spot welder, but on better models they would be brazed on. The spot welding was useless and there was many a time when the frames got all the way through the paint shop to the erecting shop and the pump pegs would drop off! They were stripped down and sent back. Nowadays they would be scrapped but not then. When I went to the steelworks at 18, with overtime and Sunday work you could double your earnings compared to Hopper's."

Brian Peeps: "Bottom English was the packing shop for UK sales and was on the corner of Brigg Road and Castedyke (Fig. 10.11). Upstairs was the showroom, then across Castledyke was the saw mill, just past where the entrance is to Castle Court, just along that wall, and the export packing department was on the right hand side. The loading dock was where the first house is. The building across Brigg Road from the office was the stores. There was everything there, inner tubes, spokes, tyres, pedals, rims, everything. It was all bought in stuff from Tom Hobson's stores on the works. The railway and BRS [British Road Services] used to come and pick up the boxes for export. For export orders we would have a box and we would stand all the rims in first, the tyres with thick string round them, and you would stand on the top pressing them down, and compressing them to get them all in. There were

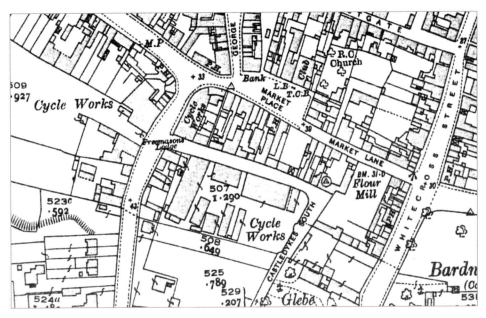

*Fig. 10.11 From a 1932 ordnance survey map Castledyke South sweeps east from the Freemasons' Lodge and then south. The sawmill and export packing shop is to the bottom of the map, below the office building and domestic packing shop on the north side of Castledyke.*

pedals, tubes, chains, saddles, spokes, tyres, seat posts. They all went in one box. A lot of exports were disassembled. The wheels were just rims, spokes, hubs, tapes and nipples in big bundles. But some went assembled, like for Sears Roebuck in the States. Muriel used to wrap the frames, the forks, the chains, the pedals. All they did was turn the handlebars sideways, turn the pedals inwards, tie the saddles on to the frame and that was it. A cardboard carton went over the top, like an envelope, well over 6 ft long, and then they were taped all the way round. We got into trouble one time: they had opened a carton in America with nothing inside it. I got called into the office – I said how can you lift an empty carton on to a lorry and not know? But it had arrived there with no bike in. Later on packing moved to the roadside machine shop, after machining had all moved to the big shop."

Muriel Peeps: "I finished up running that shop by myself. It was just a concrete floor and half of it was empty. It was mainly for export, so they would go to the railway station to be packed into vans, then to the docks. Then for some reason we went back up to Brigg Road. We sent some bikes in big crates to UK dealers from there, three in a crate, it was a skeleton crate – just held together – two bikes one way and one the other and they would go to various wholesalers in this country. Occasionally we got crates back that had been dropped in the docks, and everything was rusty!"

Brian started in about 1952. "At Christmas, when they wanted kiddies' three wheel trikes, we had to go to the Elswick building to erect them. There was no piece work by then, no pushing. They would tell you how many they needed and leave you to it." Brian went into the RAF in 1956 and after National Service worked on the railways, including picking up packages from Elswick-Hopper. "The bikes were more or less the width of the lorry, so I just put a rope round the back, took them down to the station and straight in to vans. Bikes for the passenger trains were just wrapped with brown paper and the bars turned. At the station, at half past five at night, I have seen as many as 200 bikes going into the guard's van. They all had to be labelled to say how much the carriage was. There were hundreds went by rail, especially at Christmas. Hopper's used to send a lot of bikes to India, the Far East, Malaysia; they went all over."

Muriel also remembers the CKD boxes: "There were 25 bikes to a set; you used to get 50 rims in one of those crates, and do you know I still count things. You had to count so many chains, so many this and so many that. One crate contained the rims, saddles, chains, spokes, tyres and tubes, then another crate contained the frames. The tyres, you used to roll them to make them small enough, pedals you had two in a packet, spokes, you wrapped enough for two wheels; they were always in a bundle and I suppose they weighed them, 50 cotter pins. Exports were mostly crated like that, and the Sears Roebuck consignment was not normal."

Brian added that for the partially disassembled cycles they had access to bales of wood wool to pack between them. "The bottom bracket was already in the frame, and the hubs were assembled. The rear hubs were nearly all equipped with back pedal brakes for the USA, and they had different handlebars. I remember some with a slope on the top tube down to the saddle."

Muriel remembers when they closed Castledyke packing shop and she was sent to the aerodrome. "I think they pulled out in about 1959. It was then a sprout factory. They altered it a lot and put gates across the front, but they were still using the loading bay – there was an overhead crane to handle the cases."

Brian recalled evidence of the band: "On the other side of Brigg Road I remember going up to the top of the old building and there were the remains of the old band uniforms. It was dark and light blue, and it looked as if there had been a fire there at some time."

## The Tool Room

Once Fred Hopper had decided that component manufacture could allow him to lower the price of his bicycles he became reliant on the skills of the toolmaker. They were the enablers of the factory, designing, making and setting up the jigs and tools that allowed such a large number of components to be made in-house at a lower cost than a Midlands product – at least until the 1950s.

Ray Pettit: "John Stockdale was under-foreman and took over from Harry Pond when he was away. Harry didn't come into the works until about half past eight or nine o'clock in the morning, so before then John made all the decisions. Harry was a law unto himself; he was a small chap and wore a black flat cap. He lived up Westfield Road, opposite Walt Paul. He was a very strict disciplinarian and made my life hell – I couldn't do anything right. I remember he was late one morning – it was frosty and he had fallen and broken his leg! He came back part time and then retired, and John took over. But once outside work there couldn't have been a nicer chap than Harry Pond. I appreciated his approach to discipline in later years. You called him 'Sir', no first names. John was a bit more relaxed, but I considered him my mentor. In the latter part of my apprenticeship I felt I hadn't done anything and I was always into any practical jokes that were going on. We were coming across the yard one day and he said to me, 'Don't you think it's time you took hold of yourself?' I asked what he meant. He said, 'Well, another 18 months and you are out of your apprenticeship. You are on your own then – mature a bit. Look at a person, take an image, and say, I want to be like that person. He suggested Mr Pond, but I took John as my mentor. Looking back I feel he did me the world of good with that talk, bringing me into line, from being a raw lad into a mature adult. While I was an apprentice in the tool room we built a cycle with a rickshaw at the back in anticipation of the Far Eastern market after the war. There was an interesting story on wheel building. There were nine ball bearings went into a hub and a girl called Queenie Dixon did all that and she could put her fingers into the container and pull nine balls out and put them in the hub every time. She went off sick and no one else could match her performance – they would pull out too many or too few. John Stockdale said we would build a little machine to do it, and he built a hopper with a tube just long enough to hold nine balls. But what it needed was an agitator in the hopper because they all got stuck and it never worked. By the time we had perfected it she was back again and she wouldn't use it!"

Fig. 10.12  The tool room in 1949.

Arthur Such added life to the tool room photograph (Fig 10.12): "It's 1949, and all the windows are blocked up. That's Johnny Stockdale and Walt Paul is there but you can't see him, he was a turner; there were three lathes along there. There was Alan Headley, Ray Pettit and Walt Paul, they were the turners. The small lathe nearest the office is where you got started, you all had a go on it. Up there is Barry Woods and there was an old lathe that Barry used to do some big jobs on. Rear, second from left, that's me on the milling machine. Now that's John Parsons on the universal grinder. John Carter on the shaper – we worked all the machines of course. That's Cliff Hollingsworth on the surface grinder – he was from Ferriby. That's Harold Cox in the smock. Between the drilling machine and the grinding machine there was a little cutter/grinder, which had 6" diameter blades like a thin milling cutter, used for cutting tubes. That's Clarry Brown on the drilling machine. Now this young fellow with the turned-down wellies is Keith Clark, same age as me and we went to school together. Now this lad is Bob White, he was a Scotch lad. Then Peter Warcup, and that is a band saw, and it was also a rotary filing machine. There was also a gadget for silver soldering parts together. The machine Keith is using is also a filing machine. The machine tools were all bought in, and were enough to do all the tool making you needed. That's Trevor Stow – he lives up Westfield Road. Missing is Dennis Moody, Harold Altoft, and Sid Johnson, who went to the drawing office. Steve Atkin was the wages man, and he came into the tool room office, gave the wages to John Stockdale, and then at a certain time on a Friday he had a piece of tube and a bar on the shelf where he used to hand out special tools, and he used to rattle it when it was time to collect your wages. All the drawings and designs for tools were done in the drawing office, and we made them in the tool room. We used to repair and resharpen all the tools as well, and fitted the tools in most cases and set them up. We had to try them out and check dimensions. Tools were made from stock steel and we had our own hardening equipment, for case hardening, quarter hardening, and oil hardening. There were about nine double benches. John's store had all the measuring equipment. Turning tools were made out of silver steel. I enjoyed my apprenticeship, I really did. On my first day I was shaking like a leaf, but John was a super foreman. We used to have clowning about sessions and he knew what we got up to but he took it all in his stride. Any problems, you just had to go to him and ask, and he would put it right. You went round everything, used all the machines, reading drawings, getting your measurements right. The other toolmakers would help you as well. Everybody helped everyone else and it is amazing how quickly I took to it."

Keith Clark was more involved in factory maintenance than tool making: "It meant I got round all parts of the factory and I enjoyed that. When I started the only building not in regular use was the old road side machine shop. It was still full of the old machine tools, but there was only one machine that Jack Dimoline used to work on. It was the fork crown machine, like a vertical milling machine and it used to mill round the two ends of the castings that would be inserted in the fork blades before they were brazed. They had to be machined up with a proper template to go over them to make sure they were the right size. Then the fork stem would be put on before the fork blades were bent and they would be brazed in turn and finally they were bent to the final shape. Hopper's made their own acetylene, of course, and from time to time you had to change the water pump. It was just a small cylinder that automatically fed water into the carbide. The spent carbide went into a tank outside and people used to take it for whitening. When I got a house in Finkle Lane I went back to Hopper's one afternoon and got a bucketful. It was a thick creamy paste and you got a beautiful white finish with it. You just put it straight on the walls and there was no smell."

## Long Service

A job for life was still a common idea, even in the mid 1950s, and many Hopper employees were commemorated with 50 or more years of loyal service, having joined as a 12 year old and worked into their 70s.

In April 1955 the *Lincolnshire Times* recorded the diamond wedding of Mr and Mrs Francis George Robinson. Frank was Barton born though his wife had moved there from London as a girl. He progressed to be foreman of the frame building department and retired in 1947, having completed 50 years of service. This places his initial employment at 1897, a full seven years into production, so it is surprising that he remembered the Brigg Road premises as a small concern with just eight employees. The same paper recorded the death of Fred Chappell in April 1958. He was 68 and had been at Hopper's for 55 years, finally as foreman of the wheel shop. Harry Pond died in 1961 having enjoyed just 13 years of retirement, retiring in 1948 as tool room foreman. The *Lincolnshire Times* recorded the respect and admiration of many tool makers who were trained by him.

Bill Clipson seems to have been an archetypal Barton character and in October 1960 the *Lincolnshire Times* recorded that "Old Bill Clipson, looking very much like the original Old Bill of World War I cartoons, was the oldest old boy at the 5th Lincolns annual reunion at Louth on Saturday night. Bill, who lives at 23 Beck Hill, Barton on Humber, started his soldiering in 1899, when he joined the old Barton on Humber Volunteers. A year later he was on his way to the Boer War, in the company of Mr George Peck, of Brigg. 'There were 15 of us altogether went from Barton,' he said, 'but I'm the only one left.' As a member of the Territorial Army, Bill Clipson was among the first to land in France in 1914 and was at Ypres, the Somme, the Hohernzollern Redoubt and Hell's Kitchen. 'The others went off to Egypt after the Redoubt battle,' he said, 'but I was in hospital and had to stay behind.' Then he said, with a note of disgust, 'I finished up in Skegness.' Bill tried to join up in 1939 when a third war came his way, but they told him he was too old. So he resigned himself to the fact that he had become 'Old Bill' and went on stoking boilers at the Elswick-Hopper factory. He was still stoking boilers when he was 80 and they told him he would have to retire because he was getting too old. 'I suppose I was getting old,' he agreed. 'I'll be 83 in March. Call me Old Bill if you like, but I'll still be at next year's dinner.' Old soldiers never die…"

In January 1962 the death was recorded of Teddy Lyons at the age of 75. He was a native of Wolverhampton and foreman welder at Marsh Lane. Unfortunately his tenure is not recorded, but he was probably poached from one of the several Wolverhampton firms in the years before the First World War. April of the same year saw the death of George Franklin, who had been works director of Elswick-Hopper for many years. He died suddenly at his home in Butts Road at the age of 69, having completed

56 years service with the company just a week previously – he had begun as an office boy in 1905, so would have started work at 12.

An edition of the *Lincolnshire Times* from August 1962 recorded that "Mr Walter Jennings left school at the age of 14, having joined the Elswick-Hopper cycle factory at Barton on Humber as a machinist. That was 57 years ago. At 72 years of age he is still working there as time keeper and is proud of the reputation of being the longest serving member of the firm. Mr Jennings, who lives with his wife Sarah at 150 Butts Road, stopped work for a few minutes on Wednesday and told a reporter how things had changed since he first joined the firm. 'Those were the days when we were very industrious. There were over 600 people working here around that time. But that figure has gone down a lot since.' He started at the Brigg Road factory but was transferred to the Marsh Lane factory when it was built in 1906 (sic). 'I dare say I have done everything but decorate the bicycles,' he continued. In 1943, Mr Jennings started work as a time-keeper. 'But before that we had some trouble over wages. That was in 1938, when my department came out on strike because our wages were being cut. Although there were only 14 people who came out on strike, which lasted a week, I think everybody else in the factory was in sympathy with us.' The strike was the start of the factory's trade union. Mr Jennings said they were advised to get a trade union organised. 'We called a meeting and I was appointed leader,' he said. He is still the branch leader of the National Union of General and Municipal Workers. 'You can judge how keen workers were on the union idea, because over 400 turned up for the first meeting.' Once in the union, employees received advantages of overtime rates etc. 'It was common before the union was formed for me to work for about 24 hours non-stop, especially when we had more orders than we could cope with.'

Bob Blackburn remembers his maternal grandfather, Jack Curtis, who looked after the Marsh Lane engine house. "I think he started with old Mr Hopper when he first set up. It used to be said in Barton that every other workman at Hopper's was a foreman. I know when I went there as a lad, if you needed any oil for anything you went along to the engine house (Fig. 10.13). The engine room was spotless. They were Ruston engines by the time I got there. Jack died in 1947/48. I am pretty sure he was there 51 or 52 years. He lived on Marsh Lane opposite the works and sometimes when we went round for tea, and the engines were running, he was on call. Grandad would be sitting at the table and I can remember him saying, 'I shall have to go, there's something wrong with number so and so!'"

*Fig. 10.13 An early photograph of the Marsh Lane power station with Crossley gas engines.*

## Mishaps

Perhaps surprisingly, there were few injuries in the cycle works. Walter Horne remembers one that could have been serious, "I once saw a girl get all her clothes ripped off on one of the machines. Poor lass, she was fast up. She got caught in the belt, but she was all right. I remember when George Bell lost a finger. He was setting up a tool and for some reason George had caught his foot on a pedal and the press came down and he had his finger over the die. The chap along side him bent down under the press, came up and said 'Here, George, here's your finger'. When I came out of the Army, I had some souvenirs, including a tail fin from some incendiaries that they dropped on us in Birmingham, during the Birmingham blitz. I took it into the buffing shop and asked Jack Richmond if he would buff it up and get it chromed. He said he would, and he put on the buffing wheel and it burst into flames! It was magnesium."

Ray Pettit well remembers the lay shafts in the big machine shop. "When a belt came off you just got a ladder and got the belt and slipped it on to the pulley while it was still running. There wasn't much consideration for safety. During the war I was stood by a girl, Joan Skinner, at a drilling machine and she was doing a job and I was making sure it was alright, when she leaned forward and the chuck of the drilling machine caught her hair and pulled her in. I had to stop the machine and hold her while they came and cut her hair, but it pulled a big tuft out. She was only about 17 or 18."

Eddie Gaunt remembers a near miss in the tool room: "We had a small bench with two vee blocks on it and a big screw press on the top and we used to make reamers for reaming out the bottom brackets and we had a grinding machine up there. Sometimes when you heat treated them they would distort a bit so we would put them on the blocks, heat them up a bit and flatten them out and one day someone was doing it and it smashed and a big 2" reamer flew right across the shop, missed where I was and went straight by Mick Mills and chopped half a brick out the wall. After that they thought we had better put a guard on it.

Nurse King was brilliant – she wouldn't let you in if you were bleeding – you had to stop outside. She was a smashing old lass. In the main machine shop there was an area where there was just one machine and this guy used to mill fork crowns so that the forks would fit, and he had a mandrel in the middle and had to follow a former hour after hour. You used to get cuttings off this and there was a woman in the machine shop who would get bits out of your eyes – this was before the days of safety glasses. I remember one day this man had a cutting under his thumb nail. He was ever such a quiet bloke and she said to him, 'I can't get that out, it's a hospital job', and he said, 'Get it out.' He didn't make a sound while she pulled it out. In the rough polishing shop I remember one day I had just walked in and a guy had just started up his wheel and had taken his finger end off at the first knuckle. He just picked it up and put it on his machine and went off to get it looked at. But there weren't that many accidents, given the hazards.

One of the things we had to do usually fell to the last two apprentices. On a Friday afternoon the final two hours were for cleaning up all the machines with solvent. To dispose of the used solvent we had to fill buckets of it out of a big barrel and in the courtyard area was an outside furnace with a big chimney and what we had to do was run like hell at this open furnace and as we were running past it the solvent would go in and there would be a jet of flames shoot out behind you. It was great! But one day there was just me and Roger Green, and there was no fire on. We were totally disappointed, but there were some sparks so Roger said he would get it going, and he got a little can and threw some solvent on, and there was some smoke, but it just sizzled and steamed. I was standing behind him and he said, 'I will get it going,' and he had his head stuck in this furnace. All of a sudden, whoof! There was a ball of flame came out and I just turned round and flame shot up my leg and burned all the hairs off. Roger was just coming out and he was bright red and his hair was all frizzled. But we got away with it!"

## Larks

Practical jokes appear to have been mainly the preserve of the tool makers. Ray Pettit: "Harold Altoft had been off sick and they decided to put him in the tool room. He was a great one for tales of what he had done, and of course we used to take the mickey. In the heat treatment oven there was a pre-warming chamber in the top and when we knew he was going to put a tool in there for hardening we used to fill the top oven with gas and turn it off just before he got there, and as soon as he put a light to it, it used to blow the top off. John used to create hell with Harold as to why he always blew the top off, as nobody else did! We were little devils, thinking back. When I was in the old tool room there were outside stairs that went up into the repair shop. With Eileen being in the assembly stores, the repair shop used to send out spare parts to the dealers. Eileen used to have a little low loader truck and had to carry the parts up the stairs. She used to bend over to pick them up and we had catapults didn't we? I would look out the window and ask her name, so I got to know her and took her out. Prior to that Harry Plaskitt used to have the horse and dray, and he used to pick up the parts from the repair shop for dispatch. Harry went upstairs for the big container, carried it down to the dray, and as he got there we hit the back of the horse with a ball bearing. It shot off and left Harry standing. There are many tales about that place. The tool room boys were the little devils. Having finished up my career in various management roles I think the grounding I got at Elswick-Hopper stood me in good stead. Everybody knew everybody else in Barton and as youngsters we couldn't get into trouble because, if we caused mischief, everyone knew who we were and would report us back to our parents. And we respected our parents – my mother was the disciplinarian. She told me after my dad died that he had a temper and was always afraid of losing it."

Herbert Hedley remembers Dash Ashton, "He used to work in the road side machine shop, and when I was an apprentice I saw his false teeth on the end of his lathe, and said, 'What's up with them Dash?' He said, 'I'm too busy, I haven't got me day in.' His lunch was at his side. 'I've put that there for 'em to get on with it 'cos I ain't got time to eat it!' I was only about 15 then."

Eddie Gaunt: "There were about eight apprentices when I started and one of the things they did with the last apprentice in was he had to sing carols at Christmas in front of all the women from the tube shop. You imagine, straight out of school. It was to knock any pretence out of you. But Pete Warcup had this thing; from September on it was choir practice. He had a bit of $^3/_8$" steel rod with a steel ball on the end and he made you stand on a bench and if you stopped singing you got knobbled on the knee. So you are totally embarrassed and come Christmas you didn't know what to do with yourself. And they brought all the women in and you stood up and as soon as you started they all started singing with you, and it was great. He was good was Pete. Dave Clark was also a tool room fitter but he went round the firm doing different jobs. We used to call him the Baron. They used to do things like putting marking blue behind the vice handle so that when you grabbed it, it came off on your hand. He came in this day and he checked his vice handle and spotted it and said, ah, got you! Then he went to his drawer and the handle was covered in grease. The worst thing they did was tie him to a couple of the presses in the press shop and drop a stink bomb, but he could take it, poor lad."

## War Work 1939-1945

At the outbreak of war the government began to direct labour to factories involved in war work. This involved taking workers from less critical industries, including manufacturers of bicycles. Many cycle workers found themselves living away from home, with few opportunities to see their families. Audrey Peck had already decided to volunteer and went to the Hawker Siddeley works in Lincoln. "I wasn't transferred by Hopper's – I just walked out. Well my husband had gone to the Labour Exchange and they came to Hopper's Cycle Works to see who was to be sent to various factories in Lincoln, or Leicester or anywhere. But they didn't pick my husband, I'll never know why. He never settled so he volunteered and went with the rest of them to Lincoln. So I left and we were all living in the same digs and we had only been married for six weeks. I went to work where my husband was, again in inspection and stores, which I had done at Hopper's. Anyway, I couldn't get on with the people, so I didn't stay there long and went to Smith Clayton Forge. Best job I ever had in my life. I paid more income tax there than I have ever paid anywhere. They had never employed women before the war, but they had no choice once war broke out, so that's how I got that job. It was man's work – forge work. Then I got pregnant with our first son so that was the end of that and we came back to Barton."

Ray Pettit: "A lot of men were directed away during the war, but I was too young so it left about three tradesmen and 12 apprentices. Godfrey Poole was the apprentice after me and our paths crossed all our working lives. During the war he lived in North Killingholme, cycling to and from work every day. When the daylight raids started his parents were worried about him and he came to our house and asked my mother if she could recommend any lodgings. She couldn't, as there was a lot of building work going on with aerodromes being built and a lot of labour had come in. So I persuaded my mother that we could make room for him and he stayed with us until 1947! So we more or less grew up as brothers. The old tool room was underneath the tin shop and repair shop. When Jack Walker came in 1943 they had a big reorganisation – George Franklin was the works manager, Henry Cole was in charge of wages. I heard on the grapevine that they wanted to borrow a lot of money to reorganise and the banks insisted they had a new management structure. Walker came from the Birmingham or Nottingham area, a very nice chap. The original engine house was converted to a tool room and I was the first one in because the lathe I was going to work on, a Dean, Smith and Grace 13Z, was the first machine in, and I worked there on my own for nearly a month. George Franklin was demoted at that time and reported to Walker. My wife Eileen worked for Smith Nephew in Hull until the building was bombed and they were going to move her to Manchester. Being only 16 her mother didn't want her to go and so she went to live with her cousin Edith in Barton – her husband was away, and she got a job working for Fred Green on the balcony in the stores. They had to go on the roof of the aerodrome fire watching and there were no handrails, just a ladder up and a cat walk. Ben Sharpe was on war work and we did a lot of machining work on Bren gun carrier brackets, where they fixed to the side of a truck. They also made parts for Brough aircraft works for the Swordfish and for the Blackburn Skua. The trouble was we couldn't work to the accuracy that the aircraft people needed. The equipment was late 20s early 30s machinery, probably second-hand when they bought it in the first place. We got four lathes during the war and they were installed in a corner of the Elswick shops turning out tracer bullets. They were making a lot of bicycles for the forces, especially for the air force to get around the airfields. I was going out with a girl from New Holland at the time and I used to take her home after the evening dances. Coming back I would often be met by a cycle with a front lamp on, then about 12 bikes with no lights and the last one with a rear lamp on. You had to have masked lights on during the war, and they were useless."

Herbert Hedley moved to Lincoln during the war. "I was sent to Penney and Porter, along the riverside there and we made aluminium gun carriers for the back of tanks and lorries. We used to make the base and mount the guns on them. It was only a small firm, and Fred Lovell went with me. Some went to Coventry. Harry and George Peck went to Lincoln to Hawker Siddeley, but they didn't take on extra people to replace us." Gladys worked as a machinist during the war and remembers making bullets in the roadside machine shop. "My sister Annie was on bullets, there were four of us in there, and we had to drill out these little brass cases. The girls all had short trims in those days and used to wear berets that always had to be just above their eyes." When Herbert went to Grimsby with Ralph Collingwood to volunteer the tool room lads told Gladys, but she didn't believe them, until Tup (Cyril) Franklin told her. When he came home Herbert told Gladys they had been to see 'Gone with the Wind', so she asked if he had enjoyed it. When they got to the Royal Navy recruiting office – Herbert wanted to be an engineer artificer, he was told to "bugger off home and get on with your bloody work. We'll call you buggers when we want you."

Joan Horne: "I was in the erecting shop building khaki bikes for the forces. Occasionally we did a child's tricycle, but not often – it was war time and they weren't buying them. I had been in the brake department and had been a run-around-girl in the frame department. I had been all over the place, but the main job was erecting bikes. A fellow used to come to check the khaki bikes, and he had been in a cycle factory where he had never seen bikes erected by one person."

Bertha Such was sent to Peterborough to the old BTH electrical company factory. "We were making parts for Wellington bombers. First I went to Leicester training centre and they gave you a test and then moved you out. I was there from 1942 to 1945, and I could have stayed on but I wanted to come home. I got home once a month during those years, the train stopping at every station, and then we had to wait for a train at Grimsby. We got home about half past eight. Then on a Sunday it took from about 4 o'clock to about 9 to get back."

Charles Watkinson told a story about the contribution made by Hopper's workers to the Avro factory: "It is an example of the quality of the individual they turned out. One of Avro's top executives at a dinner in Lincoln during the war made the comment that when he was told he was getting a lot of cycle workers from Barton on Humber, he thought, 'My God, what now?' But he went on to say that he wished they had had them sooner and that they had many, many more. Just based on the quality of work they turned out."

## Management & Unions

Don Tyson has an interesting story going back to the early days of the Elswick takeover. His mother in law was Annie Gertrude West, who was born in 1887 and went to work for Fred Hopper. She was an accomplished cycle racer and decided to buy a Rudge-Whitworth, to the great displeasure of her boss. Fred sacked her and then offered to take her back on the basis that he would make a special racing frame for her. Don still has this Elswick, finished in green, of course, and bearing the frame number 1097.

Audrey Peck recalled that some of the foremen lived in company houses, including a block of four detached houses on Brigg Road built at the junction of Horkstow Road on the Park Farm property bought by Fred Hopper Snr, or rather, his wife, in 1917. Jack Furniss, originally from Birmingham, lived there for a while and also Albert Wall, the long serving paint shop foreman, who had also occupied New Hall in the early part of the century.

Jack Austin observed that: "When I first started Fred Hopper [Junr] was in charge, and he had the works at his heart. I was in the Navy during the war and they had inspection rounds. Fred Hopper used to do that too. After he backed out Mr Stow took over and he was just as interested in the business and went abroad to get orders. I was a bearer at his funeral. They said his coffin was lead lined. When he died there was no-one left with the heart. It took away the guiding hand and the company was bought by outsiders, who just wanted the money."

Marjorie Kirkby recalls good times with the Hopper family: "There were wonderful parties at Mount House, which is where Freddie lived, and then he moved to a new bungalow in the gardens. Freddie wasn't the sort of chap who made waves – he wasn't flamboyant at all – he was just a very gentle, very dapper, very caring little man. He seemed to be interested in farming and he had land on the Wold Road at the top. The cycle works did not appear to be his cup of tea – he never talked about it, never. He gave my father in law, Fred Kirkby, a Hopper bicycle with an engine on it, an autocycle. They put him on it, and he went round and round the stack yard shouting, 'Whoa,' because he was a horse man. He couldn't stop it and there was my husband and Freddie and I think Laurie Kirkby too, running after him trying to stop this thing. I remember killing myself with laughter, because he ran it into the haystack and it stopped. This was in the 1940s, just at the end of the war, at Greenfield Farm, Hibaldstow. He would have been nearly 80 at the time, but after that, when he got the hang of it, he would go to Brigg on it, though it had to be mended after it finished up in the haystack.

Bob Griffiths described how one foreman discovered how to give one of his workers a better deal: "When they were taken over by Maurice Moss there were all these fancy accountants from London and they sent them to my pub [the Volunteer Arms] for a half of beer and a sandwich. There was one accountant – Vickery, he was brilliant but he was very eccentric. He came into the pub one evening and said, 'We have just solved a mystery. In looking up the records, let's say that 10,000 bicycles had gone out the door complete. But the accounts recorded 20,000 chain wheels being polished. So where was this store with 10,000 chain wheels? We made enquiries and then searched, because there was stuff in the roof and all over the place.' Eventually someone came along with a story. Frank Cooper was a polisher on chain wheels, but it was a very dangerous job and you had to go very gently with it. So when the piece work rate was organised they found they couldn't make a living. They went to the foreman – it would be Harry Osgerby – said, 'Harry, we can't make a living at this, can you get it upgraded a bit?' He said, 'It's no good going to the management, I'll tell you what, for every gross of chain wheels you polish, book two gross. This was the odd number."

Betty Clarke (née Barraclough, from the Brigg Road 'Southgarth' family) met her future husband after he moved to Barton as company secretary in 1939. George Clarke had been brought up in London, where his father was a paper bag manufacturer. His son Andrew recalls: "Once a year they went on a directors' cycling trip – to Meriden[8]. They were very entertaining – some of the directors would get their chauffeurs to pick them up half way round, and then drop them off again for lunch (Fig. 10.14). He was very bitter about his treatment at Elswick-Hopper. My understanding is that someone came in, bought a majority shareholding in the company, thought they could dispense with his services and do the job better themselves. He felt he was doing a damn good job. The senior partner of Fawley Judge and Easton said to me that the accounts were 'tickety-boo'. So I think he felt he had been given a rough deal, but he never moaned about it. I think it affected him and it knocked his confidence, definitely."

Harry Haddock also became a shop steward: "Well they originally asked my dad, so I took it over, and I knew every job with having been there for so long. The foreman said to me one day when I was too many frames in front, 'Why don't you go help so and so?' I said I would, Mr Pownell, but I'll lose money as I would be on day work. He came back one day and said, 'I have been to see Mr Cole and

*Fig. 10.14 George Clarke (rhs) at the annual May Meriden gathering.*

247

he said they will make your wages up.' That was fair enough, and so I got to know every job and I could do every job. The main union complaints were from women complaining about their quota. I would ask how many they could do and they would always tell me a lie and said they couldn't do as many as they could. They would say, 'It's no good talking to my foreman.' I could always work the problems through and sort them out. One of the old hands, after a frame had been debrassed, his job was to ream out the head and seat tubes so that the parts would fit. One time they wanted him to do a different job and they said, 'We'll give you 6d a dozen, Corney.' He said, 'That's no good', so they called him in again and said they'd give him ½d each. 'I'll accept that,' he said. There was no pension scheme in the 1930s, you worked till you dropped."

Jack Dimoline recalls the days when Arthur Stow went down to board meetings in London using the chauffeur-driven company car. "The chauffeur was in uniform with 'Elswick Hopper' across his peaked cap. The garage was along Brigg Road where Malcolm Bennett sells cars. Then in 1958 Maurice Moss came along with two chaps called Easdale and Turner. They gave us a sherry party and everyone got drunk. Mr Moss was a nice chap to talk to. He pumped a lot of money in and we made a lot of money, us lads on the assembly line. But eventually they started closing it down; the polishing shop went, the plating went, eventually, the whole lot went. The next thing we knew was that we were going to be made redundant and we got a letter. Then we got to hear that Coventry-Eagle was coming, so we cleared all our benches and we took all our stuff to a big shed and cleared everything out of the Elswick building. Then Coventry-Eagle got us all together to say what was going to happen, and we had to fetch it all back. They must have bought all the gear from Hopper's. Mr Mayo was the boss, he was the top man and ran the Coventry-Eagle side, while Mr Clements ran the Falcon side – the racing side. When they came they made out they knew a bit about bikes, but of course the people of Barton knew a bit as well! They got your back up a lot because of the attitude they adopted. He had a rum attitude did Mr Clements, but his ideas did leave us standing in some areas."

Gordon Linley recalled a lot of antipathy to management that came in from the outside, "That is why Jack Walker left and he was good. Morton took over after Walker and he didn't stay long either, and eventually they brought in McKenna to run things. I remember the Scoo-ped, or Stu-ped as it was known locally. It was Maurice Moss's idea. He had been brought up in the fabric trade, and had a funny idea about names. He wanted to name one of them the Escorto, anything Italian; the clothing trade was going through an Italian phase at the time. But that was the biggest mistake ever, the Scoo-ped. I never sold one and everyone you showed it to at the Cycle Show laughed at you. I mean you were a laughing stock with that thing. Now if it had had an engine in, it would have been OK. I am not sure if they made any other than for the Show. The frame was made in Barton but the fairings were bought in. We had an open day at the Savoy Hotel for it, and I remember Peter West and Barbara Cartland's daughter – Lady Lewisham. She was a cracking bit of stuff then. We argued about the two ranges for years but eventually managed to get them to amalgamate. You would have a Hopper dealer in a town and another shop might want to stock them as well – but you could only offer them Elswick. Hull, of course, every dealer was a Hopper. When you got up to Newcastle they were all Elswick, because that's where they started. When they did settle on Elswick-Hopper it cut down stocking. You would get a situation before when someone wanted 20 Elswick models and they would only have Hopper in stock, just barmy."

## Endnotes

1     1899 or 1900 is corroborated by the *Bicycling News and Motor Review* article from 1902, quoted in Chapter 2.

2     It would appear that John Furniss was about three years older than Hopper. It is doubtful if either could have afforded a new high bicycle in 1880, when Hopper is believed to have formed Barton and District Cycling Club (see Chapter 1), but no doubt the young journeyman would have been adept at repairing an old one.

3     *Hull Times* 7 March 1906.

4     *Hull Times* 9 February 1907.

5     *The Star* 8 February 1913. The shooting club was formed in 1913 and Captain H G Wilson presented members with a service rifle.

6     A debrassing solution is prepared by combining 285 parts concentrated ammonium hydroxide (28% ammonia ), 40 parts ammonium persulfate and 1,275 parts water for a total of 1,600 parts. The rate of brass removal is dependent on ammonium persulfate concentration. At the described concentration, residence times of ten seconds are sufficient to completely remove the excess brass. As the debrassing operation proceeds it is necessary from time to time to replenish the ammonium persulfate which has been depleted by reaction with the brass.

7     I do actually have a Hopper frame that contains a 'ringer', just a piece of loose brazing material inside the top tube that makes a noise when you shake the frame. Not something that you would notice in normal use, but proof of Rick's claim.

8     A National Cyclists' Memorial was erected at Meriden after the Great War, on the basis that it was accessible from all parts of the country. An annual rally and commemorative service is held there every year.

# APPENDIX 1

## HOPPER AND ELSWICK BICYCLES

There is not space in this book for a detailed listing and description of the many different models produced by Elswick-Hopper over a period of almost 100 years, so this appendix gives a general overview with details of some of the more distinctive machines. The first 13 years of manufacture were a time of great turmoil, as we have seen in chapter 1, with Hopper selling his company, starting again and then buying it back after the markets collapsed at the end of the 'bicycle boom'. Apart from the Ajax, of which we have both newspaper (Fig. 1.6), and, most probably, photographic evidence (Fig. 1.10), there is a dearth of printed material on Hopper's early bicycles. Indeed the earliest catalogue known to me is for the 1903 range. It is dated 21 January and the introduction records that 1902 set a new business record with the production of 13,000 frames and machines.

> 1903 Range
> We have again during the past season been compelled through the increase of our business to enlarge our Premises, so that at the present moment we have a floor area of about 2,500,000 square feet. We have also introduced labour-saving machinery of the very latest type, and we are thus able to employ every known method to cheapen the production of the Goods for which we are celebrated.

Hopper even records his 'Mission Statement', which is as meaningful now as it would have been then:

> Our aim has always been to give our customers satisfaction by –
> 1. Bestowing careful attention to even the smallest order.
> 2. Supplying Goods at absolutely Bottom Prices.
> 3. Supplying Goods of first-class Material.
> 4. Conducting our business on proper business lines.

Four ranges of frames were offered, the cheapest being for a 'second grade' machine, built from BSA fittings. Sun cycle fittings were next in price followed by Hopper's own Torpedo, which was first introduced in 1902 and for 1903 had been improved by the addition of a seat stay bridge, thus 'strengthening what has hitherto been a weak part in cycle frames'. Complete with seat post, bottom bracket and chain wheel, head set and handlebars the Torpedo sold to the trade for £2 5s 0d for up to 25 frames. Next came the top of the range frames available with BSA or Eadie fittings, selling for £4 2s 6d, complete with hubs and pedals. Complete bicycles were available in the same four frame sets, as gents' road racers, gents' roadsters and ladies' machines. The latter were fitted with full gear cases, leather for the two cheaper models and steel for the more expensive ones, and silk cord dress guards. The two lower priced ranges were offered with the wholesaler's or retailer's transfers or Hopper's own 'Advance' transfer. The Torpedo range was similarly available with customer's own or a 'Torpedo' transfer. There is no mention of transfers for the two top-end machines. By way of comparison with frame set prices a gent's Torpedo racer cost £5 12s 6d, complete with tyres, and an Eadie racer £6 17s 6d. Fitting sets were advertised for smaller builders to buy and a full range of accessories and tools was also offered, including motor jacks, the only item relating to the new mode of transport. 1903 was also the year that the speed limit for motor transport was raised from 14mph to 20mph.

## Costings

A reliable estimate of production costs has always been essential for manufacturers to price their products at a level that will yield a reasonable profit. Hopper's grip on this aspect of his business is illustrated by a 1910 breakdown for the 'Little Giant' juvenile tricycle. At this time most employee labour would have been paid on piece work, thereby giving the company a simple basis for calculating labour costs.

Quantities and costs are for a single tricycle.

| Quantity | Description | £ | s | p |
|---|---|---|---|---|
| 5 | Malleable castings | | 1 | 10½ |
| 2' 0" | 7/8" x 16g tube in seat and back tubes | | | 3 |
| 2' 6" | 7/8" x 16g tube in curved tube | | | 3¾ |
| 2' 6" | 5/8" x 16g tube in curved tube | | | 3 |
| 1 | Seat pillar lap and top piece | | | 2¾ |
| 1 | Fork stem | | | 1 |
| 1 | Fork crown | | | 2 |
| 1 pair | Fork blades | | | 3 |
| 1 | Crown ball race | | | ¾ |
| 1 | Head bolt | | | ½ |
| 1 | Lamp bracket | | | ¾ |
| 1 | Head nut | | | 1¼ |
| 1 | Handlebar complete, plated | | | 11 |
| 1 pair | Handgrips | | | 2 |
| 1 | 1" x 3/8" hex head set screw for bracket | | | ¼ |
| 2 | Bracket cups | | | 3 |
| 2 | Bracket cotter screws | | | 1½ |
| 2 | Crank cotters | | | 1 |
| 1 | Bracket axle | | | 2¾ |
| 1 | 20t x 1/8" x 1 3/8" hole cog | | | 5½ |
| 1 | 18t x 1/8" x 3/4" hole with boss | | | 6½ |
| 1 | Back axle 2 ft long x ¾" dia | | | 4 |
| 5 | Chain wheel screws | | | ½ |
| 2 | Rear hubs and caps | | 1 | ½ |
| 1 | Juvenile front hub | | | 9 |
| | Spokes, nipples and washers | | | 5¼ |
| 3 | Rims 2/20" x 1/18" | | 1 | 9½ |
| | Tyring and wire | | 3 | ¾ |
| 22 | ¼" balls | | | 1¼ |
| 40 | 1/8" balls | | | 1 |
| 1 | Seat bolt | | | ½ |
| 1 | ¼" bevel washer | | | ¼ |
| 1 | ½" x ¼" hex head screw | | | ¼ |
| 1 | Saddle | | 1 | 6 |
| | Machining castings | | | 3¾ |
| | Building and filing frame and fork | | 2 | 8½ |
| | Rough polishing frame | | | 3 |
| | Rough polishing fork | | | ½ |
| | Enamelling frame and fork | | | 6 |
| | Polishing for plating: | | | 6¼ |
| | Cutting fork | | | ¼ |
| | Machining cranks | | | 3¼ |
| | Tapping & fitting sprocket and gear | | | ¾ |
| | Erecting | | 1 | 6 |
| | Sand blasting | | | 1 |
| | Cleaning | | | 1¼ |
| | Turning stem | | | ¾ |
| | Seat pillar, making, brazing, grinding & filing | | | 1 |
| | Buffing plated parts as above | | | 1½ |
| | Enamelling rims | | | 3 |
| | Building wheels | | | 5½ |
| | Lining frame & fork | | | 5 |
| | Brazing back sprocket on boss | | | 1 |
| 1 pair | Pedals | | 1 | 4½ |
| | £ | 1 | 4 | 11¼ |
| | | | | |
| | Summary | | | |
| | Material | | 17 | 1 |
| | Labour | | 7 | 10¼ |
| | Dead charges on material @ 33⅓% | | 5 | 8½ |
| | ,,            ,,            labour            ,, | | 2 | 7½ |
| | Total production cost | 1 | 13 | 3¼ |

The 1910 trade catalogue lists the 'Little Giant' at £2 2s, yielding a profit on each tricycle of 8s 8¾d, a healthy 26% of cost. The setting of both material and labour overheads at 33⅓% appears a little arbitrary, but was presumably based on the overall running costs of the factory and offices.

## The Bicycles

I have selected just ten bicycles to illustrate almost 100 years of production, based on either unusual design, popularity or utility. At the time of writing the earliest known surviving Hopper bicycle is a Hull and Barton Cycle Manufacturing Company 'Manchester' racing model that would have been made at

*Fig. 11.1 The oldest known Hopper bicycle, a Manchester track machine, that can be seen at times on display at Barton's Baysgarth House Museum.*

*Fig. 11.2 The 'new' double top tube of 1910.*

*Fig. 11.3 French riders Paul Masson and Léon Flameng at the 1896 Olympics. Flameng's double top tube cycle bears a striking resemblance to the Manchester, apart from the chainwheel size.*

252

the Butts Road factory in 1897 or 1898. There may be earlier surviving examples but as F Hopper & Co mainly supplied to the trade during the early years, it will be a matter of luck whether any of these own brand bicycles are identified as Barton machines.

### Manchester 'Pacer'

As explained in Chapter 1 'Manchester' was the name used by Hopper for his bicycles when he set up his new company next to the MS&L railway station. The racing machine shown in Fig. 11.1 had remained in North Lincolnshire until the 1970s when it was bought at auction by a Grimsby enthusiast and subsequently swapped for a Dursley Pedersen. It migrated south and was eventually bought by the author in 2009 for museum display and the occasional rally. It is a very well made frame with a double top tube and is surprisingly light. The main drawback is the 98" fixed gear, intended for high speed track racing – possibly pacing, as it was dubbed 'The Manchester Pacer' by Boston Veteran Cycle Club founder Eric Page. Interestingly a double top tube frame was reintroduced in 1910, though with a sloping top and curved lower tube (Fig. 11.2). A Chater Lea machine with a double top tube has been dated as 1898 and is very close in angles and general construction to the Manchester. It would therefore seem likely that Chater Lea supplied the lugs for this Manchester track frame. A very similar design was used by Léon Flameng (Fig. 11.3) in the first modern Olympics of 1896, where he won the 100km track race, came second in the 10km and third in the 2km sprint. It is interesting to speculate that the 'racer' referred to in the 1895 interview with Fred Hopper (see Chapter 1) with 'an entirely new design of frame, specially adapted for racing purposes, which, in the opinion of the inventor, will become universally popular with racing men', is the double top tube design. We will never know.

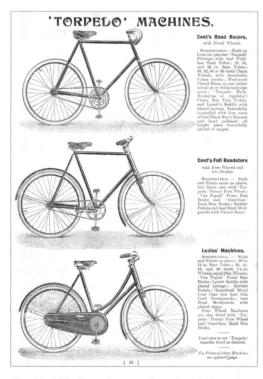

*Fig. 11.4 The Torpedo range from the 1903 catalogue.*

*Fig. 11.5 1910 'New Torpedo' lady's model.*

## Torpedo

Introduced in 1902 this name was also applied to Hopper cars and motorcycles and survived until the mid-1920s. As can be seen from the 1903 illustration (Fig. 11.4) a racing Torpedo was offered, though this had been dropped by 1905. As already mentioned it was the only named range for that year. By 1905 it had been joined by the Convincible and Enchanter. For 1910 it was renamed New Torpedo, and as described in the catalogue: 'this entirely new model is the highest grade machine we are making' (Fig. 11.5).

## Duplex

First listed in 1909 this elegant bicycle was withdrawn during the First World War. Fig. 11.6 dates from 1927 and shows a full chain case model. It was taken at Marsh Lane. Note the four frame sizes - 23", 24", 25" and 26" (Fig. 11.7). These are huge compared to modern fashion, but then frame sizes have cycled from large to small and back a few times since the mid-1880s.

## Elswick Model 6

Perhaps the best looking Barton bicycle, the Elswick cross truss design was featured in the 1908 Newcastle catalogue, which states: 'Some time since we introduced the special Cross Truss Frame.' This would indicate that the model had been in production for some years. Elswick claimed that the design

*Fig. 11.6 This photograph was dated by Charles Watkinson as 1927 and is of one of his relatives at Marsh Lane with a Hopper Duplex frame.*

*Fig 11.7 The Hopper Duplex from a 1910 catalogue.*

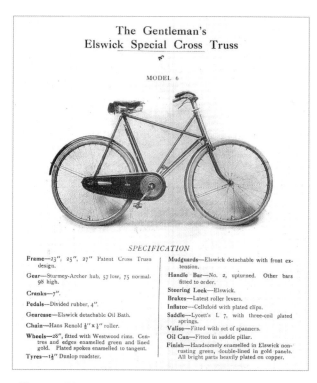

### The Gentleman's Elswick Special Cross Truss

MODEL 6

*SPECIFICATION*

**Frame**—23″, 25″, 27″ Patent Cross Truss design.

**Gear**—Sturmey-Archer hub, 57 low, 75 normal, 98 high.

**Cranks**—7″.

**Pedals**—Divided rubber, 4″.

**Gearcase**—Elswick detachable Oil Bath.

**Chain**—Hans Renold ½″ x ⅛″ roller.

**Wheels**—28″, fitted with Westwood rims. Centres and edges enamelled green and lined gold. Plated spokes enamelled to tangent.

**Tyres**—1½″ Dunlop roadster.

**Mudguards**—Elswick detachable with front extension.

**Handle Bar**—No. 2, upturned. Other bars fitted to order.

**Steering Lock**—Elswick.

**Brakes**—Latest roller levers.

**Inflator**—Celluloid with plated clips.

**Saddle**—Lycett's L 7, with three-coil plated springs.

**Valise**—Fitted with set of spanners.

**Oil Can**—Fitted in saddle pillar.

**Finish**—Handsomely enamelled in Elswick non-rusting green, double-lined in gold panels. All bright parts heavily plated on copper.

### TRICYCLES

Tricycles having given evidence of a decided return to fashion, last year we included them in our catalogue, with very gratifying results. This form of machine may be strongly recommended to those requiring a safe, reliable, and easily managed machine for either touring or town riding. We feel sure that if Agents will only make the most of the many desirable features presented by a three-wheeler they will secure many customers who would not otherwise take any interest in cycling.

SPECIFICATION

FRAME : built of weldless steel tube ; raised handlebar ; free wheel ; Perry's " Best " chain, ⅛in. by ⅛in ; rubber pedals ; pressed steel chain wheel ; wheels with double-butted spokes, British hubs and best English plated rims ; Superb front brake ; Empire de Luxe saddle ; Dunlop, Palmer or Clincher A Won tyres.

FINISH.—Black or green enamel ; all usual bright parts heavily plated on copper.

### Price Complete - £12 0 0

EXTRAS. Back Mudguards, 10 - ; Double Internal Expanding Hub Brakes, Back-pedalling, £2 7s. 6d. Hand Applied Axle Brake, £2 3s. 6d.

LESS 5% FOR CASH

*Fig. 11.8 Elswick Model 6 from the 1912 cataogue.*

*Fig. 11.9 1913 Hopper tricycle complete with Abingdon differential axle.*

resulted in an 'infinitely more rigid frame', thereby losing less power through flex. It first appeared in Barton in the 1912 catalogue and continued until 1937, making it one of the most enduring, as well as one of the most recognisable bicycles produced by Elswick-Hopper. Available in three sizes of 23" 25" and 27" and 28" wheels it was a large machine (Fig 11.8).

The 1913/14 catalogues list the following models:

| Hopper | Elswick |
|---|---|
| Duplex | Cross truss Model 6 |
| Torpedo | Universal gent's light roadster Model 19 |
| CEI (Cycles Entirely Interchangeable) | Universal lady's loop Model 20 |
| Popular | Universal road racer Model 21 |
| Torpolee carrier | Truss light roadster Model 24 |
| Box carrier tricycle | Truss racer Model 25 |
| Gent's tricycle | Popular truss lady's Model 26 |
| Little Giant juvenile bicycle (boy's and girl's) | Popular light roadster gent's Model 34 |
| | Boy's Model 24J, girl's Model 26J |

Each model was available in different frame sizes, and the Torpedo, CEI and Popular came with either gent's or lady's frames, so there was considerable complexity involved. This catalogue was also the last of its kind, with its hard cover and 140 pages offering a wide range of goods, as well as bicycles, and copious illustrations. The list clearly shows the different markets that the two ranges were aimed at

– Hopper at the agent seeking down-to-earth machines that could be sold on at a reasonable profit and Elswick at the retail customer seeking a distinctive high quality bicycle.

## Tricycle

Introduced in 1910 'to secure many customers who would not otherwise take to cycling', the full size gent's tricycle (Fig. 11.9) was listed for just four years. It is interesting to note the claim that 'tricycles had made a decided return to fashion'. Popular amongst older people and women during the high bicycle days the stability of a tricycle was no longer such an advantage for these riders once the safety bicycle became available. The Hopper tricycle illustrated is fitted with the ubiquitous Abingdon axle with differential drive. Happily, the 'Little Giant' juvenile tricycle was reintroduced in 1919 and continued to be bought by thousands of parents keen to get their children on wheels.

## Elswick Model 10

This lady's racer (Fig. 11.10) was listed in the 1927 catalogue – the earliest available at the time of writing for that decade. Produced in just a 22" frame and finished in black with a dark blue head tube and seat tube band it was instantly recognisable by the two stiffening tubes neatly triangulating the twin down tubes. It was produced until 1935, by which year it had grown ugly pump pegs on the top down

Fig. 11.10    *Model 10 Special Racer.*

Fig. 11.11    *The eight guinea Hopper Hawk.*

tube and been equipped with a front brake as standard. Women of shorter stature were catered for with a 20" frame and taller ones with a 23".

The 1930s saw a major increase in range of both Hopper and Elswick bicycles and the production of well illustrated catalogues. For 1936 there was the following line-up:

| Hopper | Elswick |
|---|---|
| Hopper Hawk Imp | Elswick Imp |
| Hopper Tandem | Elswick Tandem |
| Brighton Road Racer | Brighton Road Racer |
| Standard Racer | Standard Racer |
| Popular Racer | Popular Club Racer Model 21/22 |
| National Racer | Club Racer Model 24 RG/RL |
| Popular Light Roadster | Popular Roadster Model 12/12L |
| National Sports Light Roadster | Safety Sports Light Roadster Model 24SLG/SLL |
| National Semi-Racer | Safety Lightweight Model 24LWG/LWL |
| Popular Semi-Racer | Popular Lightweight Model 19/20 |
| National Sports Tourist | Safety Sports Tourist Model 24STG/STL |
| Popular Sports Tourist | Superb Sports Tourist Model 29/30 |
| National Light Roadster (lady's twin down tube) | Popular Model 24/24L (lady's loop) |
| National Juvenile – Boy's and Girl's | Juvenile Model 24 Boy's and Girl's |
| National Roadster | Popular Roadster Model 24/24L |
| Popular Roadster | Popular Roadster Model 12/12L |
| Popular Full Roadster | Special Full Roadster Model 31 |
| Popular All-Weather Roadster (no chrome) | All-Weather Roadster Model 32 |
| Popular 3-Speed Roadster | Popular Model 25L/25L |
| Popular 3-speed H.B. Roadster | Popular Roadster Model 26/26L |
| Popular H.B. Roadster | Popular Roadster Model 23/23L |
| Little Giant Junior LR | Junior Model 14B LR and 14G LR |
| Little Giant Junior | Junior Model 14B/G Tricycle |
| Junior Tricycle | Juvenile Model 24 Boy's/Girl's |
| Cyclette | Cyclette |
| | Deluxe Model 6 |
| | Deluxe Model 40 |

Hopper models appear in the same order as in the catalogue, while the Elswick range appeared in a different order but have been matched to the Hopper equivalent on the basis of specification and price. In the years between 1913 and 1936 the Hopper marque had changed from a predominantly wholesale range to one supplied through a network of dealers, creating the situation where most towns had both a Hopper and an Elswick agent. However, during those years all but two unique Elswick models had disappeared, and by 1938 the range was identical, a situation that continued until the names were finally merged as 'Elswick-Hopper' in 1963, a process that began in 1960.

## Hopper Hawk

Apart from the tandem the Hawk (Fig. 11.11) was the most expensive bicycle in the 1936 range at eight guineas, whereas its Elswick Imp equivalent came in third place behind the more complex Model 6 and 40. It was a classic 1930s all-rounder with two fixed cogs, quick release mudguards, 26" x 1¼" wheels and single brake – a rear mounted Resilion cantilever. With guards and the lower gear sprocket, it would be used for getting to work, then, for the weekend time trial, off with the guards, flip the wheel to the smaller sprocket and off to the start of a 25-miler, or more. Bicycles were expensive and wages low, so they had to be versatile.

*Fig. 11.12      A beautifully restored 1949 Elswick Rapier.*

## Elswick Rapier & Hopper Vampire

This 1949 Rapier (Fig. 11.12) has been painstakingly restored and is representative of the break with black frames and simple transfers and badges that had been the norm since the early days. Improved paint and transfer technology was being used to make bicycle frames stand out in the crowd, and this Rapier is still a real head-turner. These two models were made for just a few years from 1948 and were available in a range of four colours, this one being finished in what was described as 'polychromatic heliotrope'.

## Lincoln Imp

This model was introduced in 1955 and combined the older Lincoln and Imp names. Though Lincoln lies some 30 miles south of Barton it was, until the county border changes of 1974, the 'capital' of Lincolnshire. The Lincoln Imp was successfully promoted by Jim Turner and his new board of directors in 1958 with the formation of the Elswick-Hopper racing team, and was featured until the early 1970s. The question of whether the actual team bikes were made in Barton has not been resolved, and the stock frames that I have seen are not particularly light. However, the company had been in decline for some years, and Turner's decision to support a team of independents did achieve some amazing successes during the 1958 racing season under the leadership of Jim Wilson, and must have boosted sales. The retail version was supplied as a standard 5-speed, with an option of 10, and a cut-away Brooks Swallow style saddle, though probably a cheaper version, such as made by Lycett (Fig. 11.13).

## Continentale

Just why a unisex shopper with 20" wheels and a long seat pillar to accommodate a wide range of leg lengths was given the name of what, a few years previously, had been the top of the range road machine is a mystery. As noted in Chapter 7 it was intended to compete with the small wheel Moulton and was ideal for local shopping trips, with its front basket and rear carrier. It was made well into the 1970s, until replaced by the similar Cosmopolitan, made at Alveley until Phil Bradley discovered a lower cost frame made in the Far East. Uncertainty about dates is due to Elswick-Hopper not dating their catalogues after 1960. The Continentale was the last model in production at Marsh Lane. Both models were bought for their utility value and have proved reliable work horses, with many still in service as shopping bikes around the country (Fig. 11.14).

*Fig. 11.13          The 1959 Lincoln Imp, built on the record year achieved in 1958.*

*Fig. 11.14          An early leaflet for the Elswick-Hopper Continentale, probably 1965.*

## Elswick-Hopper Frame Number Key

Shortly after starting the research for this book I discovered the Veteran-Cycle Club and joined in the hope that members would be able to provide me with information about the company and its bicycles. The V-CC caters for interest in the multitude of different makers by encouraging members to become Marque Enthusiasts, the idea being that each ME becomes a single point of contact and is thereby able to build up a knowledge base on a specific marque. On discovering there was no Elswick-Hopper ME I took on the role and quickly built up a database of members' Elswick and Hopper bicycles with their frame numbers and all-important letters. I discovered that a typical frame stamping comprised a number, from three to six digits long and a single letter. Numbers collected range from 151 to 133801 and so the first frame in each year was probably numbered 101, continuing sequentially until the following year started again at 101. If this were true then the letter must represent the year. From a skeleton of letters and a collection of both hard and circumstantial evidence it became immediately clear that the letter sequence went backwards through the alphabet. After a couple of years, during which I had assumed that all 26 letters had been used, it transpired that Q and I were missing. As the purpose of frame numbers is for the maker to trace a machine back to manufacturing records it would seem that Q and I were both considered to be unreliable evidence – Q can lose its tail through a stamping error, and can fill with paint, and I is too close to 1. The table has been verified through knowledge of model changes, access to a number of original invoices, and Sturmey-Archer hub date stamps, though the latter are not always reliable due to replacement through wear and tear, or later upgrading from single speed. I am 99.99% sure that it is accurate and as I have found no company records of the system, nor any oral information, it is probably as close as anyone can get. In Chapter 2 it is recorded that by

September 1907 Fred Hopper had set up a system to trace each frame back to the workers involved in its construction so that would not 'scamp' on their work. A unique frame number would also, of course, have assisted with guarantee claims. The table starts with 'Z' for 1908, but this is speculation and the letter system may have been introduced earlier, or indeed later. The earliest letter-dated frame in my records is 'U', for 1913, so it is possible that the system was actually introduced in late 1907 with 'Z' for the new 1908 range. This would also be consistent with the formation of the limited company during 1907.

| Letter | Year | Year | Year |
| --- | --- | --- | --- |
| A | 1931 | 1955 | 1979 |
| B | 1930 | 1954 | 1978 |
| C | 1929 | 1953 | 1977 |
| D | 1928 | 1952 | 1976 |
| E | 1927 | 1951 | 1975 |
| F | 1926 | 1950 | 1974 |
| G | 1925 | 1949 | 1973 |
| H | 1924 | 1948 | 1972 |
| J | 1923 | 1947 | 1971 |
| K | 1922 | 1946 | 1970 |
| L | 1921 | 1945 | 1969 |
| M | 1920 | 1944 | 1968 |
| N | 1919 | 1943 | 1967 |
| O | 1918 | 1942 | 1966 |
| P | 1917 | 1941 | 1965 |
| R | 1916 | 1940 | 1964 |
| S | 1915 | 1939 | 1963 |
| T | 1914 | 1938 | 1962 |
| U | 1913 | 1937 | 1961 |
| V | 1912 | 1936 | 1960 |
| W | 1911 | 1935 | 1959 |
| X | 1910 | 1934 | 1958 |
| Y | 1909 | 1933 | 1957 |
| Z | 1908 | 1932 | 1956 |

## APPENDIX 2

## BARTON ON HUMBER MOTOR CYCLES

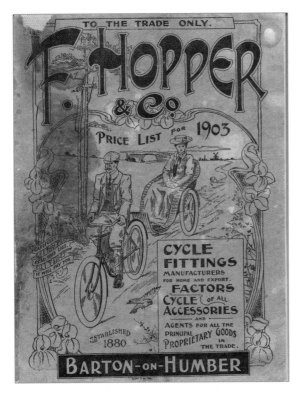

*Fig. 12.1 Front cover of the 1903 catalogue featuring a rather stylised NSU motorcycle towing a wicker trailer.*

*Fig. 12.2 1903 NSU 'Torpedo' motorcycle.*

I am indebted to Emlyn Evans, a member of the Veteran Motor Cycle Club and NSU historian, for help with this section and to John Waghorn, also of the VMCC, for loaning me his 1903 catalogue (Fig. 12.1), so far the earliest one I know of.

### NSU Imports

Fred Hopper's interest in motorised vehicles goes back at least to 1896, but by 1901 he was becoming more serious, as shown by a letter in the Lincolnshire Archives from D Citroën of 45 Holborn Viaduct, dated 5 September 1901, enclosing a 'booklet giving full particulars of the Minerva Motor for bicycles', available at a trade price of £22 10s (equivalent to £1800 in 2010 prices). The UK Minerva agent was indeed Dorus Citroën, a cousin of André Citroën, who created the eponymous car company in 1919. Dorus, or David, as he was later known, became a British citizen in 1904. The Brigg Road photograph (Fig 2.2), believed to date from 1902, shows a motorised bicycle that could indeed be evidence that he took up this offer. Not on a commercial basis, however, as in 1903 he was importing NSU machines from Germany. Records show that Hopper had bought freewheels from the Neckarsulm company during 1902, and was selling their motor cycles at the start of the 1903 season, so negotiations must have been conducted during the previous year, though whether directly, or through a British agent, has not been established. The 2hp 'Torpedo' (Fig. 12.2) was a type B NSU and the fuel tank even features an NSU badge, though the actual Torpedo version may have carried different transfers to disguise its origins. The type B was so called to differentiate it from the very first NSU motor cycle developed in 1901, with its engine mounted forward of the down tube. The type B was first available in 1902 and sold very well throughout Europe, India, and Southern Africa. The engine was actually a Swiss Zedel manufactured under licence by NSU and the 2hp version was the most powerful of the three sizes available. Starting as an agent was very much in line with his entry into bicycle manufacture: become an agent, establish a market, check out machines from different suppliers, experiment and then make your own.

No catalogue information is available for 1904 and no motor cycle was featured in 1905. It is likely that Fred Hopper had discovered that the effort required to service this more complex market was beyond his resources, given the rapid expansion of the company during the early years of the new century. Despite the move to new offices in 1905 and the factory building programme underway at Marsh Lane, it seems that during 1905 he decided to have another shot at the market with NSU, and in the 1906 catalogue offered two twin cylinder machines, one 4hp and one 5½hp, supplied with 20" and 24" frames (Fig. 12.3). Both were described as 'specially suitable for heavy riders or fore-car attachments'. There was no reference to 'Torpedo', nor in 1907, when four single cylinder touring machines, three twins and a 1¼hp lightweight were available.

The same models were available in 1908, but more significantly, these NSU machines were again referred to as Torpedo motor cycles (Fig. 12.4), possibly because NSU had produced the artwork without their name on the petrol tank, and the 1907 NSU catalogue does indeed refer to the option of tanks carrying the seller's name. The last year of NSU sourced machines was 1909, when the largest and smallest single cylinder touring models were dropped.

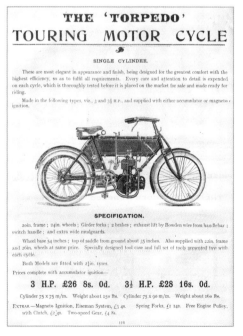

*Fig. 12.3 NSU Touring Twin from the Hopper 1906 catalogue.*
*Fig. 12.4 1908 NSU 'Torpedo' Touring Single.*

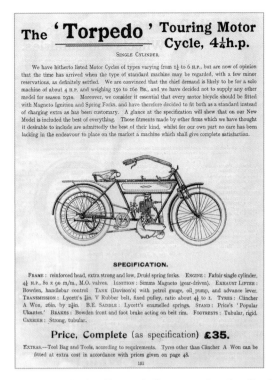

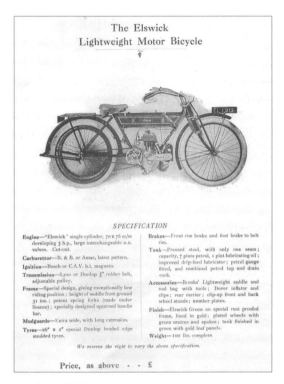

*Fig. 12.5 The first Barton-built motorcycle to be offered to the trade in 1910.*

*Fig. 12.6 From the 1912 Elswick catalogue this is the 3 hp lightweight tourer.*

## Barton-built Torpedo Motor Cycles

There is evidence from vehicle licensing records that a 2½hp Torpedo motor cycle was registered to F Hopper & Co on 1 September 1909 and given a reassigned number, BE 223. No NSU machines listed for the year were equipped with that engine size, so it may have been a prototype Barton produced machine. For 1910, Hopper did at last list his own Torpedo, a touring motor cycle equipped with a Fafnir single cylinder engine, 80mm x 90mm, 4-stroke, rated at 4¼hp and selling for £35 trade (Fig. 12.5). Probably due to lack of cash, Hopper initially produced just the one model, a significant reduction in choice compared to the NSU range, though consistent with the launch of the 'Ajax' bicycle in 1890. This lack of choice was rationally, though not at all convincingly, explained in the catalogue:

> We have hitherto listed Motor Cycles of types varying from 1¼hp to 6hp, but are now of the opinion that the time has arrived when the type of standard machine may be regarded, with a few minor reservations, as definitely settled. We are convinced that the chief demand is likely to be for a solo machine of about 4hp and weighing 150 to 160 lbs and we have decided not to supply any other model for season 1910. Moreover, we consider it essential that every motor bicycle should be fitted with Magneto Ignition and Spring Forks and have therefore decided to fit both as standard instead of charging extra as has been customary.

It is doubtful that more than a single model was practical from the sheer logistics of the production of frames and fittings and the assembly of complete machines. The decision to put all their money on 'four horses' was overturned within the year and at the November Olympia Exhibition there were two models on show, a standard 3½hp and a lightweight 2hp. These were fitted with Precision engines, a supplier that Hopper used exclusively from this time.

For the 1911 Olympia Show Hopper again displayed two Torpedo motor cycles, a 3½hp roadster model and a 2½hp lightweight roadster. The review in *Bicycling News and Motor Review* notes:

> A new form of mudguard stay-end is fitted to the front guards, which allow of instant detachability and a novelty is the Torpedo clutch, fitted on the engine shaft and controlled by Bowden wire from the left handle-grip.

Elswick motor cycles also made their first appearance at the Exhibition from their new location in Barton and a 3¾hp single and 2½hp lightweight were displayed in trademark Elswick Green livery. The larger machine was two-speed clutch driven. To create the illusion that Elswick was a separate entity the two makes occupied different stands.

Separate catalogues were produced in 1912, one for the Hopper Torpedo range and one for Elswick. The two Torpedo machines shown at Olympia were offered, and two Elswick, the smaller apparently identical to its Torpedo cousin, with the same 70 x 76mm engine, though advertised as developing 3hp (Fig. 12.6). The larger Elswick carried a 5hp Precision engine, an upgrade of the Show model and an indication that 'Elswick' was intended to be the premier marque of the company. The Hopper catalogue also offered the engines separately, the larger being advertised as the 3½hp Torpedo touring engine and the smaller as the 2½hp 'Torpedo-Precision' lightweight engine. *The Motor Cycle* of 15 August 1912 included the story of a visit to the Elswick Works at Barton. The new crankshaft free-engine clutch is referred to as having been in use on an experimental machine for some months and proven perfectly reliable. An idea of production rates is given by reference to about 30 machines a week being turned out by the motor cycle department. This undoubtedly refers to the output of both Elswick and Torpedo models combined. Production figures were reported elsewhere as 718 during the 1911/12 trading year and 324 during the last 5 months of 1912.

An article in *The Star* of 28 June 1913 indicates that the local machines were quite competitive and that Fred Hopper was confident enough in his products to allow his only son to ride them. The newly-formed Barton and District Motor Cycle Club held a hill climb at West Halton, between Scunthorpe and Barton, on the previous Saturday with five events for different classes: lightweights, touring, passenger machines, TT racing machines and unlimited. Of the 19 places listed, six were Elswick, four Torpedo, four BSA, two Clyno, one Triumph, one Riley and one Rex. Riding a 3½hp model Torpedo, Freddie, age 21, came second in the touring class, first passenger, third TT and first unlimited. The event was marred by an accident in which Herbert Barton, a young chauffeur employed by F Hopper and Co, was thrown from his machine due to a puncture at the start of the one-in-seven hill while travelling at about 50 mph. The flying start and a large quantity of loose stones on the road were said to have contributed to the accident. However, the day proved a very successful one for the locally made motor cycles.

Freddie's first motor cycle was a 110lb Torpedo motor cycle powered by a 1½hp Minerva engine. BE 413 was first registered on 26 October 1906, just 15 days after he had got his driving licence, and may have been an early development model. It was sold to a Howden man in 1909, and Freddie then bought a 3½hp Ariel. He does seem to have been something of a tear-away in his youth, and on 1 July 1913 he appeared at Hull Police Court on a charge of driving a motor cycle and side car 'in a manner dangerous to the public'. PC Downing stated that the defendant was travelling at a speed of 15mph along Carr Lane and dashed in front of a horse and rulley at the Midland Street corner, narrowly avoiding an accident. The defendant said that this was the first complaint against him during his seven years experience of motor cars and motor cycles. He said he watched Downing for a signal, when he saw it he interpreted it to relate to traffic in Midland Street. He was only travelling at 8-10mph. He never heard the officer call upon him to stop. Horace Kirk, who was riding in the side car, gave similar evidence. The Justices considered the whole of the facts and dismissed the case.[1] The fact that his father was a JP across the river would surely not have influenced the court, but he was not so fortunate

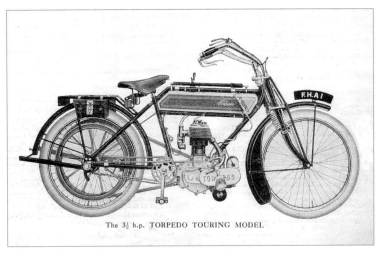

The 3½ h.p. TORPEDO TOURING MODEL

*Fig. 12.7 1913 3½ hp Torpedo as shown in the motor cycle specific catalogue of that year.*

when he had a second encounter with the law on Saturday 26 July in Bridlington. He was fined £2 and costs for riding a motor cycle at a speed estimated at 35mph.[2]

In 1913 Hopper's produced a catalogue specifically for the Torpedo motor cycle range, comprising the 2½ and 3½hp machines of the previous year (Fig. 12.7). Being specifically aimed at enthusiasts it contains many more details than the trade oriented publications. Thus, the frame is described as:

> ...considerably reduced in height and is now so low that an average sized rider can quite easily place his heels on the ground whilst seated in the saddle. Only best quality steel tubing is used and the frame is reinforced at all vital parts to secure strength. The wheel base is short enough to steady the machine on grease or round corners and yet long enough to give comfort when riding on rough roads.

We also learn that the Druid forks were made by Hopper's under licence and that the rear brake was fitted with a Hopper special patented compensating device,

> which brings the whole of the shoe into action at the same time, thus securing the maximum braking power and even-wearing of the shoe.

Testimonials were printed at the back of the catalogue from as far away as Johannesburg, Montevideo, and Burlington, Ontario. While recognising that such letters may have been embellished, they do have the ring of truth and Hopper's at this time were exporting machines to most corners of the globe. One verifiable testimonial was reprinted from the *Motor and Cycle Trader* 26 July 1912:

> Accounts are just to hand of the Cape Peninsular Club's Speed Contest, which took place at Durban. There were thirteen entries, including a 7hp machine and a 6hp, while all competitors, with one exception, were driving nothing less than machines of 3½hp. The exception was Mr T C L Smith, who was mounted on a 2½hp Torpedo. On formula, by which the event was decided, Mr Smith, with a score of 220, was far above the nearest competitor, whose score totalled 339. In actual speed the little Torpedo was fourth, being beaten by the fastest, a 7hp machine, by only 7½ seconds, while the second and third competitors, both on 3½hp machines, beat it only by 4 and 3½ seconds respectively. This is certainly an excellent performance for a machine of only 202cc, specially since it was estimated that the Torpedo attained a speed of 43 miles per hour. A Mr Hodgson of the Hull and East Riding Motor Cycle Club also had a good year on his little Torpedo as a private rider. He took the Gold Medal in the Leeds Club 24 hour run to London and back; the Gold in the Hull and ER 100 miles non-stop ride and first prize in the 100 mile Reliability Trial.

The motor cycle featured in Fig. 12.8 is clearly a Torpedo, but though registered BE 223 it is definitely not the 1909 machine. Transfer of numbers was common at the time and it is thought that this version is a development model, probably built in 1913. The photograph was taken on 16 December

*Fig. 12.8 R B Clark with a Torpedo motorcycle on 16 December 1913.*

1913 and the young man is R B Clark. Emlyn Evans observed that the frame and all the fittings are most certainly Hopper's products, with Druid side spring front forks. The dropped rear frame, to reduce saddle height, became very popular with all manufacturers post 1911. The engine is a 3½hp (499cc) Torpedo-Precision. The rear hub is an Armstrong 'Triplex' three-speed gear and clutch patented by A H Reilly in 1919 and put into production in 1911. The magneto is a Bosch ZA1 with closed magnet (early ones had an open magnet). The engine has been fitted with a Brown and Barlow track carburettor, which fits in nicely with the magneto chain drive being left open – a typical racing modification at the time, especially on Brooklands and TT bikes. Clearly, Fred Hopper had realised that racing success translated into sales.

      1914 appears to have been a good year for Elswick motor cycles despite the fact that the company was in receivership. T T Laker, secretary of Barton and District Motor Cycle Club, entered the Isle of Man Senior Tourist Trophy Race of that year on a V-twin Elswick that appears to be another development model (Fig. 12.9 ). Emlyn notes that it is fitted with a Sturmey-Archer three-speed hub as seen in the 1915 Torpedo catalogue. The clutch operating worm is operated by foot pedal on the

*Fig. 12.9 North Lincolnshire rider T T Laker at the 1914 TT.*

right hand side of the machine alongside the magneto chain case. The gear control is operated through the rear wheel spindle via a tank mounted lever that has been moved to a lower position just above the engine shaft pulley. One of the reasons for this is the position of the Best and Lloyd auxiliary hand pump that has been positioned on the top tube of the frame with what looks like an additional oil tank, as constant lubrication would be required during a race. Moving the pump from the front offside of the main oil/fuel tank to a more favourable position on the top rail was a good idea. At a pinch Laker could have operated the gear lever with his left leg – an old dodge with Sturmey boxes. It was a nice looking machine, but unfortunately Laker retired before completing the course.

The official programme for the 1914 Barton Horse Show Society athletic sports meeting on the evening of Saturday 13 June carried a back page advertisement for Elswick motor cycles and stated that the record for 1913, when 26 competitions were entered, included 23 firsts, three seconds and two 'special' awards. Mention was also made of another South African event, the Championship of the Rand, won on a 3¾hp Elswick Touring Model. This advert probably paid the cost of publication, and prizes were presented by Henry Wilson JP, a further example of the involvement of the partners in Barton's social life.

Fig. 12.10 *Torpedo combination featuring a Torpedo de luxe sidecar.*

The last Hopper's catalogue in which motor cycles appeared was for the 1915/16 season, presumably compiled in 1914, close to the start of the war. It was the most ambitious yet, with six Torpedo models available: 2 and 2½hp lightweights, 2½hp two-stroke, 3½hp touring, 4hp twin and a 4¼hp sidecar combination (Fig. 12.10). This same line-up appeared in the 1918 price list, with the note that they were 'withdrawn temporarily'. The 1919 catalogue, under the heading Motor Cycle and Side Cars stated:

> We regret having to advise our customers that we are unable to quote for these Models at present, as our Motor Cycle Department has for the last four years been engaged on important contracts with the Government, and we are not yet in a position to deliver our New Models.

Company archives record that 76 motor cycles were sold in 1913/14 and 116 in 1914/15. There is no record of motor cycle sales to the armed forces, though a Torpedo machine was tested by them during 1912. The factory did manufacture forks for Ariel motor cycles during the war, as recorded in Chapter 3. No motor cycle sales were noted after November 1916, though there were some sales in

1919 as evidenced by a report in the *Motor Cycle* of 27 November 1919 on the Olympia Exhibition, which described the Elswick-Hopper stand:

> On this stand are shown two motor cycles. Both machines are identical, except for finish, though one is known as the Elswick and the other as the Torpedo. The Elswick is an extremely neat lightweight, fitted with a Precision 3½hp two-stroke engine, which has sump lubrication. The machine is quite simple and on strictly conventional lines. It is finished in the well-known Elswick shade of green and lined with gold and this has a particularly distinctive appearance. The engine chain is neatly encased, the cover also enclosing the outside flywheel. A Sturmey-Archer two-speed gear box with kick-starter is fitted and the machine has Brampton Biflex spring forks.

The motor cycle shown in Fig. 12.11 is a 1913 3½hp Elswick owned by Alan Potts of Sussex

Fig. 12.11      *Alan Potts' 1913 Elswick motorcycle.*

Fig. 12.12      *Barton Bike Night 7 July 2004.*

and the subject of a five page article in *The Classic Motorcycle* in June 2005. Fig. 12.12 was taken at Barton Bike Night in 2004, the three Elswick motor cycles from left to right are a 1913 2½hp single speed lightweight; a 1914 model with two speed gearbox, originally exported to Australia and returning to England via Scandinavia, and a 1919 3½hp model. The moped is one of the two Lynx prototypes described in Chapter 7. They are owned by John Andrew who is pictured with his partner Leslie; the photographer on the right is local enthusiast Noel Loxley. The similarities between the frames of the machines are striking and I agree with John Andrew's assessment that the 1919 Olympia exhibits were an attempt by Elswick-Hopper to sell off whatever stock of frames they had left from before the war. Thus, John's 1919 model has the same frame as the pre-war one but is fitted with a post-war Precision engine. It is known that no further motor cycles were produced after 1919, as Fred Hopper had decided to stick to what he knew best – making bicycles. However, subsequent management had another go with motor cycles, though in the form of mopeds, as described in Chapter 7. Predictably, it was not a success.

**Endnotes**

1      *The Star* 5 July 1913.
2      *The Star* 2 August 1913.

# APPENDIX 3

## MOTOR CARS

I am indebted to Gordon Brooks of the Veteran Car Club for explaining many aspects of Hopper's venture into four-wheeled transport. He shared his deep knowledge of Edwardian cars, supplied most of the sources of information quoted, and identified the suppliers of Hopper's cars. Also my thanks to Tony Wall for his information on North Lindsey BE registered cars and motorcycles with connections to the factory.

### Background

The first mechanically driven cars produced for the market, rather than as experiments, appeared during the 1880s, with both steam, and internal combustion engines used as the motive power. However, by the late 1890s the four stroke Otto cycle internal combustion engine was well ahead, with Benz of Germany the leading manufacturer and Panhard of France not far behind. So, while Fred Hopper was setting up his business as a whitesmith during the 1880s there was massive development taking place in all three forms of personal transport – bicycles, motor cycles and motor cars. Elswick of Newcastle entered the car market in 1903, assembling cars with various engines, though advertisements in 1906 stated that they were built in London.[1]

### Fred Hopper's Automotive Ambitions

From Chapter 1 we know that one of Hopper's motives for selling his company to the Hull syndicate in 1896 was to expand into 'motors, motor cars and vehicles'. When that plan failed we know that his 1897 prospectus for the Hull and Barton Manufacturing Company Ltd refers to 'Cycles, Motor Cars etc', so there is no doubt of his plans to enter the new world of motorised transport at a very early stage of its development. There is also photographic evidence that Fred Hopper owned at least one motorcar at the turn of the century (Fig. 2.2), possibly a Delahaye c 1900, and archive evidence that they were used by his salesmen for business. We know that Fred Hopper Snr and Junr were issued with driving licences on 11 October 1906 – they had become mandatory in 1903 under the Motor Car Act of that year, so it would appear that neither father nor son actually drove before 1906. Fred Junr was just 15 and his licence limited him to motor cycles, as the age for driving cars had been set at 17 in 1903, and 14 for motor cycles. Young Fred is recorded as the owner of BE 669 from December 1908, just after his 17th birthday. This was a green Royal Starling phaeton of 12hp, swapped just three months later for a two seater 10hp Starling, BE 690.

Hopper was offered the agency for the International Motor Car Company's 'Charette' in August 1902,[2] the letter claiming a minimum profit per car of £32 10s 0d and an output of 20 cars per week with 'nothing coming from abroad'. This company did not manufacture its own cars, though may have assembled one or two at their London showroom.[3] The offer followed the collection of a 'Charette' from the West London Cycle Repository of London the previous month by his sales manager, Charles Atkinson. The letter written to his employer on the same day as the purchase tells much of the unpredictability of motor transport at the time:

Angus Hotel London 31/7/02

Dear Sir,

I have just seen Mr Patmore, the principal of the West London Cycle Repository and have bought the Charette car for £60 and promised him that he shall have [the] cheque for same by Saturday morning's post. He has also given me offer of the other De Dion car at £45 until Tuesday next. I shall wire you in the morning asking you to remit cheque tomorrow and I expect to get away from Wimbledon by about 10 am, which means it will be nearly noon by the time I get across London and on to a clear road. I shall try and reach home by Saturday evening if possible but if not I might leave the car at Sleaford or Lincoln and then go back for it on Monday.

I got here all right with the old car but it was a bit thick driving through the City, in fact Whitefriargate [centre of Hull, CHA's home town, now pedestrianised] on a Saturday night was child's play compared to it. However, I went slow and sure.

Both Mr Lovell and Mr Church are well pleased with the car and I have got them both, also one of their men, well into the art of driving.

I remain,
Yours faithfully,

C H Atkinson

This letter was written on Thursday evening, so Charles was expecting to take about 36 hours to reach home, just 160 odd miles away, at an average of less than 5 mph. Given that the London to York bicycle record set in 1900 was just 11 hours, and that York is some 30 miles further from London than Barton, it does not say much for the efficacy of early car travel, especially compared with the speed and reliability of the railways at that time. Charles had written from Lincoln the previous month with an order and commented that:

'...one of the front tyres went and I had to put two patches on the cover and one on the air tube. That was about a mile and a half from Brigg and when I got within about 10 yards of the hotel here the engine stopped of its own accord. I think it is dirt in the carburettor again.'

Hopper's interest in cars seems to have been well-known to his customers. R W Warrilow of Warrilow & Co., Weston-super-Mare, a long-standing buyer of Barton bicycles, wrote a private letter to Fred Hopper in July 1907 trying to persuade him to buy a two-cylinder Humber 10/12 for his son. As he was only 16 at the time it is doubtful the deal was accepted, though Warrilow assured him that the asking price of £95 did not in any way reflect the value of £195. Apparently Warrilow had previously sold Hopper a Darracq at a bargain price, which had proved a troublesome machine. From Tony Wall's BE registration research it is clear that Fred Hopper was seriously interested in motorised transport, and the first one recorded with a North Lindsey registration was BE479, a Brown Landaulette, 25/30hp, first registered in May 1907 and sold to Dr Loveridge of Barton in 1912.

## Car 'Manufacture'

Hopper's ambition to become a car 'manufacturer' was finally realised in 1907, with the introduction of the two-seater Torpedo light car (Fig. 13.1) in the January issue of the home trade catalogue. The export edition followed in February and included a light delivery van version on the same running gear. Surprisingly, there is nothing in the introduction to either catalogue to indicate that the Torpedo car was a new venture; perhaps he wished to hide the fact that it was just that, and perhaps because the Torpedo was primarily a bought-in kit, just assembled and finished at the Barton factory. The year 1907 was also particularly significant as F Hopper was re-formed as a limited company in order to raise cash for expansion, including, of course, the production of cars. The car kits bought by Hopper's were supplied by the Star Cycle Co of Wolverhampton, run by Edward Lisle Junr. According to *The Beaulieu Encyclopaedia of the Automobile*, a 6 hp de Dion powered 'Starling' two-seater was introduced in 1905, with a chain drive and an armoured wood frame. The Torpedo was assembled in Barton using Starling components and was described by Hopper's as 'a thoroughly reliable light car' and 'for

## THE 'TORPEDO' LIGHT CAR.

Specially designed and constructed on the very latest approved lines to meet the demand for a thoroughly reliable light car. The 'Torpedo' Light Car **is not an experiment**, but an article that, after exhaustive trials, has been found **as near perfection as it is possible to get**; for elegance, reliability, and simplicity of action **it cannot be surpassed**. It is supplied with either wire or artillery wheels, and for anyone requiring a handy and serviceable runabout, **nothing can be better**.

The 'Torpedo' Light Car, 6-h.p.

Price  - - - -  £120 0 0

### SPECIFICATION.

Engine, 6-h.p. single cylinder, balanced, 4in. bore by 4½in. stroke, water-cooled by radiator ; Carburettor, Longuemare, latest approved pattern, with automatic air regulator ; Gear, 3 speeds forward and reverse, giving speeds of 8, 16, and 24 miles per hour ; Transmission by chains ; Back Axle, live type, with very simple differential ; Steering positively irreversible, of worm and sector type ; Frame, well-seasoned ash, strongly reinforced with steel flitch plates ; Wheels, wire, for 700 by 80 mm. tyres ; Tyres, Dunlop thickened edge, 700 by 80 mm. reinforced ; Brakes, two powerful band brakes, metal to metal, one actuated by hand and the other by foot ; Body, two bucket seats, painted cream, lined blue, and richly upholstered to match. Weight, 8 cwt.

Supplied as above, complete with tool kit and tyre-repair outfit.

Lamps, horn, and jack, extra.

Artillery wheels supplied if required, at £3 extra.

*For Special Terms upon which we sell this Car, see p. 73.*

74

## STUART and STARLING CARS.

MANUFACTURED BY

## The STAR CYCLE Co., Ltd.,

WOLVERHAMPTON, England.

Telegraphic and Cable Address:—"LISLE, WOLVERHAMPTON."    Telephone Nos. 79 and 234.
Code used:—A.B.C., 5th Edition.

## THE STARLING CAR.

THE STARLING

### SPECIFICATION.

ENGINE.—6-h.p., single cylinder balanced, water-cooled, 4-in. bore x 4½-in. stroke.

GEAR.—A specially designed 3-speed and reverse gear box, giving 8, 16, and 24 miles per hour.

TRANSMISSION.—By chains.

BACK AXLE.—Live type, having very simple differential.

STEERING.—Positively irreversible. Worm and sector type.

FRAME.—Ash, strongly reinforced with steel flitch plates.

WHEELS.—Artillery, for 700 x 80-in. tyres.

BRAKES.—Two powerful band brakes, metal to metal ; one actuated by foot, the other by hand.

COOLING.—By radiator, Thermo syphon circulation.

TYRES.—Dunlop, thickened edge, 700 x 80-in., reinforced.

BODY.—Two bucket seats, painted green, lined and trimmed to match.

*Fig. 13.1 Torpedo light car from the 1907 catalogue.*

*Fig. 13.2 The Star Cycle Company Starling, identical to the 1907 Torpedo.*

anyone requiring a handy and serviceable runabout, **nothing can be better**.' Comparing the Torpedo with that from a Starling advert (Fig. 13.2) there are few differences and the specification is almost identical. The Torpedo single cylinder engine was 4" bore x 4½" stroke, water-cooled and supplied with a Longuemare carburettor. It had three forward gears and reverse, giving speeds of 8, 16 and 24mph and a well-seasoned ash frame reinforced by steel flitch plates. It would seem that the engine supplier was not de Dion as this combination of bore and stroke was not made by them. Chain drive was to the near side only. Trade price was £120 with an extra £3 for artillery wheels. The light delivery van had a strengthened chassis and was capable of carrying a load of 2½ cwt, in addition to the driver, and cost £125. The Star company was not without supply and quality problems at this time and following a complaint from Hopper this terse reply was received:

> 22 July 1907
>
> re letter of complaint
> re chassis not being tested properly and petrol tank missing, this has been a rush delivery as 3 weeks promised.
>
> E Lister
> The Star Cycle Co. Ltd.

Hopper's assembled a light van for the business, and BE 485 was registered in May 1907 for use

*Fig. 13.3 A shipment en route to Shanghai aboard ss Glen Lochy as featured in the 1908 catalogue. It was photographed along Waterside Road on the way to Barton Haven, and thence to Hull.*

initially as a light delivery van and later as a flat-bodied rulley. It was painted red with 'F Hopper' added in black and was in service until 1920. A great variety of other makes was purchased, both for hire, and for use in transporting goods, with a total of 30 recorded between 1907 and 1914. Of these no fewer than nine either started life as commercial vehicles or were converted to the carriage of goods. Typical of these was a Brown 18hp car, BE709, originally registered to Walter Boynton in 1909, purchased by Hopper later that year and converted to a flat bed rulley. Another was BE 759, a Mascot 12 seater charabanc, owned from 1909 to 1913. It was at some stage converted to a flat bed motor dray, though it probably continued to be used as a charabanc at weekends.

Letters in Lincoln Archives show that Hopper was investigating alternative suppliers. In August 1907 Rex Motor Manufacturing Co Ltd wrote reminding him that they had submitted an offer for both engines and sets and in the same month Johnson, Hurley and Martin Ltd of Gosford Street, Coventry wrote concerning drawings they had sent to Barton of a 6hp single cylinder engine.

A Hopper's publicity booklet dated 1908 and titled *A Great Barton Industry*, includes a short paragraph on the latest venture:

> Quite recently the manufacture of motor cars and motor cycles commenced, a special building being put up for the purpose of keeping the motor business separate from the parent industry and, notwithstanding the branch being in its infancy, already many cars have been shipped abroad. It may be mentioned that the company prefer to establish the same reputation for their cars as in their cycles, before turning out the cars in large numbers.

The 1908 catalogue included a photograph of a shipment of packing cases to Shanghai that apparently contained a Torpedo car (Fig. 13.3) though just how many vehicles Hopper's exported has not been discovered. The line-up for 1908 consisted of the same light cars, offered at substantially lower prices of £105 and £110 respectively. Added to the range was a 10hp two-cylinder 'Torpedo', which was identical in all respects to the 'Royal Starling' shown at the 1908 Cordingley Show. Even Hopper's artwork is identical to that in the Cordingley brochure. This car was available as a two or four-seater at trade prices of £149 15s 0d and £170 0s 0d and retail £175 and £200, respectively. The £200 price agrees with that quoted for the Royal Starling in W C Bersey's '*A List of Motor Cars Manufactured or Sold in the United Kingdom 1906-1912*', published by The Technical Publishing Company Ltd in January 1912.

For some reason the two-cylinder Torpedo was not available in 1909, probably due to supply problems from Wolverhampton, and just the light car and van were offered to the trade. By the time the 1910-11 trade catalogue was issued in January 1910 there had been a transformation in the Torpedo range:

- Two-seater Torpedo – speed 40 mph, petrol capacity 6 gallons, fitted with a two-cylinder engine of 10-12hp and Cardan shaft drive to a live back axle. Trade price £175. This was identical to the 'Little Briton', produced by the Star Cycle Co, featured at the Stanley Show of 1908.[4]
- Four-seater Torpedo – advertised as a 60mph machine, but identical to the 1909 Royal Starling.
- Torpedo Landaulette – 'A magnificently appointed car, of an appearance second to none.' It had a four-cylinder engine 100mm bore and 130mm stroke of 25-30hp. Trade price was a substantial £475, yet a lamp, horn and jack were extra (Fig. 13.4). From Gordon Brooks' detective work this car has been identified as a close relative of the 'Brown' 20hp four-cylinder Landaulette. Brown Brothers Ltd was no more a manufacturer than Hopper's, of course, but there was already a long-standing reciprocal customer/supplier relationship between the two companies. A list of possible suppliers includes Darracq, Panhard and De Dion.

Fig. 13.4 1910 Torpedo Landaulette.    Fig. 13.5 The last Torpedo car featured in the catalogues, a 1912 soft top.

By 1910 Hopper's own fleet of cars numbered nine, all available for hire. Meticulous records were kept of mileage, running costs (pence/mile) and petrol consumption. The Darracq is probably the one bought from Mr Warrilow. In 2010 values the red 'Brown' was costing £2.70/mile! Clearly, motoring was an expensive pastime for Edwardians.

| | Red 'Brown' | Landaulette | Green 'Brown' | 15 hp Humber | Belsize | Darracq | Rex | 8/10 Humber | Demeester |
|---|---|---|---|---|---|---|---|---|---|
| mileage | 230 | 412 | 245 | 118 | 28 | 169 | 10 | 30 | 22 |
| cost/mile | 7½ | 8¼ | 5½ | $5\frac{5}{8}$ | $3\frac{3}{8}$ | $19\frac{1}{8}$ | 6 | 6 | 5½ |
| mpg | 10.93 | 10.04 | 9.28 | | | 8.5 | | | 14.06 |

The final correspondence from the Briton Motor Co Ltd (the Star Cycle Co Ltd was so renamed in 1909) was dated May 1910 and related to the quite massive increase of 10% in the price of tyres.

1912 was the last year a Torpedo car was offered – a four-seater soft top with a long stroke four cylinder engine of 62mm bore and 120mm stroke of monobloc construction (Fig. 13.5), retailing at £270. The specification was word for word the same as that printed by Brown Brothers for their Albruna model – even down to the retail price.

## Elswick Cycle Car

In 1912 Hopper's finally took the plunge as an actual manufacturer, and purchased a design for a cycle car, basically a simple light weight four wheel vehicle benefiting from a reduced road tax based on its light weight, from W C Butter of Butter and Angel of London.[5] Hopper's Scottish representative, R W Gregg, wrote to his employer in December 1912, asserting:

> I am certain there is a great future for a good sensible vehicle built on small car lines. Water-cooled engine not less than 6hp – I am sure the Humber and Premier folk are out for trouble with their air-cooled ones – a good Cycle Car at about £100 will sell to cost the agent about £75. A good strong chassis with either bevel drive or central chain. I hope if you go on with the one you have that it will be turned out for hard work and not a freak, like the bulk of those at the Show.[6]

The prospectus for the new Elswick-Hopper Cycle and Motor Company, Limited, dated 23 June 1913, contains a paragraph relating to the new cycle car, which was also published in the *Cycle Trader* of 27 June 1913:

> Coincident with the progress of the Motor Industry there has been a remarkable demand for the Cycle Car. With a view to meeting this demand the company has produced a car with a water-cooled engine and a system of friction drive (dispensing with the expensive gear box and differential axle), which can be sold at a price little in excess of that asked for a Motor Cycle and Side Car and yet leave a handsome margin of profit. The demand for this Car will be beyond the present capacity of the Works and will necessitate considerable extensions and the provision of additional working capital. Owing to the great demand for this Car, the Company have to refuse to book furth**er orders for the present.**

THE ELSWICK FRICTION CAR

*Fig. 13.6 Elswick cycle car as featured in an Elswick-Hopper advertising poster*

This car was used as a central feature of a new advertising poster (Fig. 13.6), and there is a photograph of a very similar looking machine being erected in the Elswick building (Fig. 13.7). This large and extant building was erected in 1911/12. There are different versions being erected, and a twin cylinder engine can be seen at the back. How much these cycle cars were based on Butter's design has not been established and no records of that company have been found. However, the development may be partly explained by a letter to P Smith of Lincoln from John Stockdale, tool room foreman, with a 50 year employment record:

I worked with Mr Pond for over 25 years commencing in 1918 and it was in various conversations and discussions that I remember these details. Mr Pond was responsible for the development and production of the car chassis. The main frame of the chassis was of angle iron with tubular struts and stays supporting the car body.

The engines, one 6hp, another 8hp, were made by Napier Car Co of Coventry. It was a two cylinder four stroke, water cooled, coupled to a three speed gearbox also made by Napier, and the prop shaft and worm gear for the rear drive were also supplied by them. Mr C Fowler, who had been trained at the Napier company came to Hopper's for the sole purpose of fitting the engines, gearbox and final drive. I knew this man by sight, but he left Hopper's and returned to the Midlands soon after the war (1914-18). Mr F Grubert came from Wolverhampton to make the radiators and other sheet metal work. The radiator had a top and bottom tank made of sheet brass with copper tubes between and was made on the works. The tanks were supported by steel tube stays and every part was soldered together. Mr Grubert was foreman in the gear-case and sheet metal department for many years.

Only the offside rear wheel was driven as no differential gear was fitted on the early models. The only brake was a cast iron pulley, keyed on the prop shaft, with a leather lined spring clip designed to grip the pulley when the brake was applied. The near side rear wheel was a free-wheel. Later, a glass windscreen mounted in a brass frame was fitted, and a canvas hood (similar to that fitted on a pram) was also an extra.

The most comfortable cruising speed was between 12 and 16mph according to the condition of the road with a possible 20 to 25mph in favourable conditions.

*Fig. 13.7 Assembly of Elswick cycle cars in the Elswick building, © David Lee.*

While this is a second-hand record, John Stockdale is a reliable witness, given his long interest in local history through the WEA, and his engineering background. But there are anomalies – A F Grubert started at Hopper's in September 1910 according to company records, over two years before the cycle car is thought to have appeared. Engines of these ratings were produced by Napier, though the company was based in London, not Coventry. Did Hopper have firm plans for his own car production in 1910, when he hired Grubert, or was he brought in for his metal working skills, as applicable to bicycle chain cases as to radiator manufacture? The likeliest answer is that he was planning ahead and is known to have brought in several skilled workers from the Midlands. Thanks to Tony Wall's research we know that at least one cycle car was registered. BE 2216 was first registered on 26 May 1914 as a 4½hp Elswick cycle car. It was owned by Harry Boynton of Market Rasen, whose family had previously bought several cars from Hopper's. The last recorded owner is Frederick Stanley of 60 Corporation Road, Colchester, by which time it had changed from a dark blue 450lb machine to a light khaki 670lb car, no doubt due to the additional weight of a larger 8hp engine. Another anomaly is that according to John Stockdale's letter, it should have been originally a 6 or 8hp engine, though written 60 years after the event he may have misremembered.

It would appear that Fred Hopper had settled for a niche in the burgeoning car market where he could be a proud manufacturer, rather than merely an assembler. It would be interesting to know if he read *Bicycling News and Motor Review* of 12 February 1913, as an article entitled 'Has the Slump Come?' describes the rush to produce cycle cars as involving 'quite a lot of people with good, bad and indifferent manufacturing facilities (who) enrolled themselves under the little chap's banner.' The writer foresaw the future as following car practice in the production of miniature cars – a path followed after the war by Austin and Morris. There is no doubt that the company was capable of producing a good cycle car, but the craze for such vehicles soon faded and in any case, his time was fully occupied with the legal battle to reclaim his company from the receiver. When the new board was formed he was still managing director, but his freedom of action was severely curtailed. How many Elswick cycle cars were built is not known, but from photographic evidence at least three, though it is doubtful if any have survived.

## Conclusion

Some time after 1914 the fleet of cars, which by then numbered 30, was sold off. These included two charabancs, a Lancashire Motor Co steam dray, a Wolseley-Siddeley two-seater with a racing body and five Torpedo cars, one with a rulley body and used for the transport of packing cases during the week and as a charabanc at weekends (Fig. 13.8). Hopper's did retain some vehicles for the Hackney carriage business – six in 1914, four in the next two years, just two in 1917, rising to three in 1920. Given the small number of vehicles involved it would appear that this was very much a minor sideline. As for the movement of bicycles between the Marsh Lane factory and the Brigg Road packing shops, it would seem that Hopper's decided that horses were better than engines, and horse-drawn rullies were a common sight between the two locations well into the 1950s.

Fred Hopper undoubtedly had serious ambitions to become a manufacturer of cars, rather than just an assembler of badge-engineered models, and would have seen this as a natural progression for the business, in line with the rapid developments in car manufacture that had taken place in the Midlands. However, given his poor track record at attracting investment it is difficult to see how he could have developed a car factory in Barton to the extent necessary to compete with the Midlands factories. The rural location also worked against him, in that access to engines and gearboxes involved freight from the Midlands and cars would have been expensive to transport to the customers in the south who could afford them. Such was the optimism of the Edwardian years that he had a go. If he had stuck with bicycles, and perhaps motor cycles, he would probably have avoided the stress of administration, which he found quite debilitating, though he clearly had such a driven personality that a fall was perhaps inevitable.

One final encounter with cars occurred in 1981 with the development of the Elswick Envoy, see Chapter 7. This small car was designed by William Towns for rear entry by wheelchair drivers. According to the *Beaulieu Encyclopaedia of the Automobile* 'it used Mini mechanical parts in a chassis engineered by GKN Sankey. The angular glassfibre bodywork was built by Reliant at its Tamworth plant.' The most useful feature was that the car could be operated from the wheelchair, securely bolted to the chassis. Following the pattern set 70 years earlier, it was not a financial success.

*Fig. 13.8 One of the Torpedo cars used to transport cases between the works and offices, and to embarkation points. It is pictured outside the office/packing shop building and may be the one sold off in 1914.*

**Endnotes**

1    *The Beaulieu Encyclopedia of the Automobile* p 493.
2    Letter Lincolnshire Archives.
3    *The Beaulieu Encyclopaedia of the Automobile*, p 756.
4    *The Autocar* 28 November 1908 p 890.
5    F Hopper & Co – The Problems of Capital Supply in the Cycle Manufacturing Industry, 1891 – 1914. A E Harrison *Business History* vol. 24 no. 1 p 3 – 23.
6    Ibid.

# APPENDIX 4

## ST MARY'S WORKS

The full extent of the Cycle Works can best be appreciated through the plan and key produced by Royal Insurance in 1949/51 and aerial photography. The 1949 plan drawing has been digitally enhanced to make it more readable, though a magnifying glass may still be helpful. Some buildings had changed use since construction, of course, but the plan does illustrate well the departmentalised structure of the company that was set in the Edwardian years. The key contains some gaps but that is not surprising given that many buildings would have become redundant after almost half a century.

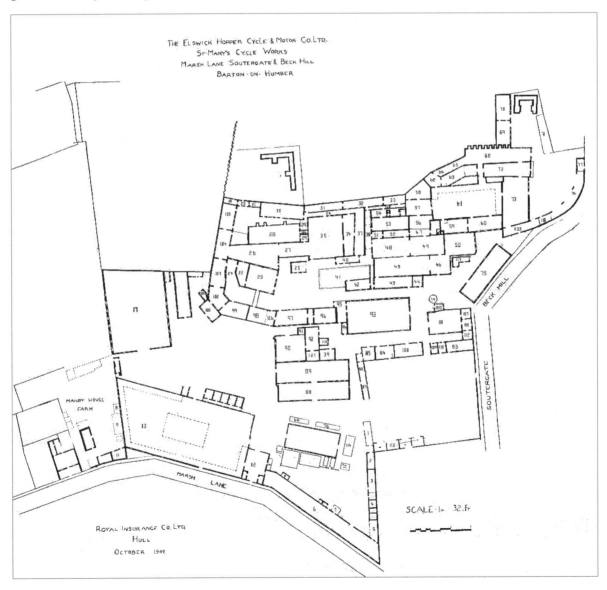

Plan key for revised plan of St Mary's Works, October 1951 by the Royal Insurance Co Ltd.

| | |
|---|---|
| 1 | First-Aid and Rest Room |
| 2 | Wash Room |
| 3 | Cellulose and Colour Enamel Store |
| 4 | Lavatory – Common Soda and Nitrate Store |
| 5 | Disused shop |
| 6 | Old Machine Shop |
| 7 | Old Machine Shop Inspection Dept |
| 8 | Boiler House |
| 9 | Official Records Store |
| 10 | Cellulose and Colour Enamel Store |
| 11 | Engine House |
| 12 | Main Entrance |
| 13 | Cycle Assembly Dept. (Elswick building, also known as Phoenix) |
| 14 | Work Offices |
| 15 | Boiler House |
| 16 | Lavatories |
| 17 | Export Dept (This building was known as the Aerodrome) |
| 18 | Boiler House |
| 19 | Lavatory (Disused) |
| 20 | Entrance to Orchard |
| 21 | Disused Boiler House |
| 22 | Stores |
| 23 | General Stores |
| 24 | Stores and Boiler House |
| 25 | Electricians Dept. |
| 26 | Conveyor Enamelling Dept (New) |
| 27 | Conveyor Enamelling Dept (Old) |
| 28 | Colour Enamel and Varnish Dept |
| 29 | Passage |
| 30 | Enamel Store |
| 31 | Mudguard Store |
| 32 | Mudguard Dept |
| 33 | Mudguard Dept |
| 34 | Disused Passage |
| 35 | Enamel and Dusting Dept |
| 36 | Drying Shop |
| 37 | Bonderize and De-Greasing Dept |
| 38 | Covered Passage Way |
| 39 | Polishing Dept. Inspection |
| 40 | Boiler House |
| 41 | Press Shop |
| 42 | Press Shop Stores |
| 43 | De-Greasing and Cleaning Dept |
| 44 | Boiler House |
| 45 | Nickel Plating Dept |

| 46 | Nickel Plating Dept |
| 47 | Plating Motor House |
| 48 | Chrome Plating Dept |
| 49 | Chrome Plating Dept |
| 50 | Buffing Dept |
| 51 | Plating Inspection |
| 52 | Plating Motor House |
| 53 | Frame Grinding Dept |
| 54 | Frame Grinding Inspection Dept |
| 55 | Lavatories |
| 56 | Compressor House |
| 57 | Covered Entrance to Frame Shop |
| 58 | Lug and Tube Store |
| 59 | Sand Blasting Dept |
| 60 | De-Brassing Dept |
| 61 | Frame Building Dept |
| 62 | Lug and Tube Store |
| 63 | Store for Fork Blades etc |
| 64 | Lug and Tube Store |
| 65 | Lug and Tube Store |
| 66 | Cycle Sheds |
| 67 | Covered Passage Way |
| 68 | Lug and Tube Store |
| 69 | Joiner's Shop |
| 70 | Joiner's Wood Store |
| 71 | Brick Layer's Shop |
| 72 | Acetylene Welding Dept |
| 73 | Tube Shop |
| 74 | Miscellaneous Storage (covered) |
| 75 | Toolroom |
| 76 | Cycle Shed |
| 77 | Liquid Oxygen Store |
| 78 | |
| 79 | Water Tank |
| 80 | Pump House |
| 81 | Steel Store |
| 82 | Staff Dining Room |
| 83 | Dining Room |
| 84 | Case Hardening Dept |
| 85 | Casting Store |
| 86 | Casting Store |
| 87 | Casting and Misc. Store |
| 88 | Barrel Polish Dept. |
| 89 | Fine Polishing Dept |
| 90 | Handlebar Bending Dept |
| 91 | Handlebar Brazing Dept |
| 92 | Carrier Rail Making |

| 93 | Machine Shop |
| 94 | Boiler House |
| 95 | Machine Shop Inspection |
| 96 | Obsolete Plant Store |
| 97 | Strip Steel Store |
| 98 | Lining Shop |
| 99 | Lining Shop |
| 100 | Lining Shop Inspection |
| 101 | Boiler House |
| 102 | Lining Shop |
| 103 | Lining Shop |
| 104 | Frame Inspection |
| 105 | Frame Store |
| 106 | Acetylene Gas Plant |
| 107 | Staff Dining Room |
| 108 | Blacksmith Shop |
| 109 | Gents Lavatory |
| 110 | Ladies Lavatory |
| 111 | |
| 112 | Canteen Kitchen |
| 113 | Scrap Sheds |
| 114 | Cycle Sheds |
| 115 | Compressor House and Day to Day Enamel Store |
| 116 | Cellulose Dept |
| 117 | Electrical Sub-Station |
| 118 | Boiler House |
| 119 | Lavatory – Common Soda and Nitrate Store |
| 120 | Lavatory |
| 121 | Cycle Shed |
| 122 | |
| 123 | |
| 124 | |
| 125 | Scrap Steel Store |
| 126 | Oxygen Cylinder Shelter |
| 127 | Polishing Shop Inspection |
| 128 | Ground Floor Passage |
| 129 | Covered Passage |
| 130 | |
| 131 | Covered Passage |
| 132 | Chrome Extractor House |
| 133 | Covered Storage |
| 134 | Coloured Frame Store |
| 135 | Acetylene Gas Generator |

The aerial photograph dates from 1936 and shows the huge physical impact of the factory on the town. The office building can be seen a third of the way in from the left of the photograph, close to the top and almost in line with the large Methodist Chapel, just to the right of centre.

St Mary's church is clearly visible in the centre with St Peter's just visible at the left hand side. The name coined for the 'Aerodrome', situated at the lower right, is appropriate.

AEROFILMS SERIES            ELSWICK CYCLE WORKS, BARTON-ON-HUMBER, FROM THE AIR        No. 12677